CW00556268

Table of Contents

Android NDK
Beginner's Guide

Discover the native side of Android and inject the power
of C/C++ in your applications

Sylvain Ratabouil

BIRMINGHAM - MUMBAI

Android NDK
Beginner's Guide

First published: January 2012

Production Reference: 1200112

Published by Packt Publishing Ltd.
Livery Place
35 Livery Street
Birmingham B3 2PB, UK.

ISBN 978-1-84969-152-9

www.packtpub.com

Cover Image by Marcus Grandon (marcusgrandon@mac.com)

Credits

Author

Sylvain Ratabouil

Reviewers

Marko Gargenta

Dr. Frank Grützmacher

Robert Mitchell

Acquisition Editor

Sarah Cullington

Lead Technical Editor

Dayan Hyames

Technical Editor

Pramila Balan

Copy Editor

Laxmi Subramanian

Project Coordinator

Jovita Pinto

Proofreader

Lynda Sliwoski

Indexer

Hemangini Bari

Graphics

Valentina D'silva

Production Coordinators

Prachali Bhiwandkar

Melwyn D'sa

Nilesh Mohite

Cover Work

Alwin Roy

About the Author

Sylvain Ratabouil is a confirmed IT consultant with experience in C++ and Java technologies. He worked for the space industry and got involved in aeronautic projects at Valtech Technologies where he now takes part in the Digital Revolution.

Sylvain earned the master's degree in IT from Paul Sabatier University in Toulouse and did M.Sc. in Computer Science from Liverpool University.

As a technology lover, he is passionate about mobile technologies and cannot live or sleep without his Android smartphone.

I would like to thank Steven Wilding for offering me to write this book; Sneha Harkut and Jovita Pinto for awaiting me with so much patience; Reshma Sundaresan, and Dayan Hyames for putting this book on the right track; Sarah Cullington for helping me finalizing this book; Dr. Frank Grützmacher, Marko Gargenta, and Robert Mitchell for all their helpful comments.

About the Reviewers

Dr. Frank Grützmacher has worked for several major German firms in the area of large distributed systems. He was an early user of different Corba implementations in the past.

He got his Ph.D. in the field of electrical engineering, but with the focus on distributed heterogeneous systems. In 2010, he was involved in a project, which changed parts of the Android platform for a manufacturer. From there, he got his knowledge about the android NDK and native processes on this platform.

He has already worked as a reviewer for another Android 3.0 book.

Robert Mitchell is an MIT graduate with over 40 years experience in Information Technology and is semiretired. He has developed software for all the big iron companies: IBM, Amdahl, Fujitsu, National Semiconductor, and Storage Technology. Software companies include Veritas and Symantec. Recent languages that he knows are Ruby and Java, with a long background in C++.

www.PacktPub.com

Support files, eBooks, discount offers and more

You might want to visit www.PacktPub.com for support files and downloads related to your book.

Did you know that Packt offers eBook versions of every book published, with PDF and ePub files available? You can upgrade to the eBook version at www.PacktPub.com and as a print book customer, you are entitled to a discount on the eBook copy. Get in touch with us at service@packtpub.com for more details.

At www.PacktPub.com, you can also read a collection of free technical articles, sign up for a range of free newsletters and receive exclusive discounts and offers on Packt books and eBooks.

http://PacktLib.PacktPub.com

Do you need instant solutions to your IT questions? PacktLib is Packt's online digital book library. Here, you can access, read and search across Packt's entire library of books.

Why Subscribe?

- Fully searchable across every book published by Packt
- Copy and paste, print and bookmark content
- On demand and accessible via web browser

Free Access for Packt account holders

If you have an account with Packt at www.PacktPub.com, you can use this to access PacktLib today and view nine entirely free books. Simply use your login credentials for immediate access.

Preface

The short history of computing machines has witnessed some major events, which forever transformed our usage of technology. From the first massive main frames to the democratization of personal computers, and then the interconnection of networks. Mobility is the next revolution. Like the primitive soup, all the ingredients are now gathered: an ubiquitous network, new social, professional and industrial usages, a powerful technology. A new period of innovation is blooming right now in front of our eyes. We can fear it or embrace it, but it is here, for good!

The mobile challenge

Today's mobile devices are the product of only a few years of evolution, from the first transportable phones to the new tiny high-tech monsters we have in our pocket. The technological time scale is definitely not the same as the human one.

Only a few years ago, surfing on the successful wave of its musical devices, Apple and its founder Steve Jobs combined the right hardware and the right software at the right time not only to satisfy our needs, but to create new ones. We are now facing a new ecosystem looking for a balance between iOS, Windows Mobile, Blackberry, WebOS, and more importantly Android! The appetite of a new market could not let Google apathetic. Standing on the shoulder of this giant Internet, Android came into the show as the best alternative to the well established iPhones and other iPads. And it is quickly becoming the number one.

In this modern Eldorado, new usages or technically speaking, applications (*activities*, if you already are an Android adept) still have to be invented. This is the mobile challenge. And the dematerialized country of Android is the perfect place to look for. Android is (mostly) an open source operating system now supported by a large panel of mobile device manufacturers.

Portability among hardware and adaptability to the constrained resources of mobile devices: this is the real essence of the mobile challenge from a technical perspective. With Android, ones has to deal with multiple screen resolutions, various CPU and GPU speed or capabilities, memory limitations, and so on, which are not topics specific to this Linux-based system, (that is, Android) but can particularly be incommoding.

To ease portability, Google engineers packaged a virtual machine with a complete framework (the Android SDK) to run programs written in one of the most spread programming language nowadays: Java. Java, augmented with the Android framework, is really powerful. But first, Java is specific to Android. Apple's products are written for example in Objective C and can be combined with C and C++. And second, a Java virtual machine does not always give you enough capability to exploit the full power of mobile devices, even with just-in-time compilation enabled. Resources are limited on these devices and have to be carefully exploited to offer the best experience. This is where the Android Native Development Kit comes into place.

What this book covers

Chapter 1, Setting Up your Environment, covers the tools required to develop an application with the Android NDK. This chapter also covers how to set up a development environment, connect your Android device, and configure the Android emulator.

Chapter 2, Creating, Compiling, and Deploying Native Projects, we will compile, package, and deploy NDK samples and create our first Android Java/C hybrid project with NDK and Eclipse.

Chapter 3, Interfacing Java and C/C++ with JNI, presents how Java integrates and communicates with C/C++ through Java Native Interface.

Chapter 4, Calling Java Back from Native Code, we will call Java from C to achieve bidirectional communication and process graphic bitmaps natively.

Chapter 5, Writing a Fully-native Application, looks into the Android NDK application life-cycle. We will also write a fully native application to get rid of Java.

Chapter 6, Rendering Graphics with OpenGL ES, teaches how to display advanced 2D and 3D graphics at full speed with OpenGL ES. We will initialize display, load textures, draw sprites and allocate vertex and index buffers to display meshes.

Chapter 7, Playing Sound with OpenSL ES, adds a musical dimension to native applications with OpenSL ES, a unique feature provided only by the Android NDK. We will also record sounds and reproduce them on the speakers.

Chapter 8, Handling Input Devices and Sensors, covers how to interact with an Android device through its multi-touch screen. We will also see how to handle keyboard events natively and apprehend the world through sensors and turn a device into a game controller.

Chapter 9, Porting Existing Libraries to Android, we will compile the indispensable C/C++ frameworks, STL and Boost. We will also see how to enable exceptions and RunTime Type Information. And also port our own or third-party libraries to Android, such as, Irrlicht 3D engine and Box2D physics engine.

Chapter 10, Towards Professional Gaming, creates a running 3D game controlled with touches and sensors using Irrlicht and Box2D.

Chapter 11, Debugging and Troubleshooting, provides an in-depth analysis of the running application with NDK debug utility. We will also analyze crash dumps and profile the performance of our application.

What you need for this book

A PC with either Windows or Linux or an Intel-based Mac. As a test machine, an Android device is highly advisable, although the Android NDK provides an emulator which can satisfy most of the needs of a hungry developer. But for 2D and 3D graphics, it is still too limited and slow.

I assume you already understand C and C++ languages, pointers, object-oriented features, and other modern language concepts. I also assume you have some knowledge about the Android platform and how to create Android Java applications. This is not a strong prerequisite, but preferable. I also guess you are not frighten by command-line terminals. The version of Eclipse used throughout this book is Helios (3.6).

Finally, bring all your enthusiasm because these little beasts can become really amazing when they demonstrate all their potential and *sense of contact*.

Who this book is for

Are you an Android Java programmer who needs more performance? Are you a C/C++ developer who doesn't want to bother with Java stuff and its out-of-control garbage collector? Do you want to create fast intensive multimedia applications or games? Answer yes to any of the above questions and this book is for you. With some general knowledge of C/C++ development, you will be able to dive head first into native Android development.

Conventions

In this book, you will find several headings appearing frequently.

To give clear instructions of how to complete a procedure or task, we use:

Time for action – heading

1. Action 1

2. Action 2

3. Action 3

Instructions often need some extra explanation so that they make sense, so they are followed with:

What just happened?

This heading explains the working of tasks or instructions that you have just completed.

You will also find some other learning aids in the book, including:

Pop quiz – heading

These are short multiple choice questions intended to help you test your own understanding.

Have a go hero – heading

These set practical challenges and give you ideas for experimenting with what you have learned.

You will also find a number of styles of text that distinguish between different kinds of information. Here are some examples of these styles, and an explanation of their meaning.

Code words in text are shown as follows: "Open a command line window and key in `java -version` to check the installation."

A block of code is set as follows:

```
export ANT_HOME=`cygpath -u "$ANT_HOME"`
export JAVA_HOME=`cygpath -u "$JAVA_HOME"`
export ANDROID_SDK=`cygpath -u "$ANDROID_SDK"`
export ANDROID_NDK=`cygpath -u "$ANDROID_NDK"`
```

When we wish to draw your attention to a particular part of a code block, the relevant lines or items are set in bold:

```xml
<?xml version="1.0" encoding="utf-8"?>
<manifest xmlns:android="http://schemas.android.com/apk/res/android"
        package="com.example.hellojni"
        android:versionCode="1"
        android:versionName="1.0">
```

Any command-line input or output is written as follows:

```
$ make –version
```

New terms and **important words** are shown in bold. Words that you see on the screen, in menus or dialog boxes for example, appear in the text like this: "When proposed, include **Devel/make** and **Shells/bash** packages".

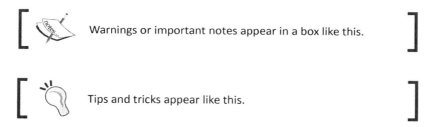

> Warnings or important notes appear in a box like this.

> Tips and tricks appear like this.

Reader feedback

Feedback from our readers is always welcome. Let us know what you think about this book—what you liked or may have disliked. Reader feedback is important for us to develop titles that you really get the most out of.

To send us general feedback, simply send an e-mail to feedback@packtpub.com, and mention the book title through the subject of your message.

If there is a topic that you have expertise in and you are interested in either writing or contributing to a book, see our author guide on www.packtpub.com/authors.

Customer support

Now that you are the proud owner of a Packt book, we have a number of things to help you to get the most from your purchase.

Downloading the example code

You can download the example code files for all Packt books you have purchased from your account at `http://www.packtpub.com`. If you purchased this book elsewhere, you can visit `http://www.packtpub.com/support` and register to have the files e-mailed directly to you.

Errata

Although we have taken every care to ensure the accuracy of our content, mistakes do happen. If you find a mistake in one of our books—maybe a mistake in the text or the code—we would be grateful if you would report this to us. By doing so, you can save other readers from frustration and help us improve subsequent versions of this book. If you find any errata, please report them by visiting `http://www.packtpub.com/support`, selecting your book, clicking on the **errata submission form** link, and entering the details of your errata. Once your errata are verified, your submission will be accepted and the errata will be uploaded to our website, or added to any list of existing errata, under the Errata section of that title.

Piracy

Piracy of copyright material on the Internet is an ongoing problem across all media. At Packt, we take the protection of our copyright and licenses very seriously. If you come across any illegal copies of our works, in any form, on the Internet, please provide us with the location address or website name immediately so that we can pursue a remedy.

Please contact us at `copyright@packtpub.com` with a link to the suspected pirated material.

We appreciate your help in protecting our authors, and our ability to bring you valuable content.

Questions

You can contact us at `questions@packtpub.com` if you are having a problem with any aspect of the book, and we will do our best to address it.

1

Setting Up your Environment

Are you ready to take up the mobile challenge? Is your computer switched on, mouse and keyboard plugged in, and screen illuminating your desk? Then let's not wait a minute more!

In this first chapter, we are going to do the following:

◆ Download and install the necessary tools to develop applications using Android

◆ Set up a development environment

◆ Connect and prepare an Android device for development

Getting started with Android development

What differentiates mankind from animals is the use of tools. Android developers, this authentic species you are about to belong to, are no different!

To develop applications on Android, we can use any of the following three platforms:

◆ Microsoft Windows PC

◆ Apple Mac OS X

◆ Linux PC

Windows 7, Vista, Mac OS X, and Linux systems are supported in both 32 and 64-bit versions, but Windows XP in 32-bit mode only. Only Mac OS X computers of version 10.5.8 or later and based on Intel architectures are supported (not PowerPC processors). Ubuntu is supported only from version 8.04 (Hardy Heron).

Right, this is a good start but unless you are able to read and write binary language like English, having an OS is not enough. We also need software dedicated to Android development:

- The **JDK** (Java Development Kit)
- The **Android SDK** (Software Development Kit)
- The **Android NDK** (Native Development Kit)
- An **IDE** (Integrated Development Environment): Eclipse

Android, and more specifically Android NDK compilation system is heavily based on Linux. So we also need to set up some utilities by default, and we need to install one environment that supports them: **Cygwin** (until NDK R7). This topic is covered in detail later in the chapter. Finally, a good old command-line Shell to manipulate all these utilities is essential: we will use **Bash** (the default on Cygwin, Ubuntu, and Mac OS X).

Now that we know what tools are necessary to work with Android, let's start with the installation and setup process.

 The following section is dedicated to Windows. If you are a Mac or Linux user, you can immediately jump to the *Setting up Mac OS X* or the *Setting up Linux* section.

Setting up Windows

Before installing the necessary tools, we need to set up Windows to host our Android development tools properly.

Time for action – preparing Windows for Android development

To work with the Android NDK, we need to set up a Cygwin Linux-like environment for Windows:

 Since NDK R7, Cygwin installation is not required anymore (steps 1 to 9). The Android NDK provides additional native Windows binaries (for example, `ndk-build.cmd`).

1. Go to `http://cygwin.com/install.html`.

2. Download **setup.exe** and execute it.

3. Select **Install from Internet**.

---

4. Follow the wizard screens.

5. Select a download site from where Cygwin packages are going to be downloaded. Consider using a server in your country:

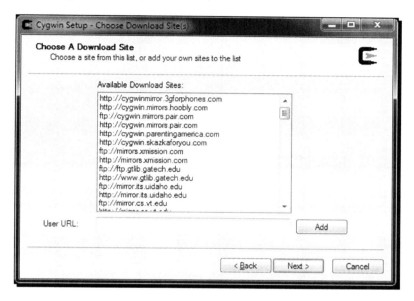

6. When proposed, include **Devel/make** and **Shells/bash** packages:

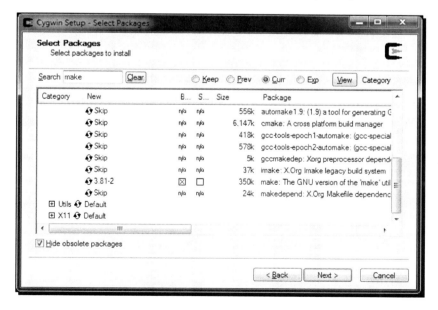

7. Follow the installation wizard until the end. This may take some time depending on your Internet connection.

8. After installation, launch Cygwin. Your profile files get created on first launch.

9. Enter the following command to check if Cygwin works:

   ```
   $ make -version
   ```

To run Eclipse and allow compilation of Android Java code to bytecode, a Java Development Kit is required. On Windows, the obvious choice is the Oracle Sun JDK:

1. Go to the **Oracle** website and download the latest Java Development Kit: `http://www.oracle.com/technetwork/java/javase/downloads/index.html`.

2. Launch the downloaded program and follow the installation wizard. At the end of the installation, a browser is opened asking for JDK registration. This step is absolutely not compulsory and can be ignored.

3. To make sure the newly installed JDK is used, let's define its location in environment variables. Open the Windows **Control panel** and go to the **System** panel (or right-click on **Computer** item in the Windows **Start** menu and select **Properties**). Then go to **Advanced system settings**. The **System Properties** window appears. Finally, select **Advanced** tab and click on the **Environment Variables** button.

4. In the **Environment Variables** window, inside the **System variables** list, insert the `JAVA_HOME` variable with JDK installation directory as value and validate. Then edit `PATH` (or `Path`) and insert the `%JAVA_HOME%\bin` directory before any other directory and separate it with a semicolon. Validate and close the window.

5. Open a command-line window and key in `java -version` to check the installation. The result should be similar to the following screenshot. Check carefully to make sure that the version number corresponds to the version of the newly installed JDK:

   ```
   $ java -version
   ```

To compile projects from the command line, the Android SDK supports **Ant**—a Java-based build automation utility. Let's install it:

1. Go to `http://ant.apache.org/bindownload.cgi` and download Ant binaries, packed within a ZIP archive.

2. Unzip Ant in the directory of your choice (for example, `C:\Ant`).

3. Go back to the **Environment Variables** window, as in step 12, and create the `ANT_HOME` variable with the `Ant` directory as the value. Append the `%ANT_HOME%\bin` directory to `PATH`:

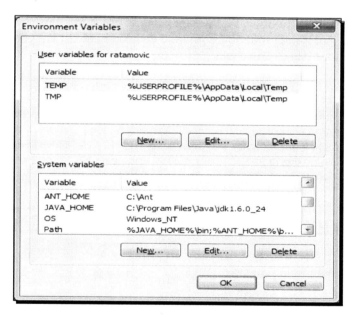

4. From a classic Windows terminal, check the Ant version to make sure it is properly working:

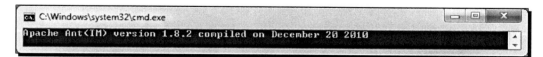

What just happened?

We have prepared Windows with the necessary underlying utilities to host Android development tools: Cygwin and Java Development Kit.

Cygwin is an open source software collection that allows the Windows platform to emulate a Unix-like environment. It aims at natively integrating software based on POSIX standard (such as Unix, Linux, and so on) into Windows. It can be considered as an intermediate layer between applications originated from Unix/Linux (but natively recompiled on Windows) and the Windows OS itself.

We have also deployed a Java Development Kit in version 1.6 and checked if it is properly working from the command line. Because Android SDK uses generics, the JDK in version 1.5 is the least required when developing with Android. JDK is simple to install on Windows but it is important to make sure a previous installation, such as JRE (Java Runtime Environment, which aims at executing applications but not developing them) is not interfering. This is why we have defined JAVA_HOME and PATH environment variables to ensure proper JDK is used.

Finally, we have installed Ant utility that we are going to use in the next chapter to build projects manually. Ant is not required for Android development but is a very good solution to set up a continuous integration chain.

Where is Java's home?

Defining the JAVA_HOME environment variable is not required. However, JAVA_HOME is a popular convention among Java applications, Ant being one of them. It first looks for the java command in JAVA_HOME (if defined) before looking in PATH. If you install an up-to-date JDK in another location later on, do not forget to update JAVA_HOME.

Installing Android development kits on Windows

Once JDK is installed on our system, we can start installing Android SDK and NDK to create, compile, and debug Android programs.

Time for action – installing Android SDK and NDK on Windows

1. Open your Web browser and go to `http://developer.android.com/sdk`. This web page lists all available SDKs, one for each platform.

2. Download Android SDK for Windows, packaged as an Exe installer.

3. Then, go to `http://developer.android.com/sdk/ndk` and download the Android NDK (not SDK!) for Windows, packaged as a ZIP archive this time.

4. Execute Android SDK installer. Select an appropriate installation location (for example, `C:\Android\android-sdk`), knowing that Android SDK and NDK together can take more than 3 GB of disk space (currently!) with all official API versions installed. As a precaution, avoid leaving any space in the target installation path.

5. Follow the installation wizard until the end. Check the **Start SDK Manager**:

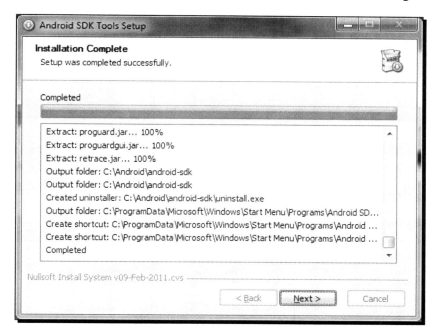

6. The **Android SDK and AVD Manager** is launched. The Package installation window appears automatically.

7. Check the **Accept All** option and click on **Install** to start the installation of Android components:

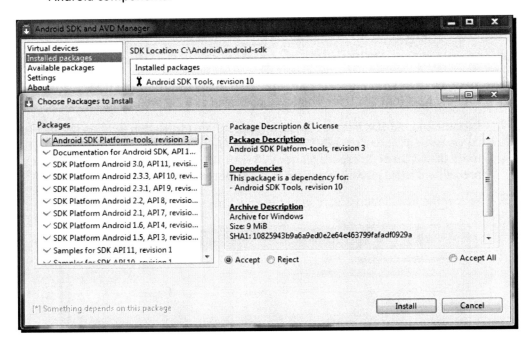

8. After a few minutes, all packages get downloaded and a message asking to restart ADB service (the Android Debug Bridge) appears. Validate by clicking on **Yes**.

9. Close the application.

10. Now, unzip Android NDK archive into its final location (for example, C:\Android\ android-ndk). Again, avoid leaving any space in the installation path (or some problems could be encountered with **Make**).

To easily access Android utilities from the command line, let's define the environment variables:

11. Open the **Environment Variables** system window, as we did in the previous part. Inside the **System variables** list, insert the ANDROID_SDK and ANDROID_NDK variables with the corresponding directories as values.

12. Append %ANDROID_SDK%\tools, %ANDROID_SDK%\platform-tools and %ANDROID_NDK%, all separated by a semicolon, to your PATH.

13. All the Windows environment variables should be imported automatically by Cygwin when launched. Let's verify this by opening a Cygwin terminal and checking whether NDK is available:

```
$ ndk-build --version
```

14. Now, check the Ant version to make sure it is properly working on Cygwin:

```
$ ant -version
```

The first time Cygwin should emit a surprising warning: paths are in MS-DOS style and not POSIX. Indeed, Cygwin paths are emulated and should look similar to /cygdrive/<Drive letter>/<Path to your directory with forward slashes>. For example, if Ant is installed in c:\ant, then the path should be indicated as /cygdrive/c/ant.

15. Let's fix this. Go to your Cygwin directory. There, you should find a directory named home/<your user name> containing a .bash_profile. Open it in edition.

16. At the end of the script, translate the Windows environment variables into Cygwin variables with the cygpath utility. PATH does not need to be translated as this essential variable is processed automatically by Cygwin. Make sure to use the prime character (`) (to execute a command inside another), which has a different meaning than the apostrophe (') (to define a variable) with Bash. An example .bash_profile is provided with this book:

```
export ANT_HOME=`cygpath -u "$ANT_HOME"`
export JAVA_HOME=`cygpath -u "$JAVA_HOME"`
export ANDROID_SDK=`cygpath -u "$ANDROID_SDK"`
export ANDROID_NDK=`cygpath -u "$ANDROID_NDK"`
```

17. Reopen a Cygwin window and check the Ant version again. No warning is issued this time:

```
$ ant -version
```

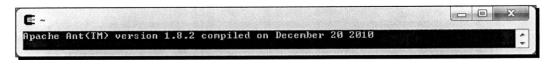

What just happened?

We have downloaded and deployed both Android SDK and NDK and made them available through command line using environment variables.

We have also launched the Android SDK and AVD manager, which aims at managing SDK components installation, updates, and emulation features. This way, new SDK API releases as well as third-party components (for example, Samsung Galaxy Tablet emulator, and so on) are made available to your development environment without having to reinstall the Android SDK.

If you have trouble connecting at step 7, then you may be located behind a proxy. In this case, Android SDK and AVD manager provide a **Settings** section where you can specify your proxy settings.

At step 16, we have converted the Windows paths defined inside the environment variables into Cygwin paths. This path form, which may look odd at first, is used by Cygwin to emulate Windows paths as if they were Unix paths. Cygdrive is similar to a **mount** or **media** directory on Unix and contains every Windows drive as a plugged file system.

Cygwin paths

The rule to remember while using paths with Cygwin is that they must contain forward slashes only and the drive letter is replaced by `/cygdrive/ [Drive Letter]`. But beware, file names in Windows and Cygwin are case-sensitive, contrary to real Unix systems.

Like any Unix system, Cygwin has a root directory named slash (/). But since there is no real root directory in Windows, Cygwin emulates it in its own installation directory. In a Cygwin command line, enter the following command to see its content:

```
$ ls /
```

These files are the ones located in your Cygwin directory (except /proc, which is an in-memory directory). This explains why we updated .bash_profile in the home directory itself, which is located inside the Cygwin directory.

Utilities packaged with Cygwin usually expect Cygwin-style paths, although Windows-style paths work most of the time. Thus, although we could have avoided the conversion in .bash_profile (at the price of a warning), the natural way to work with Cygwin and avoid future troubles is to use Cygwin paths. However, Windows utilities generally do not support Cygwin paths (for example, java.exe), in which case, an inverse path conversion is required when calling them. To perform conversion, cygpath utility provides the following options:

◆   -u: To convert Windows paths to Unix paths

◆   -w: To convert Unix paths to Windows paths

◆   -p: To convert a list of paths (separated by ; on Windows and : on Unix)

Still at step 17, you may have some difficulties when editing .bash_profile: some weird square characters may appear and the entire text is on one very long line! This is because it is encoded using Unix encoding. So use a Unix compatible file editor (such as Eclipse, PSPad, or Notepad++) when editing Cygwin files. If you already got into trouble, you can use either your editor End-Of-Line conversion feature (Notepad++ and PSPad provide one) or apply command-line **dos2unix** utility (provided with Cygwin) on the incriminated file.

Char return on Cygwin

Unix files use a simple line-feed character (better known as \n) to indicate an end of line whereas Windows uses a carriage return (CR or \r) plus a line feed. MacOS, on the other hand, uses a carriage return only. Windows newline markers can cause lots of trouble in Cygwin Shell scripts, which should be kept in Unix format.

This is the end of the section dedicated to Windows setup. If you are not a Mac or Linux user, you can jump to the *Setting up Eclipse development environment* section.

Setting up Mac OS X

Apple computers and Mac OS X have a reputation for being simple and easy to use. And honestly, this adage is rather true when it comes to Android development. Indeed, Mac OS X is based on Unix, well adapted to run the NDK toolchain, and a recent JDK is already installed by default. Mac OS X comes with almost anything we need with the exception of Developer Tools, which need to be installed separately. These Developer Tools include XCode IDE, many Mac development utilities, and also some Unix utilities, such as Make and Ant.

Time for action – preparing Mac OS X for Android development

All developer tools are included in XCode installation package (version 4, at the time this book was written). There exist four solutions to get this package, and they are as follows:

◆ If you have Mac OS X installation media, open it and look for the XCode installation package

◆ XCode is also provided on the AppStore for free (but this has changed recently and may change in the future too)

◆ XCode can also be downloaded from the Apple website with a paying program subscription at the address `http://developer.apple.com/xcode/`

◆ Older version 3, compatible with Android development tools, is available for free as a disc image from the same page with a free Apple Developer account

Using the most appropriate solution for your case, let's install XCode:

1. Find your XCode installation package and run it. Select the **UNIX Development** option when the customization screen appears. Finish installation. We are done!

2. To develop with Android NDK, we need the Make build tool for native code. Open a terminal prompt and ensure Make correctly works:

```
$ make --version
```

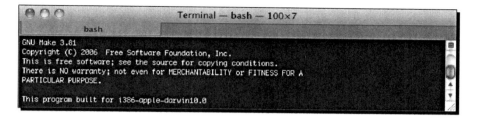

3. To run Eclipse and allow compilation of Android Java code to bytecode, Java Development Kit is required. Let's check if the default Mac OS X JDK works fine:

```
$ java -version
```

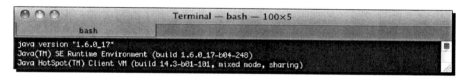

4. To compile projects from the command line, the Android SDK supports Ant, a Java-based build automation utility. Still in a terminal, ensure Ant is correctly installed:

```
$ ant -version
```

What just happened?

We have prepared our Mac OS X to host Android development tools. And as usual with Apple, that was rather easy!

We have checked if Java Development Kit in version 1.6 is properly working from the command line. Because Android SDK uses generics, a JDK in version 1.5 is the least required for Android development.

We have installed Developer Tools, which include Make—to run the NDK compiler—and Ant—that we are going to use in the next chapter to build projects manually. Ant is not required for Android development but is a very good solution to set up a continuous integration chain.

Installing Android development kits on Mac OS X

Once a JDK is installed on your system, we can start installing Android Development SDK and NDK to create, compile, and debug Android programs.

Time for action – installing Android SDK and NDK on Mac OS X

1. Open your web browser and go to `http://developer.android.com/sdk`. This web page lists all available SDKs, one for each platform.

2. Download Android SDK for Mac OS X, which is packaged as a ZIP archive.

3. Then, go to `http://developer.android.com/sdk/ndk` and download the Android NDK (not SDK!) for Mac OS X, packaged as a Tar/BZ2 archive this time.

4. Uncompress the downloaded archives separately into the directory of your choice (for example, `/Developer/AndroidSDK` and `/Developer/AndroidNDK`).

5. Let's declare these two directories as environment variables. From now on, we will refer to these directories as **$ANDROID_SDK** and **$ANDROID_NDK** throughout this book. Assuming you use the default Bash command-line shell, create or edit your **.profile** file (be careful, this is a hidden file!) in your home directory and add the following variables:

```
export ANDROID_SDK="<path to your Android SDK directory>"
export ANDROID_NDK="<path to your Android NDK directory>"
export PATH="$PATH:$ANDROID_SDK/tools:$ANDROID_SDK/platform-
tools:$ANDROID_NDK"
```

Downloading the example code

You can download the example code files for all Packt books you have purchased from your account at http://www.PacktPub.com. If you purchased this book elsewhere, you can visit http://www.PacktPub.com/support and register to have the files e-mailed directly to you.

6. Save the file and log out from your current session.

7. Log in again and open a terminal. Enter the following command:

```
$ android
```

8. The Android SDK and AVD Manager window shows up.

9. Go to the **Installed packages** section and click on **Update All**:

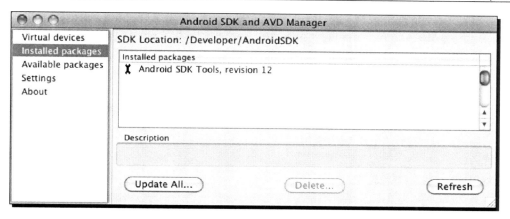

10. A package selection dialog appears. Select **Accept All** and then **Install**.

11. After few minutes, all packages get downloaded and a message asking to restart ADB service (the Android Debug Bridge) appears. Validate by clicking on **Yes**.

12. You can now close the application.

What just happened?

We have downloaded and deployed both Android SDK and NDK and made them available through the command line using environment variables.

Mac OS X and environment variables

Mac OS X is tricky when it comes to environment variables. They can be easily declared in a .profile for applications launched from a terminal, as we just did. They can also be declared using an environment.plist file for GUI applications, which are not launched from Spotlight. A more powerful way to configure them is to define or update /etc/launchd.conf system file (see http://developer.apple.com/).

We have also launched the Android SDK and AVD manager, which aims at managing the installation, updates, and emulation features of the SDK components. This way, new SDK API releases as well as third-party components (for example, Samsung Galaxy Tablet emulator, and so on) are made available to your development environment without having to reinstall the Android SDK.

If you have trouble connecting at step 9, then you may be located behind a proxy. In this case, Android SDK and AVD manager provide a **Settings** section where you can specify your proxy settings.

 This is the end of the section dedicated to Mac OS X setup. If you are not a Linux user, you can jump to the *Setting up Eclipse development environment* section.

Setting up Linux

Although Linux is more naturally suited for Android development, as the Android toolchain is Linux-based, some setup is necessary as well.

Time for action – preparing Ubuntu Linux for Android development

To work with Android NDK, we need to check and install some system packages and utilities:

1. First, Glibc (the GNU C standard library, in version 2.7 or later) must be installed. It is usually shipped with Linux systems by default. Check its version using the following command:

   ```
   $ ldd --version
   ```

   ```
   File  Edit  View  Search  Terminal  Help
   ldd (Ubuntu EGLIBC 2.13-0ubuntu13) 2.13
   Copyright (C) 2011 Free Software Foundation, Inc.
   This is free software; see the source for copying conditions.  There is NO
   warranty; not even for MERCHANTABILITY or FITNESS FOR A PARTICULAR PURPOSE.
   Written by Roland McGrath and Ulrich Drepper.
   ```

2. We also need the Make build tool for native code. Installation can be performed using the following command:

   ```
   $ sudo apt-get install build-essential
   ```

   Alternatively, Make can be installed through **Ubuntu Software Center**. Look for **build-essential** in the dedicated search box and install the packages found:

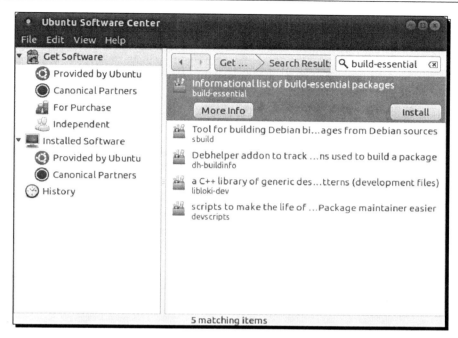

Package `build-essential` contains a minimal set of tools for compilation and packaging on Linux Systems. It also includes GCC (the GNU C Compiler), which is not required for standard Android development as Android NDK already packages its own version.

3. To ensure that Make is correctly installed, type the following command. If correctly installed, the version will be displayed:

```
$ make --version
```

Special note for 64-bit Linux owner

We also need 32-bit libraries installed to avoid compatibility problems. This can be done using the following command (to execute in a command-line prompt) or again the Ubuntu Software Center:

```
sudo apt-get install ia32-libs
```

To run Eclipse and allow compilation of Android Java code to bytecode, Java Development Kit is required. We need to download and install Oracle Sun Java Development Kit. On Ubuntu, this can be performed from the Synaptic Package Manager:

1. Open Ubuntu **System/Administration** menu and select **Synaptic Package Manager** (or open your Linux package manager if you use another Linux distros).

2. Go to the **Edit | Software Sources** menu.

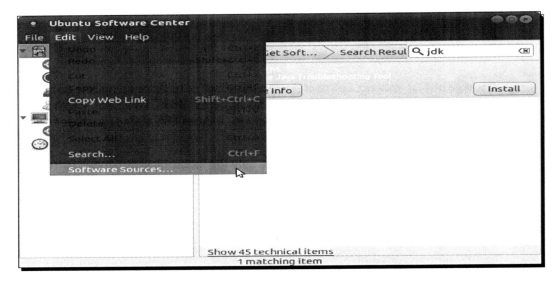

3. In the **Software Sources** dialog, open the **Other Software** tab.

4. Check the **Canonical Partners** line and close the dialog:

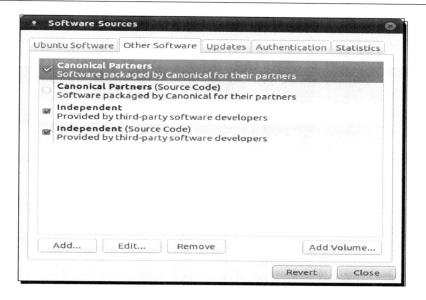

5. Package cache synchronizes automatically with the Internet, and after a few seconds or minutes some new software is made available in the **Canonical Partners** section.

6. Find **Sun Java™ Development Kit (JDK) 6** (or later) and click on **Install**. You are also advised to install Lucida TrueType fonts (from the Sun JRE), the Java(TM) Plug-in packages.

7. Accept the license (after reading it carefully of course!). Be careful as it may open in the background.

8. When installation is finished, close Ubuntu Software Center.

9. Although Sun JDK is now installed, it is not yet available. Open JDK is still used by default. Let's activate Sun JRE through the command line. First, check available JDK:

```
$ update-java-alternatives -l
```

```
File  Edit  View  Search  Terminal  Help
java-6-openjdk 1061 /usr/lib/jvm/java-6-openjdk
java-6-sun 63 /usr/lib/jvm/java-6-sun
```

10. Then, activate the Sun JRE using the identifier returned previously:

```
$ sudo update-java-alternatives -s java-6-sun
```

11. Open a terminal and check that installation is OK by typing:

```
$ java -version
```

```
File  Edit  View  Search  Terminal  Help
java version "1.6.0_26"
Java(TM) SE Runtime Environment (build 1.6.0_26-b03)
Java HotSpot(TM) 64-Bit Server VM (build 20.1-b02, mixed mode)
```

The Android SDK supports Ant, a Java-based build automation utility, to compile projects from the command line. Let's install it.

1. Install Ant with the following command or with the Ubuntu Software Center:

```
$ sudo apt-get install ant
```

2. Check whether Ant is properly working:

```
$ ant --version
```

```
File  Edit  View  Search  Terminal  Help
Apache Ant(TM) version 1.8.2 compiled on December 20 2010
```

What just happened?

We have prepared our Linux operating system with the necessary utilities to host Android development tools.

We have installed a Java Development Kit in version 1.6 and checked if it is properly working from the command line. Because Android SDK uses generics, the JDK in version 1.5 is the least required for Android development.

You may wonder why we bothered with the installation of Sun JDK while Open JDK is already ready to use. The reason is simply that Open JDK is not officially supported by Android SDK. If you want to avoid any possible interaction with Open JDK, think about removing it entirely from your system. Go to the **Provided by Ubuntu** section in the Ubuntu Software Center and click on **Remove** for each **OpenJDK** line. For more information, look for the official Ubuntu documentation: http://help.ubuntu.com/community/Java.

Finally, we have installed Ant utility that we are going to use in the next chapter to build projects manually. Ant is not required for Android development but is a very good solution to set up a continuous integration chain.

 There is no more Sun JDK on Linux repositories since Java 7. The Open JDK becomes the official Java implementation.

Installing Android development kits on Linux

Once JDK is installed on your system, we can start installing Android Development SDK and NDK to create, compile, and debug Android programs.

Time for action – installing Android SDK and NDK on Ubuntu

1. Open your web browser and go to `http://developer.android.com/sdk`. This web page lists all available SDKs, one for each platform.

2. Download Android SDK for Linux, which is packaged as a Tar/GZ archive.

3. Then, go to `http://developer.android.com/sdk/ndk` and download the Android NDK (not SDK!) for Linux, packaged as a Tar/BZ2 archive this time.

4. Uncompress the downloaded archives separately into the directories of your choice (for example, `~/AndroidSDK` and `~/AnroidNDK`). On Ubuntu, you can use **Archive Manager** (right-click on the archive file and **Extract Here**).

5. Let's declare these two directories as environment variables. From now on, we will refer to these directories as **$ANDROID_SDK** and **$ANDROID_NDK** throughout this book. Assuming you use a Bash command-line shell, edit your **.profile** file (be careful, this is a hidden file!) in your home directory and add the following variables:

    ```
    export ANDROID_SDK="<path to your Android SDK directory>"
    export ANDROID_NDK="<path to your Android NDK directory>"
    export PATH="$PATH:$ANDROID_SDK/tools:$ANDROID_SDK/platform-
    tools:$ANDROID_NDK"
    ```

6. Save the file and log out from your current session.

7. Log in again and open a terminal. Enter the following command:

    ```
    $ android
    ```

8. The Android SDK and AVD Manager window shows up.

9. Go to the **Installed packages** section and click on **Update All**:

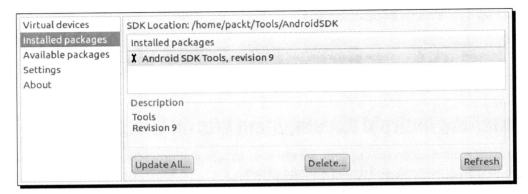

10. A package selection dialog appears. Select **Accept All** and then **Install**.

11. After a few minutes, all packages get downloaded and a message asking to restart ADB service (the Android Debug Bridge) appears. Validate by clicking on **Yes**.

12. You can now close the application.

What just happened?

We have downloaded and deployed both Android SDK and NDK and made them available through the command line using environment variables.

We have also launched the Android SDK and AVD manager, which aims at managing the installation, updates, and emulation features of the SDK components. This way, new SDK API releases as well as third-party components (for example, Samsung Galaxy Tablet emulator, and so on) are made available to your development environment without having to reinstall Android SDK.

If you have trouble connecting at step 9, then you may be located behind a proxy. In this case, Android SDK and AVD manager provide a **Settings** section where you can specify your proxy settings.

 This is the end of the section dedicated to the Linux setup. The following section is mixed.

Setting up the Eclipse development environment

Command line lovers, vi fanatics, please go to the next chapter or you may feel sick! For most humans, having a comfortable and visual-friendly IDE is essential. And hopefully, Android works with the greatest of all: Eclipse!

Eclipse is the only officially supported IDE for Android SDK through the Google official plugin named **ADT**. But ADT is only for Java. Hopefully, Eclipse supports C/C++ as well through **CDT**, a general C/C++ plugin. Although not specific to Android, it works well with the NDK. The version of Eclipse used throughout this book is Helios (3.6).

Time for action – installing Eclipse

1. Open your web browser and go to `http://www.eclipse.org/downloads/`. This web page lists all available Eclipse packages: for Java, J2EE, C++.

2. Download **Eclipse IDE for Java Developers**.

3. Extract the downloaded Tar/GZ file (on Linux and Mac OS X) or ZIP file (on Windows) with your archive manager.

4. Once extracted, run Eclipse by double-clicking on the **eclipse** executable inside its directory. On Mac OS X, make sure to execute **eclipse** alias and not **Eclipse.app** or else environment variables defined earlier in `.profile` will not be available to Eclipse.

5. If Eclipse asks for a workspace, define a custom workspace directory if you want to (default workspace is fine) and click **OK**.

6. After Eclipse has started, close the **Welcome Page**.

7. Go to the **Help | Install New Software** menu.

If a problem occurs in the next steps while accessing update sites, then check your Internet connection. You may be either disconnected or your computer is behind a proxy. In the latter case, it is possible to download ADT plugin as an archive file from the ADT web page and install it manually (or configure Eclipse to connect through a proxy but that is another matter).

8. Enter `https://dl-ssl.google.com/android/eclipse/` in the **Work with** field and validate.

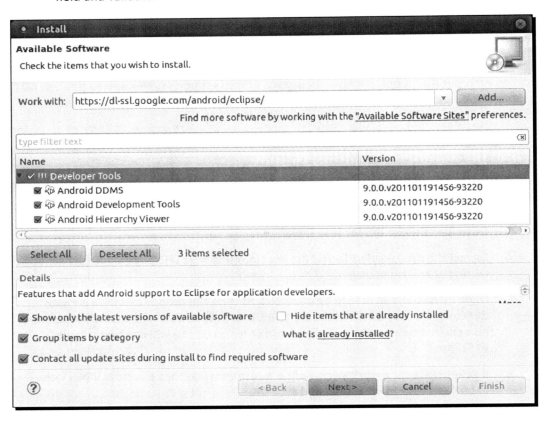

9. After a few seconds, a **Developer Tools** plugin appears; select it and click on the **Next** button.

10. Follow the wizard and accept conditions when asked. On the last wizard page, click on **Finish**.

11. ADT gets installed. A warning may appear indicating that plugin content is unsigned. Ignore it and click on **OK**.

12. When finished, restart Eclipse as requested.

13. When Eclipse is restarted, go to menu **Window | Preferences (Eclipse | Preferences** on Mac OS X) and go to the **Android** section.

14. Click on **Browse** and select the path to your Android SDK directory.

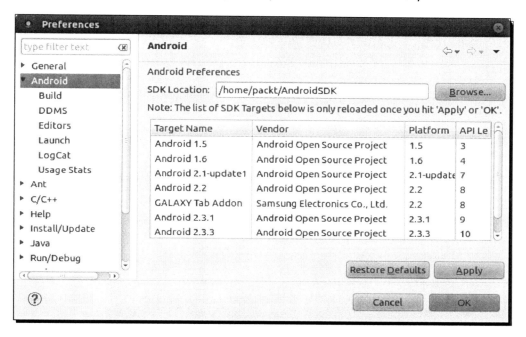

15. Validate preferences.

16. Go back to the **Help | Install New Software...** menu.

17. Open the **Work with** combobox and select the item containing Eclipse version name (here **Helios**).

18. Find **Programming Languages** in the plugin tree and open it.

19. Select CDT plugins. Incubation plugins are not essential. **C/C++ Call Graph Visualization** is for Linux only and cannot be installed on Windows or Mac OS X:

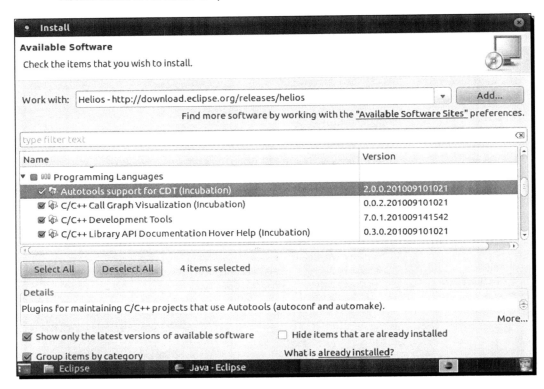

20. Follow the wizard and accept conditions when asked. On the last wizard page, click on **Finish**.

21. When finished, restart Eclipse.

What just happened?

Eclipse is now installed and official Android development plugin ADT and C/C++ plugin CDT are installed. ADT refers to the Android SDK location.

The main purpose of ADT is to ease integration of Eclipse with SDK development tools. It is perfectly possible to develop in Android without an IDE using command line only. But automatic compilation, packaging, deployment, and debugging are addictive features, which are hard to get rid of!

You may have noticed that no reference to the Android NDK is given to ADT. This is because ADT works for Java only. Hopefully, Eclipse is flexible enough to handle hybrid Java/C++ projects! We will talk about that further when creating our first Eclipse project.

In the same way, CDT allows easy integration of C/C++ compilation features into Eclipse. We also "silently" installed JDT, the Java plugin for Eclipse. It is embedded in the **Eclipse IDE for Java Developers** package. An Eclipse package including only CDT is also available on the Eclipse Website.

More on ADT

ADT update site given to Eclipse in step 8 comes from the official ADT documentation that you can find at `http://developer.android.com/sdk/eclipse-adt.html`. This page is the main information point to visit if new versions of Eclipse or Android are released.

Emulating Android

Android SDK provides an emulator to help developers who do not have a device (or are impatiently waiting for a new one!) get started quickly. Let's now see how to set it up.

Time for action – creating an Android virtual device

1. Open Android SDK and AVD Manager using either the command line (key in **android**) or the Eclipse toolbar button:

2. Click on the **New** button.

3. Give a name to this new emulated device: **Nexus_480x800HDPI**.

4. Target platform is **Android 2.3.3**.

5. Specify SD card size: **256**.

6. Enable snapshot.

7. Set **Built-in** resolution **WVGA800**.

8. Leave the **Hardware** section the way it is.

9. Click on **Create AVD**.

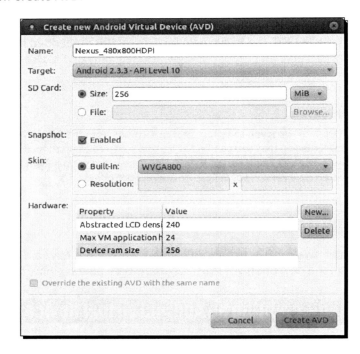

10. The newly created virtual device now appears in the list:

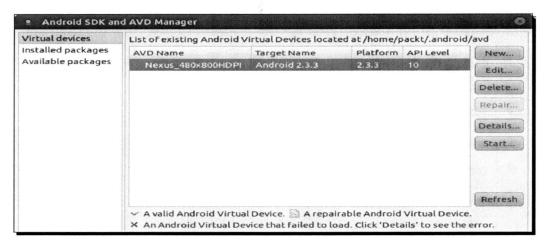

11. Let's check how it works: click on the **Start** button.

12. Click on the **Launch** button:

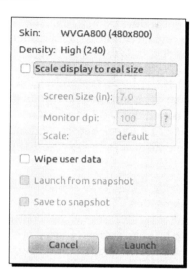

13. The emulator starts up and after a few minutes, your device is loaded:

What just happened?

We have created our Android Virtual Devices which emulate a Nexus One with an HDPI (High Density) screen of size 3.7 inches and a resolution of 480x800 pixels. So we are now able to test applications we are going develop in a representative environment. Even better, we are now able to test them in several conditions and resolutions (also called skins) without requiring a costly device.

Although this is out of the scope of this book, customizing additional options, such as the presence of a GPS, camera, and so on, is also possible when creating an AVD to test an application in limited hardware conditions. And as a final note, screen orientation can be switched with *Ctrl + F11* and *Ctrl + F12*. Check out the Android website for more information on how to use and configure the emulator (`http://developer.android.com/guide/developing/devices/emulator.html`).

Emulation is not simulation

Although emulation is a great tool when developing, there are a few important points to take into account: emulation is slow, not always perfectly representative, and some features such as GPS support may be lacking. Moreover, and this is probably the biggest drawback: Open GL ES is only partially supported. More specifically, only Open GL ES 1 currently works on the emulator.

Have a go hero

Now that you know how to install and update Android platform components and create an emulator, try to create an emulator for Android Honeycomb Tablets. Using the Android SDK and AVD Manager, you will need to do the following:

- Install Honeycomb SDK components
- Create a new AVD which targets **Honeycomb** platform
- Start the emulator and use proper screen scaling to match real tablet scale

Depending on your computer resolution, you may need to tweak AVD display scale. This can be done by checking **Scale display to real size** when starting the emulator and entering your monitor density (use the **?** button to calculate it). If you perform well, you should obtain the new Honeycomb interface at its real scale (no worries, it is also in Landscape mode on my computer):

 The following section is dedicated to Windows and Mac OS X. If you are a Linux user, you can immediately jump to the *Developing with an Android device on Linux* section.

Developing with an Android device on Windows and Mac OS X

Emulators can be of really good help, but nothing compared to a real device. Hopefully, Android provides the sufficient connectivity to develop on a real device and make the testing cycle more efficient. So take your Android in hand, switch it on and let's try to connect it to Windows or Mac OS X.

Time for action – setting up your Android device on Windows and Mac OS X

Installation of a device for development on Windows is manufacturer-specific. More information can be found at `http://developer.android.com/sdk/oem-usb.html` with a full list of device manufacturers. If you have got a driver CD with your Android device, you can use it. Note that the Android SDK also contains some Windows drivers under `$ANDROID_SDK\extras\google\usb_driver`. Specific instructions are available for Google development phones, Nexus One, and Nexus S at `http://developer.android.com/sdk/win-usb.html`.

Mac users should also refer to their Manufacturer's instructions. However, as Mac's ease of use is not only a legend, simply connecting an Android device to a Mac should be enough to get it working! Your device should be recognized immediately without installing anything.

Once the driver (if applicable) is installed on the system, do the following:

1. Go to the home menu, then go to **Settings | Application | Development** on your mobile device (may change depending on your manufacturer).

2. Enable **USB debugging** and **Stay awake**.

3. Plug your device into your computer using a data connection cable (beware some cables are alimentation cables only and will not work!). Depending on your device, it may appear as a USB disk.

4. Launch Eclipse.

5. Open the **DDMS** perspective. If working properly, your phone should be listed in the **Devices** view:

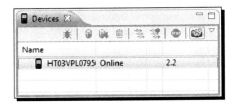

6. Say cheese and take a screen capture of your own phone by clicking the corresponding toolbar button:

Now you are sure your phone is correctly connected!

What just happened?

We have connected an Android device to a computer in development mode and enabled the **Stay awake** option to stop automatic screen shutdown when the phone is charging. If your device is still not working, go to the *Trouble shooting a device connection* section.

The device and the computer communicate through an intermediate background service: the Android Debug Bridge (ADB) (more about it in the next chapter). ADB starts automatically the first time it is called, when Eclipse ADT is launched or when invoked from the command line.

 This is the end of the section dedicated to Windows and Mac OS X. If you are not a Linux user, you can jump to the *Trouble shooting a device connection* or the *Summary* section.

Developing with an Android device on Linux

Emulators can be of really good help, but it is nothing compared to a real device. Hopefully, Android provides the sufficient connectivity to develop on a real device and make the testing cycle more efficient. So take your Android in hand, switch it on and let's try to connect it to Linux.

Time for action – setting up your Android device on Ubuntu

1. Go to **Home | Menu | Settings | Application | Development** on your mobile device (may change depending on your manufacturer).

2. Enable **USB debugging** and **Stay awake**.

3. Plugin your device to your computer using a data connection cable (beware, some cables are alimentation cables only and will not work!). Depending on your device, it may appear as a USB disk.

4. Try to run ADB and list devices. If you are lucky, your device works out of the box and the list of devices appears. In that case, you can ignore the following steps:

   ```
   $ adb devices
   ```

```
File  Edit  View  Search  Terminal  Help
List of devices attached
HT03VPL07956    device
```

5. If **????????** appears instead of your device name (which is likely), then ADB does not have proper access rights. We need to find your Vendor ID and Product ID. Because Vendor ID is a fixed value for each manufacturer, you can find it in the following list:

Manufacturer	USB Vendor ID
Acer	0502
Dell	413c
Foxconn	0489
Garmin-Asus	091E
HTC	0bb4
Huawei	12d1
Kyocera	0482
LG	1004
Motorola	22b8
Nvidia	0955
Pantech	10A9
Samsung	04e8
Sharp	04dd
Sony Ericsson	0fce
ZTE	19D2

The current list of Vendor IDs can be found on the Android website at `http://developer.android.com/guide/developing/device.html#VendorIds`.

6. The device Product ID can be found using the **lsusb** command "greped" with Vendor ID to find it more easily. In the following example, the value `0bb4` is the HTC Vendor ID and `0c87` is the HTC Desire product ID:

```
$ lsusb | grep 0bb4
```

```
File  Edit  View  Search  Terminal  Help
Bus 002 Device 013: ID 0bb4:0c87 High Tech Computer Corp.
```

7. With the root user, create a file `/etc/udev/rules.d/52-android.rules` with your Vendor and Product ID:

```
$ sudo sh -c 'echo SUBSYSTEM==\"usb\", SYSFS{idVendor}==\"<Your
Vendor ID>\", ATTRS{idProduct}=\"<Your Product ID>\",
MODE=\"0666\" > /etc/udev/rules.d/52-android.rules'
```

8. Change file rights to 644:

```
$ sudo chmod 644 /etc/udev/rules.d/52-android.rules
```

9. Restart the **udev** service (the Linux device manager):

```
$ sudo service udev restart
```

10. Relaunch the ADB server in the root mode this time:

```
$ sudo $ANDROID_SDK/tools/adb kill-server
$ sudo $ANDROID_SDK/tools/adb start-server
```

11. Check whether your device works by listing the devices again. If **?????????** appears, or worse, nothing appears, then something went wrong in the previous steps:

```
$ adb devices
```

What just happened?

We have connected an Android device to a computer in development mode and enabled the **Stay awake** option to stop automatic screen shutdown when the phone is charging. If your device is still not working, go to the *Trouble shooting a device connection* section.

We have also started the Android Debug Bridge (ADB), which is a background service used as a mediator for computer/device communication (more about it in the next chapter). ADB is started automatically the first time it is called, when Eclipse ADT is launched or when invoked from the command line.

And more important than anything, we have discovered that **HTC** means High Tech Computer! Jokes apart, the connection process can become tricky on Linux. If you belong to the unlucky group of people who need to launch ADB as the root, you are highly advised to create a startup script similar to the following one, to launch ADB. You can use it from the command line or add it to your main menu (**Menu | Preferences| Main Menu** on Ubuntu):

```
#!bin/sh
stop_command="$ANDROID_SDK/platform-tools/adb kill-server"
launch_command="$ANDROID_SDK/platform-tools/adb start-server"
/usr/bin/gksudo "/bin/bash -c '$stop_command; $launch_command'" |
zenity -text-info -title Logs
```

This script displays daemon startup message in a Zenity window (a Shell toolkit to display graphical windows using GTK+).

At step 6, if **52-android.rules** does not work, then try **50-android.rules** or **51-android.rules** (or all of them). Although **udev** (the Linux device manager) should only use the prefix number to order rule files lexicographically, that sometimes seems to do the trick. The magic of Linux!

This is the end of the section dedicated to Linux setup. The following section is mixed.

Troubleshooting a development device

Having trouble connecting an Android development device to a computer can mean any of the following:

- Your host system is not properly set up
- Your development device is not working properly
- The ADB service is malfunctioning

If the problem comes from your host system, check your device manufacturer instructions carefully to make sure any needed driver is correctly installed. Check the Hardware properties to see if it is recognized and turn on the USB storage mode (if applicable) to see if it is working properly. Indeed, after getting connected, your device may be visible in your hardware settings but not as a disk. A device can be configured as a Disk drive (if a SD-card or similar is included) or in charge-only mode. This is absolutely fine as the development mode works perfectly in the charge-only mode.

Disk-drive mode is generally activated from the Android task bar (**USB connected** item). Refer to your device documentation for the specificities of your device.

SD Card access

When the charge-only mode is activated, SD card files and directories are visible to the Android applications installed on your phone but not to your computer. On the opposite side, when Disk drive mode is activated, those are visible only from your computer. Check your connection mode when your application cannot access its resource files on a SD Card.

If problem comes from your Android device, a possible solution is to deactivate and reactivate the Debug mode on your device. This option can be switched from the **Home | Menu | Settings | Application | Development** screen on your mobile device (which may change depending on your manufacturer) or accessed more quickly from the Android task bar (**USB debugging connected** item). As a last measure, reboot your device.

Problem may also come from the ADB. In that case, check whether the ADB is working by issuing the following command from a terminal prompt:

```
$ adb devices
```

If your device is correctly listed, then ADB is working. This command will launch ADB service if it was not already. You can also restart it with commands:

```
$ adb kill-server
$ adb start-server
```

In any case, to solve a specific connection problem or get up-to-date information, visit the following web page: http://developer.android.com/guide/developing/device. html. As a feedback from experience, never neglect hardware. Always check with a second cable or device if you have one at your disposal. I once purchased a bad quality cable, which performed badly when some contortions occurred...

Summary

Setting up our Android development platform is a bit tedious but is hopefully performed once and for all! We have installed the necessary utilities using the package system on Linux, Developer Tools on Mac OS X, and Cygwin on Windows. Then we have deployed the Java and Android development kits and checked if they are working properly. Finally, we have seen how to create a phone emulator and connect a real phone for test purposes.

We now have the necessary tools in our hands to shape our mobile ideas. In the next chapter, we are going to handle them to create, compile, and deploy our first Android projects!

2

Creating, Compiling, and Deploying Native Projects

A man with the most powerful tools in hand is unarmed without the knowledge of their usage. Eclipse, GCC, Ant, Bash, Shell, Linux—any new Android programmer needs to deal with this technologic ecosystem. Depending on your background, some of these names may sound familiar to your ears. Indeed, that is a real strength; Android is based on open source bricks which have matured for years. Theses bricks are cemented by the Android Development Kits (SDK and NDK) and their set of new tools: Android Debug Bridge (ADB), Android Asset Packaging Tool (AAPT), Activity Manager (AM), ndk-build, and so on. So, since our development environment is set up, we can now get our hands dirty and start manipulating all these utilities to create, compile, and deploy projects which include native code.

In this second chapter, we are going to do the following:

◆ Compile and deploy official sample applications from the Android NDK with **Ant** build tool and native code compiler **ndk-build**

◆ Learn in more detail about **ADB**, the Android Debug Bridge, to control a development device

◆ Discover additional tools like **AM** to manage activities and **AAPT** to package applications

◆ Create our first own hybrid multi-language project using Eclipse

◆ Interface Java to C/C++ through **Java Native Interfaces** (in short **JNI**)

By the end of this chapter, you should know how to start up a new Android native project on your own.

Compiling and deploying NDK sample applications

I guess you cannot wait anymore to test your new development environment. So why not compile and deploy elementary samples provided by the Android NDK first to see it in action? To get started, I propose to run HelloJni, a sample application which retrieves a character string defined inside a native C library into a Java activity (an activity in Android being more or less equivalent to an application screen).

Time for action – compiling and deploying the hellojni sample

Let's compile and deploy the HelloJni project from command line using Ant:

1. Open a command-line prompt (or Cygwin prompt on Windows)

2. Go to `hello-jni` sample directory inside the Android NDK. All the following steps have to performed from this directory:

```
$ cd $ANDROID_NDK/samples/hello-jni
```

3. Create Ant build file and all related configuration files automatically using `android` command (`android.bat` on Windows). These files describe how to compile and package an Android application:

```
android update project -p .
```

```
File  Edit  View  Search  Terminal  Help
Updated local.properties
Added file ./build.xml
Added file ./proguard.cfg
It seems that there are sub-projects. If you want to update them
please use the --subprojects parameter.
```

4. Build `libhello-jni` native library with `ndk-build`, which is a wrapper Bash script around Make. Command `ndk-build` sets up the compilation toolchain for native C/C++ code and calls automatically GCC version featured with the NDK.

```
$ ndk-build
```

```
File  Edit  View  Search  Terminal  Help
Gdbserver    : [arm-linux-androideabi-4.4.3] libs/armeabi/gdbserver
Gdbsetup     : libs/armeabi/gdb.setup
Compile thumb : hello-jni <= hello-jni.c
SharedLibrary : libhello-jni.so
Install      : libhello-jni.so => libs/armeabi/libhello-jni.so
```

5. Make sure your Android development device or emulator is connected and running.

6. Compile, package, and install the final HelloJni APK (an Android application package). All these steps can be performed in one command, thanks to Ant build automation tool. Among other things, Ant runs `javac` to compile Java code, AAPT to package the application with its resources, and finally ADB to deploy it on the development device. Following is only a partial extract of the output:

```
$ ant install
```

The result should look like the following extract:

```
File  Edit  View  Search  Terminal  Help
Buildfile: /home/packt/Tools/AndroidNDK/samples/hello-jni/build.xml
    [setup] Android SDK Tools Revision 12
    [setup] Project Target: Android 2.2
    [setup] API level: 8
```

```
File  Edit  View  Search  Terminal  Help
compile:
    [javac] /home/packt/Tools/AndroidSDK/tools/ant/main_rules.xml:384: warning:
'includeantruntime' was not set, defaulting to build.sysclasspath=last; set to f
alse for repeatable builds
    [javac] Compiling 2 source files to /home/packt/Tools/AndroidNDK/samples/hel
lo-jni/bin/classes
```

```
File  Edit  View  Search  Terminal  Help
-package-resources:
    [echo] Packaging resources
    [aapt] Creating full resource package...
    [aapt] Warning: AndroidManifest.xml already defines debuggable (in http://s
chemas.android.com/apk/res/android); using existing value in manifest.

-package-debug-sign:
[apkbuilder] Creating HelloJni-debug-unaligned.apk and signing it with a debug k
ey...
```

```
File  Edit  View  Search  Terminal  Help
install:
    [echo] Installing /home/packt/Tools/AndroidNDK/samples/hello-jni/bin/HelloJ
ni-debug.apk onto default emulator or device...
    [exec] 984 KB/s (79163 bytes in 0.078s)
    [exec]     pkg: /data/local/tmp/HelloJni-debug.apk
    [exec] Success

BUILD SUCCESSFUL
Total time: 11 seconds
```

7. Launch a shell session using `adb` (or `adb.exe` on Windows). ADB shell is similar to shells that can be found on the Linux systems:

```
$ adb shell
```

8. From this shell, launch HelloJni application on your device or emulator. To do so, use `am`, the Android **Activity Manager**. Command `am` allows to start Android activities, services or sending intents (that is, inter-activity messages) from command line. Command parameters come from the Android manifest:

```
# am start -a android.intent.action.MAIN -n com.example.hellojni/
com.example.hellojni.HelloJni
```

9. Finally, look at your development device. **HelloJni** appears on the screen!

What just happened?

We have compiled, packaged, and deployed an official NDK sample application with Ant and SDK command-line tools. We will explore them more in later part. We have also compiled our first native C library (also called module) using the `ndk-build` command. This library simply returns a character string to the Java part of the application on request. Both sides of the application, the native and the Java one, communicate through Java Native Interface. JNI is a standard framework that allows Java code to explicitly call native C/C++ code with a dedicated API. We will see more about this at the end of this chapter and in the next one.

Finally, we have launched HelloJni on our device from an Android shell (`adb shell`) with the `am` Activity Manager command. Command parameters passed in step 8 come from the Android manifest: **com.example.hellojni** is the package name and **com.example.hellojni. HelloJni** is the main Activity class name concatenated to the main package.

```
<?xml version="1.0" encoding="utf-8"?>
<manifest xmlns:android="http://schemas.android.com/apk/res/android"
        package="com.example.hellojni"
        android:versionCode="1"
        android:versionName="1.0">
```

. . .
```
<activity android:name=".HelloJni"
                android:label="@string/app_name">
```
. . .

> **Automated build**
>
> Because Android SDK, NDK, and their open source bricks are not bound to Eclipse or any specific IDE, creating an automated build chain or setting up a continuous integration server becomes possible. A simple bash script with Ant is enough to make it work!

HelloJni sample is a little bit... let's say rustic! So what about trying something fancier? Android NDK provides a sample named **San Angeles**. San Angeles is a coding demo created in 2004 for the Assembly 2004 competition. It has been later ported to OpenGL ES and reused as a sample demonstration in several languages and systems, including Android. You can find more information by visiting one of the author's page: `http://jet.ro/visuals/4k-intros/san-angeles-observation/`.

Have a go hero – compiling san angeles OpenGL demo

To test this demo, you need to follow the same steps:

1. Go to the San Angeles sample directory.
2. Generate project files.
3. Compile and install the final San Angeles application.
4. Finally run it.

As this application uses OpenGL ES 1, AVD emulation will work, but may be somewhat slow!

You may encounter some errors while compiling the application with Ant:

```
File  Edit  View  Search  Terminal  Help
-resource-src:
     [echo] Generating R.java / Manifest.java from the resources...
     [aapt] /home/packt/Tools/AndroidNDK/samples/san-angeles/res/layout/main.xml
:2: error: Error: String types not allowed (at 'layout_width' with value 'match_
parent').
     [aapt] /home/packt/Tools/AndroidNDK/samples/san-angeles/res/layout/main.xml
:2: error: Error: String types not allowed (at 'layout_height' with value 'match
_parent').
     [aapt] /home/packt/Tools/AndroidNDK/samples/san-angeles/res/layout/main.xml
:7: error: Error: String types not allowed (at 'layout_width' with value 'match_
parent').
```

The reason is simple: in `res/layout/` directory, `main.xml` file is defined. This file usually defines the main screen layout in Java application—displayed components and how they are organized. However, when Android 2.2 (API Level 8) was released, the `layout_width` and `layout_height` enumerations, which describe the way UI components should be sized, were modified: `FILL_PARENT` became `MATCH_PARENT`. But San Angeles uses API Level 4.

There are basically two ways to overcome this problem. The first one is selecting the right Android version as the target. To do so, specify the target when creating Ant project files:

```
$ android update project -p . --target android-8
```

This way, build target is set to API Level 8 and `MATCH_PARENT` is recognized. You can also change the build target manually by editing `default.properties` at the project root and replacing:

```
target=android-4
```

with the following line:

```
target=android-8
```

The second way is more straightforward: erase the `main.xml` file! Indeed, this file is in fact not used by San Angeles demo, as only an OpenGL screen created programmatically is displayed, without any UI components.

Target right!

When compiling an Android application, always check carefully if you are using the right target platform, as some features are added or updated between Android versions. A target can also dramatically change your audience wideness because of the multiple versions of Android in the wild... Indeed, targets are moving a lot and fast on Android!

All these efforts are not in vain: it is just a pleasure to see this old-school 3D environment full of flat-shaded polygons running for the first time. So just stop reading and run it!

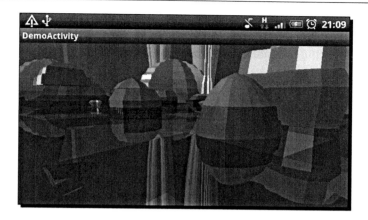

Exploring Android SDK tools

Android SDK includes tools which are quite useful for developers and integrators. We have already overlooked some of them including the Android Debug Bridge and android command. Let's explore them deeper.

Android debug bridge

You may have not noticed it specifically since the beginning but it has always been there, over your shoulder. The Android Debug Bridge is a multifaceted tool used as an intermediary between development environment and emulators/devices. More specifically, ADB is:

 ◆ A background process running on emulators and devices to receive orders or requests from an external computer.

 ◆ A background server on your development computer communicating with connected devices and emulators. When listing devices, ADB server is involved. When debugging, ADB server is involved. When any communication with a device happens, ADB server is involved!

 ◆ A client running on your development computer and communicating with devices through ADB server. That is what we have done to launch HelloJni: we got connected to our device using adb shell before issuing the required commands.

ADB shell is a real Linux shell embedded in ADB client. Although not all standard commands are available, classical commands, such as `ls`, `cd`, `pwd`, `cat`, `chmod`, `ps`, and so on are executable. A few specific commands are also provided such as:

`logcat`	To display device log messages
`dumpsys`	To dump system state
`dmesg`	To dump kernel messages

ADB shell is a real Swiss Army knife. It also allows manipulating your device in a flexible way, especially with root access. For example, it becomes possible to observe applications deployed in their "sandbox" (see directory `/data/data`) or to a list and kill currently running processes.

ADB also offers other interesting options; some of them are as follows:

`pull <device path> <local path>`	To transfer a file to your computer
`push <local path> <device path>`	To transfer a file to your device or emulator
`install <application package>`	To install an application package
`install -r <package to reinstall>`	To reinstall an application, if already deployed
`devices`	To list all Android devices currently connected, including emulators
`reboot`	To restart an Android device programmatically
`wait-for-device`	To sleep, until a device or emulator is connected to your computer (for example, in a script)
`start-server`	To launch the ADB server communicating with devices and emulators
`kill-server`	To terminate the ADB server
`bugreport`	To print the whole device state (like dumpsys)
`help`	To get an exhaustive help with all options and flags available

To ease the writing of issued command, ADB provides facultative flags to specify before options:

`-s <device id>`	To target a specific device
`-d`	To target current physical device, if only one is connected (or an error message is raised)
`-e`	To target currently running emulator, if only one is connected (or an error message is raised)

ADB client and its shell can be used for advanced manipulation on the system, but most of the time, it will not be necessary. ADB itself is generally used transparently. In addition, without root access to your phone, possible actions are limited. For more information, see http://developer.android.com/guide/developing/tools/adb.html.

Root or not root

If you know the Android ecosystem a bit, you may have heard about rooted phones and non-rooted phones. Rooting a phone means getting root access to it, either "officially" while using development phones or using hacks with an end user phone. The main interest is to upgrade your system before the manufacturer provides updates (if any!) or to use a custom version (optimized or modified, for example, CyanogenMod). You can also do any possible (especially dangerous) manipulations that an Administrator can do (for example, deploying a custom kernel).

Rooting is not an illegal operation, as you are modifying YOUR device. But not all manufacturers appreciate this practice and usually void the warranty.

Have a go hero – transferring a file to SD card from command line

Using the information provided, you should be able to connect to your phone like in the good old days of computers (I mean a few years ago!) and execute some basic manipulation using a shell prompt. I propose you to transfer a resource file by hand, like a music clip or a resource that you will be reading from a future program of yours.

To do so, you need to open a command-line prompt and perform the following steps:

1. Check if your device is available using adb from command line.
2. Connect to your device using the Android Debug Bridge shell prompt.
3. Check the content of your SD card using standard Unix ls command. Please note that ls on Android has a specific behavior as it differentiates ls mydir from ls mydir/, when mydir is a symbolic link.
4. Create a new directory on your SD card using the classic command mkdir.
5. Finally, transfer your file by issuing the appropriate adb command.

Project configuration tool

The command named `android` is the main entry point when manipulating not only projects but also AVDs and SDK updates (as seen in Chapter 1, *Setting Up your Environment*). There are few options available, which are as follows:

- `create project`: This option is used to create a new Android project through command line. A few additional options must be specified to allow proper generation:

-p	The project path
-n	The project name
-t	The Android API target
-k	The Java package, which contains application's main class
-a	The application's main class name (Activity in Android terms)

  For example:

```
$ android create project -p ./MyProjectDir -n MyProject -t
android-8 -k com.mypackage -a MyActivity
```

- `update project`: This is what we use to create Ant project files from an existing source. It can also be used to upgrade an existing project to a new version. Main parameters are as follows:

-p	The project path
-n	To change the project name
-l	To include an Android library project (that is, reusable code). The path must be relative to the project directory).
-t	To change the Android API target

There are also options to create library projects (`create lib-project`, `update lib-project`) and test projects (`create test-project`, `update test-project`). I will not go into details here as this is more related to the Java world.

 As for ADB, `android` command is your friend and can give you some help:
```
$ android create project -help
```

Command `android` is a crucial tool to implement a continuous integration toolchain in order to compile, package, deploy, and test a project automatically entirely from command line.

Have a go hero – towards continuous integration

With `adb`, `android`, and `ant` commands, you have enough knowledge to build a minimal automatic compilation and deployment script to perform some continuous integration. I assume here that you have a versioning software available and you know how to use it. **Subversion** (also known as **SVN**) is a good candidate and can work in local (without a server).

Perform the following operations:

1. Create a new project by hand using `android` command.
2. Then, create a Unix or Cygwin shell script and assign it the necessary execution rights (`chmod` command). All the following steps have to be scribbled in it.
3. In the script, check out sources from your versioning system (for example, using a `svn checkout` command) on disk. If you do not have a versioning system, you can still copy your own project directory using Unix commands.
4. Build the application using `ant`.

> Do not forget to check command results using `$?`. If the returned value is different from 0, it means an error occurred. Additionally, you can use `grep` or some custom tools to check potential error messages.

5. If needed, you can deploy resources files using `adb`.
6. Install it on your device or on the emulator (which you can launch from the script) using `ant` as shown previously.
7. You can even try to launch your application automatically and check Android logs (see `logcat` option in `adb`). Of course, your application needs to make use of logs!

> **A free monkey to test your App!**
>
> In order to automate UI testing on an Android application, an interesting utility that is provided with the Android SDK is **MonkeyRunner,** which can simulate user actions on a device to perform some automated UI testing. Have a look at `http://developer.android.com/guide/developing/tools/monkeyrunner_concepts.html`.

To favor automation, a single Android shell statement can be executed from command-line as follows:

```
adb shell ls /sdcard/
```

To execute a command on an Android device and retrieve its result back on your host shell, execute the following command: `adb shell "ls / notexistingdir/ 1> /dev/null 2>&1; echo \$?"` Redirection is necessary to avoid polluting the standard output. The escape character before `$?` is required to avoid early interpretation by the host shell.

Now you are fully prepared to automate your own build toolchain!

Creating your first Android project using eclipse

In the first part of the chapter, we have seen how to use Android command-line tools. But developing with Notepad or VI is not really attractive. Coding should be fun! And to make it so, we need our preferred IDE to perform boring or unpractical tasks. So let's see now how to create an Android project using Eclipse.

Eclipse views and perspectives

Several times in this book, I have asked you to look at an Eclipse View like the **Package Explorer View**, the **Debug View**, and so on. Usually, most of them are already visible, but sometimes they are not. In that case, open them through main menu: **Window | Show View | Other...**.

Views in Eclipse are grouped in **perspectives,** which basically store your workspace layout. They can be opened through main menu: **Window | Open Perspective | Other...**. Note that some contextual menus are available only in some perspectives.

Time for action – initiating a Java project

1. Launch Eclipse.

2. In the main menu, select **File | New | Project...**.

3. In the project wizard, select **Android | Android Project** and then **Next**.

4. In the next screen, enter project properties:

- ❑ In **Project name,** enter **MyProject**.
- ❑ Select **Create a new project in workspace**.
- ❑ Specify a new location if you want to, or keep the default location (that is, your eclipse workspace location).
- ❑ Set **Build Target** to **Android 2.3.3**.
- ❑ In **Application name**, enter (which can contain spaces): **MyProject**.
- ❑ In **Package name**, enter **com.myproject**.
- ❑ Create a new activity with the name **MyActivity**.
- ❑ Set **Min SDK Version** to **10**:

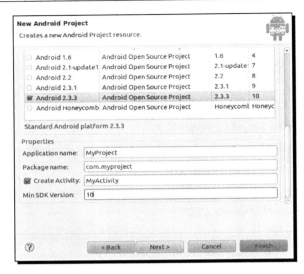

5. Click on **Finish**. The project is created. Select it in **Package Explorer** view.

6. In the main menu, select **Run | Debug As | Android Application** or click on the **Debug** button  in the toolbar.

7. Select application type **Android Application** and click **OK**:

8. Your application is launched, as shown in the following screenshot:

What just happened?

We have created our first Android project using Eclipse. In a few screens and clicks, we have been able to launch the application instead of writing long and verbose commands. Working with an IDE like Eclipse really gives a huge productivity boost and makes programming much more comfortable!

ADT plugin has an annoying bug that you may have already encountered: Eclipse complains that your Android project is missing the required source folder gen whereas this folder is clearly present. Most of the time, just recompiling the project makes this error disappear. But sometimes, Eclipse is recalcitrant and refuses to recompile projects. In that case, a little-known trick, which can be applied in many other cases, is to simply open the Problems view, select these irritating messages, delete them without mercy (*Delete* key or right-click and **Delete**) and finally recompile the incriminated project.

As you can see, this project targets Android 2.3 Gingerbread because we will access latest NDK features in the next chapters. However, you will need a proper device which hosts this OS version else testing will not be possible. If you cannot get one, then use the emulator set up in *Chapter 1, Setting Up your Environment*.

If you look at the project source code, you will notice a Java file and no C/C++ files. Android projects created with ADT are always Java projects. But thanks to Eclipse flexibility, we can turn them into C/C++ projects too; we are going to see this at the end of this chapter.

Avoiding space in file paths

When creating a new project, avoid leaving a space in the path where your project is located. Although Android SDK can handle that without any problem, Android NDK and more specifically GNU Make may not really like it.

Introducing Dalvik

It is not possible to talk about Android without touching a word about **Dalvik**. Dalvik, which is also the name of an Icelandic village, is a **Virtual Machine** on which Android bytecode is interpreted (not native code!). It is at the core of any applications running on Android. Dalvik is conceived to fit the constrained requirements of mobile devices. It is specifically optimized to use less memory and CPU. It sits on top of the Android kernel which provides the first layer of abstraction over hardware (process management, memory management, and so on).

Android has been designed with speed in mind. Because most users do not want to wait for their application to be loaded while others are still running, the system is able to instantiate multple Dalvik VMs quickly, thanks to the **Zygote** process. Zygote, whose name comes from the very first biologic cell of an organism from which daughter cells are reproduced, starts when the system boots up. It preloads (or "warms up") all core libraries shared among applications as well as a Dalvik instance. To launch a new application, Zygote is simply forked and the initial Dalvik instance is copied. Memory consumption is lowered by sharing as many libraries as possible between processes.

Dalvik operates on Android bytecode, which is different from Java bytecode. Bytecode is stored in an optimized format called **Dex** generated by an Android SDK tool named **dx**. Dex files are archived in the final APK with the application manifest and any native libraries or additional resources needed. Note that applications can get further optimized during installation on end user's device.

Interfacing Java with C/C++

Keep your Eclipse IDE opened as we are not done with it yet. We have a working project indeed. But wait, that is just a Java project, whereas we want to unleash the power of Android with native code! In this part, we are going to create C/C++ source files, compile them into a native library named `mylib` and let Java run this code.

Time for action – calling C code from Java

The native library `mylib` that we are going to create will contain one simple native method `getMyData()` that returns a basic character string. First, let's write the Java code to declare and run this method.

1. Open `MyActivity.java`. Inside main class, declare the native method with the `native` keyword and no method body:

```
public class MyActivity extends Activity {
    public native String getMyData();
...
```

2. Then, load the native library that contains this method within a static initialization block. This block will be called before `Activity` instance gets initialized:

```
...
    static {
        System.loadLibrary("mylib");
    }
...
```

3. Finally, when `Activity` instance is created, call the native method and update the screen content with its return value. You can refer to the source code provided with this book for the final listing:

```
...
    public void onCreate(Bundle savedInstanceState) {
        super.onCreate(savedInstanceState);
        setContentView(R.layout.main);

        setTitle(getMyData());
    }
}
```

Now, let's prepare the project files required to build the native code.

4. In Eclipse, create a new directory named `jni` at the project's root using menu **File | New | Folder**.

5. Inside the `jni` directory, create a new file named `Android.mk` using menu **File | New | File**. If CDT is properly installed, the file should have the following specific icon 🗋 in the **Package Explorer** view.

6. Write the following content into this file. Basically, this describes how to compile our native library named `mylib` which is composed of one source file the `com_myproject_MyActivity.c`:

```
LOCAL_PATH := $(call my-dir)

include $(CLEAR_VARS)

LOCAL_MODULE     := mylib
LOCAL_SRC_FILES := com_myproject_MyActivity.c

include $(BUILD_SHARED_LIBRARY)
```

As project files for native compilation are ready, we can write the expected native source code. Although the C implementation file must be written by hand, the corresponding header file can be generated with a helper tool provided by the JDK: `javah`.

7. In Eclipse, open **Run | External Tools | External Tools Configurations....**

8. Create a new program configuration with the following parameters:

- ◆ Name: `MyProject javah`.
- ◆ Location refers to `javah` absolute path, which is OS-specific. In Windows, you can enter `${env_var:JAVA_HOME}\bin\javah.exe`. In Mac OS X and Linux, it is usually `/usr/bin/javah`.
- ◆ Working directory: `${workspace_loc:/MyProject/bin}`.
- ◆ Arguments: `-d ${workspace_loc:/MyProject/jni} com.myproject. MyActivity}`.

> In Mac OS X, Linux, and Cygwin, you can easily find the location of an executable available in `$PATH`, by using the `which` command. For example,
>
> `$ which javah`

9. On the **Refresh** tab, check **Refresh resources upon completion** and select **Specific resources**. Using the **Specify Resources...** button, select the `jni` folder.

10. Finally, click on **Run** to save and execute `javah`. A new file `com_myproject_ MyActivity.h` is generated in the `jni` folder. It contains a prototype for the method `getMyData()` expected on the Java side:

```
/* DO NOT EDIT THIS FILE - it is machine generated */
#include <jni.h>

. . .

JNIEXPORT jstring JNICALL Java_com_myproject_MyActivity_getMyData
  (JNIEnv *, jobject);

. . .
```

11. We can now create `com_myproject_MyActivity.c` implementation inside the `jni` directory to return a raw character string. Method signature originates from the generated header file:

```
#include "com_myproject_MyActivity.h"

JNIEXPORT jstring Java_com_myproject_MyActivity_getMyData
    (JNIEnv* pEnv, jobject pThis)
{
    return (*pEnv)->NewStringUTF(pEnv,
                            "My native project talks C++");
}
```

Eclipse is not yet configured to compile native code, only Java code. Until we do that in the last part of this chapter, we can try to build native code by hand.

12. Open a terminal prompt and go inside the `MyProject` directory. Launch compilation of the native library with the command `ndk-build`:

```
$ cd <your project directory>/MyProject
$ ndk-build
```

The native library is compiled in the `libs/armeabi` directory and is named `libmylib.so`. Temporary files generated during compilation are located in the `obj/local` directory.

13. From Eclipse, launch `MyProject` again. You should obtain following result:

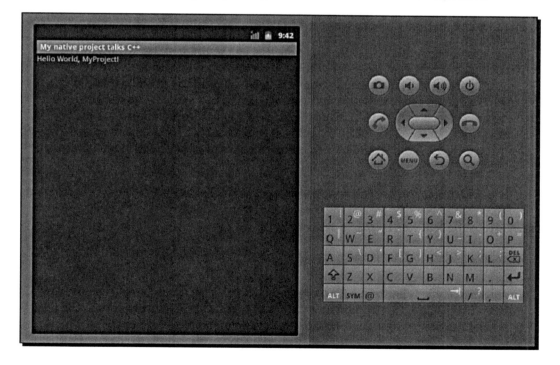

What just happened?

In the previous part, we created an Android Java project. In this second part, we have interfaced Java code to a native library compiled with the Android NDK from a C file. This binding from Java to C allows retrieving through Java Native Interfaces a simple Java string allocated in the native code. The example application shows how Java and C/C++ can cooperate together:

1. By creating UI components and code on the Java side and defining native calls.
2. Using `javah` to generate header file with corresponding C/C++ prototypes.
3. Writing native code to perform the expected operation.

Native methods are declared on the Java side with the `native` keyword. These methods have no body (like an `abstract` method) as they are implemented on the native side. Only their prototype needs to be defined. Native methods can have parameters, a return value, any visibility (`private`, `protected`, package protected or `public`) and can be static, like classic Java methods. Of course, they require the native library with method implementations to be loaded before they are called. A way to do that is to invoke `System.loadLibrary()` in a static initialization block, which is initialized when the containing class is loaded. Failure to do so results in an exception of type `java.lang.UnsatisfiedLinkError`, which is raised when the native method is invoked for the first time.

Although it is not compulsory, `javah` tool provided by the JDK is extremely useful to generate native prototypes. Indeed, JNI convention is tedious and error-prone. With generated headers, you immediately know if a native method expected by the Java side is missing or has an incorrect signature. I encourage you to use `javah` systematically in your projects, more specifically, each time native method's signature is changed. JNI code is generated from `.class` files, which means that your Java code must be first compiled before going through `javah` conversion. Implementation needs to be provided in a separate C/C++ source file.

How to write JNI code on the native side is explored in more details in the next chapter. But remember that a very specific naming convention, which is summarized by the following pattern, must be followed by native side methods:

```
<returnType> Java_<com_mypackage>_<class>_<methodName> (JNIEnv* pEnv,
<parameters>...)
```

Native method name is prefixed with `Java_` and the packages/class name (separated by `_`) containing it separated. First argument is always of type `JNIEnv` (more on this in the next chapter) and the preceding arguments are the actual parameters given to the Java method.

More on Makefiles

Native library building process is orchestrated by a Makefile named `Android.mk`. By convention, `Android.mk` is in folder `jni`, which is located inside the project's root. That way, `ndk-build` command can find this file automatically when the command is invoked. Therefore, C/C++ code is by convention also located in `jni` directory (but this can be changed by configuration).

Android Makefiles are an essential piece of the NDK building process. Thus, it is important to understand the way they work to manage a project properly. An `Android.mk` file is basically a "baking" file, which defines what to compile and how to compile. Configuration is performed using predefined variables, among which are: LOCAL_PATH, LOCAL_MODULE and LOCAL_SRC_FILES. See Chapter 9, *Porting Existing Libraries to Android*, for more explanation on Makefiles.

The `Android.mk` file presented in `MyProject` is a very simple Makefile example. Each instruction serves a specific purpose:

```
LOCAL_PATH := $(call my-dir)
```

The preceding code indicates native source files location. Instruction `$(call <function>)` allows evaluating a function and function `my-dir` returns the directory path of the last executed Makefile. Thus, as Makefiles usually share their directory with source files, this line is systematically written at the beginning of each `Android.mk` file to find their location.

```
include $(CLEAR_VARS)
```

Makes sure no "parasite" configuration disrupts compilation. When compiling an application, a few LOCAL_XXX variables need to be defined. The problem is that one module may define additional configuration settings (like a compilation MACRO or a flag) through these variables, which may not be needed by another module.

Keep your modules clean

To avoid any disruption, all necessary LOCAL_XXX variables should be cleared before any module is configured and compiled. Note that LOCAL_PATH is an exception to that rule and is never cleared out.

```
LOCAL_MODULE    := mylib
```

The preceding line of code defines your module name. After compilation, the output library is named according to the LOCAL_MODULE variable flanked by a `lib` prefix and a `.so` suffix. This LOCAL_MODULE name is also used when a module depends on another module.

```
LOCAL_SRC_FILES := com_myproject_MyActivity.c
```

The preceding line of code indicates which source files to compile. File path is expressed relative to the LOCAL_PATH directory.

```
include $(BUILD_SHARED_LIBRARY)
```

This last instruction finally launches the compilation process and indicates which type of library to generate.

With Android NDK, it is possible to produce shared libraries (also called dynamic libraries, like DLL on Windows) as well as static libraries:

◆ Shared libraries are a piece of executable loaded on demand. These are stored on disk and loaded to memory as a whole. Only shared libraries can be loaded directly from Java code.

◆ Static libraries are embedded in a shared library during compilation. Binary code is copied into a final library, without regards to code duplication (if embedded by several different modules).

In contrast with shared libraries, static libraries can be stripped, which means that unnecessary symbols (like a function which is never called from the embedding library) are removed from the final binary. They make shared libraries bigger but "all-inclusive", without dependencies. This avoids the "DLL not found" syndrome well known on Window.

Shared vs. Static modules

Whether you should use a static or shared library depends on the context:

◆ If a library is embedded in several other libraries

◆ If almost all pieces of code are required to run

◆ If a library needs to be selected dynamically at runtime

then consider turning it into a shared library because they avoid memory duplication (which is a very sensible issue on mobile devices).

On the other hand:

◆ If it is used in one or only a few places

◆ If only part of its code is necessary to run

◆ If loading it at the beginning of your application is not a concern

then consider turning it into a static library instead. It can be reduced in size at compilation-time at the price of some possible duplication.

Compiling native code from Eclipse

You probably agree with me, writing code in Eclipse but compiling it by hand is not very satisfying. Although the ADT plugin does not provide any C/C++ support, Eclipse does this through CDT. Let's use it to turn our Android project into a hybrid Java-C/C++ project.

Time for action – creating a hybrid Java/C/C++ project

To check whether Eclipse compilation works fine, let's introduce surreptitiously an error inside the `com_myproject_MyActivity.c` file. For example:

```
#include "com_myproject_MyActivity.h"

private static final String = "An error here!";

JNIEXPORT jstring Java_com_myproject_MyActivity_getMyData
...
```

Now, let's compile `MyProject` with Eclipse:

1. Open menu **File | New | Other...**.

2. Under C/C++, select **Convert to a C/C++ Project** and click on **Next**.

3. Check **MyProject**, choose **MakeFile project** and **Other Toolchain** and finally click on **Finish**.

4. Open **C/C++ perspective** when requested.

5. Right-click on **MyProject** in **Project explorer** view and select **Properties**.

6. In the **C/C++ Build** section, uncheck **Use default build command** and enter **ndk-build** as a **Build command**. Validate by clicking on **OK**:

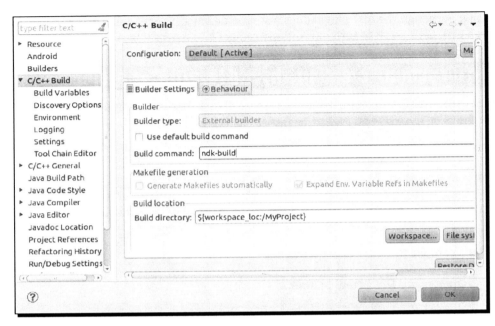

And... oops! An error got insidiously inside the code. An error? No we are not dreaming! Our Android project is compiling C/C++ code and parsing errors:

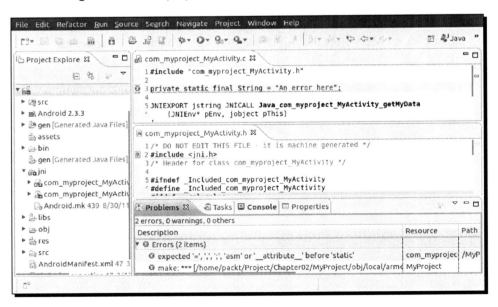

7. Let's fix it by removing the incriminated line (underlined in red) and saving the file.

8. Sadly, the error is not gone. This is because auto-build mode does not work. Go back to project properties, inside **C/C++ Settings** and then the **Behaviour** tab. Check **Build on resource save** and leave the value to **all**.

9. Go to the **Builders** section and place **CDT Builder** right above **Android Package Builder**. Validate.

10. Great! Error is gone. If you go to the **Console** view, you will see the result of `ndk-build` execution like if it was in command line. But now, we notice that the include statement of `jni.h` file is underlined in yellow. This is because it was not found by the CDT Indexer for code completion. Note that the compiler itself resolves them since there is no compilation error. Indeed, the indexer is not aware of NDK include paths, contrary to the NDK compiler

> If warnings about the include file which the CDT Indexer could not find do not appear, go to **C/C++ perspective**, then right-click on the project name in the **Project Explorer** view and select **Index/Search for Unresolved Includes** item. The **Search** view appears with all unresolved inclusions.

11. Let's go back to project properties one last time. Go to section **C/C++ General/Paths and Symbols** and then in **Includes** tab.

12. Click on **Add...** and enter the path to the directory containing this include file which is located inside NDK's `platforms` directory. In our case, we use Android 2.3.3 (API level 9), so the path is `${env_var:ANDROID_NDK}/platforms/android-9/arch-arm/usr/include`. Environment variables are authorized and encouraged! Check **Add to all languages** and validate:

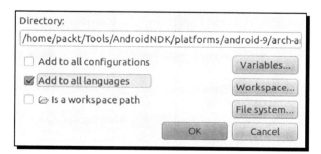

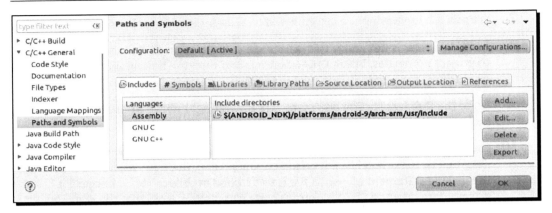

13. Because `jni.h` includes some "core" include files (for example, `stdarg.h`), also add `${env_var:ANDROID_NDK}/toolchains/arm-linux-androideabi-4.4.3/prebuilt/<your OS>/lib/gcc/arm-linux-androideabi/4.4.3/include` path and close the **Properties** window. When Eclipse proposes to rebuild its index, say **Yes**.

14. Yellow lines are now gone. If you press *Ctrl* and click simultaneously on `string.h`, the file gets automatically opened. Your project is now fully integrated in Eclipse.

What just happened?

We managed to integrate Eclipse CDT plugin with an Android project using CDT conversion wizard. In a few clicks, we have turned a Java project into a hybrid Java/C/C++ project! By tweaking CDT project properties, we managed to launch `ndk-build` command to produce the library `mylib` defined in `Android.mk`. After getting compiled, this native library is packaged automatically into the final Android application by ADT.

Running javah automatically while building

If you do not want to bother executing manually `javah` each time native methods changes, you can create an Eclipse builder:

1. Open your project **Properties** window and go to the **Builder** section.

2. Click on **New...** and create a new builder of type **Program**.

3. Enter configuration like done at step 8 with the **External tool configuration**.

4. Validate and position it after **Java Builder** in the list (because JNI files are generated from Java `.class` files).

5. Finally, move CDT Builder right after this new builder (and before **Android Package Builder**).

JNI header files will now be generated automatically each a time project is compiled.

In step 8 and 9, we enabled **Building on resource save** option. This allows automatic compilation to occur without human intervention, for example, when a save operation is triggered. This feature is really nice but can sometimes cause a build cycle: Eclipse keeps compiling code so we moved CDT Builder just before Android Package Builder, in step 9, to avoid Android Pre Compiler and Java Builder to triggering CDT uselessly. But this is not always enough and you should be prepared to deactivate it temporarily or definitely as soon as you are fed up!

Automatic building

Build command invocation is performed automatically when a file is saved. This is practical but can be resource and time consuming and can cause some build cycle. That is why it is sometimes appropriate to deactivate the **Build automatically** option from main menu through **Project**. A new button: appears in the toolbar to trigger a build manually. You can then re-enable automatic building.

Summary

Although setting up, packaging, and deploying an application project are not the most exciting tasks, but they cannot be avoided. Mastering them will allow being productive and focused on the real objective: producing code.

In this chapter, we have seen how to use NDK command tools to compile and deploy Android projects manually. This experience will be useful to make use of continuous integration in your project. We have also seen how to make both Java and C/C++ talk together in a single application using JNI. Finally we have created a hybrid Java/C/C++ project using Eclipse to develop more efficiently.

With this first experiment in mind, you got a good overview of how the NDK works. In the next chapter, we are going to focus on code and discover in more detail the JNI protocol for bidirectional Java to C/C++ communication.

3

Interfacing Java and C/C++ with JNI

Android is inseparable from Java. Although its kernel and its critical libraries are native, the Android application framework is almost entirely written in Java or wrapped inside a thin layer of Java. Obviously, a few libraries are directly accessible from native code, such as Open GL (as we will see in Chapter 6, Rendering Graphics with OpenGL ES). However, most APIs are available only from Java. Do not expect to build your Android GUI directly in C/C++. Technically speaking, it is not yet possible to completely get rid of Java in an Android application. At best, we can hide it under the cover!

Thus, native C/C++ code on Android would be nonsense if it is was not possible to tie Java and C/C++ together. This role is devoted to the Java Native Interface framework, which has been introduced in the previous chapter. JNI is a specification standardized by Sun that is implemented by JVMs with two purposes in mind: allowing Java to call native code and native code to call Java. It is a two-way bridge between the Java and native side and the only way to inject the power of C/C++ into your Java application.

*Thanks to JNI, one can call C/C++ functions from Java like any Java method, passing Java primitives or objects as parameters and receiving them as result. In turn, native code can access, inspect, modify, and call Java objects or raise exceptions with a **reflection-like** API. JNI is a subtle framework which requires care as any misuse can result in a dramatic ending...*

In this chapter, we are going to learn how to do the following:

- Pass and return Java primitives, objects, and arrays to/from native code
- Handle Java objects references inside native code
- Raise exceptions from native code

JNI is a vast and highly technical subject, which could require a whole book to be covered exhaustively. Instead, the present chapter focuses on the essential knowledge to bridge the gap between Java and C++.

Working with Java primitives

You are probably hungry to see more than the simple MyProject created in previous chapter: passing parameters, retrieving results, raising exceptions... to pursue this objective, we will see through this chapter how to implement a basic key/value store with various data types, starting with primitive types and strings.

A simple Java GUI will allow defining an "entry" composed of a key (a character string), a type (an integer, a string, and so on), and a value related to the selected type. An entry is inserted or updated inside the data store which will reside on the native side (actually a simple fixed-size array of entries). Entries can be retrieved back by the Java client. The following diagram presents an overall view of how the program will be structured:

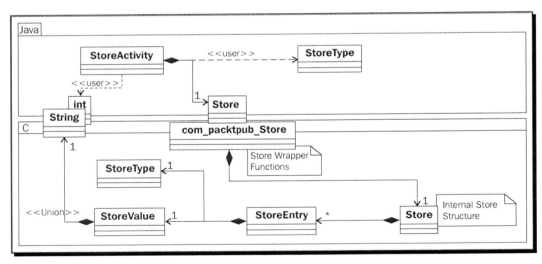

The resulting project is provided with this book under the name Store_Part3-1.

Time for action – building a native key/value store

Let's take care of the Java side first:

1. Create a new hybrid Java/C++ project like shown in the previous chapter:

    ❏   Name it `Store`.

    ❏   Its main package is `com.packtpub`.

    ❏   Its main activity is `StoreActivity`.

    ❏   Do not forget to create a `jni` directory at project's root.

    Let's work on the Java side first, which is going to contain three source files: `Store.java`, `StoreType.java`, and `StoreActivity.java`.

2. Create a new class `Store` which loads the eponym native library and defines the functionalities our key/value store provides. `Store` is a front-end to our native code. To get started, it supports only integers and strings:

    ```
    public class Store {
        static {
            System.loadLibrary("store");
        }

        public native int getInteger(String pKey);
        public native void setInteger(String pKey, int pInt);

        public native String getString(String pKey);
        public native void setString(String pKey, String pString);
    }
    ```

3. Create `StoreType.java` with an enumeration specifying supported data types:

    ```
    public enum StoreType {
        Integer, String
    }
    ```

4. Design a Java GUI in `res/layout/main.xml` similar to the following screenshot. You can make use of the ADT Graphical Layout designer included in ADT or simply copy it from project Store_Part3-1. GUI must allow defining an entry with a key (`TextView`, id `uiKeyEdit`), a value (`TextView`, id `uiValueEdit`) and a type (`Spinner`, id `uiTypeSpinner`). Entries can be saved or retrieved:

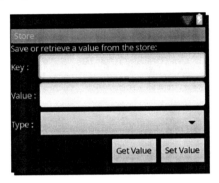

5. Application GUI and `Store` need to be bound together. That is the role devoted to the `StoreActivity` class. When activity is created, set up GUI components: **Type** spinner content is bound to the `StoreType` enum. **Get Value** and **Set Value** buttons trigger private methods `onGetValue()` and `onSetValue()` defined in the next steps. Have a look at final project Store_Part3-1 if you need some help.

Finally, initialize a new instance of the store:

```
public class StoreActivity extends Activity {
    private EditText mUIKeyEdit, mUIValueEdit;
    private Spinner mUITypeSpinner;
    private Button mUIGetButton, mUISetButton;
    private Store mStore;

    @Override
    public void onCreate(Bundle savedInstanceState) {
        super.onCreate(savedInstanceState);
        setContentView(R.layout.main);

        // Initializes components and binds buttons to handlers.
        ...

        mStore = new Store();
    }
```

6. Define method `onGetValue()`, which retrieves an entry from the store according to type `StoreType` currently selected in the GUI:

```
private void onGetValue() {
String lKey = mUIKeyEdit.getText().toString();
StoreType lType = (StoreType) mUITypeSpinner
                .getSelectedItem();

switch (lType) {
case Integer:
    mUIValueEdit.setText(Integer.toString(mStore
                    .getInteger(lKey)));
    break;
case String:
    mUIValueEdit.setText(mStore.getString(lKey));
    break;
}
}
```

7. Add method `onSetValue()` in `StoreActivity` to insert or update an entry into the store. Entry data needs to be parsed according to its type. If value format is incorrect, an Android `Toast` message is displayed:

```
...
private void onSetValue() {
    String lKey = mUIKeyEdit.getText().toString();
    String lValue = mUIValueEdit.getText().toString();
    StoreType lType = (StoreType) mUITypeSpinner
                    .getSelectedItem();

    try {
        switch (lType) {
        case Integer:
            mStore.setInteger(lKey, Integer.parseInt(lValue));
            break;
        case String:
            mStore.setString(lKey, lValue);
            break;
        }
    } catch (NumberFormatException eNumberFormatException) {
        displayError("Incorrect value.");
    }
}

private void displayError(String pError) {
    Toast.makeText(getApplicationContext(), pError,
                Toast.LENGTH_LONG).show();
}
}
```

The Java side is ready and native method prototypes defined. We can switch to the native side.

8. In the `jni` directory, create `Store.h` which defines store data structures. Create a `StoreType` enumerate that matches exactly the Java enumeration. Also create the main structure `Store`, which contains a fixed size array of entries. A `StoreEntry` is composed of a key (a C string), a type, and a value. `StoreValue` is simply the union of any of the possible values (that is, an integer or a C string pointer):

```c
#ifndef _STORE_H_
#define _STORE_H_

#include "jni.h"
#include <stdint.h>

#define STORE_MAX_CAPACITY 16

typedef enum {
    StoreType_Integer, StoreType_String
} StoreType;

typedef union {
    int32_t mInteger;
    char* mString;
} StoreValue;

typedef struct {
    char* mKey;
    StoreType mType;
    StoreValue mValue;
} StoreEntry;

typedef struct {
    StoreEntry mEntries[STORE_MAX_CAPACITY];
    int32_t mLength;
} Store;
...
```

9. Terminate the `Store.h` file by declaring utility methods to create, find, and destroy an entry. `JNIEnv` and `jstring` types are defined in header `jni.h` already included in the previous step:

```c
...
int32_t isEntryValid(JNIEnv* pEnv, StoreEntry* pEntry,
                     StoreType pType);
StoreEntry* allocateEntry(JNIEnv* pEnv, Store* pStore,
jstring pKey);
```

```
StoreEntry* findEntry(JNIEnv* pEnv, Store* pStore, jstring pKey,
                      int32_t* pError);
void releaseEntryValue(JNIEnv* pEnv, StoreEntry* pEntry);
```

All these utility methods are implemented in file `jni/Store.c`. First,
`isEntryValid()` simply checks an entry is allocated and has the expected type:

```
#include "Store.h"
#include <string.h>

int32_t isEntryValid(JNIEnv* pEnv, StoreEntry* pEntry,
                     StoreType pType) {
    if ((pEntry != NULL) && (pEntry->mType == pType)) {
        return 1;
    }
    return 0;
}
...
```

10. Method `findEntry()` compares the key passed as parameter with every entry
key currently stored until it finds a matching one. Instead of working with classic C
strings, it receives directly a `jstring` parameter, which is the native representation
of a Java `String`.

A `jstring` cannot be manipulated directly in native code. Indeed, Java and C
strings are completely different beasts. In Java, `String` is a real object with
member methods whereas in C, strings are raw character arrays.

To recover a C string from a Java `String`, one can use JNI API method
`GetStringUTFChars()` to get a temporary character buffer. Its content can
then be manipulated using standard C routines. `GetStringUTFChars()` must be
systematically coupled with a call to `ReleaseStringUTFChars()` to release the
temporary buffer:

```
...
StoreEntry* findEntry(JNIEnv* pEnv, Store* pStore, jstring pKey,
                      Int32_t* pError) {
    StoreEntry* lEntry = pStore->mEntries;
    StoreEntry* lEntryEnd = lEntry + pStore->mLength;

    const char* lKeyTmp = (*pEnv)->GetStringUTFChars(pEnv, pKey,
                                                      NULL);
    if (lKeyTmp == NULL) {
        if (pError != NULL) {
            *pError = 1;
        }
```

```
        return;
    }

    while ((lEntry < lEntryEnd)
        && (strcmp(lEntry->mKey, lKeyTmp) != 0)) {
        ++lEntry;
    }
    (*pEnv)->ReleaseStringUTFChars(pEnv, pKey, lKeyTmp);

    return (lEntry == lEntryEnd) ? NULL : lEntry;
}
...
```

11. Still in `Store.c`, implement `allocateEntry()` which either creates a new entry (that is, increments store length and returns last array element) or returns an existing one (after releasing its previous value) if key already exists. If entry is new, convert the key to a C string kept in memory outside method scope. Indeed, raw JNI objects live for the time of a method and cannot be kept outside its scope:

> It is a good practice to check that `GetStringUTFChars()` does not return a NULL value which would indicate that the operation has failed (for example, if temporary buffer cannot be allocated because of memory limitations). This should theoretically be checked for `malloc` too, although not done here for simplicity purposes.

```
...
StoreEntry* allocateEntry(JNIEnv* pEnv, Store* pStore, jstring
pKey)
{
    Int32_t lError = 0;
    StoreEntry* lEntry = findEntry(pEnv, pStore, pKey, &lError);
    if (lEntry != NULL) {
        releaseEntryValue(pEnv, lEntry);
    } else if (!lError) {
        if (pStore->mLength >= STORE_MAX_CAPACITY) {
            return NULL;
        }
        lEntry = pStore->mEntries + pStore->mLength;

        const char* lKeyTmp = (*pEnv)->GetStringUTFChars
                                     (pEnv, pKey, NULL);

        if (lKeyTmp == NULL) {
            return;
```

```
        }

        lEntry->mKey = (char*) malloc(strlen(lKeyTmp));
        strcpy(lEntry->mKey, lKeyTmp);
        (*pEnv)->ReleaseStringUTFChars(pEnv, pKey, lKeyTmp);

        ++pStore->mLength;
    }
    return lEntry;
}
...
```

12. The last method of `Store.c` is `releaseEntryValue()`, which frees memory allocated for a value if needed. Currently, only strings are dynamically allocated and need to be freed:

```
...
void releaseEntryValue(JNIEnv* pEnv, StoreEntry* pEntry) {
    int i;
    switch (pEntry->mType) {
        case StoreType_String:
            free(pEntry->mValue.mString);
            break;
    }
}
#endif
```

13. Generate JNI header file for the class `com.packtpub.Store` with `javah` as seen in Chapter 2, *Creating, Compiling, and Deploying Native Projects*. A file `jni/com_packtpub_Store.h` should be generated.

14. Now that our utility methods and JNI header are generated, we need to write the JNI source file `com_packtpub_Store.c`. The unique `Store` instance is saved in a static variable which is created when library is loaded:

```
#include "com_packtpub_Store.h"
#include "Store.h"
#include <stdint.h>
#include <string.h>

static Store gStore = { {}, 0 };
...
```

15. With the help of the generated JNI header, implement `getInteger()` and `setInteger()` in `com_packtpub_Store.c`.

The first method looks for the passed key in the store and returns its value (which needs to be of type integer). If any problem happens, a default value is returned.

The second method allocates an entry (that is, creates a new entry in the store or reuses an existing one if it has the same key) and stores the new integer value in it.

Note here how mInteger, which is a C int, can be "casted" directly to a Java jint primitive and vice versa. They are in fact of the same type:

```
. . .
JNIEXPORT jint JNICALL Java_com_packtpub_Store_getInteger
   (JNIEnv* pEnv, jobject pThis, jstring pKey) {
      StoreEntry* lEntry = findEntry(pEnv, &gStore, pKey, NULL);
      if (isEntryValid(pEnv, lEntry, StoreType_Integer)) {
          return lEntry->mValue.mInteger;
      } else {
          return 0.0f;
      }
}
JNIEXPORT void JNICALL Java_com_packtpub_Store_setInteger
   (JNIEnv* pEnv, jobject pThis, jstring pKey, jint pInteger) {
      StoreEntry* lEntry = allocateEntry(pEnv, &gStore, pKey);
      if (lEntry != NULL) {
          lEntry->mType = StoreType_Integer;
          lEntry->mValue.mInteger = pInteger;
      }
}
. . .
```

16. Strings have to be handled with more care. Java strings are not real primitives. Types jstring and char* cannot be used interchangeably as seen in step 11.

To create a Java String object from a C string, use NewStringUTF().

In second method setString(), convert a Java string into a C string with GetStringUTFChars() and SetStringUTFChars() as seen previously.

```
. . .
JNIEXPORT jstring JNICALL Java_com_packtpub_Store_getString
   (JNIEnv* pEnv, jobject pThis, jstring pKey) {
      StoreEntry* lEntry = findEntry(pEnv, &gStore, pKey, NULL);
      if (isEntryValid(pEnv, lEntry, StoreType_String)) {
        return (*pEnv)->NewStringUTF(pEnv, lEntry->mValue.mString);
      }
      else {
        return NULL;
      }
}
```

```
JNIEXPORT void JNICALL Java_com_packtpub_Store_setString
  (JNIEnv* pEnv, jobject pThis, jstring pKey, jstring pString) {
    const char* lStringTmp = (*pEnv)->GetStringUTFChars(pEnv,
                                                    pString, NULL);
    if (lStringTmp == NULL) {
        return;
    }

    StoreEntry* lEntry = allocateEntry(pEnv, &gStore, pKey);
    if (lEntry != NULL) {
        lEntry->mType = StoreType_String;
        jsize lStringLength = (*pEnv)->GetStringUTFLength(pEnv,
                                                    pString);
        lEntry->mValue.mString =
            (char*) malloc(sizeof(char) * (lStringLength + 1));
        strcpy(lEntry->mValue.mString, lStringTmp);
    }
    (*pEnv)->ReleaseStringUTFChars(pEnv, pString, lStringTmp);
}
```

17. Finally, write the `Android.mk` file as follows. Library name is `store` and the two C files are listed. To compile C code, run `ndk-build` inside project's root:

```
LOCAL_PATH := $(call my-dir)

include $(CLEAR_VARS)

LOCAL_CFLAGS    := -DHAVE_INTTYPES_H
LOCAL_MODULE    := store
LOCAL_SRC_FILES := com_packtpub_Store.c Store.c

include $(BUILD_SHARED_LIBRARY)
```

What just happened?

Run the application, save a few entries with different keys, types, and values and try to get them back from the native store. We have managed to pass and retrieve `int` primitives and strings from Java to C. These values are saved in a data store indexed by a string key. Entries can be retrieved from the store with respect to their key and type.

Integer primitives wear several dresses during native calls: first an int in Java code, then a jint during transfer from/to Java code and finally an int/int32_t in native code. Obviously, we could have kept the JNI representation jint in native code since both types are equivalent.

 Type int32_t is a typedef refering to int introduced by the **C99 standard library** with the aim at more portability. More numeric types are available in stdint.h. to force their use in JNI, declare -DHAVE_INTTYPES_H macro in Android.mk.

More generally, primitive types have all their proper representations:

Java type	JNI type	C type	Stdint C type
boolean	Jboolean	unsigned char	uint8_t
byte	Jbyte	signed char	int8_t
char	Jchar	unsigned short	uint16_t
double	Jdouble	double	double
float	jfloat	float	float
int	jint	Int	int32_t
long	jlong	long long	int64_t
short	jshort	Short	int16_t

On the other hand, Java strings need a concrete conversion to C strings to allow processing using standard C string routines. Indeed, jstring is not a representation of a classic char* array but of a reference to a Java String object, accessible from Java code only.

Conversion is performed with JNI method GetStringUTFChars() which must match with a call to ReleaseStringUTFChars(). Internally, this conversion allocates a new string buffer. The resulting C string is encoded in modified UTF-8 format (a slightly different flavor of UTF-8) that allows processing with standard C routine. Modified UTF-8 can represent standard ASCII characters (that is, on one byte) and can grow to several bytes for extended characters. This format is different than Java string, which uses an UTF-16 representation (which explains why Java characters are 16-bit, as shown in the preceding table). To avoid an internal conversion when getting native strings, JNI also provides GetStringChars() and ReleaseStringChars(), which returns an UTF-16 representation instead. This format is not zero-terminated like classic C strings. Thus, it is compulsory to use them in conjunction with GetStringLength() (whereas GetStringUTFLength() can be replaced by a classic strlen() with modified UTF-8).

See JNI specification at `http://java.sun.com/docs/books/jni/html/jniTOC.html` for more details on the subject. Refer to `http://java.sun.com/docs/books/jni/html/types.html` for details to know more about JNI types and to `http://java.sun.com/developer/technicalArticles/Intl/Supplementary` for an interesting discussion about strings in Java.

Have a go hero – passing and returning other primitive types

The current store deals only with integers and strings. Based on this model, try to implement store methods for other primitive types: `boolean`, `byte`, `char`, `double`, `float`, `long`, and `short`.

 Project Store_Part3-Final provided with this book implements these cases.

Referencing Java objects from native code

We know from a previous part that a string is represented in JNI as a `jstring`, which is in fact a Java object which means that it is possible to exchange Java objects through JNI! But because native code cannot understand or access Java directly, all Java objects have the same representation: a `jobject`.

In this part, we are going to focus on how to save an object on the native side and how to send it back to Java. In the next project, we are going to work with colors, although any other type of object would work.

 Project Store_Part3-1 can be used as a starting point for this part. The resulting project is provided with this book under the name Store_Part3-2.

Time for action – saving a reference to an object in the Store

First, let's append the `Color` data type to the Java client:

1. In `package com.packtpub`, create a new class `Color` that contains an integer representation of a color. This integer is parsed from a `String` (HTML codes such as #FF0000) thanks to the Android `android.graphics.Color` class:

```
public class Color {
    private int mColor;
```

```java
        public Color(String pColor) {
            super();
            mColor = android.graphics.Color.parseColor(pColor);
        }

        @Override
        public String toString() {
            return String.format("#%06X", mColor);
        }
    }
```

2. Change `StoreType` enumeration to include the new `Color` data type:

```java
public enum StoreType {
    Integer, String, Color
}
```

3. Open the `Store.java` file created in the previous part and add two new methods to retrieve and save a `Color` object in the native store:

```java
public class Store {
    static {
        System.loadLibrary("store");
    }
    ...

    public native Color getColor(String pKey);
    public native void setColor(String pKey, Color pColor);
}
```

4. Open the existing file `StoreActivity.java` and update methods `onGetValue()` and `onSetValue()` to display and parse `Color` instances. Note that color parsing can generate an `IllegalArgumentException` if color code is incorrect:

```java
public class StoreActivity extends Activity {
    ...
    private void onGetValue() {
        String lKey = mUIKeyEdit.getText().toString();
        StoreType lType = (StoreType) mUITypeSpinner
                            .getSelectedItem();

        switch (lType) {
        ...
        case Color:
            mUIValueEdit.setText(mStore.getColor(lKey).toString());
            break;
        }
    }
```

```
private void onSetValue() {
    String lKey = mUIKeyEdit.getText().toString();
    String lValue = mUIValueEdit.getText().toString();
    StoreType lType = (StoreType) mUITypeSpinner
                        .getSelectedItem();

    try {
        switch (lType) {
        ...
        case Color:
            mStore.setColor(lKey, new Color(lValue));
            break;
        }
    }
    catch (NumberFormatException eNumberFormatException) {
        displayError("Incorrect value.");
    } catch (IllegalArgumentException eIllegalArgumentException)
    {
        displayError("Incorrect value.");
    }
}
...
}
```

The Java side is now ready. Let's write the necessary code to retrieve and store a Color entry inside native code.

5. In jni/Store.h, append the new color type to the StoreType enumeration and add a new member to the StoreValue union. But what type to use, since Color is an object known only from Java? In JNI, all java objects have the same type: jobject, an (indirect) object reference:

```
...
typedef enum {
    StoreType_Integer, StoreType_String, StoreType_Color
} StoreType;


typedef union {
    int32_t   mInteger;
    char*     mString;
    jobject   mColor;
} StoreValue;
...
```

6. Re-generate JNI header file `jni/com_packtpub_Store.h` with `javah`.

7. Two new method prototypes `getColor()` and `setColor()` have been freshly generated. We have to implement them. First one simply returns the Java `Color` object kept in the store entry. No difficulties here.

The real subtleties are introduced in the second method `setColor()`. Indeed, at first sight, simply saving the `jobject` value in the store entry would seem sufficient. But this assumption is wrong. Objects passed in parameters or created inside a JNI method are **local references**. Local references cannot be kept in native code outside method scope.

To be allowed to keep a Java object reference in native code after method returns, they must be turned into **global references** to inform the Dalvik VM that they cannot be garbage collected. To do so, JNI API provides `NewGlobalRef()` and its counterpart `DeleteGlobalRef()`. Here, global reference is deleted if entry allocation fails:

```
#include "com_packtpub_Store.h"
#include "Store.h"
...

JNIEXPORT jobject JNICALL Java_com_packtpub_Store_getColor
  (JNIEnv* pEnv, jobject pThis, jstring pKey) {
    StoreEntry* lEntry = findEntry(pEnv, &gStore, pKey, NULL);
    if (isEntryValid(pEnv, lEntry, StoreType_Color)) {
        return lEntry->mValue.mColor;
    } else {
        return NULL;
    }
}

JNIEXPORT void JNICALL Java_com_packtpub_Store_setColor
  (JNIEnv* pEnv, jobject pThis, jstring pKey, jobject pColor) {
    jobject lColor = (*pEnv)->NewGlobalRef(pEnv, pColor);
    if (lColor == NULL) {
        return;
    }

    StoreEntry* lEntry = allocateEntry(pEnv, &gStore, pKey);
    if (lEntry != NULL) {
        lEntry->mType = StoreType_Color;
        lEntry->mValue.mColor = lColor;
    } else {
        (*pEnv)->DeleteGlobalRef(pEnv, lColor);
    }
}
...
```

8. A call to `NewGlobalRef()` must always match with a call to `DeleteGlobalRef()`. In our example, global reference should be deleted when entry is replaced by a new one (removal is not implemented). Do it in `Store.c` by updating `releaseEntryValue()`:

```
...
void releaseEntryValue(JNIEnv* pEnv, StoreEntry* pEntry) {
    switch (pEntry->mType) {
        ...
        case StoreType_Color:
            (*pEnv)->DeleteGlobalRef(pEnv, pEntry->mValue.mColor);
            break;
    }
}
```

What just happened?

Run the application, enter and save a color value such as **#FF0000** or **red** (which is a predefined value allowed by the Android color parser) and get the entry back from the store. We have managed to store a Java object on the native side.

All objects coming from Java are represented by a `jobject`. Even `jstring`, which is in fact a `typedef` over `jobject`, can be used as such. Because native code invocation is limited to method boundaries, JNI keeps object references local to this method by default. This means that a `jobject` can only be used safely inside the method it was transmitted to. Indeed, the Dalvik VM is in charge of invoking native methods and can manage Java object references before and after method is run. But a `jobject` is just a "pointer" without any smart or garbage collection mechanism (after all, we want to get rid of Java, at least partially). Once native method returns, the Dalvik VM has no way to know if native code still holds object references and can decide to collect them at any time.

 Global references are also the only way to share variables between threads because JNI contexts are always thread local.

To be able to use an object reference outside its scope, reference must be made global with `NewGlobalRef()` and "unreferenced" with `DeleteGlobalRef()`. Without the latter, the Dalvik VM would consider objects to still be referenced and would never collect them.

Have a look at JNI specification at `http://java.sun.com/docs/books/jni/html/jniTOC.html` for more information on the subject.

Local and global JNI references

When getting an object reference from JNI, this reference is said to be **Local**. It is automatically freed (the reference not the object) when native method returns to allow proper garbage collection later in the Java code. Thus, by default, an object reference cannot be kept outside the lifetime of a native call. For example:

```
static jobject gMyReference;
JNIEXPORT void JNICALL Java_MyClass_myMethod(JNIEnv* pEnv,
                                        jobject pThis, jobject pRef) {
    gMyReference = pRef;
}
```

The piece of code above should be strictly prohibited. Keeping such a reference outside JNI method will eventually lead to a disaster (memory corruption or a crash).

Local references can be deleted when they are no longer used:

```
pEnv->DeleteLocalRef(lReference);
```

A JVM is required to store at least 16 references at the same time and can refuse to create more. To do so, explicitly inform it, for example:

```
pEnv->EnsureLocalCapacity(30)
```

It is a rather good practice to eliminate references when they are no longer needed. There are two benefits to act as such:

Because the number of local references in a method is finite. When a piece of code contains and manipulates many objects such as an array, keep your number of simultaneous local references low by deleting them as soon as possible.

Because released local references can be garbage collected immediately and memory freed if no other references exist.

To keep object references for a longer period of time, one needs to create a global reference:

```
JNIEXPORT void JNICALL Java_MyClass_myStartMethod (JNIEnv* pEnv,
                                        jobject pThis, jobject pRef) {
    . . .
    gMyReference = pEnv->NewGlobalRef(pEnv, pRef<);
    . . .
}
```

And then delete it for proper garbage collection:

```
JNIEXPORT void JNICALL Java_MyClass_myEndMethod (JNIEnv* pEnv,
                                      jobject pThis, jobject pRef) {
    ...
    gMyReference = pEnv->DeleteGlobalRef(gMyReference)
    ...
}
```

Global reference can now be safely shared between two different JNI calls or threads.

Throwing exceptions from native code

Error handling in the Store project is not really satisfying. If the requested key cannot be found or if the retrieved value type does not match the requested type, a default value is returned. We definitely need a way to indicate an error happened! And what better (note that I do not say faster...) to indicate an error than an exception?

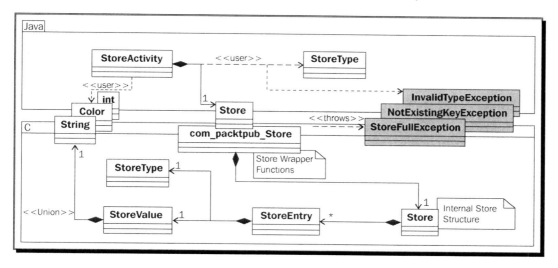

 Project Store_Part3-2 can be used as a starting point for this part. The resulting project is provided with this book under the name Store_Part3-3.

Time for action – raising exceptions from the Store

Let's start by creating and catching exceptions on the Java side:

1. Create a new exception class `InvalidTypeException` of type `Exception` in package `com.packtpub.exception` as follows:

```
public class InvalidTypeException extends Exception {
    public InvalidTypeException(String pDetailMessage) {
        super(pDetailMessage);
    }
}
```

2. Repeat the operation for two other exceptions: `NotExistingKeyException` of type `Exception` and `StoreFullException` of type `RuntimeException` instead.

3. Open existing file `Store.java` and declare thrown exceptions on getter prototypes only (`StoreFullException` is a `RuntimeException` and does not need declaration):

```
public class Store {
    static {
        System.loadLibrary("store");
    }

    public native int getInteger(String pKey)
        throws NotExistingKeyException, InvalidTypeException;
    public native void setInteger(String pKey, int pInt);

    public native String getString(String pKey)
        throws NotExistingKeyException, InvalidTypeException;
    public native void setString(String pKey, String pString);

    public native Color getColor(String pKey)
        throws NotExistingKeyException, InvalidTypeException;
    public native void setColor(String pKey, Color pColor);
}
```

4. Exceptions need to be caught. Catch `NotExistingKeyException` and `InvalidTypeException` in `onGetValue()`. Catch `StoreFullException` in `onSetValue()` in case entry cannot be inserted:

```
public class StoreActivity extends Activity {
    ...
    private void onGetValue() {
```

```java
        String lKey = mUIKeyEdit.getText().toString();
        StoreType lType = (StoreType) mUITypeSpinner
                        .getSelectedItem();

        try {
            switch (lType) {
            ...
            }
        }
        catch (NotExistingKeyException eNotExistingKeyException) {
            displayError("Key does not exist in store");
        } catch (InvalidTypeException eInvalidTypeException) {
            displayError("Incorrect type.");
        }
    }

    private void onSetValue() {
        String lKey = mUIKeyEdit.getText().toString();
        String lValue = mUIValueEdit.getText().toString();
        StoreType lType = (StoreType) mUITypeSpinner
                        .getSelectedItem();

        try {
            switch (lType) {
            ...
            }
        }
        catch (NumberFormatException eNumberFormatException) {
            displayError("Incorrect value.");
        } catch (IllegalArgumentException eIllegalArgumentException)
        {
            displayError("Incorrect value.");
        } catch (StoreFullException eStoreFullException) {
            displayError("Store is full.");
        }
    }
    ...
}
```

Let's throw these exceptions from native code. As exceptions are not part of the C language, JNI exceptions cannot be declared on C method prototypes (the same goes for C++ which has a different exception model than Java). Thus, there is no need to re-generate JNI header.

5. Open `jni/Store.h` created in previous parts and define three new helper methods to throw exceptions:

```
#ifndef _STORE_H_
#define _STORE_H_

. . .

void throwInvalidTypeException(JNIEnv* pEnv);
void throwNotExistingKeyException(JNIEnv* pEnv);
void throwStoreFullException(JNIEnv* pEnv);
#endif
```

6. `NotExistingKeyException` and `InvalidTypeException` are only thrown when getting a value from the store. A good place to raise them is when checking an entry with `isEntryValid()`. Open and change the `jni/Store.c` file accordingly:

```
#include "Store.h"
#include <string.h>

int32_t isEntryValid(JNIEnv* pEnv, StoreEntry* pEntry,
                     StoreType pType) {
    if (pEntry == NULL) {
        throwNotExistingKeyException(pEnv);
    } else if (pEntry->mType != pType) {
        throwInvalidTypeException(pEnv);
    } else {
        return 1;
    }
    return 0;
}
. . .
```

7. `StoreFullException` is obviously raised when a new entry is inserted. Modify `allocateEntry()` in the same file to check entry insertions:

```
. . .
StoreEntry* allocateEntry(JNIEnv* pEnv, Store* pStore, jstring
pKey){
    StoreEntry* lEntry = findEntry(pEnv, pStore, pKey);
    if (lEntry != NULL) {
        releaseEntryValue(pEnv, lEntry);
    } else {
        if (pStore->mLength >= STORE_MAX_CAPACITY) {
            throwStoreFullException(pEnv);
            return NULL;
        }
```

```
        // Initializes and insert the new entry.
        . . .
    }
    return lEntry;
}
. . .
```

8. We must implement `throwNotExistingException()`. To throw a Java exception, the first task is to find the corresponding class (like with the Java Reflection API). A Java class reference is represented in JNI with the specific type `jclass`. Then, raise the exception with `ThrowNew()`. Once we no longer need the exception class reference, we can get rid of it with `DeleteLocalRef()`:

```
. . .
void throwNotExistingKeyException(JNIEnv* pEnv) {
    jclass lClass = (*pEnv)->FindClass(pEnv,
        "com/packtpub/exception/NotExistingKeyException");
    if (lClass != NULL) {
        (*pEnv)->ThrowNew(pEnv, lClass, "Key does not exist.");
    }
    (*pEnv)->DeleteLocalRef(pEnv, lClass);
}
```

9. Repeat the operation for the two other exceptions. The code is identical (even to throw a runtime exception), only the class name changes.

What just happened?

Launch the application and try to get an entry with a non-existing key. Repeat the operation with an entry which exists in the store but with a different type then the one selected in the GUI. In both cases, there is an error message because of the raised exception. Try to save more than 16 references in the store and you will get an error again.

Raising exception is a not a complex task. In addition, it is a good introduction to the Java call-back mechanism provided by JNI. An exception is instantiated with a class descriptor of type `jclass` (which is also a `jobject` behind the scenes). Class descriptor is searched in the current class loader according to its complete name (package path included).

Do not forget about return codes

`FindClass()` and JNI methods in general can fail for several reasons (not enough memory is available, class not found, and so on). Thus checking their result is highly advised.

Once an exception is raised, do not make further call to JNI except cleaning methods (`DeleteLocalRef()`, `DeleteGlobalRef()`, and so on). Native code should clean its resources and give control back to Java, although it is possible to continue "pure" native processing if no Java is invoked. When native method returns, exception is propagated by the VM to Java.

We have also deleted a local reference, the one pointing to the class descriptor because it was not needed any more after its use (step 8). When JNI lends you something, do not forget to give it back!

JNI in C++

C is not an object-oriented language but C++ is. This is why you do not write JNI in C like in C++.

In C, `JNIEnv` is in fact a structure containing function pointer. Of course, when a `JNIEnv` is given to you, all these pointers are initialized so that you can call them a bit like an object. However, the `this` parameter, which is implicit in an object-oriented language, is given as first parameter in C (`pJNIEnv` in the following code). Also, `JNIEnv` needs to be dereferenced the first time to run a method:

```
jclass ClassContext = (*pJNIEnv)->FindClass(pJNIEnv,
    "android/content/Context");
```

C++ code is more natural and simple. The `this` parameter is implicit and there is no need to dereference `JNIEnv`, as methods are not declared as function pointer anymore but as real member methods:

```
jclass ClassContext = lJNIEnv->FindClass(
    "android/content/Context");
```

Handling Java arrays

There is one type we have not talked about yet: arrays. Arrays have a specific place in JNI like in Java. They have their proper types and their proper API, although Java arrays are also objects at their root. Let's improve the Store project by letting users enter a set of values simultaneously in an entry. Then, this set is going to be communicated to the native backend in a Java array which is then going to be stored as a classic C array.

 Project Store_Part3-3 can be used as a starting point for this part. The resulting project is provided with this book under the name Store_Part3-4.

Time for action – saving a reference to an object in the Store

Let's start again with the Java code:

1. To help us handling operations on arrays, let's download a helper library: **Google Guava** (release r09 in this book) at `http://code.google.com/p/guava-libraries`. Guava offers many useful methods to deal primitives and arrays and perform "pseudo-functional" programming. Copy `guava-r09 jar` contained in the downloaded ZIP in `libs`.

2. Open project `Properties` and go to the `Java Build Path` section. In the Libraries tab, reference Guava jar by clicking on the `Add JARs...` button. Validate.

3. Edit `StoreType` enumeration initiated in previous parts and add two new values the `IntegerArray` and `ColorArray`:

```
public enum StoreType {
    Integer, String, Color,
    IntegerArray, ColorArray
}
```

4. Open `Store.java` and add new methods to retrieve and save `int` and `Color` arrays:

```
public class Store {
    static {
        System.loadLibrary("store");
    }
    ...


    public native int[] getIntegerArray(String pKey)
        throws NotExistingKeyException;
    public native void setIntegerArray(String pKey,
int[] pIntArray);

    public native Color[] getColorArray(String pKey)
        throws NotExistingKeyException;
    public native void setColorArray(String pKey,
                    Color[] pColorArray);
}
```

5. Finally, connect native methods to the GUI in file `StoreActivity.java`. First, `onGetValue()` retrieves an array from the store, concatenates its values with a semicolon separator thanks to Guava joiners (more information can be found in Guava Javadoc at `http://guava-libraries.googlecode.com/svn`) and finally displays them:

```
public class StoreActivity extends Activity {
    ...
    private void onGetValue() {
        String lKey = mUIKeyEdit.getText().toString();
        StoreType lType = (StoreType) mUITypeSpinner
                        .getSelectedItem();

        try {
            switch (lType) {
            ...
            case IntegerArray:
                mUIValueEdit.setText(Ints.join(";",
                            mStore.getIntegerArray(lKey)));
                break;

            case ColorArray:
                mUIValueEdit.setText(Joiner.on(";").join(
                            mStore.getColorArray(lKey)));
                break;
            }
        }
        catch (NotExistingKeyException eNotExistingKeyException) {
            displayError("Key does not exist in store");
        } catch (InvalidTypeException eInvalidTypeException) {
            displayError("Incorrect type.");
        }
    }
    ...
```

6. In `StoreActivity.java`, improve `onSetValue()` to convert a list of user entered values into an array before sending it to the `Store`. Use the Guava transformation feature to accomplish this task: a `Function` object (or **functor**) converting a string value into the target type is passed to the helper method `stringToList()`. The latter splits the user string on the semicolon separator before running transformations:

```
    ...
    private void onSetValue() {
        String lKey = mUIKeyEdit.getText().toString();
```

```
            String lValue = mUIValueEdit.getText().toString();
            StoreType lType = (StoreType) mUITypeSpinner
                            .getSelectedItem();

        try {
            switch (lType) {
            ...
            case IntegerArray:
                mStore.setIntegerArray(lKey,
                    Ints.toArray(stringToList(
                    new Function<String, Integer>() {
                        public Integer apply(String pSubValue) {
                            return Integer.parseInt(pSubValue);
                        }
                    }, lValue)));
                break;
            case ColorArray:
                List<Color> lIdList = stringToList(
                    new Function<String, Color>() {
                        public Color apply(String pSubValue) {
                            return new Color(pSubValue);
                        }
                    }, lValue);
                Color[] lIdArray = lIdList.toArray(
                                    new Color[lIdList.size()]);
                mStore.setColorArray(lKey, lIdArray);
                break;
            }
        }
        catch (NumberFormatException eNumberFormatException) {
            displayError("Incorrect value.");
        } catch (IllegalArgumentException eIllegalArgumentException)
        {
            displayError("Incorrect value.");
        } catch (StoreFullException eStoreFullException) {
            displayError("Store is full.");
        }
    }

    private <TType> List<TType> stringToList(
                    Function<String, TType> pConversion,
                    String pValue) {
        String[] lSplitArray = pValue.split(";");
        List<String> lSplitList = Arrays.asList(lSplitArray);
        return Lists.transform(lSplitList, pConversion);
    }
}
```

Switch back to the native side.

7. In jni/Store.h, add the new array types to the enumeration StoreType.

Also declare two new fields mIntegerArray and mColorArray in StoreValue union. Store arrays are represented as raw C arrays (that is, a pointer).

We also need to remember the length of these arrays. Put this information in a new field mLength in StoreEntry.

```
#ifndef _STORE_H_
#define _STORE_H_

#include "jni.h"
#include <stdint.h>

#define STORE_MAX_CAPACITY 16

typedef enum {
    StoreType_Integer, StoreType_String, StoreType_Color,
    StoreType_IntegerArray, StoreType_ColorArray
} StoreType;

typedef union {
    int32_t  mInteger;
    char*    mString;
    jobject  mColor;
    int32_t* mIntegerArray;
    jobject* mColorArray;
} StoreValue;

typedef struct {
    char* mKey;
    StoreType mType;
    StoreValue mValue;
    int32_t mLength;
} StoreEntry;
...
```

8. Open jni/Store.c and insert new cases in releaseEntryValue() for arrays. Array allocated memory has to be freed when corresponding entry is released. As colors are Java objects, delete global references or garbage collection will never happen:

```
...
void releaseEntryValue(JNIEnv* pEnv, StoreEntry* pEntry) {
    int32_t i;
    switch (pEntry->mType) {
```

```
    . . .
    case StoreType_IntegerArray:
        free(pEntry->mValue.mIntegerArray);
        break;
    case StoreType_ColorArray:
        for (i = 0; i < pEntry->mLength; ++i) {
            (*pEnv)->DeleteGlobalRef(pEnv,
                        pEntry->mValue.mColorArray[i]);
        }
        free(pEntry->mValue.mColorArray);
        break;
    }
}
. . .
```

9. Re-generate JNI header `jni/com_packtpub_Store.h`.

10. Implement all these new store methods in `com_packtpub_Store.c`, starting with `getIntegerArray()`. A JNI array of integers is represented with type `jintArray`. If an `int` is equivalent to a `jint`, an `int*` array is absolutely not equivalent to a `jintArray`. The first is a pointer to a memory buffer whereas the second is a reference to an object.

Thus, to return a `jintArray` here, instantiate a new Java integer array with JNI API method `NewIntArray()`. Then, use `SetIntArrayRegion()` to copy the native `int` buffer content into the `jintArray`.

`SetIntArrayRegion()` performs bound checking to prevent buffer overflows and can return an `ArrayIndexOutOfBoundsException()`. However, there is no need to check it since there is no statement further in the method to be executed (exceptions will be propagated automatically by the JNI framework):

```
#include "com_packtpub_Store.h"
#include "Store.h"
. . .


JNIEXPORT jintArray JNICALL Java_com_packtpub_Store_
getIntegerArray
  (JNIEnv* pEnv, jobject pThis, jstring pKey) {
    StoreEntry* lEntry = findEntry(pEnv, &gStore, pKey, NULL);
    if (isEntryValid(pEnv, lEntry, StoreType_IntegerArray)) {
        jintArray lJavaArray = (*pEnv)->NewIntArray(pEnv,
                                        lEntry->mLength);
        if (lJavaArray == NULL) {
            return;
        }
```

```
            (*pEnv)->SetIntArrayRegion(pEnv, lJavaArray, 0,
                lEntry->mLength, lEntry->mValue.mIntegerArray);
        return lJavaArray;
    } else {
        return NULL;
    }
}
...
```

11. To save a Java array in native code, the inverse operation `GetIntArrayRegion()` exists. The only way to allocate a suitable target memory buffer is to measure array size with `GetArrayLength()`. `GetIntArrayRegion()` also performs bound checking and can raise an exception. So method flow needs to be stopped immediately when detecting one with `ExceptionCheck()`. Although `GetIntArrayRegion()` is not the only method to raise exceptions, it has the particularity with `SetIntArrayRegion()` to return `void`. There is no way to check return code. Hence the exception check:

```
...
JNIEXPORT void JNICALL Java_com_packtpub_Store_setIntegerArray
    (JNIEnv* pEnv, jobject pThis, jstring pKey, jintArray
pIntegerArray) {
    jsize lLength = (*pEnv)->GetArrayLength(pEnv, pIntegerArray);
    int32_t* lArray = (int32_t*) malloc(lLength *
sizeof(int32_t));
    (*pEnv)->GetIntArrayRegion(pEnv, pIntegerArray, 0, lLength,
                              lArray);
    if ((*pEnv)->ExceptionCheck(pEnv)) {
        free(lArray);
        return;
    }

    StoreEntry* lEntry = allocateEntry(pEnv, &gStore, pKey);
    if (lEntry != NULL) {
        lEntry->mType = StoreType_IntegerArray;
        lEntry->mLength = lLength;
        lEntry->mValue.mIntegerArray = lArray;
    } else {
        free(lArray);
        return;
    }
}
...
```

12. Object arrays are different than primitive arrays. They are instantiated with a `Class` type (here `com/packtpub/Color`) because Java arrays are mono-type. Object arrays are represented with type `jobjectArray`.

On the opposite of primitive arrays, it is not possible to work on all elements at the same time. Instead, objects are set one by one with `SetObjectArrayElement()`. Here, array is filled with `Color` objects stored on the native side, which keeps global references to them. So there is no need to delete or create any reference here (except the class descriptor).

 Remember that an object array keep references to the objects it holds. Thus, local as well as global references can be inserted in an array and deleted safely right after.

```
. . .
JNIEXPORT jobjectArray JNICALL Java_com_packtpub_Store_
getColorArray
                        (JNIEnv* pEnv, jobject pThis, jstring
pKey) {
    StoreEntry* lEntry = findEntry(pEnv, &gStore, pKey, NULL);
    if (isEntryValid(pEnv, lEntry, StoreType_ColorArray)) {
        jclass lColorClass = (*pEnv)->FindClass(pEnv,
                                    "com/packtpub/Color");
        if (lColorClass == NULL) {
            return NULL;
        }
        jobjectArray lJavaArray = (*pEnv)->NewObjectArray(
            pEnv, lEntry->mLength, lColorClass, NULL);
        (*pEnv)->DeleteLocalRef(pEnv, lColorClass);
        if (lJavaArray == NULL) {
            return NULL;
        }

        int32_t i;
        for (i = 0; i < lEntry->mLength; ++i) {
            (*pEnv)->SetObjectArrayElement(pEnv, lJavaArray, i,
            lEntry->mValue.mColorArray[i]);
            if ((*pEnv)->ExceptionCheck(pEnv)) {
                return NULL;
            }
        }
        return lJavaArray;
    } else {
        return NULL;
    } }
. . .
```

13. In `setColorArray()`, array elements are also retrieved one by one with `GetObjectArrayElement()`. Returned references are local and should be made global to store them safely in a memory buffer. If a problem happens, global references must be carefully destroyed to allow garbage collection, as we decide to interrupt processing.

```
...
JNIEXPORT void JNICALL Java_com_packtpub_Store_setColorArray
(JNIEnv*
        pEnv, jobject pThis, jstring pKey, jobjectArray
pColorArray) {
    jsize lLength = (*pEnv)->GetArrayLength(pEnv, pColorArray);
    jobject* lArray = (jobject*) malloc(lLength *
sizeof(jobject));
    int32_t i, j;
    for (i = 0; i < lLength; ++i) {
        jobject lLocalColor = (*pEnv)->GetObjectArrayElement(pEnv,
                                        pColorArray, i);
        if (lLocalColor == NULL) {
            for (j = 0; j < i; ++j) {
                (*pEnv)->DeleteGlobalRef(pEnv, lArray[j]);
            }
            free(lArray);
            return;
        }

        lArray[i] = (*pEnv)->NewGlobalRef(pEnv, lLocalColor);
        if (lArray[i] == NULL) {
            for (j = 0; j < i; ++j) {
                (*pEnv)->DeleteGlobalRef(pEnv, lArray[j]);
            }
            free(lArray);
            return;
        }
        (*pEnv)->DeleteLocalRef(pEnv, lLocalColor);
    }

    StoreEntry* lEntry = allocateEntry(pEnv, &gStore, pKey);
    if (lEntry != NULL) {
        lEntry->mType = StoreType_ColorArray;
        lEntry->mLength = lLength;
        lEntry->mValue.mColorArray = lArray;
    } else {
        for (j = 0; j < i; ++j) {
```

```
                    (*pEnv)->DeleteGlobalRef(pEnv, lArray[j]);
            }
            free(lArray);
            return;
        }
    }
```

What just happened?

We have transmitted Java arrays from native to C code and vice versa. Java arrays are objects which cannot be manipulated natively in C code but only through a dedicated API.

Primitives array types available are `jbooleanArray`, `jbyteArray`, `jcharArray`, `jdoubleArray`, `jfloatArray`, `jlongArray`, and `jshortArray`. These arrays are manipulated "by set", that is, several elements at a time. There are several ways to access array content:

Get<Primitive>ArrayRegion() and Set<Primitive>ArrayRegion()	Copy the content of a Java array into a native array or reciprocally. This is the best solution when a local copy is necessary to native code.
Get<Primitive>ArrayElements(), Set<Primitive>ArrayElements(), and Release<Primitive>ArrayElements()	These methods are similar but work on a buffer either temporarily allocated by them or pointing directly on the target array. This buffer must be released after use. These are interesting to use if no local data copy is needed.
Get<Primitive>ArrayCritical() and Release<Primitive>ArrayCritical()	These are more likely to provide a direct access to the target array (instead of a copy). However, their usage is restricted: JNI functions and Java callbacks must not be performed..

> The final project `Store` provides an example of `Get<Primitives>ArrayElements()` usage for `setBooleanArray()`.

Objects arrays are specific because on the opposite of primitive arrays each array element is a reference which can be garbage collected. As a consequence, a new reference is automatically registered when inserted inside the array. That way, even if calling code removes its references, array still references them. Object arrays are manipulated with `GetObjectArrayElement()` and `SetObjectArrayElement()`.

See `http://download.oracle.com/javase/1.5.0/docs/guide/jni/spec/functions.html` for a more exhaustive list of JNI functions.

Checking JNI exceptions

In JNI, methods which can raise an exception (most of them actually) should be carefully checked. If a return code or pointer is given back, checking it is sufficient to know if something happened. But sometimes, with Java callbacks or methods like `GetIntArrayRegion()`, we have no return code. In that case, exceptions should be checked systematically with `ExceptionOccured()` or `ExceptionCheck()`. The first returns a `jthrowable` type containing a reference to the raised exception whereas the latter just returns a Boolean indicator.

When an exception is raised, any subsequent call fails until either:

- method returns and exception is propagated.

- or exception is cleared. Clearing an exception mean that the exception is handled and thus not propagated to Java. For example:

```
Jthrowable lException;
pEnv->CallObjectMethod(pJNIEnv, ...);
lException = pEnv->ExceptionOccurred(pEnv);
if (lException) {
    // Do something...
    pEnv->ExceptionDescribe();
    pEnv->ExceptionClear();
    (*pEnv)->DeleteLocalRef(pEnv, lException);
}
```

Here, `ExceptionDescribe()` is a utility routine to dump exception content like done by `printStackTrace()` in Java. Only a few JNI methods are still safe to call when handling an exception:

`DeleteLocalRef()`	`PushLocalFrame()`
`DeleteGlobalRef()`	`PopLocalFrame()`
`ExceptionOccured()`	`ReleaseStringChars()`
`ExceptionDescribe()`	`ReleaseStringUTFChars()`
`ExceptionOccured()`	`ReleaseStringCritical()`
`ExceptionDescribe()`	`Release<Primitive>ArrayElements()`
`MonitorExit()`	`ReleasePrimitiveArrayCritical()`

Have a go hero – handling other array types

With the knowledge freshly acquired, implement store methods for other array types: jbooleanArray, jbyteArray, jcharArray, jdoubleArray, jfloatArray, jlongArray, and jshortArray. When you are done, write operations for string arrays.

 The final project Store implementing these cases is provided with this book.

Summary

In this chapter, we have seen how to make Java communicate with C/C++. Android is now almost bilingual! Java can call C/C++ code with any type of data or objects. More specifically, we have seen how to call native code with primitive types. These primitives have their C/C++ equivalent type they can can be casted to. Then, we have passed objects and handled their references. References are local to a method by default and should not be shared outside method scope. They should be managed carefully as their number is limited (this limit can still be manually increased). After that, we have shared and stored objects with global references. Global references need to be carefully deleted to ensure proper garbage collection. We have also raised exceptions from native code to notify Java if a problem occurred and check exceptions occurring in JNI. When an exception occurs, only a few cleaning JNI methods are safe to call. Finally, we have manipulated primitive and objects arrays. Arrays may or may not be copied by the VM when manipulated in native code. The performance penalty has to be taken into account.

But there is still more to come: how to call Java from C/C++ code. We got a partial overview with exceptions. But actually, any Java object, method, or field can be handled by native code. Let's see this in the next chapter.

4

Calling Java Back from Native Code

To reach its full potential, JNI allows calling Java code from C/C++. This is often referred to as a callback since native code is itself invoked from Java. Such calls are performed through a reflective API, which allows doing almost anything that can be done directly in Java. Another important matter to consider with JNI is threading. Native code can be run on a Java thread, managed by the Dalvik VM, and also from a native thread created with standard POSIX primitives. Obviously, a native thread cannot call JNI code unless it is turned into a managed thread! Programming with JNI necessitates knowledge of all these subtleties. This chapter will guide you through the main ones.

Since version R5, the Android NDK also proposes a new API to access natively an important type of Java objects: bitmaps. This bitmap API is Android-specific and aims at giving full processing power to graphics applications running on these tiny (but powerful) devices. To illustrate this topic, we will see how to decode a camera feed directly inside native code.

To summarize, in this chapter, we are going to learn how to:

◆ Attach a JNI context to a native thread

◆ Handle synchronization with Java threads

◆ Call Java back from native code

◆ Process Java bitmaps in native code

By the end of the chapter, you should be able to make Java and C/C++ communicate together in both directions.

Synchronizing Java and native threads

In this part, we are going to create a background thread, the *watcher*, which keeps an eye constantly on what is inside the data store. It iterates through all entries and then sleeps for a fixed amount of time. When the watcher thread finds a specific key, value, or type predefined in code, it acts accordingly. For this first part, we are just going to increment a *watcher counter* each time the watcher thread iterates over entries. In next part, we will see how to react by calling back Java.

Of course, threads also needs synchronization. The native thread will be allowed to access and update the store only when a user (understand the UI thread) is not modifying it. The native thread is in C but the UI thread in Java. Thus, we have two options here:

- Use native mutexes as our UI thread makes native calls when getting and setting values anyway
- Use Java monitors and synchronize native thread with JNI

Of course, in a chapter dedicated to JNI, we can only choose the second option! The final application structure will look as follows:

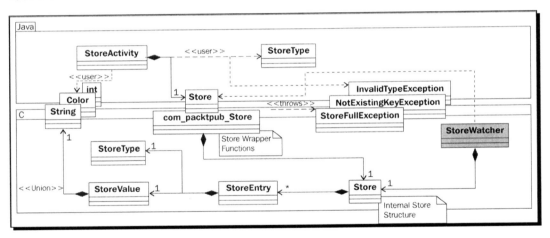

 Project Store_Part3-4 can be used as a starting point for this part. The resulting project is provided with this book under the name Project Store_Part4-1.

Time for action – running a background thread

Let's add some synchronization capabilities on the Java first:

1. Open `Store.java` created in the previous chapter. Create two new native methods, `initializeStore()` and `finalizeStore()`, to start/stop the watcher thread and initialize/destroy the store when activity is started and stopped, respectively.

    Make every `Store` class's getter and setter synchronized, as they are not allowed to access and modify store entries while the watcher thread iterates through them:

    ```java
    public class Store {
        static {
            System.loadLibrary("store");
        }

        public native void initializeStore();
        public native void finalizeStore();

        public native synchronized int getInteger(String pKey)
            throws NotExistingKeyException, InvalidTypeException;
        public native synchronized void setInteger(String pKey,
                        int pInt);

        // Other getters and setters are synchronized too.
        ...
    }
    ```

2. Call initialization and finalization methods when activity is started and stopped. Create a `watcherCounter` entry of type integer when store is initialized. This entry will be updated automatically by the watcher:

    ```java
    public class StoreActivity extends Activity {
        private EditText mUIKeyEdit, mUIValueEdit;
        private Spinner mUITypeSpinner;
        private Button mUIGetButton, mUISetButton;
        private Store mStore;

        @Override
        public void onCreate(Bundle savedInstanceState) {
            super.onCreate(savedInstanceState);
            setContentView(R.layout.main);

            // Initializes components and binds buttons to handlers.
            ...
            // Initializes the native side store.
    ```

```
        mStore = new Store();
    }

    @Override
    protected void onStart() {
        super.onStart();
        mStore.initializeStore();
        mStore.setInteger("watcherCounter", 0);
    }

    @Override
    protected void onStop() {
        super.onStop();
        mStore.finalizeStore();
    }
    ...
}
```

The Java side is ready to initialize and destroy the native thread... Let's switch to the native side to implement it:

3. Create a new file `StoreWatcher.h` in folder `jni`. Include `Store`, JNI, and native threads headers.

   The watcher works on a `Store` instance updated at regular intervals of time (three seconds here). It needs:

   ❑ A `JavaVM`, which is the only object safely shareable among threads from which a JNI environment can be safely retrieved.

   ❑ A Java object to synchronize on, here the Java `Store` frontend object because it has synchronized methods.

   ❑ Variables dedicated to thread management.

4. Finally, define two methods to start the native thread after initialization and stop it:

```
#ifndef _STOREWATCHER_H_
#define _STOREWATCHER_H_

#include "Store.h"
#include <jni.h>
#include <stdint.h>
#include <pthread.h>

#define SLEEP_DURATION 5
#define STATE_OK 0
```

```
#define STATE_KO 1

typedef struct {
    // Native variables.
    Store* mStore;
    // Cached JNI references.
    JavaVM* mJavaVM;
    jobject mStoreFront;
    // Thread variables.
    pthread_t mThread;
    int32_t mState;
} StoreWatcher;

void startWatcher(JNIEnv* pEnv, StoreWatcher* pWatcher,
    Store* pStore, jobject pStoreFront);
void stopWatcher(JNIEnv* pEnv, StoreWatcher* pWatcher);

#endif
```

5. Create `jni/StoreWatcher.h` and declare additional private methods:

    ❑ `runWatcher()`: This represents the native thread main loop.

    ❑ `processEntry()`: This is invoked while a watcher iterates through entries.

    ❑ `getJNIEnv()`: This retrieves a JNI environment for the current thread.

    ❑ `deleteGlobalRef()`: This helps delete global references previously
        created.

    ```
    #include "StoreWatcher.h"
    #include <unistd.h>

    void deleteGlobalRef(JNIEnv* pEnv, jobject* pRef);
    JNIEnv* getJNIEnv(JavaVM* pJavaVM);

    void* runWatcher(void* pArgs);
    void processEntry(JNIEnv* pEnv, StoreWatcher* pWatcher,
                      StoreEntry* pEntry);
    ...
    ```

6. In `jni/StoreWatcher.c`, implement `startWatcher()`, invoked from the UI
    thread, that set up the `StoreWatcher` structure and starts the watcher thread,
    thanks to POSIX primitives.

7. Because the UI thread may access store content at the same time the watcher thread checks entries, we need to keep an object to synchronize on. Let's use Store class itself since its getters and setters are synchronized:

In Java, synchronization is always performed on an object. When a Java method is defined with the `synchronized` keyword, then Java synchronizes on `this` (the current object) behind the scene: `synchronized(this) { doSomething(); ... }`.

```
...
void startWatcher(JNIEnv* pEnv, StoreWatcher* pWatcher,
    Store* pStore, jobject pStoreFront) {
    // Erases the StoreWatcher structure.
    memset(pWatcher, 0, sizeof(StoreWatcher));
    pWatcher->mState = STATE_OK;
    pWatcher->mStore = pStore;
    // Caches the VM.
    if ((*pEnv)->GetJavaVM(pEnv, &pWatcher->mJavaVM) != JNI_OK) {
        goto ERROR;
    }

    // Caches objects.
    pWatcher->mStoreFront = (*pEnv)->NewGlobalRef
      (pEnv, pStoreFront);
    if (pWatcher->mStoreFront == NULL) goto ERROR;

    // Initializes and launches the native thread. For simplicity
    // purpose, error results are not checked (but we should...).
    pthread_attr_t lAttributes;
    int lError = pthread_attr_init(&lAttributes);
    if (lError) goto ERROR;

    lError = pthread_create(&pWatcher->mThread, &lAttributes,
                            runWatcher, pWatcher);
    if (lError) goto ERROR;
    return;

ERROR:
    stopWatcher(pEnv, pWatcher);
    return;
}

...
```

8. In `StoreWatcher.c`, implement helper method `getJNIEnv()`, which is called when the thread starts. The watcher thread is native, which means that:

- No JNI environment is attached. Thus, JNI is not activated by default for the thread.

- It is not instantiated by Java and has no "Java root", that is, if you look at the call stack, you never find a Java method.

> Having no Java root is an important property of native threads because it impacts directly the ability of JNI to load Java classes. Indeed, it is not possible from a native thread to access the Java application **class loader**. Only a bootstrap class loader with system classes is available. A Java thread on the opposite always has a Java root and thus can access the application class loader with its application classes.
>
> A solution to that problem is to load classes in an appropriate Java thread and to share them later with native threads.

9. The native thread is attached to the VM with `AttachCurrentThread()` in order to retrieve a `JNIEnv`. This JNI environment is specific to the current thread and cannot be shared with others (he opposite of a `JavaVM` object which can be shared safely). Internally, the VM builds a new `Thread` object and adds it to the main thread group, like any other Java thread:

```
. . .
JNIEnv* getJNIEnv(JavaVM* pJavaVM) {
    JavaVMAttachArgs lJavaVMAttachArgs;
    lJavaVMAttachArgs.version = JNI_VERSION_1_6;
    lJavaVMAttachArgs.name = "NativeThread";
    lJavaVMAttachArgs.group = NULL;

    JNIEnv* lEnv;
    if ((*pJavaVM)->AttachCurrentThread(pJavaVM, &lEnv,
                        &lJavaVMAttachArgs) != JNI_OK) {
        lEnv = NULL;
    }
    return lEnv;
}
. . .
```

10. The most important method is `runWatcher()`, the main thread loop. Here, we are not anymore on the UI thread but on the watcher thread. Thus we need to attach it to the VM in order to get a working JNI environment.

11. The thread works only at regular intervals of time and sleeps meanwhile. When it leaves its nap, the thread starts looping over each entry individually in a critical section (that is, synchronized) to access them safely. Indeed, the UI thread (that is, the user) may change an entry value at any time.

12. Critical section is delimited with a JNI monitor which has exactly the same properties as the synchronized keyword in Java. Obviously, MonitorEnter() and MonitorExit() have to lock/unlock on the object mStoreFront to synchronize properly with its getters and setters. These instructions ensure that the first thread to reach a monitor/synchronized block will enter the section while the other will wait in front of the door until the first has finished.

13. Thread leaves the loop and exits when state variable is changed by the UI thread (in stopWatcher()). An attached thread which dies must eventually detach from the VM so that the latter can release resources properly:

```
...
void* runWatcher(void* pArgs) {
    StoreWatcher* lWatcher = (StoreWatcher*) pArgs;
    Store* lStore = lWatcher->mStore;
    JavaVM* lJavaVM = lWatcher->mJavaVM;

    JNIEnv* lEnv = getJNIEnv(lJavaVM);
    if (lEnv == NULL) goto ERROR;

    int32_t lRunning = 1;
    while (lRunning) {
        sleep(SLEEP_DURATION);

        StoreEntry* lEntry = lWatcher->mStore->mEntries;
        int32_t lScanning = 1;
        while (lScanning) {
            // Critical section begining, one thread at a time.
            // Entries cannot be added or modified.
            (*lEnv)->MonitorEnter(lEnv, lWatcher->mStoreFront);
            lRunning = (lWatcher->mState == STATE_OK);
            StoreEntry* lEntryEnd = lWatcher->mStore->mEntries
                                  + lWatcher->mStore->mLength;
            lScanning = (lEntry < lEntryEnd);

            if (lRunning && lScanning) {
                processEntry(lEnv, lWatcher, lEntry);
            }

            // Critical section end.
```

```
                    (*lEnv)->MonitorExit(lEnv, lWatcher->mStoreFront);
                    // Goes to next element.
                    ++lEntry;
                }
            }

    ERROR:
        (*lJavaVM)->DetachCurrentThread(lJavaVM);
        pthread_exit(NULL);
    }
    ...
```

14. In StoreWatcher, write processEntry() which detects the watcherCounter
entry and increment its value. Thus, watcherCounter contains how many
iterations the watcher thread has performed since the beginning:

```
    ...
    void processEntry(JNIEnv* pEnv, StoreWatcher* pWatcher,
                      StoreEntry* pEntry) {
        if ((pEntry->mType == StoreType_Integer)
         && (strcmp(pEntry->mKey, "watcherCounter") == 0)   {
            ++pEntry->mValue.mInteger;
        }
    }
    ...
```

15. To finish with jni/StoreWatcher.c, write stopWatcher(), also executed on the
UI thread, which terminates the watcher thread and releases all global references.
To help releasing them, implement deleteGlobalRef() helper utility which will
help us make the code more consise in the next part. Note that mState is a shared
variable among threads and need to be accessed inside a critical section:

```
    ...
    void deleteGlobalRef(JNIEnv* pEnv, jobject* pRef) {
        if (*pRef != NULL) {
            (*pEnv)->DeleteGlobalRef(pEnv, *pRef);
            *pRef = NULL;
        }
    }

    void stopWatcher(JNIEnv* pEnv, StoreWatcher* pWatcher) {
        if (pWatcher->mState == STATE_OK) {
            // Waits for the watcher thread to stop.
            (*pEnv)->MonitorEnter(pEnv, pWatcher->mStoreFront);
            pWatcher->mState = STATE_KO;
```

```
        (*pEnv)->MonitorExit(pEnv, pWatcher->mStoreFront);
        pthread_join(pWatcher->mThread, NULL);

        deleteGlobalRef(pEnv, &pWatcher->mStoreFront);
    }
}
```

16. Generate JNI header file with `javah`.

17. Finally, open existing file `jni/com_packtpub_Store.c`, declare a static `Store`
    variable containing store content and define `initializeStore()` to create and
    run the watcher thread and `finalizeStore()` to stop it and release entries:

```c
#include "com_packtpub_Store.h"
#include "Store.h"
#include "StoreWatcher.h"
#include <stdint.h>
#include <string.h>


static Store mStore;
static StoreWatcher mStoreWatcher;

JNIEXPORT void JNICALL Java_com_packtpub_Store_initializeStore
  (JNIEnv* pEnv, jobject pThis) {
    mStore.mLength = 0;
    startWatcher(pEnv, &mStoreWatcher, &mStore, pThis);
}

JNIEXPORT void JNICALL Java_com_packtpub_Store_finalizeStore
  (JNIEnv* pEnv, jobject pThis) {
    stopWatcher(pEnv, &mStoreWatcher);

    StoreEntry* lEntry = mStore.mEntries;
    StoreEntry* lEntryEnd = lEntry + mStore.mLength;
    while (lEntry < lEntryEnd) {
        free(lEntry->mKey);
        releaseEntryValue(pEnv, lEntry);

        ++lEntry;
    }
    mStore.mLength = 0;
}
...
```

18. Do not forget to add `StoreWatcher.c` to the `Android.mk` file as usual.

19. Compile and run the application.

What just happened?

We have created a background native thread and managed to attach it to the Dalvik VM, allowing us to get a JNI environment. Then we have synchronized Java and native threads together to handle concurrency issues properly. Store is initialized when application starts and when it stops.

On the native side, synchronization is performed with a JNI monitor equivalent to the `synchronized` keyword. Because Java threads are based on POSIX primitives internally, it would also be possible to implement thread synchronization completely natively (that is, without relying on Java primitive) with POSIX mutexes:

```
pthread_mutex_t lMutex;
pthread_cond_t lCond;

// Initializes synchronization variables
pthread_mutex_init(&lMutex, NULL);
pthread_cond_init(&lCond, NULL);

// Enters critical section.
pthread_mutex_lock(&lMutex);

// Waits for a condition
While (needToWait)
    pthread_cond_wait(&lCond, &lMutex);

// Does something...

// Wakes-up other threads.
pthread_cond_broadcast(&lCond);

// Leaves critical section.
pthread_mutex_unlock(&lMutex);
```

Depending on the platform, mixing Java thread synchronization and native synchronization based on different models is considered as a harmful practice (for example, platforms which implement green threads). Android is not concerned by this problem but keep it in mind if you plan to write portable native code.

As a last note I would like to point out that Java and C/C++ are different languages, with similar but somewhat different semantics. Thus, always be careful not to expect C/C++ to behave like Java. As an example, the `volatile` has a different semantic in Java and C/C++ since both follow a different memory model.

Attaching and detaching threads

A good place to get `JavaVM` instance is from `JNI_OnLoad()`, a callback that a native library can declare and implement to get notified when library is loaded in memory (when `System.loadLibrary()` is called from Java). This is also a good place to do some JNI descriptor caching as we will see in next part:

```
JavaVM* myGlobalJavaVM;

jint JNI_OnLoad(JavaVM* pVM, void* reserved) {
    myGlobalJavaVM = pVM;

    JNIEnv *lEnv;
    if (pVM->GetEnv((void**) &lEnv, JNI_VERSION_1_6) != JNI_OK) {
        // A problem occured
        return -1;
    }
    return JNI_VERSION_1_6;
}
```

An attached thread like the watcher thread must be eventually unattached before activity is destroyed. Dalvik detects threads which are not detached and reacts by aborting and leaving a dirty crash dump in your logs! When getting detached, any monitor held is released and any waiting thread is notified.

Since Android 2.0, a technique to make sure a thread is systematically detached is to bind a destructor callback to the native thread with `pthread_key_create()` and `DetachCurrentThread()`. A JNI environment can be saved into thread local storage with `pthread_setspecific()` to pass it as an argument to the destructor.

 Although attaching/detaching can be performed at any time, these operations are expensive and should be performed once or punctually rather than constantly.

More on Java and native code lifecycles

If you compare Store_Part3-4 and Store_Part4-1, you will discover that values remain between executions in the first one. This is because native libraries have a different lifecycle than usual Android activities. When an activity is destroyed and recreated for any reason (for example, screen reorientation), any data is lost in the Java activity.

But native library and its global data are likely to remain in memory! Data persists between executions. This has implications in terms of memory management. Carefully release memory when an application is destroyed if you do not want to keep it between executions.

Take care with create and destroy events

In some configurations, onDestroy() event has the reputation of sometimes being executed after an activity instance is recreated. This means that destruction of an activity may occur unexpectedly after the second instance is recreated. Obviously, this can lead to memory corruption or leak.

Several strategies exist to overcome this problem:

◆ Create and destroy data in other events if possible (like onStart() and onStop()). But you will probably need to persist your data somewhere meanwhile (Java file), which may impact responsiveness.

◆ Destroy data only in onCreate(). This has the major inconvenience of not releasing memory while an application is running in the background.

◆ Never allocate global data on the native side (that is, static variables) but save the pointer to your native data on the Java side: allocate memory when activity is created and send back your pointer to Java casted as an int (or even better a long for future compatibility reasons). Any futher JNI call must be performed with this pointer as parameter.

◆ Use a variable on the Java side to detect the case where destruction of an activity (onDestroy()) happens after a new instance has been recreated (onCreate()).

Do not cache JNIEnv between executions!

Android applications can be destroyed and recreated at any time. If a JNIEnv is cached on the native side and the application gets closed meanwhile, then its reference may become invalid. So get back a new reference each time an application is recreated.

Calling Java back from native code

In the previous chapter, we have discovered how to get a Java class descriptor with JNI method `FindClass()`. But we can get much more! Actually, if you are a regular Java developer, this should remind you of something: the Java reflection API. Similarly, JNI can modify Java object fields, run Java methods, access static members... but from native code. This is often referred to as a Java callback, because Java code is run from native code which descends itself from Java. But this is the simple case. Since JNI is tightly coupled with threads, calling Java code from native threads is slightly more difficult. Attaching a thread to a VM is only part of the solution.

For this last part with the Store project, let's enhance the watcher thread so that it warns the Java activity when it detects a value it does not like (for example, an integer outside a defined range). We are going to use JNI callback capabilities to initiate communication from native code to Java.

 Project Store_Part4-1 can be used as a starting point for this part. The resulting project is provided with this book under the name Project Store_Part4-2.

Time for action – invoking Java code from a native thread

Let's make a few changes on the Java side:

1. Create a `StoreListener` interface as follows to define methods through which native code is going to communicate with Java code:

```
public interface StoreListener {
    public void onAlert(int pValue);

    public void onAlert(String pValue);

    public void onAlert(Color pValue);
}
```

2. Open `Store.java` and make a few changes:

   □ Declare one `Handler` member. A `Handler` is a message queue associated with the thread it was created on (here, it will be the UI thread). Any message posted from whatever thread is received in an internal queue processed magically on the initial thread. Handlers are a popular and easy inter-thread communication technique on Android.

- Declare a delegate StoreListener to which messages (that is, a method call) received from the watcher thread are going to be posted. This will be the `StoreActivity`.

- Change `Store` constructor to inject the target delegate listener.

- Implement `StoreListener` interface and its corresponding methods. Alert messages are recorded as `Runnable` tasks and posted to the target thread, on which the final listener works safely.

```
public class Store implements StoreListener {
    static {
        System.loadLibrary("store");
    }

    private Handler mHandler;
    private StoreListener mDelegateListener;

    public Store(StoreListener pListener) {
        mHandler = new Handler();
        mDelegateListener = pListener;
    }

    public void onAlert(final int pValue) {
        mHandler.post(new Runnable() {
            public void run() {
                mDelegateListener.onAlert(pValue);
            }
        });
    }

    public void onAlert(final String pValue) {
        mHandler.post(new Runnable() {
            public void run() {
                mDelegateListener.onAlert(pValue);
            }
        });
    }

    public void onAlert(final Color pValue) {
        mHandler.post(new Runnable() {
            public void run() {
                mDelegateListener.onAlert(pValue);
            }
        });
    }
    ...
}
```

3. Update the existing class `Color` and add methods to check equality. This will later allow the watcher thread to compare an entry to a reference color:

```java
public class Color {
    private int mColor;

    public Color(String pColor) {
        super();
        mColor = android.graphics.Color.parseColor(pColor);
    }

    @Override
    public String toString() {
        return String.format("#%06X", mColor);
    }

    @Override
    public int hashCode() {
        return mColor;
    }

    @Override
    public boolean equals(Object pOther) {
        if (this == pOther) { return true; }
        if (pOther == null) { return false; }
        if (getClass() != pOther.getClass()) { return false; }
        Color pColor = (Color) pOther;
        return (mColor == pColor.mColor);
    }
}
```

4. Open `StoreActivity.java` and implement `StoreListener` interface. When an alert is received, a simple toast message is raised. Change `Store` constructor call accordingly. Note that this is the moment where the thread on which the internal `Handler` processes messages is determined:

```java
public class StoreActivity extends Activity implements
StoreListener{
    private EditText mUIKeyEdit, mUIValueEdit;
    private Spinner mUITypeSpinner;
    private Button mUIGetButton, mUISetButton;
    private Store mStore;

    @Override
```

```
public void onCreate(Bundle savedInstanceState) {
    super.onCreate(savedInstanceState);
    setContentView(R.layout.main);

    // Initializes components and binds buttons to handlers.
    ...

    // Initializes the native side store.
    mStore = new Store(this);
}

...

public void onAlert(int pValue) {
    displayError(String.format("%1$d is not an allowed integer",
                    pValue));
}

public void onAlert(String pValue) {
    displayError(String.format("%1$s is not an allowed string",
                    pValue));
}

public void onAlert(Color pValue) {
    displayError(String.format("%1$s is not an allowed color",
                    pValue.toString()));
}
}
```

The Java side is ready to receive callbacks. Let's go back to native code to emit them:

5. Open existing file `jni/StoreWatcher.c`. The `StoreWatcher` structure already has access to the Java Store frontend. But to call its methods (for example, `Store.onAlert()`), we need a few more items: declare the appropriate class and method descriptors like if you were working with the reflection API. Do the same for `Color.equals()`.

6. In addition, declare a a reference to a `Color` object which is going to be used as a base for color comparison by the watcher. Any identical color will be considered as an alert:

What we do here is cache references so that we do not have to find them again for each JNI call. Caching has two main benefits: it improves performances (JNI lookups are quite expensive compare to a cached access) and readability.

Caching is also the only way to provide JNI references to native threads as they do not have access to the application class loader (only the system one).

```c
#ifndef _STOREWATCHER_H_
#define _STOREWATCHER_H_

...

typedef struct {
    // Native variables.
    Store* mStore;

    // Cached JNI references.
    JavaVM* mJavaVM;
    jobject mStoreFront;
    jobject mColor;
    // Classes.
    jclass ClassStore;
    jclass ClassColor;
    // Methods.
    jmethodID MethodOnAlertInt;
    jmethodID MethodOnAlertString;
    jmethodID MethodOnAlertColor;
    jmethodID MethodColorEquals;

    // Thread variables.
    pthread_t mThread;
    int32_t mState;
} StoreWatcher;
...
```

7. In `jni` directory, open implementation file `StoreWatcher.c`. Declare helper methods to create a global reference and process entries.

8. Implement `makeGlobalRef()`, which turns a local into a global reference. This is a "shortcut" to ensure proper deletion of local references and NULL value handling (if an error occurs in a previous instruction):

```c
#include "StoreWatcher.h"
```

```
#include <unistd.h>

void makeGlobalRef(JNIEnv* pEnv, jobject* pRef);
void deleteGlobalRef(JNIEnv* pEnv, jobject* pRef);
JNIEnv* getJNIEnv(JavaVM* pJavaVM);

void* runWatcher(void* pArgs);
void processEntry(JNIEnv* pEnv, StoreWatcher* pWatcher,
                  StoreEntry* pEntry);
void processEntryInt(JNIEnv* pEnv, StoreWatcher* pWatcher,
                  StoreEntry* pEntry);
void processEntryString(JNIEnv* pEnv, StoreWatcher* pWatcher,
                  StoreEntry* pEntry);
void processEntryColor(JNIEnv* pEnv, StoreWatcher* pWatcher,
                  StoreEntry* pEntry);

void makeGlobalRef(JNIEnv* pEnv, jobject* pRef) {
    if (*pRef != NULL) {
        jobject lGlobalRef = (*pEnv)->NewGlobalRef(pEnv, *pRef);
        // No need for a local reference any more.
        (*pEnv)->DeleteLocalRef(pEnv, *pRef);
        // Here, lGlobalRef may be null.
        *pRef = lGlobalRef;
    }
}

void deleteGlobalRef(JNIEnv* pEnv, jobject* pRef) {
    if (*pRef != NULL) {
        (*pEnv)->DeleteGlobalRef(pEnv, *pRef);
        *pRef = NULL;
    }
}
...
```

9. Here is the big piece, still in `StoreWatcher.c`. If you remember the previous part, method `startWatcher()` is called from the UI thread to initialize and start the watcher. Thus, this is a perfect place to cache JNI descriptors. Actually, this is almost one of the only places because as the UI thread is a Java thread, we have total access to the application class loader. But if we were trying to cache them inside the native thread, the latter would have access only to the system class loader and nothing else!

10. One can find a class descriptor thanks to its absolute package path (for example, `com./packtpub/Store`). Because classes are objects, the only way to share them safely with the native thread is to turn them into global references. This is not the case for "IDs" such as `jmethodID` and `jfieldID` which are in now way references:

```
...
void startWatcher(JNIEnv* pEnv, StoreWatcher* pWatcher,
    Store* pStore, jobject pStoreFront) {
    // Erases the StoreWatcher structure.
    memset(pWatcher, 0, sizeof(StoreWatcher));
    pWatcher->mState = STATE_OK;
    pWatcher->mStore = pStore;
    // Caches the VM.
    if ((*pEnv)->GetJavaVM(pEnv, &pWatcher->mJavaVM) != JNI_OK) {
        goto ERROR;
    }

    // Caches classes.
    pWatcher->ClassStore = (*pEnv)->FindClass(pEnv,
        "com/packtpub/Store");
    makeGlobalRef(pEnv, &pWatcher->ClassStore);
    if (pWatcher->ClassStore == NULL) goto ERROR;

    pWatcher->ClassColor = (*pEnv)->FindClass(pEnv,
        "com/packtpub/Color");
    makeGlobalRef(pEnv, &pWatcher->ClassColor);
    if (pWatcher->ClassColor == NULL) goto ERROR;
...
```

11. In `start_watcher()`, method descriptors are retrieved with JNI from a class descriptor. To differentiate different overloads with the same name, a description of the method with a simple predefined formalism is necessary. For example, `(I)V` which means an integer is expected and a void returned or `(Ljava/lang/String;)V` which means a `String` is passed in parameter). Constructor descriptors are retrieved in the same way except that their name is always `<init>` and they do not return a value:

```
...
    // Caches Java methods.
    pWatcher->MethodOnAlertInt = (*pEnv)->GetMethodID(pEnv,
        pWatcher->ClassStore, "onAlert", "(I)V");
    if (pWatcher->MethodOnAlertInt == NULL) goto ERROR;

    pWatcher->MethodOnAlertString = (*pEnv)->GetMethodID(pEnv,
```

```
        pWatcher->ClassStore, "onAlert", "(Ljava/lang/String;)V");
    if (pWatcher->MethodOnAlertString == NULL) goto ERROR;

    pWatcher->MethodOnAlertColor = (*pEnv)->GetMethodID(pEnv,
      pWatcher->ClassStore, "onAlert","(Lcom/packtpub/Color;)V");
    if (pWatcher->MethodOnAlertColor == NULL) goto ERROR;

    pWatcher->MethodColorEquals = (*pEnv)->GetMethodID(pEnv,
        pWatcher->ClassColor, "equals", "(Ljava/lang/Object;)Z");
    if (pWatcher->MethodColorEquals == NULL) goto ERROR;

    jmethodID ConstructorColor = (*pEnv)->GetMethodID(pEnv,
        pWatcher->ClassColor, "<init>", "(Ljava/lang/String;)V");
    if (ConstructorColor == NULL) goto ERROR;
    ...
```

12. Again in the same method `start_watcher()`, cache object instances with a global reference. Do not use `makeGlobalRef()` utility on the Java store frontend because local reference is actually a parameter and does not need to be released.

13. The color is not an outside object referenced and cached like others. It is instantiated with JNI by a call to `NewObject()`, which takes a constructor descriptor in parameter.

```
    ...
    // Caches objects.
    pWatcher->mStoreFront = (*pEnv)->NewGlobalRef(pEnv, pStoreFront);
    if (pWatcher->mStoreFront == NULL) goto ERROR;
    // Creates a new white color and keeps a global reference.
    jstring lColor = (*pEnv)->NewStringUTF(pEnv, "white");
    if (lColor == NULL) goto ERROR;

    pWatcher->mColor = (*pEnv)->NewObject(pEnv,pWatcher->ClassColor,
        ConstructorColor, lColor);
    makeGlobalRef(pEnv, &pWatcher->mColor);
    if (pWatcher->mColor == NULL) goto ERROR;

    // Launches the native thread.
    ...
    return;

ERROR:
    stopWatcher(pEnv, pWatcher);
    return;
}
...
```

14. In the same file, rewrite `processEntry()` to process each type of entry separately. Check that integers are in the range [-1000, 1000] and send an alert if that is not the case. To invoke a Java method on a Java object, simply use `CallVoidMethod()` on a JNI environment. This means that the called Java method returns `void`. If Java method was returning an `int`, we would call `CallIntMethod()`. Like with the reflection API, invoking a Java method requires:

❑ An object instance (except for static methods, in which case we would provide a class instance and use `CallStaticVoidMethod()`).

❑ A method descriptor.

❑ Parameters (if applicable, here an integer value).

```
. . .
void processEntry(JNIEnv* pEnv, StoreWatcher* pWatcher,
                  StoreEntry* pEntry) {
    switch (pEntry->mType) {
    case StoreType_Integer:
        processEntryInt(pEnv, pWatcher, pEntry);
        break;
    case StoreType_String:
        processEntryString(pEnv, pWatcher, pEntry);
        break;
    case StoreType_Color:
        processEntryColor(pEnv, pWatcher, pEntry);
        break;
    }
}

void processEntryInt(JNIEnv* pEnv,StoreWatcher* pWatcher,
                     StoreEntry* pEntry) {
    if(strcmp(pEntry->mKey, "watcherCounter") == 0) {
        ++pEntry->mValue.mInteger;
    } else if ((pEntry->mValue.mInteger > 1000) ||
        (pEntry->mValue.mInteger < -1000)) {
        (*pEnv)->CallVoidMethod(pEnv,
            pWatcher->mStoreFront,pWatcher->MethodOnAlertInt,
                (jint) pEntry->mValue.mInteger);
    }
}
. . .
```

15. Repeat the operation for strings. Strings require allocating a new Java string. We do not need to generate a global reference as it is used immediately in the Java callback. But if you have kept in mind previous lessons, you know we can release the local reference right after it is used. Indeed, we are in a utility method and we do not always know the context they may be used in. In addition, whereas in a classic JNI method, local references are deleted when method returns, here we are in an attached native thread. Thus, local references would get deleted only when thread is detached (that is, when activity leaves). JNI memory would leak meanwhile:

```
. . .
void processEntryString(JNIEnv* pEnv, StoreWatcher* pWatcher,
                        StoreEntry* pEntry) {
    if (strcmp(pEntry->mValue.mString, "apple")) {
        jstring lValue = (*pEnv)->NewStringUTF(
            pEnv, pEntry->mValue.mString);
        (*pEnv)->CallVoidMethod(pEnv,
            pWatcher->mStoreFront, pWatcher->MethodOnAlertString,
            lValue);
        (*pEnv)->DeleteLocalRef(pEnv, lValue);
    }
}
```

16. Finally, process colors. To check if a color is identical to the reference color, invoke the equality method provided by Java and reimplemented in our `Color` class. Because it returns a Boolean value, `CallVoidMethod()` is inappropriate for the first test. But `CallBooleanMethod()` is:

```
void processEntryColor(JNIEnv* pEnv, StoreWatcher* pWatcher,
                       StoreEntry* pEntry) {
    jboolean lResult = (*pEnv)->CallBooleanMethod(
            pEnv, pWatcher->mColor,
            pWatcher->MethodColorEquals, pEntry->mValue.mColor);
    if (lResult) {
        (*pEnv)->CallVoidMethod(pEnv,
            pWatcher->mStoreFront, pWatcher->MethodOnAlertColor,
            pEntry->mValue.mColor);
    }
}
. . .
```

17. We are almost done. Do not forget to release global references when a thread exits!

```
...
void stopWatcher(JNIEnv* pEnv, StoreWatcher* pWatcher) {
    if (pWatcher->mState == STATE_OK) {
        // Waits for the watcher thread to stop.
        ...

        deleteGlobalRef(pEnv, &pWatcher->mStoreFront);
        deleteGlobalRef(pEnv, &pWatcher->mColor);
        deleteGlobalRef(pEnv, &pWatcher->ClassStore);
        deleteGlobalRef(pEnv, &pWatcher->ClassColor);
    }
}
```

18. Compile and run.

What just happened?

Launch the application and create a string entry with the value `apple`. Then try to create an entry with `white` color. Finally, enter an integer value outside the [-1000, 1000] range. In each case, a message should be raised on screen (every time the watcher iterates).

In this part, we have seen how to cache JNI descriptors and perform callbacks to Java. We have also introduced a way to send messages between threads with handlers, invoked indirectly in Java. Android features several other communication means, such as AsyncTask. Have a look at `http://developer.android.com/resources/articles/painless-threading.html` for more information.

Java callbacks are not only useful to execute a Java piece of code, they are also the only way to analyze `jobject` parameters passed to a native method. But if calling C/C++ code from Java is rather easy, performing Java operations from C/C++ is bit more involving! Performing a single Java call that holds in one single line of Java code requires lots of work! Why? Simply because JNI is a reflective API.

To get a field value, one needs to get its containing class descriptor and its field descriptor before actually retrieving its value. To call a method, one needs to retrieve class descriptor and method descriptor before calling the method with the necessary parameters. The process is always the same.

Caching definitions

Retrieving all these element definitions is not only tedious, it is absolutely not optimal in terms of performance. Thus, JNI definitions used frequently should be cached for reuse. Cached elements can be kept safely for the lifetime of an activity (not of the native library) and shared between threads with global references (for example, for class descriptors).

Caching is the only solution to communicate with native threads, which do not have access to the application class loader. But there is a way to limit the amount of definitions to prepare: instead of caching classes, methods, and fields, simply cache the application class loader itself.

Do not call back in callbacks!

Calling native code from Java through JNI works perfectly. Calling Java code from native works perfect too. However, interleaving several levels of Java and native calls should be avoided.

More on callbacks

The central object in JNI is `JNIEnv`. It is provided systematically as first parameter to JNI C/C++ methods called from Java. We have seen:

```
jclass FindClass(const char* name);
jclass GetObjectClass(jobject obj);
jmethodID GetMethodID(jclass clazz, const char* name,
                      const char* sig) ;
jfieldID GetStaticFieldID(jclass clazz, const char* name,
                          const char* sig);
```

but also:

```
jfieldID GetFieldID(jclass clazz, const char* name, const char* sig);
jmethodID GetStaticMethodID(jclass clazz, const char* name,
                            const char* sig);
```

These allow retrieving JNI descriptors: classes, methods, and fields, static and instance members having different accessors. Note that `FindClass()` and `GetObjectClass()` have the same purpose except that `FindClass` finds class definitions according to their absolute path whereas the other finds the class of an object directly.

There is a second set of methods to actually execute methods or retrieve field values. There is one method per primitive types plus one for objects.

```
jobject GetObjectField(jobject obj, jfieldID fieldID);
jboolean GetBooleanField(jobject obj, jfieldID fieldID);
void SetObjectField(jobject obj, jfieldID fieldID, jobject value);
void SetBooleanField(jobject obj, jfieldID fieldID, jboolean value);
```

The same goes for methods according to their return values:

```
jobject CallObjectMethod(JNIEnv*, jobject, jmethodID, ...)
jboolean CallBooleanMethod(JNIEnv*, jobject, jmethodID, ...);
```

Variants of call methods exist, with an A and V postfix. Behavior is identical except that arguments are specified using a va_list (that is, variable argument list) or a jvalue array (jvalue being an union of all JNI types):

```
jobject CallObjectMethodV(JNIEnv*, jobject, jmethodID, va_list);
jobject CallObjectMethodA(JNIEnv*, jobject, jmethodID, jvalue*);
```

Parameters passed to a Java method through JNI must use the available JNI type: jobject for any object, jboolean for a boolean value, and so on. See the following table for a more detailed list.

Look for jni.h in the Android NDK include directory to feel all the possibilities by JNI reflective API.

JNI method definitions

Methods in Java can be overloaded. That means that there can be two methods with the same name but different parameters. This is why a signature needs to be passed to GetMethodID() and GetStaticMethodID().

Formally speaking, a signature is declared in the following way:

```
(<Parameter 1 Type Code>[<Parameter 1 Class>];...)<Return Type Code>
```

For example:

```
(Landroid/view/View;I)Z
```

The following table summarizes the various types available in JNI with their code:

Java type	Native type	Native array type	Type code	Array type code
boolean	jboolean	jbooleanArray	Z	[Z
byte	jbyte	jbyteArray	B	[B
char	jchar	jcharArray	C	[C
double	jdouble	jdoubleArray	D	[D
float	jfloat	jfloatArray	F	[F
int	jint	jintArray	I	[I
long	jlong	jlongArray	J	[J
short	jshort	jshortArray	S	[S
Object	jobject	jobjectArray	L	[L
String	jstring	N/A	L	[L
Class	jclass	N/A	L	[L
Throwable	jthrowable	N/A	L	[L
void	void	N/A	V	N/A

Processing bitmaps natively

Android NDK proposes an API dedicated to bitmap processing which allows accessing bitmap surface directly. This API is specific to Android and is not related to the JNI specification. However, bitmaps are Java objects and will need to be treated as such in native code.

To see more concretely how bitmaps can be modified from native code, let's try to decode a camera feed from native code. Android already features a Camera API on the Java side to display a video feed. However, there is absolutely no flexibility on how the feed is displayed—it is drawn directly on a GUI component. To overcome this problem, snapshots can be recorded into a data buffer encoded in a specific format, **YUV**, which is not compatible with classic RGB images! This is a situation where native code comes to the rescue and can help us improve performances.

 The final project is provided with this book under the name LiveCamera.

Time for action – decoding camera feed from native code

1. Create a new hybrid Java/C++ project like shown in Chapter 2, *Creating, Compiling, and Deploying Native Projects*:

   ❏ Name it `LiveCamera`.

   ❏ Its main package is `com.packtpub`.

   ❏ Its main activity is `LiveCameraActivity`.

   ❏ Get rid of `res/main.xml` as we will not create a GUI this time.

   ❏ Do not forget to create a `jni` directory at project's root.

2. In the application manifest, set the activity style to fullscreen and its orientation to landscape. Landscape orientation avoids most camera orientation problems that can be met on Android devices. Also request acces permission to the Android camera:

```xml
<?xml version="1.0" encoding="utf-8"?>
<manifest xmlns:android="http://schemas.android.com/apk/res/
android"
        package="com.packtpub" android:versionCode="1"
        android:versionName="1.0">
    <uses-sdk android:minSdkVersion="10" />

    <application android:icon="@drawable/icon"
                android:label="@string/app_name">
        <activity android:name=".LiveCameraActivity"
        android:label="@string/app_name"
        android:theme="@android:style/Theme.NoTitleBar.Fullscreen"
         android:screenOrientation="landscape">
            . . .
        </activity>
    </application>
    <uses-permission android:name="android.permission.CAMERA" />
</manifest>
```

   Let's take care of the Java side. We need to create a component to display the camera feed captured from the Android system class `android.hardware.Camera`.

3. Create a new class `CameraView` which extends `andoid.View.SurfaceView` and implements `Camera.PreviewCallback` and `SurfaceHolder.Callback`. `SurfaceView` is a visual component provided by Android to perform custom rendering.

Give `CameraView` the responsibility to load `livecamera` library, the native video decoding library we are about to create. This library will contain one method `decode()` which will take raw video feed data in input and decode it into a target Java bitmap:

```
public class CameraView extends SurfaceView implements
                SurfaceHolder.Callback, Camera.PreviewCallback {
    static {
        System.loadLibrary("livecamera");
    }

    public native void decode(Bitmap pTarget, byte[] pSource);
...
```

4. Initialize `CameraView` component.

In its constructor, register it as a listener of its own surface events, that is, surface creation, destruction, and change. Disable the `willNotDraw` flag to ensure its `onDraw()` event is triggered as we are going to render the camera feed from the main UI thread.

 Render a `SurfaceView` from the main UI thread only if a rendering operation is not too time consuming or for prototyping purposes. This can simplify code and avoid synchronization concerns. However, `SurfaceView` is designed to be rendered from a separate thread and should be generally used that way.

```
...
    private Camera mCamera;
    private byte[] mVideoSource;
    private Bitmap mBackBuffer;
    private Paint mPaint;

    public CameraView(Context context) {
        super(context);

        getHolder().addCallback(this);
        setWillNotDraw(false);
    }
...
```

5. When surface is created, acquire the default camera (there can be a front and rear camera, for example) and set its orientation to landscape (like the activity). To draw the camera feed ourself, deactivate automatic preview (that is, `setPreviewDisplay()`, which causes the video feed to be automatically drawn into `SurfaceView`) and request the use of data buffers for recording instead:

```
. . .
    public void surfaceCreated(SurfaceHolder holder) {
        try {
            mCamera = Camera.open();
            mCamera.setDisplayOrientation(0);
            mCamera.setPreviewDisplay(null);
            mCamera.setPreviewCallbackWithBuffer(this);
        } catch (IOException eIOException) {
            mCamera.release();
            mCamera = null;
            throw new IllegalStateException();
        }
    }
. . .
```

6. Method `surfaceChanged()` is triggered (potentially several times) after surface is created and, of course, before it is destroyed. This is the place where surface dimensions and pixel format get known.

First, find the resolution that is closest to the surface. Then create a byte buffer to capture a raw camera snapshot and a backbuffer bitmap to store the conversion result. Set up camera parameters: the selected resolution and the video format (`YCbCr_420_SP`, which is the default on Android) and finally, start the recording. Before a frame is recorded, a data buffer must be enqueued to capture a snapshot:

```
. . .
    public void surfaceChanged(SurfaceHolder pHolder, int pFormat,
                    int pWidth, int pHeight) {
        mCamera.stopPreview();
        Size lSize = findBestResolution(pWidth, pHeight);
        PixelFormat lPixelFormat = new PixelFormat();
        PixelFormat.getPixelFormatInfo(mCamera.getParameters()
                        .getPreviewFormat(), lPixelFormat);
        int lSourceSize = lSize.width * lSize.height
                        * lPixelFormat.bitsPerPixel / 8;
        mVideoSource = new byte[lSourceSize];
        mBackBuffer = Bitmap.createBitmap(lSize.width,
    lSize.height,Bitmap.Config.ARGB_8888);
```

```
Camera.Parameters lParameters = mCamera.getParameters();
lParameters.setPreviewSize(lSize.width, lSize.height);
lParameters.setPreviewFormat(PixelFormat.YCbCr_420_SP);
mCamera.setParameters(lParameters);

mCamera.addCallbackBuffer(mVideoSource);
mCamera.startPreview();
    }
...
```

7. An Android camera can support various resolutions which are highly dependent on the device. As there is no rule on what could be the default resolution, we need to look for a suitable one. Here, we select the biggest resolution that fits the display surface or the default one if none can be found.

```
...
    private Size findBestResolution(int pWidth, int pHeight) {
        List<Size> lSizes = mCamera.getParameters()
                                    .getSupportedPreviewSizes();
        Size lSelectedSize = mCamera.new Size(0, 0);
        for (Size lSize : lSizes) {
            if ((lSize.width <= pWidth)
            && (lSize.height <= pHeight)
            && (lSize.width >= lSelectedSize.width)
            && (lSize.height >= lSelectedSize.height)) {
                lSelectedSize = lSize;
            }
        }
        if ((lSelectedSize.width == 0)
                        || (lSelectedSize.height == 0)) {
            lSelectedSize = lSizes.get(0);
        }
        return lSelectedSize;
    }
...
```

8. In `CameraView.java`, release camera when surface is destroyed as it is a shared resource. In memory, buffers can also be nullified to facilitate garbage collector work:

```
...
    public void surfaceDestroyed(SurfaceHolder holder) {
        if (mCamera != null) {
            mCamera.stopPreview();
            mCamera.release();
```

```
                            mCamera = null;
                            mVideoSource = null;
                            mBackBuffer = null;
                    }
            }
    . . .
```

9. Now that surface is set up, decode video frames in `onPreviewFrame()` and store the result in the backbuffer bitmap. This handler is triggered by the `Camera` class when a new frame is ready. Once decoded, invalidate the surface to redraw it.

To draw a video frame, override `onDraw()` and draw the backbuffer into the target canvas. Once done, we can *re-enqueue* the raw video buffer to capture a new image.

 The `Camera` component can enqueue several buffers to process a frame while others are getting captured. Although this approach is more complex as it implies threading and synchronization, it can achieve better performance and can handle punctual slow down. The single-threaded capture algorithm shown here is simpler but much less efficient since a new frame can only be recorded after the previous one is drawn.

```
    . . .
        public void onPreviewFrame(byte[] pData, Camera pCamera) {
            decode(mBackBuffer, pData);
            invalidate();
        }

        @Override
        protected void onDraw(Canvas pCanvas) {
            if (mCamera != null) {
                pCanvas.drawBitmap(mBackBuffer, 0, 0, mPaint);
                mCamera.addCallbackBuffer(mVideoSource);
            }
        }
    }
```

10. Open the `LiveCameraActivity.java` file, which should have been created by the Android project creation wizard. Initialize the GUI with a new `CameraView` instance.

```java
public class LiveCameraActivity extends Activity {
    @Override
    protected void onCreate(Bundle savedInstanceState) {
        super.onCreate(savedInstanceState);
        setContentView(new CameraView(this));
    }
}
```

Now that the Java side is ready, we can write the `decode()` method on the native side.

11. Generate JNI header file with `javah`.

12. Create corresponding implementation file `com_packtpub_CameraView.c`. Include `android/bitmap.h`, which defines the NDK bitmap processing API. The following are a few utility methods to help decode video:

- ❑ `toInt()`: This converts a jbyte to an integer, erasing all useless bits with a mask.
- ❑ `max()`: This gets the maximum between two values.
- ❑ `clamp()`: This method is used to clamp a value inside a defined interval.
- ❑ `color()`: This method builds an ARGB color from its component.

13. Make them `inline` to gain a bit of performance:

```c
#include "com_packtpub_CameraView.h"
#include <android/bitmap.h>

inline int32_t toInt(jbyte pValue) {
    return (0xff & (int32_t) pValue);
}

inline int32_t max(int32_t pValue1, int32_t pValue2) {
    if (pValue1 < pValue2) {
        return pValue2;
    } else {
        return pValue1;
    }
}
```

```
inline int32_t clamp(int32_t pValue, int32_t pLowest, int32_t
pHighest) {
    if (pValue < 0) {
        return pLowest;
    } else if (pValue > pHighest) {
        return pHighest;
    } else {
        return pValue;
    }
}

inline int32_t color(pColorR, pColorG, pColorB) {
    return 0xFF000000 | ((pColorB << 6)  & 0x00FF0000)
                      | ((pColorG >> 2)  & 0x0000FF00)
                      | ((pColorR >> 10) & 0x000000FF);
}
...
```

14. Still in the same file, implement `decode()`. First, retrieve bitmap information and lock it for drawing with the `AndroidBitmap_*` API.

Then, gain access to the input Java byte array with `GetPrimitiveArrayCritical()`. This JNI method is similar to `Get<Primitive>ArrayElements()` except that the acquired array is less likely to be a temporary copy. In return, no JNI or thread-blocking calls can be performed until the array is released.

```
...
JNIEXPORT void JNICALL Java_com_packtpub_CameraView_decode
(JNIEnv * pEnv, jclass pClass, jobject pTarget, jbyteArray
pSource) {
    AndroidBitmapInfo lBitmapInfo;
    if (AndroidBitmap_getInfo(pEnv, pTarget, &lBitmapInfo) < 0) {
        return;
    }
    if (lBitmapInfo.format != ANDROID_BITMAP_FORMAT_RGBA_8888) {
        return;
    }

    uint32_t* lBitmapContent;
    if (AndroidBitmap_lockPixels(pEnv, pTarget,
                                (void**)&lBitmapContent) < 0) {
        return;
    }
```

```
jbyte* lSource = (*pEnv)->GetPrimitiveArrayCritical(pEnv,
    pSource, 0);
if (lSource == NULL) {
    return;
}
```
. . .

15. Continue `decode()` method. We have access to the input video buffer with a video frame inside and to the backbuffer bitmap surface. So we can decode the video feed into the output backbuffer.

The video frame is encoded in the YUV format, which is quite different from RGB. YUV format encodes a color in three components:

❑   One **luminance** component, that is, the grayscale representation of a color.

❑   Two **chrominance** components which encode the color information (also called Cb and Cr as they represent the blue-difference and red-difference).

16. There are many frames available whose format is based on YUV colors. Here, we convert frames following the **YCbCr 420 SP** (or **NV21**) format. This kind of image frame is composed of a buffer of 8 bits Y luminance samples followed by a second buffer of interleaved 8 bits V and U chrominance samples. The VU buffer is subsampled, which means that there are less U and V samples compared to Y samples (1 U and 1 V for 4 Y). The following algorithm processes each pixel and converts each YUV pixel to RGB using the appropriate formula (see `http://www.fourcecc.org/fccyvrgb.php` for more information).

17. Terminate `decode()` method by unlocking the backbuffer bitmap and releasing the Java array acquired earlier:

. . .

```
int32_t lFrameSize = lBitmapInfo.width * lBitmapInfo.height;
int32_t lYIndex, lUVIndex;
int32_t lX, lY;
int32_t lColorY, lColorU, lColorV;
int32_t lColorR, lColorG, lColorB;
int32_t y1192;

// Processes each pixel and converts YUV to RGB color.
for (lY = 0, lYIndex = 0; lY < lBitmapInfo.height; ++lY) {
    lColorU = 0; lColorV = 0;
    // Y is divided by 2 because UVs are subsampled vertically.
    // This means that two consecutives iterations refer to the
```

```
                    // same UV line (e.g when Y=0 and Y=1).
                    lUVIndex = lFrameSize + (lY >> 1) * lBitmapInfo.width;

                    for (lX = 0; lX < lBitmapInfo.width; ++lX, ++lYIndex) {
                        // Retrieves YUV components. UVs are subsampled
                        // horizontally too, hence %2 (1 UV for 2 Y).
                        lColorY = max(toInt(lSource[lYIndex]) - 16, 0);
                        if (!(lX % 2)) {
                            lColorV = toInt(lSource[lUVIndex++]) - 128;
                            lColorU = toInt(lSource[lUVIndex++]) - 128;
                        }

                        // Computes R, G and B from Y, U and V.
                        y1192 = 1192 * lColorY;
                        lColorR = (y1192 + 1634 * lColorV);
                        lColorG = (y1192 - 833  * lColorV - 400 * lColorU);
                        lColorB = (y1192 + 2066 * lColorU);

                        lColorR = clamp(lColorR, 0, 262143);
                        lColorG = clamp(lColorG, 0, 262143);
                        lColorB = clamp(lColorB, 0, 262143);

                        // Combines R, G, B and A into the final pixel color.
                        lBitmapContent[lYIndex] = color(lColorR,lColorG,lColorB);
                    }
                }
            (*pEnv)-> ReleasePrimitiveArrayCritical(pEnv,pSource,lSource,0);
            AndroidBitmap_unlockPixels(pEnv, pTarget);
        }
```

18. Write `livecamera` library `Android.mk`. Link it to `jnigraphics` NDK module:

```
LOCAL_PATH := $(call my-dir)

include $(CLEAR_VARS)

LOCAL_MODULE    := livecamera
LOCAL_SRC_FILES := com_packtpub_CameraView.c
LOCAL_LDLIBS    := -ljnigraphics

include $(BUILD_SHARED_LIBRARY)
```

19. Compile and run the application.

What just happened?

Right after starting the application, the camera feed should appear on your device screen. Video is decoded in native code into a Java bitmap which is then drawn into the display surface. Accessing the video feed natively allow much faster processing than what could be done with classic Java code (see *Chapter 11, Debugging and Troubleshooting* for further optimizations with the NEON instruction set). It opens many new possibilities: image processing, pattern recognition, augmented reality, and so on.

Bitmap surface is accessed directly by native code thanks to the Android NDK Bitmap library defined in library in `jnigraphics`. Drawing occurs in three steps:

1. Bitmap surface is acquired.
2. Video pixels are converted to RGB and written to bitmap surface.
3. Bitmap surface is released.

Bitmaps must be systematically locked and then released to access them natively. Drawing operations must occur between a lock/release pair.

Video decoding and rendering is performed with with a non-threaded `SurfaceView`, although this process could be made more efficient with a second thread. Multithreading can be introduced thanks to the buffer queue system introduced in latest releases of the Android `Camera` component. Do not forget that YUV to RGB is an expensive operation that is likely to remain a point of contention in your program.

Adapt snapshot size to your needs. Indeed, beware of the surface to process quadruple when snapshot's size doubles. If feedback is not too important, snapshot size can be partially reduced (for example, for pattern recognition in Augmented Reality). If you can, draw directly to the display window surface instead of going through a temporary buffer.

The video feed is encoded in the YUV NV21 format. YUV is a color format originally invented in the old days of electronics to make black-and-white video receivers compatible with color transmissions and still commonly used nowadays. Default frame format is guaranteed by the Android specification to be **YCbCr 420 SP** (or **NV21**) on Android. The algorithm used to decode the YUV frame originates from the Ketai open source project, an image and sensor processing library for Android. See `http://ketai.googlecode.com/` for more information.

Although **YCbCr 420 SP** is the default video format on Android, the emulator only supports **YCbCr 422 SP**. This defect should not cause much trouble as it basically swaps colors. This problem should not occur on real devices.

Summary

We have seen more in-depth how to make Java and C/C++ communicate together. Android is now fully bilingual! Java can call C/C++ code with any type of data or object and native code can call Java back. We have discovered, in more detail, how to attach and detach a thread to the VM and synchronize Java and native threads together with JNI monitors. Then we saw how to call Java code from native code with the JNI Reflection API. Practically any Java operation can be performed from native code thanks to it. However, for best performance, class, method, or fields descriptor must be cached. Finally, we have processed bitmaps natively thanks to JNI and decoded a video feed manually. But an expensive conversion is needed from default YUV format (which should be supported on every device according to Android specification) to RGB.

When dealing with native code on Android, JNI is almost always somewhere in the way. Sadly, it is a verbose and cumbersome API which requires lot of setup and care. JNI is full of subtleties and would require a whole book for an in-depth understanding. This chapter gave you the essential knowledge to get started. In the next chapter, we are going to see how to create a fully native application, which gets completely rid of JNI.

5
Writing a Fully-native Application

*In previous chapters, we have breached Android NDK's surface using JNI. But there is much more to find inside! NDK R5 is a major release which has seen several long-awaited features finally delivered, one of them is **native activities**. Native activities allow creating applications based only on native code, without a single line of Java. No more JNI! No more references! No more Java!*

*In addition to native activities, NDK R5 has brought some APIs for native access to some Android resources such as **display windows**, **assets**, **device configuration**... These APIs help dismantle the JNI bridge, often necessary to develop native applications opened to their host environment. Although still a lot is missing and is not likely to be available (Java remains the main platform language for GUIs and most frameworks), multimedia applications are a perfect target to apply them.*

I propose now to enter into the heart of the Android NDK by:

♦ Creating a fully native activity

♦ Handling main activity events

♦ Accessing display window natively

♦ Retrieving time and calculating delays

The present chapter initiates a native C++ project developed progressively throughout this book: `DroidBlaster`. Based on a top-down viewpoint, this sample scrolling shooter will feature 2D graphics, and later on 3D graphics, sound, input, and sensor management. In this chapter, we are going to create its base structure.

Creating a native activity

The class `NativeActivity` provides a facility to minimize the work necessary to create a native application. It lets the developer get rid of all the boilerplate code to initialize and communicate with native code and concentrate on core functionalities. In this first part, we are going to see how to create a minimal native activity that runs an event loop.

 The resulting project is provided with this book under the name DroidBlaster_Part5-1.

Time for action – creating a basic native activity

First, let's create `DroidBlaster` project:

1. In Eclipse, create a new project **Android project** with the following settings:

- ❑ Enter Eclipse project name: `DroidBlaster`.
- ❑ Set **Build target** to **Android 2.3.3**.
- ❑ Enter **Application name**: `DroidBlaster`.
- ❑ Enter **Package name**: `com.packtpub.droidblaster`.
- ❑ Uncheck **Create Activity**.
- ❑ Set **Min SDK Version** to `10`.

2. Once the project is created, go to the `res/layout` directory and remove `main.xml`. This UI description file is not needed in our native application. You can also remove `src` directory as `DroidBlaster` will not contain even a piece of Java code.

3. The application is compilable and deployable, but not runnable simply because we have not created an activity yet. Let's declare `NativeActivity` in the `AndroidManifest.xml` file at the project's root. The declared native activity refers to a native module named `droidblaster` (property `android.app.lib_name`):

```
<?xml version="1.0" encoding="utf-8"?>
<manifest xmlns:android="http://schemas.android.com/apk/res/
android"
    package="com.packtpub.droidblaster" android:versionCode="1"
    android:versionName="1.0">
  <uses-sdk android:minSdkVersion="10"/>

  <application android:icon="@drawable/icon"
      android:label="@string/app_name">
```

```
<activity android:name="android.app.NativeActivity"
  android:label="@string/app_name">
<meta-data android:name="android.app.lib_name"
            android:value="droidblaster"/>
<intent-filter>
   <action android:name="android.intent.action.MAIN"/>
   <categoryandroid:name="android.intent.category.LAUNCHER"/>
      </intent-filter>
   </activity>
</application>
</manifest>
```

Let's set up the Eclipse project to compile native code:

4. Convert the project to a hybrid **C++ project** (not C) using **Convert C/C++ Project** wizard.

5. Then, go to project, select **Properties** in **C/C++ Build** section and change default build command to `ndk-build`.

6. In the **Path and Symbols/Includes** section, add Android NDK include directories to all languages as seen in Chapter 2, *Creating, Compiling, and Deploying Native Projects*:

```
${env_var:ANDROID_NDK}/platforms/android-9/arch-arm/usr/include
```

```
${env_var:ANDROID_NDK}/toolchains/arm-linux-androideabi-4.4.3/
prebuilt/<your OS>/lib/gcc/arm-linux-androideabi/4.4.3/include
```

7. Still in the same section, add native app glue directory to all languages. Validate and close the project **Properties** dialog:

```
${env_var:ANDROID_NDK}/sources/android/native_app_glue
```

8. Create directory `jni` at the project's root containing the following `Android.mk` file. It describes the C++ files to compile and the `native_app_glue` module to link to. The native glue binds together native code and `NativeActivity`:

```
LOCAL_PATH := $(call my-dir)

include $(CLEAR_VARS)

LOCAL_MODULE     := droidblaster
LOCAL_SRC_FILES := Main.cpp EventLoop.cpp Log.cpp
LOCAL_LDLIBS    := -landroid -llog
LOCAL_STATIC_LIBRARIES := android_native_app_glue
```

```
include $(BUILD_SHARED_LIBRARY)
```

```
$(call import-module,android/native_app_glue)
```

Now we can start writing some native code that runs inside the native activity. Let's begin with some utility code:

9. In `jni` directory, create a file `Types.hpp`. This header will contain common types and the header `stdint.h`:

```
#ifndef _PACKT_TYPES_HPP_
#define _PACKT_TYPES_HPP_

#include <stdint.h>

#endif
```

10. To still get some feedback without the ability to input or output anything from or to the screen, let's write a logging class. Create `Log.hpp` and declare a new class `Log`. You can define `packt_Log_debug` macro to activate debug messages with a simple flag:

```
#ifndef PACKT_LOG_HPP
#define PACKT_LOG_HPP

namespace packt {
    class Log {
    public:
        static void error(const char* pMessage, ...);
        static void warn(const char* pMessage, ...);
        static void info(const char* pMessage, ...);
        static void debug(const char* pMessage, ...);
    };
}

#ifndef NDEBUG
    #define packt_Log_debug(...) packt::Log::debug(__VA_ARGS__)
#else
    #define packt_Log_debug(...)
#endif

#endif
```

By default, NDEBUG macro is defined by the NDK compilation toolchain. To undefined it, the application has to be made debuggable in its manifest: `<application android:debuggable="true" ...>`

11. Create `Log.cpp` file and implement method `info()`. To write messages to Android logs, the NDK provides a dedicated logging API in header `android/log.h.` which can be used similarly to `printf()` and `vprintf()` (with `varargs`) in C:

```cpp
#include "Log.hpp"

#include <stdarg.h>
#include <android/log.h>

namespace packt {
    void Log::info(const char* pMessage, ...) {
        va_list lVarArgs;
        va_start(lVarArgs, pMessage);
        __android_log_vprint(ANDROID_LOG_INFO, "PACKT", pMessage,
            lVarArgs);
        __android_log_print(ANDROID_LOG_INFO, "PACKT", "\n");
        va_end(lVarArgs);
    }
}
```

12. Other log methods are almost identical. The only piece of code which changes between each method is the level macro: `ANDROID_LOG_ERROR`, `ANDROID_LOG_WARN`, and `ANDROID_LOG_DEBUG` instead.

Finally, we can write the code to poll activity events:

13. Application events have to be processed in an event loop. To do so, still in `jni` directory, create `EventLoop.hpp` defining the eponym class with a unique method `run()`.

Included header `android_native_app_glue.h` defines `android_app` structure, which represents what could be called an "applicative context", with all information related to the native activity: its state, its window, its event queue, and so on:

```cpp
#ifndef _PACKT_EVENTLOOP_HPP_
#define _PACKT_EVENTLOOP_HPP_

#include "Types.hpp"
```

```
#include <android_native_app_glue.h>

namespace packt {
    class EventLoop {
    public:
        EventLoop(android_app* pApplication);

        void run();

    private:
        android_app* mApplication;
    };
}
#endif
```

14. Create `EventLoop.cpp` and implement activity event loop in method `run
()` as follows. Include a few log events to get some feedback in Android log.

During the whole activity lifetime, `run()` loops continuously over events
until it is requested to terminate. When an activity is about to be destroyed,
`destroyRequested` value in `android_app` structure is changed internally
to notify the event loop:

```
#include "EventLoop.hpp"
#include "Log.hpp"

namespace packt {
    EventLoop::EventLoop(android_app* pApplication) :
        mApplication(pApplication)
    {}

    void EventLoop::run() {
        int32_t lResult;
        int32_t lEvents;
        android_poll_source* lSource;

        app_dummy();

        packt::Log::info("Starting event loop");
        while (true) {
            while ((lResult = ALooper_pollAll(-1, NULL, &lEvents,
                                    (void**) &lSource)) >= 0)
{
                if (lSource != NULL) {
                    packt::Log::info("Processing an event");
```

```
                        lSource->process(mApplication, lSource);
            }
            if (mApplication->destroyRequested) {
                packt::Log::info("Exiting event loop");
                return;
            }
          }
        }
      }
    }
```

15. Finally, create the main entry point running the event loop in a new file Main.cpp:

```
#include "EventLoop.hpp"

void android_main(android_app* pApplication) {
    packt::EventLoop lEventLoop(pApplication);
    lEventLoop.run();
}
```

16. Compile and run the application.

What just happened?

Of course, you will not see anything tremendous when starting this application. Actually, you will just see a black screen! But if you look carefully at the **LogCat** view in Eclipse (or command adb logcat), you will discover a few interesting messages that have been emitted by your native application in reaction to activity events:

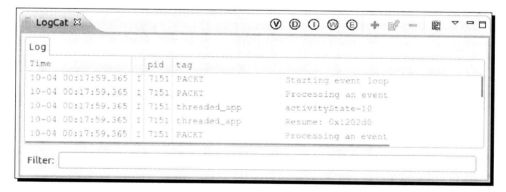

We have initiated a Java Android project without a single line of Java code! Instead of a new Java Activity child class, in AndroidManifest.xml, we have referenced the android. app.NativeActivity class, which is launched like any other Android activity.

NativeActivity is a Java class. Yes, a Java class. But we never confronted to it directly. NativeActivity is in fact a helper class provided with Android SDK and which contains all the necessary glue code to handle application lifecycle and events and broadcast them transparently to native code. Being a Java class, NativeActivity runs, of course, on the Dalvik Virtual Machine and is interpreted like any Java class.

A native activity does not eliminate the need for JNI. In fact, it just hides it! Hopefully, we never face NativeActivity directly. Even better, the C/C++ module run by a NativeActivity runs outside Dalvik boundaries in its own thread... entirely natively!

NativeActivity and native code are connected together through the native_app_glue module. Native glue has the responsibility of:

- ◆ launching the native thread which runs our own native code
- ◆ receiving events from NativeActivity
- ◆ routing these events to the native thread event loop for further processing

Our own native code entry point is declared at step 15 with an android_main() method similar to main methods in desktop applications. It is called once when a native application is launched and loops over application events until NativeActivity is terminated by user (for example, when pressing device back button). The android_main() method runs the native event loop, which is itself composed of two nested while loops. The outer one is an infinite loop, terminated only when application destruction is requested. Destruction request flag can be found in android_app "application context" provided as an argument to the android_main() method by the native glue.

Inside the main loop is an inner loop which processes all pending events with a call to ALooper_pollAll(). This method is part of the ALooper API which is a general-purpose event loop manager provided by Android. When timeout is -1 like at step 14, ALooper_pollAll() remains blocked while waiting for events. When at least one is received, ALooper_pollAll() returns and code flow continues. The android_poll_source structure describing the event is filled and used for further processing.

If an event loop was a heart, then event polling would be a heartbeat. In other words, polling makes your application alive and reactive to the outside world. It is not even possible to leave a native activity without polling events; destruction is itself an event!

Handling activity events

In the first part, we have run a native event loop which flushes events without really processing them. In this second part, we are going to discover more about these events occurring during activity lifecycle. Let's extend the previous example to log all events that a native activity is confronted to.

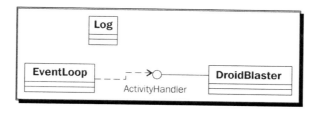

 Project DroidBlaster_Part5-1 can be used as a starting point for this part. The resulting project is provided with this book under the name DroidBlaster_Part5-2.

Time for action – handling activity events

Let's improve the code created in the previous part:

1. Open `Types.hpp` and define a new type `status` to represent return codes:

```
#ifndef _PACKT_TYPES_HPP_
#define _PACKT_TYPES_HPP_

#include <stdint.h>

typedef int32_t status;

const status STATUS_OK   = 0;
const status STATUS_KO   = -1;
const status STATUS_EXIT = -2;
#endif
```

2. Create `ActivityHandler.hpp` in `jni` directory. This header defines an interface to observe native activity events. Each possible event has its own handler method: `onStart()`, `onResume()`, `onPause()`, `onStop()`, `onDestroy()`, and so on. However, we are generally interested in three specific moments in the activity lifecycle:

   - `onActivate()`: This method is invoked when activity is resumed and its window is available and focused.

- ❑ `onDeactivate()`: This activity is invoked when activity is paused or the display window loses its focus or is destroyed.

- ❑ `onStep()`: This activity is invoked when no event has to be processed and computations can take place.

```cpp
#ifndef _PACKT_EVENTHANDLER_HPP_
#define _PACKT_EVENTHANDLER_HPP_

#include "Types.hpp"

namespace packt {
    class EventHandler {
    public:
        virtual status onActivate() = 0;
        virtual void onDeactivate() = 0;
        virtual status onStep() = 0;

        virtual void onStart() {};
        virtual void onResume() {};
        virtual void onPause() {};
        virtual void onStop() {};
        virtual void onDestroy() {};

        virtual void onSaveState(void** pData,
          int32_t* pSize) {};
        virtual void onConfigurationChanged() {};
        virtual void onLowMemory() {};

        virtual void onCreateWindow() {};
        virtual void onDestroyWindow() {};
        virtual void onGainFocus() {};
        virtual void onLostFocus() {};
    };
}
#endif
```

All these events have to be triggered from the activity event loop.

3. Open existing file `EventLoop.hpp`. Although its public face is conserved, `EventLoop` class is enhanced with two internal methods (`activate()` and `deactivate()`) and two state variables (`mEnabled` and `mQuit`) to save activity activation state. Real activity events are handled in `processActivityEvent()` and its corresponding callback `activityCallback()`. These events are routed to `mActivityHandler` event observer:

```
#ifndef _PACKT_EVENTLOOP_HPP_
#define _PACKT_EVENTLOOP_HPP_

#include "EventHandler.hpp"
#include "Types.hpp"

#include <android_native_app_glue.h>

namespace packt {
    class EventLoop {
    public:
        EventLoop(android_app* pApplication);

        void run(EventHandler& pEventHandler);

    protected:
        void activate();
        void deactivate();

        void processActivityEvent(int32_t pCommand);

    private:
        static void activityCallback(android_app* pApplication,
            int32_t pCommand);

    private:
        bool mEnabled; bool mQuit;
        ActivityHandler* mActivityHandler;
        android_app* mApplication;
    };
}
#endif
```

4. Open and edit EventLoop.cpp. Constructor initialization list is trivial to implement. However, the android_app application context needs to be filled with some additional information:

   ❏ onAppCmd: This points to an internal callback triggered each time an event occurs. In our case, this is the role devoted to the static method activityCallback.

   ❏ userData: This is a pointer in which you can assign any data you want. This piece of data is the only information accessible from the callback declared previously (except global variables). In our case, this is the EventLoop instance (this).

```
#include "EventLoop.hpp"
#include "Log.hpp"

namespace packt {
    EventLoop::EventLoop(android_app* pApplication) :
        mEnabled(false), mQuit(false),
        mApplication(pApplication),
        mActivityHandler(NULL) {
        mApplication->onAppCmd = activityCallback;
        mApplication->userData = this;
    }
...
```

5. Update the `run()` main event loop to stop blocking while polling events. Indeed, `ALooper_pollAll()` behavior is defined by its first parameter, timeout:

   ❑ When timeout is `-1` like at step 14, call is blocking until events are received.

   ❑ When timeout is `0`, call is non-blocking so that if nothing remains in the queue, program flow continues (inner `while` loop is terminated) and makes it possible to perform recurrent processing.

   ❑ When timeout is greater than `0`, then we have a blocking call which remains until an event is received or the duration is elapsed.

     ❑ Here, we want to step the activity (that is, perform computations) when it is in active state (`mEnabled` is true): in that case, timeout is `0`. When activity is in deactivated state (`mEnabled` is false), events are still processed (for example, to resurrect the activity) but nothing needs to get computed. The thread has to be blocked to avoid consuming battery and processor time uselessly: timeout is `-1`.

     ❑ To leave the application programmatically, NDK API provides `ANativeActivity_finish()` method to request activity termination. Termination does not occur immediately but after a few events (pause, stop, and so on)!

```
...
   void EventLoop::run(ActivityHandler& pActivityHandler)
{
    int32_t lResult;
    int32_t lEvents;
    android_poll_source* lSource;

    app_dummy();
    mActivityHandler = &pActivityHandler;
```

```
packt::Log::info("Starting event loop");
while (true) {
  while ((lResult = ALooper_pollAll(mEnabled ? 0 : -1,
              NULL, &lEvents, (void**) &lSource)) >= 0) {
        if (lSource != NULL) {
          packt::Log::info("Processing an event");
          lSource->process(mApplication, lSource);
        }
        if (mApplication->destroyRequested) {
          packt::Log::info("Exiting event loop");
            return;
        }
      }

    if ((mEnabled) && (!mQuit)) {
        if (mActivityHandler->onStep() != STATUS_OK) {
          mQuit = true;
          ANativeActivity_finish(mApplication->activity);
          }
        }
      }
    }
  ...
```

6. Still in `EventLoop.cpp`, implement `activate()` and `deactivate()`. Both check activity state before notifying the observer (to avoid untimely triggering). As stated earlier, activation requires a window to be available before going further:

```
...
    void EventLoop::activate() {
        if ((!mEnabled) && (mApplication->window != NULL)) {
            mQuit = false; mEnabled = true;
            if (mActivityHandler->onActivate() != STATUS_OK) {
                mQuit = true;
                ANativeActivity_finish(mApplication->activity);
            }
        }
    }

    void EventLoop::deactivate()
    {
        if (mEnabled) {
            mActivityHandler->onDeactivate();
            mEnabled = false;
        }
    }
...
```

7. Finally, implement `processActivityEvent()` and its companion callback `activityCallback()`. Do you remember the `onAppCmd` and `userData` fields from `android_app` structure that we initialized in the constructor? They are used internally by the native glue to trigger the right callback (here `activityCallback()`) when an event occurs. The `EventLoop` object is gotten back thanks to the `userData` pointer (`this` being unavailable from a static method). Effective event processing is then delegated to `processActivityEvent()`, which brings us back into the object-oriented world.

Parameter `pCommand` contains an enumeration value (`APP_CMD_*`) which describes the occurring event (`APP_CMD_START`, `APP_CMD_GAINED_FOCUS`, and so on). Once an event is analyzed, activity is activated or deactivated depending on the event and the observer is notified.

A few events such as APP_CMD_WINDOW_RESIZED are available but never triggered. Do not listen to them unless you are ready to stick your hands in the glue...

Activation occurs when activity gains focus. This event is always the last event that occurs after activity is resumed and window is created. Getting focus means that activity can receive input events. Thus, it would be possible to activate the event loop as soon as window is created.

Deactivation occurs when window loses focus or application is paused (both can occur first). By security, deactivation is also performed when window is destroyed although this should always occur after focus is lost. Losing focus means that application does not receive input events anymore. Thus, it would also be possible to deactivate the event loop only when window is destroyed instead:

To make your activity lose and gain focus easily, just press your device home button to display the **Recent** applications pop up (which may be manufacturer specific). If activation and deactivation occur on a focus change, activity pauses immediately. Otherwise, it would keep working in the background until another activity is selected (which could be desirable).

```
. . .
void EventLoop::processActivityEvent(int32_t pCommand) {
  switch (pCommand) {
    case APP_CMD_CONFIG_CHANGED:
      mActivityHandler->onConfigurationChanged();
      break;
    case APP_CMD_INIT_WINDOW:
```

```
        mActivityHandler->onCreateWindow();
        break;
      case APP_CMD_DESTROY:
        mActivityHandler->onDestroy();
        break;
      case APP_CMD_GAINED_FOCUS:
        activate();
        mActivityHandler->onGainFocus();
        break;
      case APP_CMD_LOST_FOCUS:
        mActivityHandler->onLostFocus();
        deactivate();
        break;
      case APP_CMD_LOW_MEMORY:
        mActivityHandler->onLowMemory();
        break;
      case APP_CMD_PAUSE:
        mActivityHandler->onPause();
        deactivate();
        break;
      case APP_CMD_RESUME:
        mActivityHandler->onResume();
        break;
      case APP_CMD_SAVE_STATE:
        mActivityHandler->onSaveState(&mApplication->savedState,
          &mApplication->savedStateSize);
        break;
      case APP_CMD_START:
        mActivityHandler->onStart();
        break;
      case APP_CMD_STOP:
        mActivityHandler->onStop();
        break;
      case APP_CMD_TERM_WINDOW:
        mActivityHandler->onDestroyWindow();
      deactivate();
        break;
        default:
        break;
          }
}

void EventLoop::activityCallback(android_app* pApplication,
    int32_t pCommand)
```

```
      {
        EventLoop& lEventLoop = *(EventLoop*) pApplication->userData;
          lEventLoop.processActivityEvent(pCommand);
      }
}
```

Finally, we can implement application-specific code.

8. Create a `DroidBlaster.hpp` file which implements `ActivityHandler` interface:

```
#ifndef _PACKT_DROIDBLASTER_HPP_
#define _PACKT_DROIDBLASTER_HPP_

#include "ActivityHandler.hpp"
#include "Types.hpp"

namespace dbs {
    class DroidBlaster : public packt::ActivityHandler {
    public:
        DroidBlaster();
        virtual ~DroidBlaster();

    protected:
        status onActivate();
        void onDeactivate();
        status onStep();

        void onStart();
        void onResume();
        void onPause();
        void onStop();
        void onDestroy();

        void onSaveState(void** pData; int32_t* pSize);
        void onConfigurationChanged();
        void onLowMemory();

        void onCreateWindow();
        void onDestroyWindow();
        void onGainFocus();
        void onLostFocus();
    };
}
#endif
```

9. Create `DroidBlaster.cpp` implementation. To keep this introduction to the activity lifecycle simple, we are just going to log events for each occurring event. Computations are limited to a simple thread sleep:

```cpp
#include "DroidBlaster.hpp"
#include "DroidBlaster.hpp"
#include "Log.hpp"

#include <unistd.h>

namespace dbs {
    DroidBlaster::DroidBlaster() {
        packt::Log::info("Creating DroidBlaster");
    }

    DroidBlaster::~DroidBlaster() {
        packt::Log::info("Destructing DroidBlaster");
    }


    status DroidBlaster::onActivate() {
        packt::Log::info("Activating DroidBlaster");
        return STATUS_OK;
    }

    void DroidBlaster::onDeactivate() {
        packt::Log::info("Deactivating DroidBlaster");
    }


    status DroidBlaster::onStep() {
        packt::Log::info("Starting step");
        usleep(300000);
        packt::Log::info("Stepping done");
        return STATUS_OK;
    }

    void DroidBlaster::onStart() {
        packt::Log::info("onStart");
    }
    ...
}
```

10. Let's not forget to initialize our activity and its new event handler DroidBlaster:

```
#include "DroidBlaster.hpp"
#include "EventLoop.hpp"

void android_main(android_app* pApplication) {
    packt::EventLoop lEventLoop(pApplication);
    dbs::DroidBlaster lDroidBlaster;
    lEventLoop.run(lDroidBlaster);
}
```

11. Update the Android.mk Makefile to include all the new .cpp files created in the present part. Then compile and run the application.

What just happened?

If you like black screen, you are served! Again, everything happens in the Eclipse **LogCat** view. All messages that have been emitted by your native application in reaction to application events are displayed there:

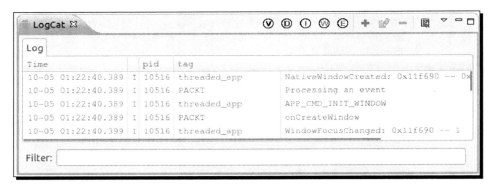

We have created a minimalist framework which handles application events in the native thread using an event-driven approach. These events are redirected to an observer object which performs its own specific computations. Native activity events correspond mostly to Java activity events. Following is an important schematic inspired from official Android documentation showing events that can happen during an activity lifecycle:

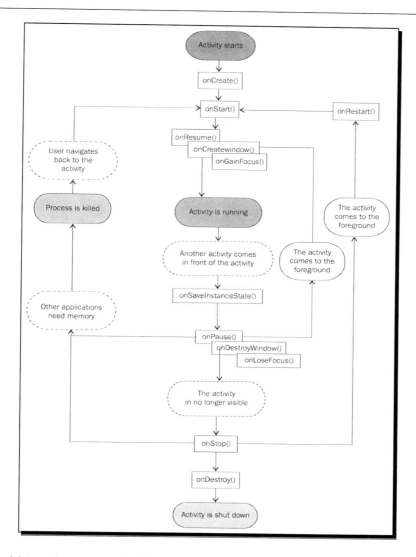

See `http://developer.android.com/reference/android/app/Activity.html` for more information.

Events are a critical point that any application needs to handle properly. Although event pairs, that is, start/stop, resume/pause, create/destroy window, and gain/lose focus occur most of the time in a predetermined order, some specific cases generate different behaviors, for example:

- Pressing for a long time the device home button and then getting back should cause a loss and gain of focus only

- Shutting down phone screen and switching it back on should cause window to be terminated and reinitialized immediately right after activity is resumed

- When changing screen orientation, the whole activity may not lose its focus although it will regain it after activity is recreated

Choice has been made to use a simplified event handling model in `DroidBlaster`, with only three main events occurring in the application lifecycle (activation, deactivation, and stepping). However, an application can be made more efficient by performing more subtle event handling. For example, pausing an activity may not release resources whereas a stop event should.

Have a look at the NVIDIA developer site where you will find interesting documents about Android events and even more: `http://developer.nvidia.com/content/resources-android-native-game-development-available`.

More on Native App Glue

You may still wonder what the native glue framework does exactly behind your back and how. The truth is `android_main()` is not the real native application entry point. The real entry point is `ANativeActivity_onCreate()` method hidden in the `android_native_app_glue` module. The event loop we have seen until now is in fact a *delegate* event loop launched in its own native thread by the glue code so that your `android_main()` is not correlated anymore to `NativeActivity` on the Java side. Thus, even if your code takes a long time to handle an event, `NativeActivity` is not blocked and your Android device still remains responsive. Native glue module code is located in `${ANDROID_NDK}/sources/android/native_app_glue` and can be modified or forked at will (see *Chapter 9, Porting Existing Libraries to Android*).

android_native_app_glue ease your life

The native glue really simplifies code by handling initialization and system-related stuff that most applications do not need to worry about (synchronization with **mutexes, pipe communication**, and so on). It frees the UI thread from its load to keep device ability to handle unexpected events such as a sudden phone call.

UI thread

The following call hierarchy is an overview of how Native App Glue proceeds internally on the UI thread (that is, on the Java side):

```
Main Thread
NativeActivity
+___ANativeActivity_onCreate(ANativeActivity, void*, size_t)
    +___android_app_create(ANativeActivity*, void*, size_t)
```

ANativeActivity_onCreate() is the real native-side entry point and is executed on the UI thread. The given ANativeActivity structure is filled with event callbacks used in the native glue code: onDestroy, onStart, onResume, and so on. So when something happens in NativeActivity on the Java side, callback handlers are immediately triggered on the native side but still on the UI thread. Processing performed by these handlers is very simple: they notify the native thread by calling internal method android_app_write_cmd(). Here is a list of some of the occurring events:

onStart, onResume, onPause, onStop	changes the application state by setting android_app.activityState with the appropriate APP_CMD_* value.
onSaveInstance	sets the application state to APP_CMD_SAVE_STATE and waits for the native application to save its state. Custom saving has to be implemented by Native App Glue client in its own command callback.
onDestroy	notifies the native thread that destruction is pending, and then frees memory when native thread acknowledges (and does what it needs to frees resources!). Structure android_app is not useable anymore and application itself terminates.
onConfigurationChanged, onWindowFocusedChanged, onLowMemory	notifies the native-side thread of the event (APP_CMD_GAINED_FOCUS, APP_CMD_LOST_FOCUS, and so on).
onNativeWindowCreated and onNativeWindowDestroyed	calls function android_app_set_window() which provides and requests the native thread to change its display window.
onInputQueueCreated and onInputQueueDestoyed	uses a specfic method android_app_set_input() to register an input queue. Input queue comes from NativeActivity and is usually provided after native thread loop has started.

`ANativeActivity_onCreate()` also allocates memory and initializes the application context `android_app` and all the synchronization stuff. Then the native thread itself is "forked", so that it can live its life. Thread is created with entry point `android_app_entry`. Main UI thread and native thread communicates via Unix pipes and mutexes to ensure proper synchronization.

Native thread

The native thread call tree is a bit harsher! If you plan to create your own glue code, you will probably need to implement something similar:

```
+___android_app_entry(void*)
        +___AConfiguration_new()
        +___AConfiguration_fromAssetManager(AConfiguration*,
        |                               AAssetManager*)
        +___print_cur_config(android_app*)
        +___process_cmd(android_app*, android_poll_source*)
        |   +___android_app_read_cmd(android_app*)
        |   +___android_app_pre_exec_cmd(android_app*, int8_t)
        |   |   +___AInputQueue_detachLooper(AInputQueue*)
        |   |   +___AInputQueue_attachLooper(AInputQueue*,
        |   |   |       ALooper*, int, ALooper_callbackFunc, void*)
        |   |   +___AConfiguration_fromAssetManager(AConfiguration*,
        |   |   |                               AAssetManager*)
        |   |   +___print_cur_config(android_app*)
        |   +___android_app_post_exec_cmd(android_app*, int8_t)
        +___process_input(android_app*, android_poll_source*)
        |   +___AInputQueue_getEvent(AInputQueue*, AInputEvent**)
        |   +___AInputEvent_getType(const AInputEvent*)
        |   +___AInputQueue_preDispatchEvent(AInputQueue*,
        |   |                               AInputEvent*)
        |   +___AInputQueue_finishEvent(AInputQueue*,
        |                               AInputEvent*, int)
        +___ALooper_prepare(int)
        +___ALooper_addFd(ALooper*, int, int, int,
        |               ALooper_callbackFunc, void*)
        +___android_main(android_app*)
        +___android_app_destroy(android_app*)
            +___AInputQueue_detachLooper(AInputQueue*)
            +___AConfiguration_delete(AConfiguration*)
```

Let's see in detail what this means. Method `android_app_entry()` is executed exclusively on the native thread and performs several tasks. First, it creates the **Looper**, which processes the event queue by reading data coming into the pipe (identified by a Unix **File Descriptor**). Creation of the command queue Looper is performed by `ALooper_prepare()` when native thread starts (something similar exists in Java in the equivalent class `Looper`). Attachment of the Looper to the pipe is performed by `ALooper_addFd()`.

Queues are processed by Native App Glue internal methods `process_cmd()` and `process_input()` for the command and input queue, respectively. However both are triggered by your own code when you write `lSource->process()` in your `android_main()`. Then, internally, `process_cmd()` and `process_input()` calls itself your own callback, the one we created in `Activity.cpp`. So finally we know what is happening when we receive an event in our main loop!

The input queue is also attached to the looper, but not immediately inside thread entry point. Instead, it is sent in *differed-time* from the main UI thread to the native thread using the pipe mechanism explained before. That explains why command queue is attached to the looper and not the input queue. Input queue is attached to the looper through a specific API: `AInputQueue_attachLooper()` and `AInputQueue_detachLooper()`.

We have not talked about it yet but a third queue, the user queue, can be attached to the looper. This queue is a custom one, unused by default and which can be used for your own purpose. More generally, your application can use the same `ALooper` to listen to additional file-descriptors.

Now, the big part: `android_main()`. Our method! Our code! As you now know, it is executed on the native thread and loops infinitely until destruction is requested. Destruction requests as well as all others events are detected by polling them, hence the method `ALooper_pollAll()` used in `DroidBlaster`. We need to check each event that happens until nothing remains in the queue, then we can do whatever we want, like redrawing the window surface, and then we go back to the wait state until new events arrive.

Android_app structure

The native event loop receives an `android_app` structure in parameter. This structure, described in `android_native_app_glue.h`, contains some contextual information such as:

◆ `void* userData`: This is a pointer to any data you want. This is essential to give some contextual information to the activity event callback.

◆ `void (*pnAppCmd)(...) int32_t (*onInputEvent)(...)`: These are callbacks triggered respectively when an activity and an input event occur. We will see input events in *Chapter 8, Handling Input Devices and Sensors*.

◆ `ANativeActivity* activity`: This describes the Java native activity (its class as a JNI object, its data directories, and so on) and gives the necessary information to retrieve a JNI context.

◆ `AConfiguration* config`: This contains information about current hardware and system state, such as the current language and country, the current screen orientation, density, size, and so on This is a place of choice to learn more about the host device.

◆ `void* savedState size_t savedStateSize`: This is used to save a buffer of data when an activity (and thus its native thread) is destroyed and restored later.

◆ `AInputQueue* inputQueue`: This handles input events (used internally by the native glue). We will see input events in Chapter 8.

◆ `ALooper* looper`: This allows attaching and detaching event listeners (used internally by the native glue). The listeners poll and wait for events represented as data on a Unix file descriptor.

◆ `ANativeWindow* window ARect contentRect`: This represents the "drawable" area, in which graphics can be drawn. The `ANativeWindow` API declared in `native_window.h` allows retrieving window width, height and pixel format and changing these settings.

◆ `int activityState`: This describes the current activity state, that is, `APP_CMD_START`, `APP_CMD_RESUME`, `APP_CMD_PAUSE`, and so on.

◆ `int destroyRequested`: This is a flag when equals to `1`, indicates that application is about to be destroyed and native thread must be terminated immediately. This flag has to be checked in the event loop.

The `android_app` structure also contains some internal data that should not be changed.

Have a go hero – saving activity state

It is very surprising for many new Android developers, but when screen orientation changes, an Android activity needs to be completely recreated. Native activities and their native thread are no exception. To handle this case properly, the native glue triggers an APP_CMD_SAVE_STATE event to leave you a chance to save your activity state before it is destroyed.

Based on DroidBlaster current code, the challenge is to track the number of times activity is recreated by:

1. Creating a state structure to save the activation counter.

2. Saving the counter when activity requests it. A new state structure will need to be allocated each time with malloc() (memory is released with free()) and returned via savedState and savedStateSize fields in the android_app structure.

3. Restoring the counter when activity is recreated. State will need to be checked: if it is NULL, then the activity is created for the first time. If it is not, then activity is recreated.

Because the state structure is copied and freed internally by the native glue, no pointers can be saved in the structure.

 Project DroidBlaster_Part5-2 can be used as a starting point for this part. The resulting project project is provided with this book under the name DroidBlaster_Part5-SaveState.

Accessing window and time natively

Application events are essential to understand. But they are only a part of the puzzle and will not get your users much excited. An interesting feature of the Android NDK is the ability to access display window natively to draw graphics. But who talks about graphics talks also about timing. Indeed, Android devices have different capabilities. Animations should be adapted to their speed. To help us in this task, Android gives access to time primitives thanks to its good support of Posix APIs.

We are now going to exploit these features to get a graphic feedback in our application: a red square moving on the screen. This square is going to be animated according to time to get a reproducible result.

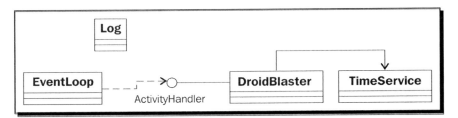

 Project DroidBlaster_Part5-2 can be used as a starting point for this part. The resulting project project is provided with this book under the name DroidBlaster_Part5-3.

Time for action – displaying raw graphics and implementing a timer

First, let's implement a timer in a dedicated module:

 Throughout this book, we will implement several modules named with the postfix `Service`. These services are purely design concepts and are not related to Android services.

1. In the `jni` directory, create `TimeService.hpp` which includes `time.h` Posix header.

   It contains methods `reset()` and `update()` to manage timer state and two interrogation methods to read current time (method `now()`) and the time elapsed in seconds between the last two updates (method `elapsed()`):

```cpp
#ifndef _PACKT_TIMESERVICE_HPP_
#define _PACKT_TIMESERVICE_HPP_

#include "Types.hpp"

#include <time.h>

namespace packt {
    class TimeService {
    public:
```

```
        TimeService();

        void reset();
        void update();

        double now();
        float elapsed();

    private:
        float mElapsed;
        double mLastTime;
    };
}
#endif
```

2. Create a new `TimeService.cpp` file in `jni`. Use Posix primitive `clock_gettime()` to retrieve current time in `now()` method implementation. A **monotonic** clock is essential to ensure time always goes forward and is not subject to system changes (for example, if user change its settings).

    To accommodate the need of graphics applications, define method `elapsed()` to check elapsed time since last update. This allows adapting application behavior according to device speed. It is important to work on doubles when manipulating *absolute* time to avoid losing accuracy. Then the resulting delay can be converted back to float:

```
#include "TimeService.hpp"
#include "Log.hpp"

namespace packt {
    TimeService::TimeService() :
        mElapsed(0.0f),
        mLastTime(0.0f)
    {}

    void TimeService::reset() {
        Log::info("Resetting TimeService.");
        mElapsed = 0.0f;
        mLastTime = now();
    }

    void TimeService::update() {
        double lCurrentTime = now();
        mElapsed = (lCurrentTime - mLastTime);
        mLastTime = lCurrentTime;
```

```
    }

    double TimeService::now() {
        timespec lTimeVal;
        clock_gettime(CLOCK_MONOTONIC, &lTimeVal);
        return lTimeVal.tv_sec + (lTimeVal.tv_nsec * 1.0e-9);
    }

    float TimeService::elapsed() {
        return mElapsed;
    }
}
```

3. Create a new header file `Context.hpp`. Define `Context` helper structure to hold and share all `DroidBlaster` modules, starting with `TimeService`. This structure is going to be enhanced throughout the next chapters:

```
#ifndef _PACKT_CONTEXT_HPP_
#define _PACKT_CONTEXT_HPP_

#include "Types.hpp"

namespace packt
{
    class TimeService;

    struct Context {
        TimeService* mTimeService;
    };
}
#endif
```

The time module can now be embedded in the application code:

4. Open already existing file `DroidBlaster.hpp`. Define two internal methods `clear()` and `draw()` to erase the screen and draw the square cursor on it. Declare a few member variables to store activity and display state as well as cursor position, size, and speed:

```
#ifndef _PACKT_DROIDBLASTER_HPP_
#define _PACKT_DROIDBLASTER_HPP_

#include "ActivityHandler.hpp"
#include "Context.hpp"
#include "TimeService.hpp"
#include "Types.hpp"
```

```
#include <android_native_app_glue.h>

namespace dbs {
    class DroidBlaster : public packt::ActivityHandler {
    public:
        DroidBlaster(packt::Context& pContext,
                    android_app* pApplication);
        ~DroidBlaster();

    protected:
        status onActivate();
        void onDeactivate();
        status onStep();

        ...

    private:
        void clear();
        void drawCursor(int pSize, int pX, int pY);

    private:
        android_app* mApplication;
        ANativeWindow_Buffer mWindowBuffer;
        packt::TimeService* mTimeService;

        bool mInitialized;

        float mPosX;
        float mPosY;
        const int32_t mSize;
        const float mSpeed;
    };
}
#endif
```

5. Now, open `DroidBlaster.cpp` implementation file. Update its constructor and destructor. Cursor is 24 pixels large and moves at 100 pixels per second. `TimeService` (and in near future all other services) is transmitted in the `Context` structure:

```
#include "DroidBlaster.hpp"
#include "Log.hpp"

#include <math.h>
```

```
namespace dbs {
    DroidBlaster::DroidBlaster(packt::Context& pContext,
                                android_app* pApplication) :
        mApplication(pApplication),
        mTimeService(pContext.mTimeService),
        mInitialized(false),
        mPosX(0), mPosY(0), mSize(24), mSpeed(100.0f) {
        packt::Log::info("Creating DroidBlaster");
    }

    DroidBlaster::~DroidBlaster() {
        packt::Log::info("Destructing DroidBlaster");
    }
...
```

6. Still in `DroidBlaster.cpp`, re-implement activation handler to:

   ❑ Initialize the timer.

   ❑ Force the window format in 32-bit with `ANativeWindow_setBuffersGeometry()`. The two zeros passed in parameters are the wanted window width and height. They are ignored unless initialized with a positive value. Note that window area defined by width and height is scaled to match screen size.

   ❑ Retrieve all the necessary window information in an `ANativeWindow_Buffer` structure to allow drawing. To fill this structure, window must be locked.

   ❑ Initialize cursor position the first time activity is launched.

   ```
   ...
       status DroidBlaster::onActivate() {
           packt::Log::info("Activating DroidBlaster");

           mTimeService->reset();

           // Forces 32 bits format.
           ANativeWindow* lWindow = mApplication->window;
           if (ANativeWindow_setBuffersGeometry(lWindow, 0,
   0,
               WINDOW_FORMAT_RGBX_8888) < 0) {
               return STATUS_KO;
           }

           // Needs to lock the window buffer to get its
   properties.
   ```

```
            if (ANativeWindow_lock
                (lWindow, &mWindowBuffer, NULL) >= 0) {
                ANativeWindow_unlockAndPost(lWindow);
            } else {
                return STATUS_KO;
            }

            // Position the mark in the center.
            if (!mInitialized) {
                mPosX = mWindowBuffer.width / 2;
                mPosY = mWindowBuffer.height / 2;
                mInitialized = true;
            }
            return STATUS_OK;
        }
    ...
```

7. Continue with `DroidBlaster.cpp` and step the application by moving the cursor at a constant rate (here 100 pixels per second). The window buffer has to be locked to draw on it (method `ANativeWindow_lock()`) and unlocked when drawing is finished (method `ANativeWindow_unlockAndPost()`):

```
    ...
    status DroidBlaster::onStep() {
        mTimeService->update();

        // Moves the mark at 100 pixels per second.
        mPosX = fmod(mPosX + mSpeed * mTimeService->elapsed(),
                     mWindowBuffer.width);

        // Locks the window buffer and draws on it.
        ANativeWindow* lWindow = mApplication->window;
    if (ANativeWindow_lock(lWindow, &mWindowBuffer, NULL) >= 0) {
            clear();
            drawCursor(mSize, mPosX, mPosY);
            ANativeWindow_unlockAndPost(lWindow);
            return STATUS_OK;
        } else {
            return STATUS_KO;
        }
    }
    ...
```

8. Finally, implement the drawing methods. Clear the screen with a brute-force approach using `memset()`. This operation is supported by display window surface which is in fact just a big continuous memory buffer.

Drawing the cursor is not much more difficult Like for bitmaps processed natively, display window surface is directly accessible via the `bits` field (only when surface is locked!) and can be modified pixel by pixel. Here, a red square is rendered line by line at the requested position. The `stride` allows jumping directly from one line to another.

 Note that no boundary check is performed. This is not a problem for such a simple example but a memory overflow can happen really quickly and cause a violent crash.

```cpp
...
    void DroidBlaster::clear() {
        memset(mWindowBuffer.bits, 0, mWindowBuffer.stride
                    * mWindowBuffer.height * sizeof(uint32_t*));
    }

    void DroidBlaster::drawCursor(int pSize, int pX, int pY) {
        const int lHalfSize = pSize / 2;

        const int lUpLeftX = pX - lHalfSize;
        const int lUpLeftY = pY - lHalfSize;
        const int lDownRightX = pX + lHalfSize;
        const int lDownRightY = pY + lHalfSize;

        uint32_t* lLine =
            reinterpret_cast<uint32_t*> (mWindowBuffer.bits)
                            + (mWindowBuffer.stride * lUpLeftY);
        for (int iY = lUpLeftY; iY <= lDownRightY; iY++) {
            for (int iX = lUpLeftX; iX <= lDownRightX; iX++) {
                lLine[iX] = 255;
            }
            lLine = lLine + mWindowBuffer.stride;
        }
    }
}
```

The test code must be launched from the main entry point.

9. Update `android_main` in file `Main.cpp` to launch the `DroidBlaster` activity handler. You can temporarily comment `DroidBlaster` declaration:

```
#include "Context.hpp"
#include "DroidBlaster.hpp"
#include "EventLoop.hpp"
#include "TimeService.hpp"

void android_main(android_app* pApplication) {
    packt::TimeService lTimeService;
    packt::Context lContext = { &lTimeService };

    packt::EventLoop lEventLoop(pApplication);
    dbs::DroidBlaster lDroidBlaster(lContext, pApplication);
    lEventLoop.run(lDroidBlaster);
}
```

10. Are you fed up with adding new `.cpp` files each time you create a new one? Then change the `Android.mk` file to define a Make macro `LS_CPP` that lists all `.cpp` files in `jni` directory automatically. This macro is invoked when `LOCAL_SRC_FILES` variable is initialized. Please refer to *Chapter 9, Porting Existing Libraries to Android* for more information on the Makefile language:

```
LOCAL_PATH := $(call my-dir)

include $(CLEAR_VARS)

LS_CPP=$(subst $(1)/,,$(wildcard $(1)/*.cpp))
LOCAL_MODULE      := droidblaster
LOCAL_SRC_FILES := $(call LS_CPP,$(LOCAL_PATH))
LOCAL_LDLIBS      := -landroid -llog

LOCAL_STATIC_LIBRARIES := android_native_app_glue

include $(BUILD_SHARED_LIBRARY)

$(call import-module,android/native_app_glue)
```

11. Compile and run the application.

What just happened?

If you run `DroidBlaster`, you will discover the following result. The red square crosses the screen at a constant rhythm. Result should be reproducible among each run:

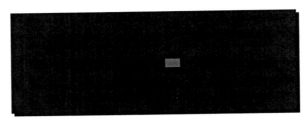

Graphic feedback is performed through the `ANativeWindow_*` API which gives native access to the display window and allow manipulating its surface like a bitmap. Like with bitmaps, accessing window surface requires locking and unlocking before and after processing.

Be safe!

Native applications can crash. They can crash badly and although there are means to detect where an application crashed (like core dumps in Android logs, see Chapter 11, *Debugging and Troubleshooting*), it is always better to develop carefully and protect your program code. Here, if the cursor was drawn outside surface memory buffer, a sudden crash would be very likely to happen.

You can start experimenting more concretely with application events by pressing the power button, leaving to the home screen. Several situations can occur and should be systematically tested carefully:

◆ Leaving the application using the **Back** button (which destroys the native thread)

◆ Leaving the application using the **Home** button (does not destroy the native thread but stops the application and releases the window)

◆ Long press on the power button to open the **Power** menu (application loses focus)

◆ Long press on the **Home** button to show application switching menu (loses focus)

◆ An unexpected phone call

Leaving the application using the **Back** button, reinitializes the mark in the middle; this is because the native thread gets destructed. This is not the case in other scenarios (for example, pressing the **Home** button).

More on time primitives

Timers are essential to display animations and movement at correct speed. They can be implemented with the POSIX method `clock_gettime()` which retrieves time with a high precision, theoretically until the nanosecond.

Clock has been configured with the option `CLOCK_MONOTONIC`. A monotonic timer gives the elapsed clock time since an arbitrary starting point in the past. It is unaffected by potential system date change and thus cannot go back in the past compared to other options. The downside with `CLOCK_MONOTONIC` is that it is system specific and it is not guaranteed to be supported. Hopefully, Android supports it but care should be taken when porting Android code to other platforms.

An alternative, less precise but which is affected by changes in the system time, is `gettimeofday()`, also provided in `time.h`. Usage is similar but precision is in microseconds instead of nanoseconds. Here could be an usage example that could replace the current `now()` implementation in `TimeService`:

```
double TimeService::now() {
    timeval lTimeVal;
    gettimeofday(&lTimeVal, NULL);
    return (lTimeVal.tv_sec * 1000.0) + (lTimeVal.tv_usec / 1000.0);
}
```

Summary

In this chapter, we created our first fully native application without a line of Java code and started to implement the skeleton of an event loop which processes events. More specifically, we have seen how to poll events accordingly and make an application alive. We have also handled events occurring during activity lifecycle to activate and deactivate activity as soon as it is idling.

We have locked and unlocked natively the display window to display raw graphics. We can now draw graphics directly without a temporary back buffer. Finally, we have retrieved time to make the application adapt to device speed, thanks to a monotonic clock.

The basic framework initiated here will form the base of the 2D/3D game that we will develop throughout this book. However, although nowadays simplicity is fashion, we need something a bit fancier than just a red square! Follow me into the next chapter and discover how to render advanced graphics with OpenGL ES for Android.

Rendering Graphics with OpenGL ES

6

Let's face it: one of the main interests of the Android NDK is to write multimedia applications and games. Indeed, these programs consume lots of resources and need responsiveness. That is why one of the first available APIs (and almost the only one until recently) in Android NDK is an API for graphics: the **Open Graphics Library for Embedded Systems** *(abbreviated* **OpenGL ES***).*

OpenGL is a standard API created by Silicon Graphics and now managed by the Khronos Group (see `http://www.khronos.org/`*). OpenGL ES derivative is available on many platforms such as iOS or Blackberry OS and is the best hope for writing portable and efficient graphics code. OpenGL can do both 2D and 3D graphics with programmable shaders (if hardware supports it). There are two main releases of OpenGL ES currently supported by Android:*

- OpenGL ES 1.1: This is the most supported API on Android devices. It offers an old school graphic API with a **fixed pipeline** (that is, a fixed set of configurable operations to transform and render geometry). Although specification is not fully implemented, its current implementation is perfectly sufficient. This is a good choice to write 2D games or 3D games targeting older devices.

- OpenGL ES 2: This is not supported on old phones (like the antic HTC G1) but more recent ones (at least not so old like the Nexus One... time goes fast in the mobile world) support it. OpenGL ES 2 replaces the fixed pipeline with a modern programmable pipeline with vertex and pixel shaders. This is the best choice for advanced 3D games. Note that OpenGL ES 1.X is frequently emulated by an OpenGL 2 implementation behind the scene.

This chapter teaches how to create 2D graphics. More specifically, it shows how to do the following:

- Initialize OpenGL ES and bind it to an Android window
- Load a texture from a PNG file
- Draw sprites using OpenGL ES 1.1 extensions
- Display a tile map using vertex and index buffers

OpenGL ES and graphics in general is a wide subject. This chapter covers the essential basics to get started with OpenGL ES 1.1, largely enough to create the next mind-blowing app!

Initializing OpenGL ES

The first step to create awesome graphics is to initialize OpenGL ES. Although not terribly complex, this task is a little bit involving when binding to an Android window (that is, attaching a rendering context to a window). These pieces are glued together with the help of the **Embedded-System Graphics Library** (or **EGL**), a companion API of OpenGL ES.

For this first part, I propose to replace the raw drawing system implemented in a previous chapter with OpenGL ES. We are going to take care of EGL initialization and finalization and try to fade screen color from black to white to ensure everything works properly.

> Project DroidBlaster_Part5-3 can be used as a starting point for this part. The resulting project is provided with this book under the name DroidBlaster_Part6-1.

Time for action – initializing OpenGL ES

First, let's encapsulate OpenGL ES initialization code in a dedicated C++ class:

1. Create header file `GraphicsService.hpp` in `jni` folder. It needs to include `EGL/egl.h` which defines EGL API to bind OpenGL ES to the Android platform. This header declares among others `EGLDisplay`, `EGLSurface`, and `EGLContext` types which are handles to system resources.

Our `GrapicsService` lifecycle is composed of three main steps:

- `start()`: This binds an OpenGL rendering context to the Android native window and loads graphic resources (textures and meshes later in this chapter).

❑ `stop()`: This unbinds rendering context from Android window and frees allocated graphic resources.

❑ `update()`: This performs rendering operations during each refresh iteration.

```
#define _PACKT_GRAPHICSSERVICE_HPP_

#include "TimeService.hpp"
#include "Types.hpp"

#include <android_native_app_glue.h>
#include <EGL/egl.h>

namespace packt {
    class GraphicsService {
    public:
        GraphicsService(android_app* pApplication,
                        TimeService* pTimeService);

        const char* getPath();
        const int32_t& getHeight();
        const int32_t& getWidth();

        status start();
        void stop();
        status update();

    private:
        android_app* mApplication;
        TimeService* mTimeService;

        int32_t mWidth, mHeight;
        EGLDisplay mDisplay;
        EGLSurface mSurface;
        EGLContext mContext;
    };
}
#endif
```

2. Create `jni/Graphics.Service.cpp`. Include `GLES/gl.h` and `GLES/glext.h`, which are the official OpenGL include files for Android. Write constructor, destructor, and getter methods:

```
#include "GraphicsService.hpp"
#include "Log.hpp"

#include <GLES/gl.h>
#include <GLES/glext.h>


namespace packt
{
    GraphicsService::GraphicsService(android_app* pApplication,
                                     TimeService* pTimeService) :
        mApplication(pApplication),
        mTimeService(pTimeService),
        mWidth(0), mHeight(0),
        mDisplay(EGL_NO_DISPLAY),
        mSurface(EGL_NO_CONTEXT),
        mContext(EGL_NO_SURFACE)
    {}

    int32_t GraphicsService::getPath() {
        return mResource.getPath();
    }

    const int32_t& GraphicsService::getHeight() {
        return mHeight;
    }

    const int32_t& GraphicsService::getWidth() {
        return mWidth;
    }
...
```

3. In the same file, carry out the bulk of the work by writing `start()`. The first initialization steps consist of the following:

   ❑ Connecting to a **display**, that is, an Android window, with `eglGetDisplay()` and `eglInitialize()`.

❑ Finding an appropriate **framebuffer** configuration with
`eglChooseConfig()` for the display. Framebuffer is an OpenGL term
referring to a rendering surface (including additional elements like a
Z-buffer). Configurations are selected according to requested attributes:
OpenGL ES 1 and a 16 bits surface (5 bits for red, 6 for green, and 5 for
blue). The attribute list is terminated by `EGL_NONE` sentinel. Here, we
choose the default configuration.

❑ Re-configuring the Android window according to selected configuration
attributes (retrieved with `eglGetConfigAttrib()`). This operation is
Android-specific and is performed with Android `ANativeWindow` API.

A list of all available framebuffer configurations is also available through
`eglGetConfigs()` which can then be parsed with `eglGetConfigAttrib()`.
Note how EGL defines its own types and re-declares primitive types `EGLint`
and `EGLBoolean` to favor platform independence:

```
...
    status GraphicsService::start() {
        EGLint lFormat, lNumConfigs, lErrorResult;
        EGLConfig lConfig;
        const EGLint lAttributes[] = {
            EGL_RENDERABLE_TYPE, EGL_OPENGL_ES_BIT,
            EGL_BLUE_SIZE, 5, EGL_GREEN_SIZE, 6, EGL_RED_SIZE, 5,
            EGL_SURFACE_TYPE, EGL_WINDOW_BIT,
            EGL_NONE
        };

        mDisplay = eglGetDisplay(EGL_DEFAULT_DISPLAY);
        if (mDisplay == EGL_NO_DISPLAY) goto ERROR;
        if (!eglInitialize(mDisplay, NULL, NULL)) goto ERROR;

        if(!eglChooseConfig(mDisplay, lAttributes, &lConfig, 1,
            &lNumConfigs) || (lNumConfigs <= 0)) goto ERROR;

        if (!eglGetConfigAttrib(mDisplay, lConfig,
            EGL_NATIVE_VISUAL_ID, &lFormat)) goto ERROR;
    ANativeWindow_setBuffersGeometry(mApplication->window, 0, 0,
            lFormat);
...
```

4. Continue `start()` method to create the display surface according to the configuration selected previously and context. A context contains all data related to OpenGL state (enabled and disabled settings, matrix stack, and so on).

 OpenGL ES supports the creation of multiple contexts for one display surface. This allows dividing rendering operations among threads or rendering to several windows. However, it is not well supported on Android hardware and should be avoided.

Finally, activate the created rendering context (`eglMakeCurrent()`) and define the display viewport according to surface attributes (retrieved with `eglQuerySurface()`).

```
. . .
        mSurface = eglCreateWindowSurface(mDisplay, lConfig,
            mApplication->window, NULL);
    if (mSurface == EGL_NO_SURFACE) goto ERROR;
        mContext = eglCreateContext(mDisplay, lConfig,
                    EGL_NO_CONTEXT, NULL);
    if (mContext == EGL_NO_CONTEXT) goto ERROR;

    if (!eglMakeCurrent (mDisplay, mSurface, mSurface, mContext)
      || !eglQuerySurface(mDisplay, mSurface, EGL_WIDTH,   &mWidth)
      || !eglQuerySurface(mDisplay, mSurface, EGL_HEIGHT, &mHeight)
          || (mWidth <= 0) || (mHeight <= 0)) goto ERROR;
        glViewport(0, 0, mWidth, mHeight);

        return STATUS_OK;

ERROR:
    Log::error("Error while starting GraphicsService");
    stop();
    return STATUS_KO;
}
. . .
```

5. In `GraphicsService.cpp`, unbind the application from the android window and release EGL resources when the application stops running:

 OpenGL contexts are lost frequently on Android applications (when leaving or going back to the home screen, when a call is received, when devices go to sleep, and so on). As a lost context becomes unusable, it is important to release resources as soon as possible.

```
...
    void GraphicsService::stop() {
        if (mDisplay != EGL_NO_DISPLAY) {
            eglMakeCurrent(mDisplay, EGL_NO_SURFACE, EGL_NO_
SURFACE,
                           EGL_NO_CONTEXT);
            if (mContext != EGL_NO_CONTEXT) {
                eglDestroyContext(mDisplay, mContext);
                mContext = EGL_NO_CONTEXT;
            }
            if (mSurface != EGL_NO_SURFACE) {
                eglDestroySurface(mDisplay, mSurface);
                mSurface = EGL_NO_SURFACE;
            }
            eglTerminate(mDisplay);
            mDisplay = EGL_NO_DISPLAY;
        }
    }
...
```

6. Finally, implement the last method `update()` to refresh the screen during each step with `eglSwapBuffers()`. To have a concrete visual feedback, change the display background color gradually according to the time step with `glClearColor()` and erase the framebuffer with `glClear()`. Internally, rendering is performed on a **back buffer** which is *swapped* with the **front buffer** shown to the user meanwhile. The front buffer becomes the back buffer and vice versa (pointers are switched):

 This technique is more commonly referred to as **page flipping**. Front and back buffers form a swap chain. According to driver implementation, they can be extended with a third buffer, in which case we talk about **triple buffering**. Swapping is often synchronized with the screen refresh rate to avoid image tearing: this is a **VSync**.

```
. . .
    status GraphicsService::update() {
        float lTimeStep = mTimeService->elapsed();

        static float lClearColor = 0.0f;
        lClearColor += lTimeStep * 0.01f;
        glClearColor(lClearColor, lClearColor, lClearColor, 1.0f);
        glClear(GL_COLOR_BUFFER_BIT);

        if (eglSwapBuffers(mDisplay, mSurface) != EGL_TRUE) {
          Log::error("Error %d swapping buffers.", eglGetError());
            return STATUS_KO;
        }
        return STATUS_OK;
    }
}
```

We are done with `GraphicsService`. Let's use it in the final application.

7. Add `GraphicsService` to the `Context` structure in existing file
    `jni/Context.hpp`:

```
. . .
namespace packt
{
    class GraphicsService;
    class TimeService;

    struct Context
    {
        GraphicsService* mGraphicsService;
        TimeService*     mTimeService;
    };
}
. . .
```

8. Now, modify `DroidBlaster.hpp` to include `GraphicsService` as a member
    variable. You can get rid of previous members `mApplication`, `mPosX`, `mPosY`,
    `mSize`, `mSpeed`, and methods `clear()` and `drawCursor()` created in the
    previous chapter:

```
#ifndef _PACKT_DROIDBLASTER_HPP_
#define _PACKT_DROIDBLASTER_HPP_

#include "ActivityHandler.hpp"
```

```
#include "Context.hpp"
#include "GraphicsService.hpp"
#include "TimeService.hpp"
#include "Types.hpp"

namespace dbs {
    class DroidBlaster : public packt::ActivityHandler {
    public:
        DroidBlaster(packt::Context* pContext);
        ...

    private:
        packt::GraphicsService* mGraphicsService;
        packt::TimeService*     mTimeService;
    };
}
#endif
```

9. And obviously, rewrite `jni/DroidBlaster.cpp`. Method `onStep()` is completely rewritten and do not make use of `DrawingUtil` or `ANativeWindow` locking and unlocking features anymore. This is completely replaced by `GraphicsService`, which is started when the application is made available. The same goes for `TimeService`:

```
#include "DroidBlaster.hpp"
#include "Log.hpp"

namespace dbs {
    DroidBlaster::DroidBlaster(packt::Context* pContext) :
        mGraphicsService(pContext->mGraphicsService),
        mTimeService(pContext->mTimeService)
    {}

    packt::status DroidBlaster::onActivate() {
        if (mGraphicsService->start() != packt::STATUS_OK) {
            return packt::STATUS_KO;
        }

        mTimeService->reset();
        return packt::STATUS_OK;
    }

    void DroidBlaster::onDeactivate() {
        mGraphicsService->stop();
    }
```

```
      packt::status DroidBlaster::onStep() {
          mTimeService->update();

          if (mGraphicsService->update() != packt::STATUS_OK) {
              return packt::STATUS_KO;
          }
          return packt::STATUS_OK;
      }
      ...
}
```

10. Finally, update the main loop in existing file `Main.cpp` to instantiate `GraphicsService`:

```
#include "Context.hpp"
#include "DroidBlaster.hpp"
#include "EventLoop.hpp"
#include "GraphicsService.hpp"
#include "TimeService.hpp"

void android_main(android_app* pApplication) {
    packt::TimeService lTimeService;
    packt::GraphicsService lGraphicsService(pApplication,
        &lTimeService);

    packt::Context lContext = { &lGraphicsService, &lTimeService
};

    packt::EventLoop lEventLoop(pApplication);
    dbs::DroidBlaster lDroidBlaster(&lContext);
    lEventLoop.run(&lDroidBlaster);
}
```

11. Let's not forget compilation. OpenGL ES 1.x libraries need to be included: `libEGL` for device initialization and `libGLESv1_CM` for drawing calls:

```
LOCAL_PATH := $(call my-dir)

include $(CLEAR_VARS)

LS_CPP=$(subst $(1)/,,$(wildcard $(1)/*.cpp))
LOCAL_MODULE    := droidblaster
LOCAL_SRC_FILES := $(call LS_CPP,$(LOCAL_PATH))
LOCAL_LDLIBS    := -landroid -llog -lEGL -lGLESv1_CM
```

```
LOCAL_STATIC_LIBRARIES := android_native_app_glue

include $(BUILD_SHARED_LIBRARY)

$(call import-module,android/native_app_glue)
```

What just happened?

Launch the application. If everything works fine, your device screen will progressively fade from black to white. But instead of clearing display with a raw `memset()` or setting pixels one by one like seen in previous chapter, efficient OpenGL ES drawing primitives are invoked instead. Note that the effect appears only the first time the application is started because the clear color is stored in a static variable, which has a different lifecycle than local and Java variables on Android (see *Chapter 4, Calling Back Java from Native Code*). To make it appear again, kill the application or relaunch it in Debug mode.

We have initialized and connected OpenGL ES and the Android native window system together with EGL. Thanks to this API, we have queried a display configuration that matches our expectations and created a framebuffer to render our scene on. We have taken care of releasing resources when the application is deactivated, as OpenGL contexts are lost frequently on mobile systems. Although EGL is a standard API, specified by the Khronos group like OpenGL, platforms often implement their own variant (haphazardly, EAGL on iOS). Portability is also limited by the fact that display window initialization remains the responsibility of client application.

Reading PNG textures with the asset manager

I guess you need something more consistent than just changing the screen color! But before showing awesome graphics in our application, we need to load some external resources.

In this second part, we are going to load a texture into OpenGL ES thanks to the Android **asset manager**, an API provided since NDK R5. It allows programmers to access any resources stored in the `assets` folder of their project folder. Assets stored there are then packaged into the final APK archive during application compilation. Asset resources are considered as raw binary files that your application needs to interpret and access using their filename relative to the `assets` folder (a file `assets/mydir/myfile` can be accessed with `mydir/myfile` path). Files are read-only and likely to be compressed.

If you have already written some Java Android application, then you know that Android also provides resources accessible through compile-time generated IDs inside the `res` project folder. This is not directly available on the Android NDK and unless you are ready to use a JNI bridge, assets are the only way to package resources in your APK.

In the current part, we are going to load a texture encoded in one of the most popular picture formats used nowadays: **Portable Network Graphics** or more commonly known as **PNG**. To help us in this task, we are going to integrate **libpng** NDK to interpret a PNG file added to our assets. The resulting application will look like the following diagram:

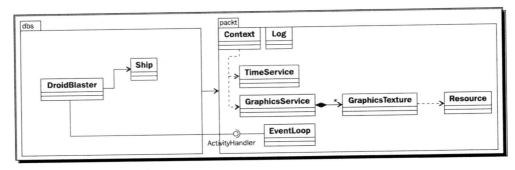

 Project DroidBlaster_Part6-1 can be used as a starting point for this part. The resulting project is provided with this book under the name DroidBlaster_Part6-2.

Time for action – loading a texture in OpenGL ES

PNG is a complex format to read. So let's embed libpng third-party library:

1. Go to the libpng website at `http://www.libpng.org/pub/png/libpng.html` and download the libpng source package (version 1.5.2 in this book).

 Original libpng 1.5.2 archive is provided with this book in `Chapter6/ Resource` folder under the name `lpng152.zip`. A second archive `lpng152_ndk.zip` with the modifications made in the following steps is also available.

2. Create a folder `libpng` inside `$ANDROID_NDK/sources/`. Move all files from the libpng package in it.

3. Copy file `libpng/scripts/pnglibconf.h.prebuilt` into root folder `libpng` with other source files. Rename it `pnglibconf.h`.

4. Write an `Android.mk` file inside `$ANDROID_NDK/sources` with the content as follows. This Makefile compiles all C files (macro `LS_C` called from `LOCAL_SRC_FILES` directive) inside `libpng` folder, excluding `example.c` and `pngtest.c`. The library is linked with prerequisite library **libzip** (option `-lz`) and packaged as a static library. All include files are made available with directive `LOCAL_EXPORT_C_INCLUDES` to clients.

 Folder `$ANDROID_NDK/sources` is a special folder considered by default as a module folder (which contains reusable libraries. See *Chapter 9, Porting Existing Libraries to Android* for more information).

```
LOCAL_PATH:= $(call my-dir)

include $(CLEAR_VARS)

LS_C=$(subst $(1)/,,$(wildcard $(1)/*.c))

LOCAL_MODULE := png
LOCAL_SRC_FILES := \
    $(filter-out example.c pngtest.c,$(call LS_C,$(LOCAL_PATH)))
LOCAL_EXPORT_C_INCLUDES := $(LOCAL_PATH)
LOCAL_EXPORT_LDLIBS := -lz

include $(BUILD_STATIC_LIBRARY)
```

5. Now, open `jni/Android.mk` in DroidBlaster. Link and import `libpng` thanks to the `LOCAL_STATIC_LIBRARIES` and `import-module` directives:

```
LOCAL_PATH := $(call my-dir)

include $(CLEAR_VARS)

LS_CPP=$(subst $(1)/,,$(wildcard $(1)/*.cpp))
LOCAL_MODULE    := droidblaster
LOCAL_SRC_FILES := $(call LS_CPP,$(LOCAL_PATH))
LOCAL_LDLIBS    := -landroid -llog -lEGL -lGLESv1_CM
LOCAL_STATIC_LIBRARIES := android_native_app_glue png

include $(BUILD_SHARED_LIBRARY)

$(call import-module,android/native_app_glue)
$(call import-module,libpng)
```

6. Add `libpng` folder (`${env_var:ANDROID_NDK}/sources/libpng`) to your project paths in the **Project | Properties | Path and Symbols | Includes** tab.

7. Ensure your module works by compiling `DroidBlaster`. If everything works fine, `libpng` source files should get compiled (note that NDK will not recompile already compiled sources). Some warnings are likely to appear. You can safely ignore them:

```
Console 23

C-Build [DroidBlaster_Part6-4]
Compile thumb  : png <= pngwtran.c
Compile thumb  : png <= pngwutil.c
StaticLibrary  : libpng.a
SharedLibrary  : libdroidblaster.so
Install        : libdroidblaster.so => libs/armeabi/libdroidblaster.so
```

Library `libpng` is now included in our project. So let's now try to read a PNG image file.

8. First, create in `jni/Resource.hpp` a new class `Resource` to access asset files. We need three simple operations: `open()`, `close()`, and `read()`.

Resource will encapsulate calls to the native Android asset management API. This API is defined in `android/asset_manager.hpp` which is already included in header `android_native_app_glue.h`. Its main entry point is an `AAsetMAnager` opaque pointer, from which we can access an asset file represented by an `AAsset`:

```
#ifndef _PACKT_RESOURCE_HPP_
#define _PACKT_RESOURCE_HPP_

#include "Types.hpp"

#include <android_native_app_glue.h>

namespace packt {
    class Resource {
    public:
        Resource(android_app* pApplication, const char* pPath);

        const char* getPath();

        status open();
        void close();
        status read(void* pBuffer, size_t pCount);

    private:
        const char* mPath;
```

```
        AAssetManager* mAssetManager;
        AAsset* mAsset;
    };
}
#endif
```

Implement class `Resource` in `jni/Resource.cpp`. The asset manager opens
assets with `AAssetManager_open()`. This is its sole responsibility apart from
listing folders. Assets are opened in default `AASSET_MODE_UNKNOWN` mode.
Other possibilities are:

❑   `AASSET_MODE_BUFFER`: This performs fast small reads

❑   `AASSET_MODE_RANDOM`: This reads chunks of data forward and backward

❑   `AASSET_MODE_STREAMING`: This reads data sequentially with occasional
    forward seeks

Then, code operates on asset files with `AAsset_read()` to read data and
`AAsset_close()` to close the asset:

```cpp
#include "Resource.hpp"
#include "Log.hpp"

namespace packt {
    Resource::Resource(android_app* pApplication, const char*
pPath):
        mPath(pPath),
        mAssetManager(pApplication->activity->assetManager),
        mAsset(NULL)
    {}

    const char* Resource::getPath() {
        return mPath;
    }

    status Resource::open() {
        mAsset = AAssetManager_open(mAssetManager, mPath,
                            AASSET_MODE_UNKNOWN);
        return (mAsset != NULL) ? STATUS_OK : STATUS_KO;
    }

    void Resource::close() {
        if (mAsset != NULL) {
            AAsset_close(mAsset);
            mAsset = NULL;
        }
```

```
        }

        status Resource::read(void* pBuffer, size_t pCount) {
            int32_t lReadCount = AAsset_read(mAsset, pBuffer, pCount);
            return (lReadCount == pCount) ? STATUS_OK : STATUS_KO;
        }
    }
```

9. Create `jni/GraphicsTexture.hpp` as follows. Include OpenGL and PNG header `GLES/gl.h` and `png.h`. A texture is loaded from a PNG file with `loadImage()` and `callback_read()`, pushed into OpenGL with `load()` and released in `unload()`.

    A texture is accessible through a simple identifier and has a format (RGB, RGBA, and so on). Texture width and height have to be stored when as image is loaded from file:

```
#ifndef _PACKT_GRAPHICSTEXTURE_HPP_
#define _PACKT_GRAPHICSTEXTURE_HPP_

#include "Context.hpp"
#include "Resource.hpp"
#include "Types.hpp"

#include <android_native_app_glue.h>
#include <GLES/gl.h>
#include <png.h>

namespace packt {
    class GraphicsTexture {
    public:
        GraphicsTexture(android_app* pApplication, const char*
pPath);
        ~GraphicsTexture();

        int32_t getHeight();
        int32_t getWidth();

        status load();
        void unload();
        void apply();

    protected:
        uint8_t* loadImage();

    private:
        static void callback_read(png_structp pStruct,
```

```
                    png_bytep pData, png_size_t pSize);

        private:
            Resource mResource;
            GLuint mTextureId;
            int32_t mWidth, mHeight;
            GLint mFormat;
        };
    }
    #endif
```

10. Create the C++ source counterpart `jni/GraphicsTexture.cpp` with a constructor, a destructor, and getters:

```
#include "Log.hpp"
#include "GraphicsTexture.hpp"

namespace packt {
    GraphicsTexture::GraphicsTexture(android_app* pApplication,
        const char* pPath) :
        mResource(pApplication, pPath),
        mTextureId(0),
        mWidth(0), mHeight(0)
    {}

    int32_t GraphicsTexture::getHeight() {
        return mHeight;
    }

    int32_t GraphicsTexture::getWidth() {
        return mWidth;
    }
    ...
```

11. Then, in the same file, implement `loadImage()` method to load a PNG file. File is first opened through our `Resource` class and then its signature (the first 8 bytes) is checked to ensure file is a PNG (note that it can still be corrupted):

```
    ...
    uint8_t* GraphicsTexture::loadImage() {
        png_byte lHeader[8];
        png_structp lPngPtr = NULL; png_infop lInfoPtr = NULL;
        png_byte* lImageBuffer = NULL; png_bytep* lRowPtrs = NULL;
        png_int_32 lRowSize; bool lTransparency;
```

```
if (mResource.open() != STATUS_OK) goto ERROR;
if (mResource.read(lHeader, sizeof(lHeader)) != STATUS_OK)
    goto ERROR;
if (png_sig_cmp(lHeader, 0, 8) != 0) goto ERROR;
```
. . .

12. In the same method, create all structures necessary to read a PNG image.

After that, prepare reading operations by giving our `callback_read()` (implemented later in this tutorial) to libpng with our `Resource` reader.

Set up error management with `setjmp()`. This mechanism allows jumping like a `goto` but through the call stack. If an error occurs, control flow comes back at the point where `setjmp()` has been called first, but enters the `if` block instead (here `goto ERROR`):

. . .

```
lPngPtr = png_create_read_struct(PNG_LIBPNG_VER_STRING,
    NULL, NULL, NULL);
if (!lPngPtr) goto ERROR;
lInfoPtr = png_create_info_struct(lPngPtr);
if (!lInfoPtr) goto ERROR;

png_set_read_fn(lPngPtr, &mResource, callback_read);
if (setjmp(png_jmpbuf(lPngPtr))) goto ERROR;
```
. . .

13. In `loadImage()`, start reading PNG file header with `png_read_info()`, ignoring the first 8 bytes read for file signature with `png_set_sig_bytes()`.

PNG files can be encoded in several formats: RGB, RGBA, 256 colors with a palette, grayscale... R,G, and B color channels can be encoded on up to 16 bits. Hopefully, libpng provides transformation functions to decode unusual formats to more classical RGB and luminance formats with 8 bits per channel with or without an alpha channel. Transformations are validated with `png_read_update_info()`:

. . .

```
png_set_sig_bytes(lPngPtr, 8);
png_read_info(lPngPtr, lInfoPtr);

png_int_32 lDepth, lColorType;
png_uint_32 lWidth, lHeight;
png_get_IHDR(lPngPtr, lInfoPtr, &lWidth, &lHeight,
    &lDepth, &lColorType, NULL, NULL, NULL);
mWidth = lWidth; mHeight = lHeight;
```

```
// Creates a full alpha channel if transparency is encoded as
// an array of palette entries or a single transparent color.
   lTransparency = false;
   if (png_get_valid(lPngPtr, lInfoPtr, PNG_INFO_tRNS)) {
       png_set_tRNS_to_alpha(lPngPtr);
       lTransparency = true;
       goto ERROR;
   }
   // Expands PNG with less than 8bits per channel to 8bits.
   if (lDepth < 8) {
       png_set_packing (lPngPtr);
   // Shrinks PNG with 16bits per color channel down to
8bits.
   } else if (lDepth == 16) {
       png_set_strip_16(lPngPtr);
   }
   // Indicates that image needs conversion to RGBA if
needed.
   switch (lColorType) {
   case PNG_COLOR_TYPE_PALETTE:
       png_set_palette_to_rgb(lPngPtr);
       mFormat = lTransparency ? GL_RGBA : GL_RGB;
       break;
   case PNG_COLOR_TYPE_RGB:
       mFormat = lTransparency ? GL_RGBA : GL_RGB;
       break;
   case PNG_COLOR_TYPE_RGBA:
       mFormat = GL_RGBA;
       break;
   case PNG_COLOR_TYPE_GRAY:
       png_set_expand_gray_1_2_4_to_8(lPngPtr);
       mFormat = lTransparency ? GL_LUMINANCE_ALPHA:GL_
LUMINANCE;
       break;
   case PNG_COLOR_TYPE_GA:
       png_set_expand_gray_1_2_4_to_8(lPngPtr);
       mFormat = GL_LUMINANCE_ALPHA;
       break;
   }
   png_read_update_info(lPngPtr, lInfoPtr);
...
```

14. Allocate the necessary temporary buffer to hold image data and a second one with the address of each output image row for libpng. Note that row order is inverted because OpenGL uses a different coordinate system (first pixel is at bottom-left) then PNG (first pixel at top-left). Then start reading effectively image content with `png_read_image()`.

```
...
    lRowSize = png_get_rowbytes(lPngPtr, lInfoPtr);
    if (lRowSize <= 0) goto ERROR;
    lImageBuffer = new png_byte[lRowSize * lHeight];
    if (!lImageBuffer) goto ERROR;

    lRowPtrs = new png_bytep[lHeight];
    if (!lRowPtrs) goto ERROR;
    for (int32_t i = 0; i < lHeight; ++i) {
      lRowPtrs[lHeight - (i + 1)] = lImageBuffer + i * lRowSize;
      }

    png_read_image(lPngPtr, lRowPtrs);
...
```

15. Finally, release resources(whether an error occurs or not) and return loaded data.

```
...
        mResource.close();
        png_destroy_read_struct(&lPngPtr, &lInfoPtr, NULL);
        delete[] lRowPtrs;
        return lImageBuffer;

ERROR:
    Log::error("Error while reading PNG file");
    mResource.close();
    delete[] lRowPtrs; delete[] lImageBuffer;
    if (lPngPtr != NULL) {
      png_infop* lInfoPtrP = lInfoPtr != NULL ? &lInfoPtr: NULL;
          png_destroy_read_struct(&lPngPtr, lInfoPtrP, NULL);
      }
      return NULL;
    }
...
```

16. We are almost done with `loadImage()`... almost because libpng still requires `callback_read()` to be implemented. This callback method, passed to libpng at step 11, is a mechanism designed to integrate custom read operations... like the Android asset management API! The asset file is read through `Resource` instance transmitted as an untyped pointer at step 11:

```
. . .
    void png_read_callback(png_structp png, png_bytep data,
        png_size_t size) {
        ResourceReader& lReader =
                        *((ResourceReader*) png_get_io_ptr(png));
        if (lReader.read(data, size) != STATUS_OK) {
            lReader.close();
            png_error(png, "Error while reading PNG file");
        }
    }
. . .
```

17. We are done with PNG loading! In `GraphicsTexture.hpp`, get the temporary image buffer loaded in `loadImage()` back in method `load()`. Creating a texture once image data is in memory is easy:

- ❑ Generate a new texture ID with `glGenTextures()`.

- ❑ Tell OpenGL we are working on a new texture with `glBindTexture()`.

- ❑ Configure texture parameters, which need to be set only when texture is created. `GL_LINEAR` smooths textures drawn on screen. This is not essential for a 2D game which does not scale textures but the smallest zoom effect will require it. Texture repetition is prevented with `GL_CLAMP_TO_EDGE`.

- ❑ Push image data into current OpenGL texture with `glTexImage2D()`.

- ❑ And, of course, do not forget to free the temporary image buffer!

```
. . .
    status GraphicsTexture::load() {
        uint8_t* lImageBuffer = loadImage();
        if (lImageBuffer == NULL) {
            return STATUS_KO;
        }

        // Creates a new OpenGL texture.
        GLenum lErrorResult;
        glGenTextures(1, &mTextureId);
        glBindTexture(GL_TEXTURE_2D, mTextureId);
```

```
        // Set-up texture properties.
        glTexParameteri(GL_TEXTURE_2D, GL_TEXTURE_MIN_FILTER,
            GL_NEAREST);
        glTexParameteri(GL_TEXTURE_2D, GL_TEXTURE_MAG_FILTER,
            GL_NEAREST);
        glTexParameteri(GL_TEXTURE_2D, GL_TEXTURE_WRAP_S,
            GL_CLAMP_TO_EDGE);
        glTexParameteri(GL_TEXTURE_2D, GL_TEXTURE_WRAP_T,
            GL_CLAMP_TO_EDGE);

        // Loads image data into OpenGL.
        glTexImage2D(GL_TEXTURE_2D, 0, mFormat, mWidth, mHeight,
0,
                    mFormat, GL_UNSIGNED_BYTE, lImageBuffer);
        delete[] lImageBuffer;
        if (glGetError() != GL_NO_ERROR) {
            Log::error("Error loading texture into OpenGL.");
            unload();
            return STATUS_KO;
        }
        return STATUS_OK;
    }
...
```

18. The rest of the code is much simpler. Method `unload()` releases Open GL texture resources when application exits with `glDeleteTextures()`:

```
...
    void GraphicsTexture::unload() {
        if (mTextureId != 0) {
            glDeleteTextures(1, &mTextureId);
            mTextureId = 0;
        }
        mWidth = 0; mHeight = 0; mFormat = 0;
    }
...
```

19. Finally, implement method `apply()` to indicate to OpenGL ES which texture to draw on screen when refreshing the scene:

```
...
    void GraphicsTexture::apply() {
        glActiveTexture( GL_TEXTURE0);
        glBindTexture(GL_TEXTURE_2D, mTextureId);
    }
}
```

Code to properly load textures is ready. Let's manage them in GraphicsService:

20. Open jni/GraphicsService.hpp. Add a destructor and create a method registerTexture() to allow clients to create new textures by passing an asset path. Textures are stored in a C++ array. They are loaded when GraphicsService starts (with loadResources()) and unloaded when it stops (with unloadResources()):

```
#ifndef _PACKT_GRAPHICSSERVICE_HPP_
#define _PACKT_GRAPHICSSERVICE_HPP_

#include "GraphicsTexture.hpp"
#include "TimeService.hpp"
#include "Types.hpp"

...

namespace packt {
    class GraphicsService
    {
    public:
        GraphicsService(android_app* pApplication,
                        TimeService* pTimeService);
        ~GraphicsService();
        ...

        status start();
        void stop();
        status update();

        GraphicsTexture* registerTexture(const char* pPath);

    protected:
        status loadResources();
        status unloadResources();

    private:
        ...

        GraphicsTexture* mTextures[32]; int32_t mTextureCount;
    };
}
#endif
```

21. In `jni/GraphicsService.cpp`, implementation of the constructor, destructor, `start()` and `stop()` is rather trivial:

```cpp
...
namespace packt
{
    GraphicsService::GraphicsService(android_app* pApplication,
                                     TimeService* pTimeService) :

        ...,
        mTextures(), mTextureCount(0)
    {}

    GraphicsService::~GraphicsService() {
        for (int32_t i = 0; i < mTextureCount; ++i) {
            delete mTextures[i];
            mTextures[i] = NULL;
        }
        mTextureCount = 0;
    }

    ...

    status GraphicsService::start() {
        ...
        glViewport(0, 0, mWidth, mHeight);

        if (loadResources() != STATUS_OK) goto ERROR;
        return STATUS_OK;

ERROR:
        Log::error("Error while starting GraphicsService");
        stop();
        return STATUS_KO;
    }

    void GraphicsService::stop() {
        unloadResources();

        if (mDisplay != EGL_NO_DISPLAY) {
            ...
        }
    ...
```

22. To finish with `jni/GraphicsService.cpp`, append new methods for texture resource management. There is no specific difficulty here. A lookup is performed when registering a texture to prevent duplication:

```
...
    status GraphicsService::loadResources() {
        for (int32_t i = 0; i < mTextureCount; ++i) {
            if (mTextures[i]->load() != STATUS_OK) {
                return STATUS_KO;
            }
        }
        return STATUS_OK;
    }

    status GraphicsService::unloadResources() {
        for (int32_t i = 0; i < mTextureCount; ++i) {
            mTextures[i]->unload();
        }
        return STATUS_OK;
    }

    GraphicsTexture* GraphicsService::registerTexture(
        const char* pPath) {
        for (int32_t i = 0; i < mTextureCount; ++i) {
            if (strcmp(pPath, mTextures[i]->getPath()) == 0) {
                return mTextures[i];
            }
        }

        GraphicsTexture* lTexture = new GraphicsTexture(
            mApplication, pPath);
        mTextures[mTextureCount++] = lTexture;
        return lTexture;
    }
}
```

What just happened?

In the previous chapter, we have just embedded existing module `NativeAppGlue` to create a fully native application. This time, we have created our first reusable module to integrate `libpng`. Combined with the Android asset manager, we are now able to create an OpenGL texture from a PNG file packaged as an asset. The only drawback is that PNG does not support 16 bits RGB.

Do not be greedy with assets

Assets take space, lots of space. Installing large APK size can be problematic, even when they are deployed on a SD Card (see the `installLocation` option in the Android manifest). Moreover, opening assets of more than 1 MB or which were compressed was problematic in OS prior to version 2.3. Thus, a good strategy to deal with tons of megabytes of resources is to keep essential assets in your APK and download remaining files to SD Card at runtime the first time application is launched.

To test if code loads textures without error, you can insert the following lines in `jni/DroidBlaster.cpp`. Texture must be located in the assets project folder:

File `ship.png` loaded is provided with this book in `Chapter6/Resource`.

```
. . .
    packt::GraphicsTexture* lShipTex =
        mGraphicsService->registerTexture("ship.png");
. . .
```

When dealing with textures, an important requirement to remember is that OpenGL textures must have a power of two dimensions (for example, 128 or 256 pixels). This allows, for example, the generation of **mipmaps**, that is, smaller versions of the same texture, to increase performance and reduce aliasing artifacts when rendered object distance changes. Other dimensions will fail on most devices. In addition, textures consume a lot of memory and bandwidth. So consider using a compressed texture format such as ETC1 which is getting wider support (but cannot handle alpha channels natively). Have a look at `http://blog.tewdew.com/post/7362195285/the-android-texture-decision` for an interesting article about texture compression.

Drawing a sprite

The base of 2D games is sprites, pieces of images composited (or **blitted**) on screen and which represent an object, character, or anything else animated or not. Sprites can be displayed with a transparency effect using the Alpha channel of an image. Typically, an image will contain several **frames** for a sprite, each frame representing a different animation step or different objects.

Editing sprite images

If you need a powerful multiplatform image editor, consider using GIMP, the GNU Image Manipulation Program. This program available on Windows, Linux and Mac OS X is really powerful and open source. You can download it at http://www.gimp.org/.

To implement sprites, we are going to rely on an OpenGL ES extension generally supported on Android devices : GL_OES_draw_texture. It allows drawing pictures directly onto the screen from an texture. This is one of the most efficient technique when creating a 2D game.

Project DroidBlaster_Part6-2 can be used as a starting point for this part. The resulting project is provided with this book under the name DroidBlaster_Part6-3.

Time for action – drawing a Ship sprite

Let's write the necessary code to handle a sprite first:

1. First, we need a class to contain sprites coordinates. Update jni/Types.hpp to define a new structure Location:

```
...
namespace packt {
    typedef int32_t status;

    const status STATUS_OK   = 0;
    const status STATUS_KO   = -1;
    const status STATUS_EXIT = -2;

    struct Location {
        Location(): mPosX(0), mPosY(0) {};
        void setPosition(float pPosX, float pPosY)
        { mPosX = pPosX; mPosY = pPosY; }

        void translate(float pAmountX, float pAmountY)
        { mPosX += pAmountX; mPosY += pAmountY; }

        float mPosX; float mPosY;
    };
}
...
```

2. Create `GraphicsSprite.hpp` in folder `jni`. A sprite is loaded when `GraphicsService` starts with `load()` and rendered when screen is refreshed with `draw()`. It is possible to set an animation with `setAnimation()` and play it infinitely or not by drawing sprite frames consecutively in time.

A sprite requires several properties:

❑ A texture containing the sprite sheet (`mTexture`).

❑ A location to draw on screen (`mLocation`).

❑ Information about sprite frames: `mWidth` and `mHeight`, horizontal, vertical, and total number of frames in `mFrameXCount`, `mFrameYCount`, and `mFrameCount`.

❑ Animation information: first and total number of frames of an animation in `mAnimStartFrame` and `mAnimFrameCount`, animation speed in `mAnimSpeed`, currently shown frame in `mAnimFrame`, and a looping indicator in `mAnimLoop`.

```cpp
#ifndef _PACKT_GRAPHICSSPRITE_HPP_
#define _PACKT_GRAPHICSSPRITE_HPP_

#include "GraphicsTexture.hpp"
#include "TimeService.hpp"
#include "Types.hpp"

namespace packt {
    class GraphicsSprite {
    public:
        GraphicsSprite(GraphicsTexture* pTexture,
            int32_t pHeight, int32_t pWidth, Location*
pLocation);

        void load();
        void draw(float pTimeStep);

        void setAnimation(int32_t pStartFrame, int32_t
pFrameCount,
            float pSpeed, bool pLoop);
        bool animationEnded();

    private:
        GraphicsTexture* mTexture;
        Location* mLocation;
        // Frame.
        int32_t mHeight, mWidth;
```

```
                              int32_t mFrameXCount, mFrameYCount, mFrameCount;
                              // Animation.
                              int32_t mAnimStartFrame, mAnimFrameCount;
                              float mAnimSpeed, mAnimFrame;
                              bool mAnimLoop;
                    };
          }
          #endif
```

3. Write `GraphicsSprite.cpp` in `jni` folder. Frame information (horizontal, vertical, and total number of frames) needs to be recomputed in `load()` as texture dimensions are known only at load time.

When setting up an animation with `setAnimation()`, compute the first frame index `mAnimStartFrame` inside the sprite sheet and the number of images composing the animation, `mAnimFrameCount`. The animation speed is set through `mAnimSpeed` and current animation frame (updated at each step) is saved in `mAnimFrame`:

```
include "GraphicsSprite.hpp"
#include "Log.hpp"

#include <GLES/gl.h>
#include <GLES/glext.h>

namespace packt {
    GraphicsSprite::GraphicsSprite(GraphicsTexture* pTexture,
        int32_t pHeight, int32_t pWidth, Location* pLocation) :
        mTexture(pTexture), mLocation(pLocation),
        mHeight(pHeight), mWidth(pWidth),
        mFrameCount(0), mFrameXCount(0), mFrameYCount(0),
        mAnimStartFrame(0), mAnimFrameCount(0),
        mAnimSpeed(0), mAnimFrame(0), mAnimLoop(false)
    {}

    void GraphicsSprite::load() {
        mFrameXCount = mTexture->getWidth() / mWidth;
        mFrameYCount = mTexture->getHeight() / mHeight;
        mFrameCount = (mTexture->getHeight() / mHeight)
                    * (mTexture->getWidth() / mWidth);
    }

    void GraphicsSprite::setAnimation(int32_t pStartFrame,
        int32_t pFrameCount, float pSpeed, bool pLoop) {
        mAnimStartFrame = pStartFrame;
        mAnimFrame = 0.0f, mAnimSpeed = pSpeed, mAnimLoop = pLoop;
```

```cpp
        int32_t lMaxFrameCount = mFrameCount - pStartFrame;
        if ((pFrameCount > -1) && (pFrameCount <= lMaxFrameCount))
{
            mAnimFrameCount = pFrameCount;
        } else {
            mAnimFrameCount = lMaxFrameCount;
        }
    }

    bool GraphicsSprite::animationEnded() {
        return mAnimFrame > (mAnimFrameCount - 1);
    }
...
```

4. In `GraphicsSprite.cpp`, implement last method `draw()`. First, compute the current frame to display depending on the animation state and then draw it with OpenGL. They are three main steps involved to draw a sprite:

   ❑ Ensure OpenGL draws the right texture with `apply()` (that is, `glBindTexture()`).

   ❑ Crop texture to draw only the required sprite frame with `glTexParameteriv()` and `GL_TEXTURE_CROP_RECT_OES`.

   ❑ Finally send a draw order to OpenGL ES with `glDrawTexfOES()`.

```cpp
        ...
            void GraphicsSprite::draw(float pTimeStep) {
                int32_t lCurrentFrame, lCurrentFrameX,
        lCurrentFrameY;

                // Updates animation in loop mode.
                mAnimFrame += pTimeStep * mAnimSpeed;
                if (mAnimLoop) {
                    lCurrentFrame = (mAnimStartFrame +
                                    int32_t(mAnimFrame) %
        mAnimFrameCount);
                }
                // Updates animation in one-shot mode.
                else {
                    // If animation ended.
                    if (animationEnded()) {
                        lCurrentFrame = mAnimStartFrame +
        (mAnimFrameCount-1);
                    } else {
                        lCurrentFrame = mAnimStartFrame +
        int32_t(mAnimFrame);
```

```
                }
            }
            // Computes frame X and Y indexes from its id.
            lCurrentFrameX = lCurrentFrame % mFrameXCount;
            // lCurrentFrameY is converted from OpenGL
        coordinates
            // to top-left coordinates.
            lCurrentFrameY = mFrameYCount - 1
                            - (lCurrentFrame /
        mFrameXCount);

            // Draws selected sprite frame.
            mTexture->apply();
            int32_t lCrop[] = { lCurrentFrameX * mWidth,
                                lCurrentFrameY * mHeight,
                                mWidth, mHeight };
            glTexParameteriv(GL_TEXTURE_2D,
                            GL_TEXTURE_CROP_RECT_OES,
                            lCrop);
            glDrawTexfOES(mLocation->mPosX - (mWidth / 2),
                          mLocation->mPosY - (mHeight / 2),
                          0.0f, mWidth, mHeight);
        }
    }
```

Code to render sprites is ready. Let's make use of it:

5. Modify `GraphicsService` to manage sprite resources (like textures in the previous part):

```
#ifndef _PACKT_GRAPHICSSERVICE_HPP_
#define _PACKT_GRAPHICSSERVICE_HPP_

#include "GraphicsSprite.hpp"
#include "GraphicsTexture.hpp"

...


namespace packt {
    class GraphicsService {
    public:
        ...
        GraphicsTexture* registerTexture(const char* pPath);
        GraphicsSprite* registerSprite(GraphicsTexture* pTexture,
            int32_t pHeight, int32_t pWidth, Location* pLocation);
```

```
    protected:
        status loadResources();
        status unloadResources();
        void setup();

    private:
        ...

        GraphicsTexture* mTextures[32]; int32_t mTextureCount;
        GraphicsSprite*  mSprites[256]; int32_t mSpriteCount;
    };
}
#endif
```

6. Modify `GraphicsService.cpp` so that it creates a buffer of sprite to draw while operating. We define a method `registerSprite` for this purpose:

```
...

namespace packt {
    GraphicsService::GraphicsService(android_app* pApplication,
                                     TimeService* pTimeService) :
        ...,
        mTextures(), mTextureCount(0),
        mSprites(), mSpriteCount(0)
    {}

    GraphicsService::~GraphicsService() {
        for (int32_t i = 0; i < mSpriteCount; ++i) {
            delete mSprites[i];
            mSprites[i] = NULL;
        }
        mSpriteCount = 0;

        for (int32_t i = 0; i < mTextureCount; ++i) {
            delete mTextures[i];
            mTextures[i] = NULL;
        }
        mTextureCount = 0;
    }

    ...

    status GraphicsService::start() {
        ...
```

```
            if (loadResources() != STATUS_OK) goto ERROR;
            setup();
            return STATUS_OK;

        ERROR:
            Log::error("Error while starting GraphicsService");
            stop();
            return STATUS_KO;
        }
    ...
```

7. Erase screen with black and draw sprites over using the method `update()`.
Transparency is enabled with `glBlendFunc()` which blends source texture pixel
with final framebuffer according to the specified formula. Here, source pixel affects
destination pixel according to its alpha channel (`GL_SRC_ALPHA`/`GL_ONE_MINUS_`
`SRC_ALPHA`). This is commonly referred to as **alpha blending**:

```
    ...
        status GraphicsService::update() {
            float lTimeStep = mTimeService->elapsed();

            glClearColor(0.0f, 0.0f, 0.0f, 1.0f);
            glClear(GL_COLOR_BUFFER_BIT);

            glEnable(GL_BLEND);
            glBlendFunc(GL_SRC_ALPHA, GL_ONE_MINUS_SRC_ALPHA);
            for (int32_t i = 0; i < mSpriteCount; ++i) {
                mSprites[i]->draw(lTimeStep);
            }
            glDisable(GL_BLEND);

            if (eglSwapBuffers(mDisplay, mSurface) != EGL_TRUE) {
              Log::error("Error %d swapping buffers.", eglGetError());
                return STATUS_KO;
            }
            return STATUS_OK;
        }

        status GraphicsService::loadResources() {
            for (int32_t i = 0; i < mTextureCount; ++i) {
                if (mTextures[i]->load() != STATUS_OK) {
                    return STATUS_KO;
                }
            }
```

```
        for (int32_t i = 0; i < mSpriteCount; ++i) {
            mSprites[i]->load();
        }
        return STATUS_OK;
    }
...
```

8. To finish with `jni/GraphicsService.cpp`, implement `setup()` to initialize main OpenGL settings. Here, enable texturing but disable the Z-buffer which is not needed in a simple 2D game. Ensure sprites are rendered (for the emulator) with `glColor4f()`:

```
...
    void GraphicsService::setup() {
        glEnable(GL_TEXTURE_2D);
        glDisable(GL_DEPTH_TEST);
        glColor4f(1.0f, 1.0f, 1.0f, 1.0f);
    }


    ...

    GraphicsSprite* GraphicsService::registerSprite(
        GraphicsTexture* pTexture, int32_t pHeight,
        int32_t pWidth, Location* pLocation) {
        GraphicsSprite* lSprite = new GraphicsSprite(pTexture,
            pHeight, pWidth, pLocation);
        mSprites[mSpriteCount++] = lSprite;
        return lSprite;
    }
}
```

We are almost done! Let's use our engine drawing capabilities to render a spaceship:

9. Create a `Ship` game object in `jni/Ship.hpp` file:

```
#ifndef _DBS_SHIP_HPP_
#define _DBS_SHIP_HPP_

#include "Context.hpp"
#include "GraphicsService.hpp"
#include "GraphicsSprite.hpp"
#include "Types.hpp"

namespace dbs {
    class Ship {
```

```
    public:
        Ship(packt::Context* pContext);

        void spawn();

    private:
        packt::GraphicsService* mGraphicsService;

        packt::GraphicsSprite* mSprite;
        packt::Location mLocation;
        float mAnimSpeed;
    };
}
#endif
```

10. The `Ship` class registers the resource it needs when it is created, here `ship.png` sprite (which must be located in the `assets` folder) contains 64x64 pixel frames. It is initialized in `spawn()` in the lower quarter of the screen and uses an 8-frame animation:

 File `ship.png` is provided with this book in the `Chapter6/ Resource` folder.

```
#include "Ship.hpp"
#include "Log.hpp"

namespace dbs {
    Ship::Ship(packt::Context* pContext) :
        mGraphicsService(pContext->mGraphicsService),
        mLocation(), mAnimSpeed(8.0f) {
        mSprite = pContext->mGraphicsService->registerSprite(
            mGraphicsService->registerTexture("ship.png"), 64, 64,
            &mLocation);
    }

    void Ship::spawn() {
        const int32_t FRAME_1 = 0; const int32_t FRAME_NB = 8;
        mSprite->setAnimation(FRAME_1, FRAME_NB, mAnimSpeed, true);
        mLocation.setPosition(mGraphicsService->getWidth() * 1 / 2,
```

```
                                   mGraphicsService->getHeight() * 1 / 4);
        }
    }
```

11. Include the new `Ship` class in `jni/DroidBlaster.hpp`:

```
#ifndef _PACKT_DROIDBLASTER_HPP_
#define _PACKT_DROIDBLASTER_HPP_

#include "ActivityHandler.hpp"
#include "Context.hpp"
#include "GraphicsService.hpp"
#include "Ship.hpp"
#include "TimeService.hpp"
#include "Types.hpp"

namespace dbs {
    class DroidBlaster : public packt::ActivityHandler {
        ...
    private:
        packt::GraphicsService* mGraphicsService;
        packt::TimeService*     mTimeService;

        Ship mShip;
    };
}
#endif
```

12. Modify `jni/DroidBlaster.cpp` accordingly. Implementation is trivial:

```
#include "DroidBlaster.hpp"
#include "Log.hpp"

namespace dbs {
    DroidBlaster::DroidBlaster(packt::Context* pContext) :
        mGraphicsService(pContext->mGraphicsService),
        mTimeService(pContext->mTimeService),
        mShip(pContext)
    {}

    ...

    packt::status DroidBlaster::onActivate() {
```

```
    if (mGraphicsService->start() != packt::STATUS_OK) {
        return packt::STATUS_KO;
    }

    mShip.spawn();

    mTimeService->reset();
    return packt::STATUS_OK;
}
...
}
```

What just happened?

Launch DroidBlaster now to see the following screen with the ship animated at a rate of 8 FPS:

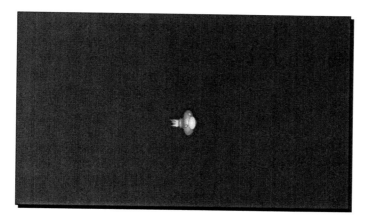

In this part, we have seen how to draw a sprite efficiently with a common OpenGL ES extension GL_OES_draw_texture. This technique is simple to use and is generally the way to go to render sprites. However, it suffers from a few caveats that can be solved only by going back to polygons:

- glDrawTexOES() is available on OpenGL ES 1.1! OpenGL ES 2.0 and some old devices do not support it.
- Sprite cannot be rotated.
- This technique may cause lots of state changes when drawing many different sprites (like a background) which could impact performance.

A common cause of bad performance in OpenGL programs relies in state changes. Changing OpenGL device state (for example, binding a new buffer or texture, changing an option with `glEnable()`, and so on) is a costly operation and should be avoided as much as possible, for example, by sorting draw calls and changing only the needed states. For example, we could improve our `Texture::apply()` method by checking the texture currently set before binding it.

One of the best OpenGL ES documentation is available, well... from the Apple developer site: `http://developer.apple.com/library/IOS/#documentation/3DDrawing/Conceptual/OpenGLES_ProgrammingGuide/`.

Rendering a tile map with vertex buffer objects

What would a 2D game be without a map; more precisely a tile map. A **tile map** is a full-size map composed of small quad polygons or **tiles** mapped with a piece of image. These tiles are made so that they can be pasted beside, repeatedly. We are now going to implement a tile map to draw a background. The rendering technique is inspired from the Android game Replica Island (see `http://replicaisland.net`). It is based on **vertex** and **index buffer** to batch tile rendering in a few OpenGL calls (thus minimizing state changes).

Tiled map editor

Tiled is an open source program available on Windows, Linux, and Mac OS X to create your own custom tile maps with a friendly editor. Tiled exports XML-based files with the TMX extension. Download it from `http://www.mapeditor.org/`.

Let's now implement our own tile map. The final application should look like the following:

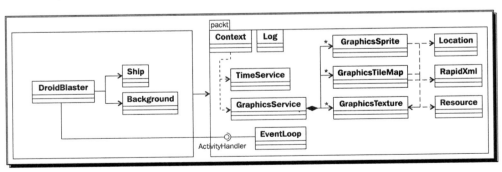

Project DroidBlaster_Part6-3 can be used as a starting point for this part. The resulting project is provided with this book under the name DroidBlaster_Part6-4.

Time for action – drawing a tile-based background

First, let's embed RapidXml library to read XML files:

1. Download RapidXml (version 1.1.13 in this book) at `http://rapidxml.sourceforge.net/`.

RapidXml archive is provided with this book in the `Chapter6/Resource` folder.

2. Find `rapidxml.hpp` in the downloaded archive and copy it into your `jni` folder.

3. RapidXml works with exceptions by default. As we will study exception handling later in this book, deactivate them in `jni/Android.mk` with a predefined macro:

```
...
LS_CPP=$(subst $(1)/,,$(wildcard $(1)/*.cpp))
LOCAL_CFLAGS     := -DRAPIDXML_NO_EXCEPTIONS
LOCAL_MODULE     := droidblaster
LOCAL_SRC_FILES  := $(call LS_CPP,$(LOCAL_PATH))
LOCAL_LDLIBS     := -landroid -llog -lEGL -lGLESv1_CM
...
```

4. For efficiency reasons, RapidXml read XML files directly from a memory buffer containing the whole file. So open `Resource.hpp` and add a new method to get a full buffer from an asset (`bufferize()`) and retrieve its length (`getLength()`):

```
...
namespace packt {
    class Resource {
    public:
        ...

        off_t getLength();
        const void* bufferize();

    private:
        ...
```

```
    };
}
. . .
```

5. The asset management API offers all the required stuff to implement these methods:

```
. . .
namespace packt {

    . . .

    off_t Resource::getLength() {
        return AAsset_getLength(mAsset);
    }

    const void* Resource::bufferize() {
        return AAsset_getBuffer(mAsset);
    }
}
```

Now, let's write the code necessary to handle a simple TMX tile map:

6. Create a new header file `jni/GraphicsTileMap.hpp` as follows. A `GraphicsTileMap` is first loaded, then drawn when the screen refreshes and finally unloaded. Loading itself occurs in three steps:

   ❑ `loadFile()`: This loads a Tiled TMX file with RapidXml

   ❑ `loadVertices()`: This sets up an OpenGL Vertex Buffer Object and generate vertices from file data

   ❑ `loadIndexes()`: This generates an index buffer with indexes delimitating two triangle polygons for each tile

A tile map requires the following:

   ❑ A texture containing the sprite sheet.

   ❑ Two resource handles (`mVertexBuffer`, `mIndexBuffer`) pointing to OpenGL vertex and index buffers, the number of elements they contain (`mVertexCount`, `mIndexCount`) and the number of coordinate components (X/Y/Z and U/V coordinates in `mVertexComponent`).

   ❑ Information about the number of tiles in the final map (`mWidth` and `mHeight`).

   ❑ A description of tile width and height in pixels (`mTileHeight` and `mTileHeight`) and count (`mTileCount` and `mTileXCount`).

```
#ifndef _PACKT_GRAPHICSTILEMAP_HPP_
#define _PACKT_GRAPHICSTILEMAP_HPP_

#include "GraphicsTexture.hpp"
#include "Types.hpp"

#include <android_native_app_glue.h>

namespace packt {
    class GraphicsTileMap {
    public:
        GraphicsTileMap(android_app* pApplication, const
char* pPath,
            GraphicsTexture* pTexture, Location*
pLocation);

        status load();
        void unload();
        void draw();

    private:
        int32_t* loadFile();
        void loadVertices(int32_t* pTiles, uint8_t**
pVertexBuffer,
                          uint32_t* pVertexBufferSize);
        void loadIndexes(uint8_t** pIndexBuffer,
                         uint32_t* pIndexBufferSize);

    private:
        Resource mResource;
        Location* mLocation;
        // OpenGL resources.
        GraphicsTexture* mTexture;
        GLuint mVertexBuffer, mIndexBuffer;
        int32_t mVertexCount, mIndexCount;
        const int32_t mVertexComponents;
        // Tile map description.
        int32_t mHeight, mWidth;
        int32_t mTileHeight, mTileWidth;
        int32_t mTileCount, mTileXCount;
    };
}
#endif
```

7. Start implementing `GraphicsTileMap` in `jni/GraphicsTileMap.cpp`. Because exceptions are not supported in the current project, define `parse_error_handler()` method to handle parsing problems. By design, result of this handler is undefined (that is, a crash). So implement a non-local jump instead, similar to what we have done for `libpng`:

```cpp
#include "GraphicsTileMap.hpp"
#include "Log.hpp"

#include <GLES/gl.h>
#include <GLES/glext.h>

#include "rapidxml.hpp"

namespace rapidxml {
    static jmp_buf sJmpBuffer;

    void parse_error_handler(const char* pWhat, void* pWhere) {
        packt::Log::error("Error while parsing TMX file.");
        packt::Log::error(pWhat);
        longjmp(sJmpBuffer, 0);
    }
}

namespace packt {
    GraphicsTileMap::GraphicsTileMap(android_app* pApplication,
        const char* pPath, GraphicsTexture* pTexture,
        Location* pLocation) :
        mResource(pApplication, pPath), mLocation(pLocation),
        mTexture(pTexture), mVertexBuffer(0), mIndexBuffer(0),
        mVertexCount(0), mIndexCount(0), mVertexComponents(5),
        mHeight(0), mWidth(0),
        mTileHeight(0), mTileWidth(0), mTileCount(0),
mTileXCount(0)
    {}
    ...
```

8. Let's write the code necessary to read a TMX file exported by Tiled. Asset file is read with resource and copied into a temporary buffer which is not modifiable (the opposite of the buffer returned by `bufferize()`, which is flagged with `const`).

   RapidXml parses XML files through an `xml_document` instance. It works directly on the provided buffer, which it may modify to normalize space, translate character entities, or terminate strings with zero. A non-destructive mode without these features is also available. XML nodes and attributes can then be retrieved easily:

...

```cpp
int32_t* GraphicsTileMap::loadFile() {
    using namespace rapidxml;
    xml_document<> lXmlDocument;
    xml_node<>* lXmlMap, *lXmlTileset, *lXmlLayer;
    xml_node<>* lXmlTile, *lXmlData;
    xml_attribute<>* lXmlTileWidth, *lXmlTileHeight;
    xml_attribute<>* lXmlWidth, *lXmlHeight, *lXmlGID;
    char* lFileBuffer = NULL; int32_t* lTiles = NULL;

    if (mResource.open() != STATUS_OK) goto ERROR;
    {
    int32_t lLength = mResource.getLength();
    if (lLength <= 0) goto ERROR;
    const void* lFileBufferTmp = mResource.bufferize();
    if (lFileBufferTmp == NULL) goto ERROR;
    lFileBuffer = new char[mResource.getLength() + 1];
    memcpy(lFileBuffer, lFileBufferTmp,mResource.getLength());
        lFileBuffer[mResource.getLength()] = '\0';
        mResource.close();
    }
    // Parses the document. Jumps back here if an error occurs
    if (setjmp(sJmpBuffer)) goto ERROR;
    lXmlDocument.parse<parse_default>(lFileBuffer);

// Reads XML tags.
lXmlMap = lXmlDocument.first_node("map");
if (lXmlMap == NULL) goto ERROR;
lXmlTileset = lXmlMap->first_node("tileset");
if (lXmlTileset == NULL) goto ERROR;
lXmlTileWidth = lXmlTileset->first_attribute("tilewidth");
if (lXmlTileWidth == NULL) goto ERROR;
lXmlTileHeight = lXmlTileset->first_attribute("tileheight");
if (lXmlTileHeight == NULL) goto ERROR;

lXmlLayer = lXmlMap->first_node("layer");
if (lXmlLayer == NULL) goto ERROR;
lXmlWidth = lXmlLayer->first_attribute("width");
if (lXmlWidth == NULL) goto ERROR;
lXmlHeight = lXmlLayer->first_attribute("height");
if (lXmlHeight == NULL) goto ERROR;
```

```
      lXmlData = lXmlLayer->first_node("data");
      if (lXmlData == NULL) goto ERROR;
  ...
```

9. Continue implementing `loadFile()` by initializing member data. After that, load each tile index into a new memory buffer that we will use later to create a vertex buffer. Note that vertical coordinates are reversed between TMX and OpenGL coordinates and that TMX files first tile index is 1 instead of 0 (hence `-1` when setting `lTiles[]` value):

```
  ...
    mWidth      = atoi(lXmlWidth->value());
    mHeight     = atoi(lXmlHeight->value());
    mTileWidth  = atoi(lXmlTileWidth->value());
    mTileHeight = atoi(lXmlTileHeight->value());
    if ((mWidth <= 0) || (mHeight <= 0)
     || (mTileWidth <= 0) || (mTileHeight <= 0)) goto ERROR;
    mTileXCount = mTexture->getWidth()/mTileWidth;
    mTileCount = mTexture->getHeight()/mTileHeight * mTileXCount;

      lTiles = new int32_t[mWidth * mHeight];
      lXmlTile = lXmlData->first_node("tile");
      for (int32_t lY = mHeight - 1; lY >= 0; --lY) {
        for (int32_t lX = 0; lX < mWidth; ++lX) {
          if (lXmlTile == NULL) goto ERROR;
          lXmlGID = lXmlTile->first_attribute("gid");
          lTiles[lX + (lY * mWidth)] = atoi(lXmlGID->value())-1;
              if (lTiles[lX + (lY * mWidth)] < 0) goto ERROR;

              lXmlTile = lXmlTile->next_sibling("tile");
          }
      }
      delete[] lFileBuffer;
      return lTiles;

  ERROR:
      mResource.close();
      delete[] lFileBuffer; delete[] lTiles;
      mHeight = 0;       mWidth = 0;
      mTileHeight = 0; mTileWidth = 0;
      return NULL;
  }
  ...
```

10. Now the big piece: `loadVertices()`, populating a temporary memory buffer with vertices. First we need to compute some information such as the total number of vertices and allocate the buffer accordingly, knowing that it contains four vertices composed of five float components (X/Y/Z and U/V) per tile. We also need to know the size of a **texel**, that is, the size of one pixel in **UV** coordinates. UV coordinates are bound to [0,1] where 0 means texture left or bottom and 1 texture right or bottom.

Then, we basically loop over each tile and compute vertex coordinates (X/Y position and UV coordinates) at the right offset (that is, location) in the buffer. UV coordinates are slightly shifted to avoid seams at tile edges especially when using bilinear filtering which can cause adjacent tile textures to be blended:

```
. . .
    void GraphicsTileMap::loadVertices(int32_t* pTiles,
            uint8_t** pVertexBuffer, uint32_t*
pVertexBufferSize) {
        mVertexCount = mHeight * mWidth * 4;
        *pVertexBufferSize = mVertexCount * mVertexComponents;
        GLfloat* lVBuffer = new GLfloat[*pVertexBufferSize];
        *pVertexBuffer = reinterpret_cast<uint8_t*>(lVBuffer);
        int32_t lRowStride = mWidth * 2;
        GLfloat lTexelWidth = 1.0f / mTexture->getWidth();
        GLfloat lTexelHeight = 1.0f / mTexture->getHeight();

        int32_t i;
        for (int32_t tileY = 0; tileY < mHeight; ++tileY) {
            for (int32_t tileX = 0; tileX < mWidth; ++tileX) {
                // Finds current tile index (0 for 1st tile, 1...).
                int32_t lTileSprite = pTiles[tileY * mWidth + tileX]
                                % mTileCount;
                int32_t lTileSpriteX = (lTileSprite % mTileXCount)
                                * mTileWidth;
                int32_t lTileSpriteY = (lTileSprite / mTileXCount)
                                * mTileHeight;

                // Values to compute vertex offsets in the buffer.
                int32_t lOffsetX1 = tileX * 2;
                int32_t lOffsetX2 = tileX * 2 + 1;
                int32_t lOffsetY1 = (tileY * 2) * (mWidth * 2);
                int32_t lOffsetY2 = (tileY * 2 + 1) * (mWidth * 2);
                // Vertex positions in the scene.
                GLfloat lPosX1 = tileX * mTileWidth;
```

```
                          GLfloat lPosX2 = (tileX + 1) * mTileWidth;
                          GLfloat lPosY1 = tileY * mTileHeight;
                          GLfloat lPosY2 = (tileY + 1) * mTileHeight;
                  // Tile UV coordinates (coordinates origin needs to be
                  // translated from top-left to bottom-left origin).
                          GLfloat lU1 = (lTileSpriteX) * lTexelWidth;
                          GLfloat lU2 = lU1 + (mTileWidth * lTexelWidth);
                          GLfloat lV2 = 1.0f - (lTileSpriteY) * lTexelHeight;
                          GLfloat lV1 = lV2 - (mTileHeight * lTexelHeight);
                  // Small shift to limit edge artifacts (1/4 of texel).
                          lU1 += lTexelWidth/4.0f;  lU2 -= lTexelWidth/4.0f;
                          lV1 += lTexelHeight/4.0f; lV2 -=
lTexelHeight/4.0f;

                          // 4 vertices per tile in the vertex buffer.
                          i = mVertexComponents * (lOffsetY1 + lOffsetX1);
                          lVBuffer[i++] = lPosX1; lVBuffer[i++] = lPosY1;
                          lVBuffer[i++] = 0.0f;
                          lVBuffer[i++] = lU1;    lVBuffer[i++] = lV1;
                          i = mVertexComponents * (lOffsetY1 + lOffsetX2);
                          lVBuffer[i++] = lPosX2; lVBuffer[i++] = lPosY1;
                          lVBuffer[i++] = 0.0f;
                          lVBuffer[i++] = lU2;    lVBuffer[i++] = lV1;
                          i = mVertexComponents * (lOffsetY2 + lOffsetX1);
                          lVBuffer[i++] = lPosX1; lVBuffer[i++] = lPosY2;
                          lVBuffer[i++] = 0.0f;
                          lVBuffer[i++] = lU1;    lVBuffer[i++] = lV2;
                          i = mVertexComponents * (lOffsetY2 + lOffsetX2);
                          lVBuffer[i++] = lPosX2; lVBuffer[i++] = lPosY2;
                          lVBuffer[i++] = 0.0f;
                          lVBuffer[i++] = lU2;    lVBuffer[i++] = lV2;
                  }
              }
          }
      ...
```

11. Our vertex buffer is pretty useless without its index buffer companion. Populate it with two triangle polygons per tile (that is, 6 indexes) to form quad:

```
    ...
    void GraphicsTileMap::loadIndexes(uint8_t** pIndexBuffer,
                                      uint32_t* pIndexBufferSize)
{
        mIndexCount = mHeight * mWidth * 6;
        *pIndexBufferSize = mIndexCount;
        GLushort* lIBuffer = new GLushort[*pIndexBufferSize];
```

```
*pIndexBuffer   = reinterpret_cast<uint8_t*>(lIBuffer);
int32_t lRowStride = mWidth * 2;

int32_t i = 0;
for (int32_t tileY = 0; tileY < mHeight; tileY++) {
    int32_t lIndexY = tileY * 2;
    for (int32_t tileX = 0; tileX < mWidth; tileX++) {
        int32_t lIndexX = tileX * 2;

        // Values to compute vertex offsets in the buffer.
        GLshort lVertIndexY1 = lIndexY * lRowStride;
        GLshort lVertIndexY2 = (lIndexY + 1) * lRowStride;
        GLshort lVertIndexX1 = lIndexX;
        GLshort lVertIndexX2 = lIndexX + 1;

        // 2 triangles per tile in the index buffer.
        lIBuffer[i++] = lVertIndexY1 + lVertIndexX1;
        lIBuffer[i++] = lVertIndexY1 + lVertIndexX2;
        lIBuffer[i++] = lVertIndexY2 + lVertIndexX1;

        lIBuffer[i++] = lVertIndexY2 + lVertIndexX1;
        lIBuffer[i++] = lVertIndexY1 + lVertIndexX2;
        lIBuffer[i++] = lVertIndexY2 + lVertIndexX2;
    }
}
...
```

12. In GraphicsTileMap.cpp, terminate loading code by generating final buffers with glGenBuffers() and binding them (to indicate we are working on them) with glBindBuffer(). Then, push vertex and index buffer data into graphics memory through glBufferData(). Our temporary buffers can then be discarded:

```
status GraphicsTileMap::load() {
    GLenum lErrorResult;
    uint8_t* lVertexBuffer = NULL, *lIndexBuffer = NULL;
    uint32_t lVertexBufferSize, lIndexBufferSize;

    // Loads tiles and creates temporary vertex/index buffers.
    int32_t* lTiles = loadFile();
```

```
if (lTiles == NULL) goto ERROR;
loadVertices(lTiles, &lVertexBuffer, &lVertexBufferSize);
if (lVertexBuffer == NULL) goto ERROR;
loadIndexes(&lIndexBuffer,  &lIndexBufferSize);
if (lIndexBuffer == NULL) goto ERROR;

// Generates new buffer names.
glGenBuffers(1, &mVertexBuffer);
glGenBuffers(1, &mIndexBuffer);
glBindBuffer(GL_ARRAY_BUFFER, mVertexBuffer);
glBindBuffer(GL_ELEMENT_ARRAY_BUFFER, mIndexBuffer);

// Loads buffers into OpenGL.
glBufferData(GL_ARRAY_BUFFER, lVertexBufferSize *
        sizeof(GLfloat), lVertexBuffer, GL_STATIC_DRAW);
lErrorResult = glGetError();
if (lErrorResult != GL_NO_ERROR) goto ERROR;

glBufferData(GL_ELEMENT_ARRAY_BUFFER, lIndexBufferSize *
        sizeof(GLushort), lIndexBuffer, GL_STATIC_DRAW);
lErrorResult = glGetError();
if (lErrorResult != GL_NO_ERROR) goto ERROR;

// Unbinds buffers.
glBindBuffer(GL_ARRAY_BUFFER, 0);
glBindBuffer(GL_ELEMENT_ARRAY_BUFFER, 0);

delete[] lTiles; delete[] lVertexBuffer;
delete[] lIndexBuffer;
return STATUS_OK;

ERROR:
    Log::error("Error loading tilemap");
    unload();
    delete[] lTiles; delete[] lVertexBuffer;
    delete[] lIndexBuffer;
    return STATUS_KO;
}
...
```

13. We are done with resource loading. Take care of unloading them in `unload()`:

```
...
    void GraphicsTileMap::unload() {
        mHeight      = 0, mWidth      = 0;
        mTileHeight  = 0, mTileWidth  = 0;
        mTileCount   = 0, mTileXCount = 0;

        if (mVertexBuffer != 0) {
            glDeleteBuffers(1, &mVertexBuffer);
            mVertexBuffer = 0; mVertexCount = 0;
        }
        if (mIndexBuffer != 0) {
            glDeleteBuffers(1, &mIndexBuffer);
            mIndexBuffer = 0; mIndexCount = 0;
        }
    }
...
```

14. To finish with `GraphicsTileMap.cpp`, write `draw()` method to render the tile map:

- Bind the tile sheet texture for rendering.

- Set up geometry transformations with `glTranslatef()` to position the map to its final coordinates in the scene. Note that matrices are hierarchical, hence the preliminary call to `glPushMatrix()` to stack tile map matrix on top of the projection and world matrices. Position coordinates are rounded to prevent seams from appearing between tiles because of rendering interpolation.

- Enable, bind, and describe vertex and index buffer contents with `glEnableClientState()`, `glVertexPointer()`, and `glTexCoordPointer()`.

- Issue a rendering call to draw the whole map mesh with `glDrawElements()`.

- Reset OpenGL machine state when done.

```
    ...
        void GraphicsTileMap::draw() {
            int32_t lVertexSize      = mVertexComponents *
    sizeof(GLfloat);
            GLvoid* lVertexOffset    = (GLvoid*) 0;
            GLvoid* lTexCoordOffset = (GLvoid*)
    (sizeof(GLfloat) * 3);
            mTexture->apply();
```

```
glPushMatrix();
        glTranslatef(int32_t(mLocation->mPosX + 0.5f),
                        int32_t(mLocation->mPosY + 0.5f),
    0.0f);

        // Draws using hardware buffers
        glEnableClientState(GL_VERTEX_ARRAY);
        glEnableClientState(GL_TEXTURE_COORD_ARRAY);
        glBindBuffer(GL_ARRAY_BUFFER, mVertexBuffer);
        glBindBuffer(GL_ELEMENT_ARRAY_BUFFER,
    mIndexBuffer);
        glVertexPointer(3, GL_FLOAT, lVertexSize,
    lVertexOffset);
        glTexCoordPointer(2, GL_FLOAT, lVertexSize,
    lTexCoordOffset);

        glDrawElements(GL_TRIANGLES, mIndexCount,
            GL_UNSIGNED_SHORT, 0 * sizeof(GLushort));

        glBindBuffer(GL_ARRAY_BUFFER, 0);
        glBindBuffer(GL_ELEMENT_ARRAY_BUFFER, 0);
        glPopMatrix();
        glDisableClientState(GL_VERTEX_ARRAY);
        glDisableClientState(GL_TEXTURE_COORD_ARRAY);
    }
}
```

Let's append our new tile map module to the application:

15. Like for textures and sprites, let GraphicsService manage tile maps:

```
#ifndef _PACKT_GRAPHICSSERVICE_HPP_
#define _PACKT_GRAPHICSSERVICE_HPP_

#include "GraphicsSprite.hpp"
#include "GraphicsTexture.hpp"
#include "GraphicsTileMap.hpp"
#include "TimeService.hpp"
#include "Types.hpp"

#include <android_native_app_glue.h>
#include <EGL/egl.h>

namespace packt {
    class GraphicsService {
```

```
    public:
        ...
        GraphicsTexture* registerTexture(const char* pPath);
        GraphicsSprite* registerSprite(GraphicsTexture* pTexture,
            int32_t pHeight, int32_t pWidth, Location* pLocation);
        GraphicsTileMap* registerTileMap(const char* pPath,
            GraphicsTexture* pTexture, Location* pLocation);
        ...

    private:
        ...
        GraphicsTexture* mTextures[32]; int32_t mTextureCount;
        GraphicsSprite*  mSprites[256]; int32_t mSpriteCount;
        GraphicsTileMap* mTileMaps[8]; int32_t mTileMapCount;
    };
}
#endif
```

16. In `jni/GraphicsService.cpp`, implement `registerTileMap()` and update `load()`, `unload()`, and class destructor like for sprites previous tutorial.

Change `setup()` to push a projection and ModelView matrix in the matrix stack:

❑   Projection is orthographic since 2D games do not need a perspective effect.

❑   ModelView matrix describes basically the position and orientation of the *camera*. Here, camera (that is, the whole scene) does not move; only the background tile map moves to simulate a scrolling effect. Thus, a simple identity matrix is sufficient.

Then, modify `update()` to effectively draw tile maps:

```
...
namespace packt {
    ...
    void GraphicsService::setup() {
        glEnable(GL_TEXTURE_2D);
        glDisable(GL_DEPTH_TEST);
        glColor4f(1.0f, 1.0f, 1.0f, 1.0f);

        glMatrixMode(GL_PROJECTION);
        glLoadIdentity();
        glOrthof(0.0f, mWidth, 0.0f, mHeight, 0.0f, 1.0f);

        glMatrixMode( GL_MODELVIEW);
        glLoadIdentity();
    }
```

```
status GraphicsService::update() {
    float lTimeStep = mTimeService->elapsed();

    for (int32_t i = 0; i < mTileMapCount; ++i) {
        mTileMaps[i]->draw();
    }

    glEnable(GL_BLEND);
    glBlendFunc(GL_SRC_ALPHA, GL_ONE_MINUS_SRC_ALPHA);
    for (int32_t i = 0; i < mSpriteCount; ++i) {
        mSprites[i]->draw(lTimeStep);
    }
    glDisable(GL_BLEND);

    if (eglSwapBuffers(mDisplay, mSurface) != EGL_TRUE) {
      Log::error("Error %d swapping buffers.", eglGetError());
        return STATUS_KO;
    }
    return STATUS_OK;
  }
}
```

17. Write `jni/Background.hpp` to declare a game object drawing a background tile map:

```
#ifndef _DBS_BACKGROUND_HPP_
#define _DBS_BACKGROUND_HPP_

#include "Context.hpp"
#include "GraphicsService.hpp"
#include "GraphicsTileMap.hpp"
#include "Types.hpp"

namespace dbs {
    class Background {
    public:
        Background(packt::Context* pContext);

        void spawn();
        void update();

    private:
```

```
            packt::TimeService* mTimeService;
            packt::GraphicsService* mGraphicsService;

            packt::GraphicsTileMap* mTileMap;
            packt::Location mLocation; float mAnimSpeed;
        };
    }
    #endif
```

18. Then implement this class in `jni/Background.cpp`. Register a tile map `tilemap.tmx` which must be copied in `asset` project folder:

 File `tilemap.tmx` is provided with this book in the `Chapter6/Resource` folder.

```
#include "Background.hpp"
#include "Log.hpp"

namespace dbs {
    Background::Background(packt::Context* pContext) :
        mTimeService(pContext->mTimeService),
        mGraphicsService(pContext->mGraphicsService),
        mLocation(), mAnimSpeed(8.0f) {
        mTileMap = mGraphicsService->registerTileMap("tilemap.tmx",
            mGraphicsService->registerTexture("tilemap.png"),
            &mLocation);
    }

    void Background::update() {
        const float SCROLL_PER_SEC = -64.0f;
        float lScrolling = mTimeService->elapsed() * SCROLL_PER_SEC;
        mLocation.translate(0.0f, lScrolling);
    }
}
```

19. We are close to the end. Add a `Background` object in `jni/DroidBlaster.hpp`:

```
#ifndef _PACKT_DROIDBLASTER_HPP_
#define _PACKT_DROIDBLASTER_HPP_

#include "ActivityHandler.hpp"
```

```cpp
#include "Background.hpp"
#include "Context.hpp"
#include "GraphicsService.hpp"
#include "Ship.hpp"
#include "TimeService.hpp"
#include "Types.hpp"

namespace dbs {
    class DroidBlaster : public packt::ActivityHandler {
        ...
        Background mBackground;
        Ship mShip;
    };
}
#endif
```

20. Finally, initialize, and update this `Background` object in `jni/DroidBlaster.cpp`:

```cpp
#include "DroidBlaster.hpp"
#include "Log.hpp"

namespace dbs {
    DroidBlaster::DroidBlaster(packt::Context* pContext) :
        mGraphicsService(pContext->mGraphicsService),
        mTimeService(pContext->mTimeService),
        mBackground(pContext), mShip(pContext)
    {}

    packt::status DroidBlaster::onActivate() {
        if (mGraphicsService->start() != packt::STATUS_OK) {
            return packt::STATUS_KO;
        }

        mBackground.spawn();
        mShip.spawn();

        mTimeService->reset();
        return packt::STATUS_OK;
    }

    status DroidBlaster::onStep() {
        mTimeService->update();

        mBackground.update();
```

```
        if (mGraphicsService->update() != packt::STATUS_OK) {
            return packt::STATUS_KO;
        }
        return packt::STATUS_OK;
    }
}
```

What just happened?

The final result should look like the following. The terrain is scrolling below the ship:

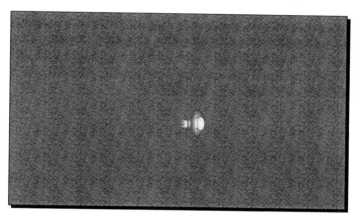

Vertex Buffer Objects, coupled with index buffers, are a really efficient way to render lots of polygons in a single call, by pre-computing vertices and textures coordinates in advance. They largely minimize the number of necessary state changes. Buffer objects are also definitely the way to go for 3D rendering. Note however that if this technique is efficient when many tiles are rendered, it will be much less interesting if your background is only composed of only a few tiles, in which case sprites may be more appropriate.

However, the work done in this part can still be vastly improved. The tile map rendering method here is inefficient: it draws the whole vertex buffer systematically. Hopefully, today's graphic drivers are optimized to clip invisible vertices, which still gives us good performance. But an algorithm could, for example, issue draw calls only for the visible portions of the vertex buffer.

This tile map technique also allows multiple extensions. For example, several tile maps scrolled at different speeds can be superposed to create a **parallax effect**. Of course, one would need to enable alpha blending (at step 16 in `GraphicsService::update()`) to properly blend layers. Let your imagination do the rest!

Summary

OpenGL and graphics, in general, is a really vast domain. One book is not enough to cover it entirely. But drawing 2D graphics with textures and buffer objects opens the door to much more advanced stuff! In more detail, we have learned how to initialize and bind OpenGL ES to the Android windows with EGL. We have also loaded a PNG texture packaged as assets with an external library. Then, we have drawn sprites efficiently with OpenGL ES extensions. This technique should not be overused as it can impact performance when many sprites are *blitted*. Finally, we have rendered a tile map efficiently by pre-computing rendered tiles in vertex and index buffers.

With the knowledge acquired here, the road to OpenGL ES 2 is at a perfectly walkable distance! But if you cannot wait to see 3D graphics, Chapter 9, *Porting Existing Libraries to Android* and Chapter 10, *Towards Professional Gaming*, are your next destination to discover how to embed a 3D engine. But if you are a bit more patient, let's discover how to reach the fourth dimension, the musical one, with OpenSL ES.

7

Playing Sound with OpenSL ES

Multimedia is not only about graphics; it is also about sound and music. Applications in this domain are among the most popular in the Android market. Indeed, music has always been a strong engine for mobile devices sales and music lovers are a target of choice. This is why an OS like Android could probably not go far without some musical talent!

When talking about sound on Android, we should distinguish Java from the native world. Indeed, both sides feature completely different APIs: **MediaPlayer,** **SoundPool, AudioTrack,** *and* **JetPlayer** *on one hand,* **Open SL for Embedded Systems** *(also abbreviated* **OpenSL ES***) on the other hand:*

- ◆ MediaPlayer is more high-level and easy to use. It handles not only music but also video. It is the way to go when simple file playback is sufficient.

- ◆ SoundPool and AudioTrack are more low-level and closer to low latency when playing sound. AudioTrack is the most flexible but also complex to use and allows sound buffer modifications on the fly (by hand!).

- ◆ JetPlayer is more dedicated to the playback of MIDI files. This API can be interesting for dynamic musing synthesis in a multimedia application or game (the see JetBoy example provided with Android SDK).

- ◆ OpenSL ES which aims at offering a cross-platform API to manage audio on embedded systems. In other words, the OpenGL ES for audio. Like GLES, its specification is led by the Khronos Group. On Android, OpenSL ES is in fact implemented on top of AudioTrack API.

OpenSL ES was first released on Android 2.3 Gingerbread and is not available on previous releases (Android 2.2 and lower). While there is a profusion of APIs in Java, OpenSL ES is the only one provided on the native side and is exclusively available on it.

However, OpenSL ES is still immature. The OpenSL specification is still incompletely supported and several limitations shall be expected. In addition, OpenSL specification is implemented in its version 1.0.1 on Android although version 1.1 is already out. Thus, OpenSL ES implementation is not frozen yet and should continue evolving. Some subsequent change may have to be expected in the future.

For this reason, 3D Audio features are available starting from Android 2.3 through OpenSL ES, but only for devices whose system is compiled with the appropriate profile. Indeed, current OpenSL ES specification provides three different profiles, Game, Music, and Phone for different types of devices. At the time this book is written, none of these profiles are supported.

Another important point to consider is that Android is currently not suited for low latency! OpenSL ES API does not improve this situation. This issue is not only related to the system itself but also to the hardware. And if latency is becoming a concern for the Android development team and manufacturers, months will be needed to see decent progress. Anyway, expect OpenSL ES and low-level Java APIs SoundPool and AudioTrack to support low latency sooner or later.

But OpenSL ES has qualities. First, it may be easier to integrate in the architecture of a native application, since it is itself written in C/C++. It does not have to carry a garbage collector on its back. Native code is not interpreted and can be optimized in-depth through assembly code (and the NEON instruction set). These are some of the many reasons to consider it.

The OpenMAX AL low-level multimedia API is also available since NDK R7 (although not fully supported). This API is, however, more related to video/ sound playback and is less powerful than Open SL ES for sound and music. It is somewhat similar to the `android.media.MediaPlayer` on the Java side. Have a look at `http://www.khronos.org/openmax/` for more information.

This chapter is an introduction to the musical capabilities of OpenSL ES on the Android NDK. We are about to discover how to do the following:

◆ Initialize OpenSL ES on Android

◆ Play background music

◆ Play sounds with a sound buffer queue

◆ Record sounds and play them

Initializing OpenSL ES

Let's start this chapter smoothly by initializing OpenSL ES inside a new service, which we are going to call `SoundService` (the term *service* is just a design choice and should not be confused with Android Java services).

 Project DroidBlaster_Part6-4 can be used as a starting point for this part. The resulting project is provided with this book under the name DroidBlaster_Part7-1.

Time for action – creating OpenSL ES engine and output

First, let's create this new class to manage sounds:

1. Open project `DroidBlaster` and create a new file `jni/SoundService.hpp`. First, include OpenSL ES headers: the standard header `OpenSLES.h`, `OpenSLES_Android.h`, and `OpenSLES_AndroidConfiguration.h`. The two latter define objects and methods , and are specifically created for Android. Then create `SoundService` class to do the following:

  ❏ Initialize OpenSL ES with the method `start()`

  ❏ Stop the sound and release OpenSL ES with the method `stop()`

There are two main kinds of *pseudo-object* structures (that is, containing function pointers applied on the structure itself like a C++ object with `this`) in OpenSL ES:

  ❏ **Objects**: These are represented by a `SLObjectItf`, which provides a few common methods to get allocated resources and get object interfaces. This could be roughly compared to an `Object` in Java.

  ❏ **Interfaces**: These give access to object features. There can be several interfaces for an object. Depending on the host device, some interfaces may or may not be available. These are very roughly comparable to interfaces in Java.

In `SoundService`, declare two `SLObjectItf` instances, one for the OpenSL ES engine and other for the speakers. Engines are available through an `SLEngineItf` interface:

```
#ifndef _PACKT_SOUNDSERVICE_HPP_
#define _PACKT_SOUNDSERVICE_HPP_

#include "Types.hpp"

#include <android_native_app_glue.h>
#include <SLES/OpenSLES.h>
#include <SLES/OpenSLES_Android.h>
#include <SLES/OpenSLES_AndroidConfiguration.h>

namespace packt {
    class SoundService {
    public:
        SoundService(android_app* pApplication);

        status start();
        void stop();

    private:
        android_app* mApplication;

        SLObjectItf mEngineObj; SLEngineItf mEngine;
        SLObjectItf mOutputMixObj;
    };
}
#endif
```

2. Implement `SoundService` in `jni/SoundService.cpp`. Write method `start()`:

   ❏ Initialize OpenSL ES engine object (that is, the basic type `SLObjectItf`) with method `slCreateEngine()`. When we create an OpenSL ES object, the specific interfaces we are going to use have to be indicated. Here, we request (as compulsory) the `SL_IID_ENGINE` interface to create other OpenSL ES objects, the engine being the central object of the OpenSL ES API.

 Android OpenSL ES implementation is not really strict. Forgetting to declare some required interfaces does not mean you will not be allowed to access them later.

❏ Then, invoke `Realize()` on the engine object. Any OpenSL ES object needs to be **realized** to allocate required internal resources before use.

❏ Finally, retrieve `SLEngineItf`-specific interface.

❏ The engine interface gives us the possibility to instantiate an audio output mix with the method `CreateOutputMix()`. The audio output mix defined here delivers sound to default speakers. It is rather autonomous (played sound is sent automatically to the speaker), so there is no need to request any specific interface here.

```cpp
#include "SoundService.hpp"
#include "Log.hpp"

namespace packt {
    SoundService::SoundService(android_app* pApplication):
        mApplication(pApplication),
        mEngineObj(NULL), mEngine(NULL),
        mOutputMixObj(NULL)
    {}

    status SoundService::start() {
        Log::info("Starting SoundService.");
        SLresult lRes;
        const SLuint32      lEngineMixIIDCount = 1;
const SLInterfaceID lEngineMixIIDs[]={SL_IID_ENGINE};
const SLboolean lEngineMixReqs[]={SL_BOOLEAN_TRUE};
const SLuint32 lOutputMixIIDCount=0;
const SLInterfaceID lOutputMixIIDs[]={};
const SLboolean lOutputMixReqs[]={};

lRes = slCreateEngine(&mEngineObj, 0, NULL,
    lEngineMixIIDCount, lEngineMixIIDs, lEngineMixReqs);
if (lRes != SL_RESULT_SUCCESS) goto ERROR;
lRes=(*mEngineObj)->Realize(mEngineObj,SL_BOOLEAN_FALSE);
if (lRes != SL_RESULT_SUCCESS) goto ERROR;
lRes=(*mEngineObj)->GetInterface(mEngineObj,
    SL_IID_ENGINE, &mEngine);
if (lRes != SL_RESULT_SUCCESS) goto ERROR;

lRes=(*mEngine)->CreateOutputMix(mEngine,
 &mOutputMixObj,lOutputMixIIDCount,lOutputMixIIDs,
  lOutputMixReqs);
```

```
                    lRes=(*mOutputMixObj)->Realize(mOutputMixObj,
                      SL_BOOLEAN_FALSE);

                   return STATUS_OK;

                 ERROR:
                  Packt::Log::error("Error while starting SoundService.");
                  stop();
                  return STATUS_KO;
                 }
                 ...
```

3. Write the `stop()` method to destroy what has been created in `start()`:

    ```
    ...
        void SoundService::stop() {
            if (mOutputMixObj != NULL) {
                (*mOutputMixObj)->Destroy(mOutputMixObj);
                mOutputMixObj = NULL;
            }
            if (mEngineObj != NULL) {
                (*mEngineObj)->Destroy(mEngineObj);
                mEngineObj = NULL; mEngine = NULL;
            }
        }
    }
    ```

    Now, we can embed our new service:

4. Open existing file `jni/Context.hpp` and define a new entry for
    SoundService:

    ```
    #ifndef _PACKT_CONTEXT_HPP_
    #define _PACKT_CONTEXT_HPP_

    #include "Types.hpp"

    namespace packt {
        class GraphicsService;
        class SoundService;
        class TimeService;

        struct Context {
            GraphicsService* mGraphicsService;
    ```

```
        SoundService*      mSoundService;
        TimeService*       mTimeService;
    };
}
#endif
```

5. Then, **append** SoundService inside jni/DroidBlaster.hpp:

```
#ifndef _PACKT_DROIDBLASTER_HPP_
#define _PACKT_DROIDBLASTER_HPP_

#include "ActivityHandler.hpp"
#include "Background.hpp"
#include "Context.hpp"
#include "GraphicsService.hpp"
#include "Ship.hpp"
#include "SoundService.hpp"
#include "TimeService.hpp"
#include "Types.hpp"

namespace dbs {
    class DroidBlaster : public packt::ActivityHandler {
        ...

    private:
        packt::GraphicsService* mGraphicsService;
        packt::SoundService*    mSoundService;
        packt::TimeService*     mTimeService;

        Background mBackground;
        Ship mShip;
    };
}
#endif
```

6. Create, start, and stop the sound service in jni/DroidBlaster.cpp source file. Code implementation should be trivial:

```
#include "DroidBlaster.hpp"
#include "Log.hpp"

namespace dbs {
    DroidBlaster::DroidBlaster(packt::Context* pContext) :
        mGraphicsService(pContext->mGraphicsService),
        mSoundService(pContext->mSoundService),
```

```
        mTimeService(pContext->mTimeService),
        mBackground(pContext), mShip(pContext)
{}

packt::status DroidBlaster::onActivate() {
    if (mGraphicsService->start() != packt::STATUS_OK) {
        return packt::STATUS_KO;
    }
    if (mSoundService->start() != packt::STATUS_OK) {
        return packt::STATUS_KO;
    }

    mBackground.spawn();
    mShip.spawn();

    mTimeService->reset();
    return packt::STATUS_OK;
}

void DroidBlaster::onDeactivate() {
    mGraphicsService->stop();
    mSoundService->stop();
}
...
}
```

7. Finally, instantiate the sound service in `jni/Main.cpp`:

```
#include "Context.hpp"
#include "DroidBlaster.hpp"
#include "EventLoop.hpp"
#include "GraphicsService.hpp"
#include "SoundService.hpp"
#include "TimeService.hpp"

void android_main(android_app* pApplication) {
    packt::TimeService lTimeService;
    packt::GraphicsService lGraphicsService(pApplication,
        &lTimeService);
    packt::SoundService lSoundService(pApplication);

    packt::Context lContext = { &lGraphicsService, &lSoundService,
```

```
                  &lTimeService };

          packt::EventLoop lEventLoop(pApplication);
          dbs::DroidBlaster lDroidBlaster(&lContext);
          lEventLoop.run(&lDroidBlaster);
     }
Link to libOpenSLES.so in the jni/Android.mk file:
LOCAL_PATH := $(call my-dir)

include $(CLEAR_VARS)

LS_CPP=$(subst $(1)/,,$(wildcard $(1)/*.cpp))
LOCAL_CFLAGS       := -DRAPIDXML_NO_EXCEPTIONS
LOCAL_MODULE       := droidblaster
LOCAL_SRC_FILES := $(call LS_CPP,$(LOCAL_PATH))
LOCAL_LDLIBS       := -landroid -llog -lEGL -lGLESv1_CM -lOpenSLES

LOCAL_STATIC_LIBRARIES := android_native_app_glue png

include $(BUILD_SHARED_LIBRARY)

$(call import-module,android/native_app_glue)
$(call import-module,libpng)
```

What just happened?

Run the application and check that no error is logged. We have initialized OpenSL ES library which gives us access to efficient sound handling primitives directly from native code. The current code does not perform anything apart from initialization. No sound comes out from the speakers yet.

The entry point to OpenSL ES here is the SLEngineItf, which is mainly an OpenSL ES object factory. It can create a *channel* to an output device (a speaker or anything else) as well as sound players or recorders (and even more!), as we will see later in this chapter.

The SLOutputMixItf is the object representing the audio output. Generally, this will be the device speaker or headset. Although OpenSL ES specification allows enumerating available output (and also input) devices, NDK implementation is not mature enough to obtain or select proper one (SLAudioIODeviceCapabilitiesItf, the official interface to obtain such an information). So when dealing with output and input device selection (only input device for recorders needs to be specified currently), prefer sticking to default values: SL_DEFAULTDEVICEID_AUDIOINPUT and SL_DEFAULTDEVICEID_AUDIOOUTPUT defined in OpenSLES.h.

Current Android NDK implementation allows only one engine per application (this should not be an issue) and at most 32 created objects. Beware however that creation of any object can fail as this is dependent on available system resources.

More on OpenSL ES philosophy

OpenSL ES is different from its graphics compatriot GLES, partly because it does not have a long history to carry. It is constructed on an (more or less...) object-oriented principle based on Objects and Interfaces. The following definitions come from the official specification:

> An **object** is an abstraction of a set of resources, assigned for a well-defined set of tasks, and the state of these resources. An object has a type determined on its creation. The object type determines the set of tasks that an object can perform. This can be considered similar to a class in C++.

> An **interface** is an abstraction of a set of related features that a certain object provides. An interface includes a set of methods, which are functions of the interface. An interface also has a type which determines the exact set of methods of the interface. We can define the interface itself as a combination of its type and the object to which it is related.

> An **interface ID** identifies an interface type. This identifier is used within the source code to refer to the interface type.

An OpenSL ES object is set up in few steps as follows:

1. Instantiating it through a build method (belonging usually to the engine).
2. Realizing it to allocate necessary resources.
3. Retrieving object interfaces. A basic object only has a very limited set of operations (`Realize()`, `Resume()`, `Destroy()`, and so on). Interfaces give access to real object features and describes what operations can be performed on an object, for example, a Play interface to play or pause a sound.

Any interfaces can be requested but only the one supported by the object is going to be successfully retrieved. You cannot retrieve the record interface for an audio player because it returns (sometimes it is annoying!) `SL_RESULT_FEATURE_UNSUPPORTED` (error code 12). In technical terms, an OpenSL ES interface is a structure containing function pointers (initialized by OpenSL ES implementation) with a self parameter to simulate C++ objects and `this`, for example:

```
struct SLObjectItf_ {
    SLresult (*Realize) (SLObjectItf self, SLboolean async);
    SLresult (*Resume) ( SLObjectItf self, SLboolean async);
    ...
}
```

Here, `Realize()`, `Resume()`, and so on are object methods that can be applied on an `SLObjectItf` object. The approach is identical for interfaces.

For more detailed information on what OpenSL ES can provide, refer to the specification on Khronos web site: `http://www.khronos.org/opensles` as well as the OpenSL ES documentation in Android NDK `docs` directory. Android implementation does not fully respect the specification, at least for now. So do not be disappointed when discovering that only a limited subset of the specification (especially sample codes) works on Android.

Playing music files

OpenSL ES is initialized, but the only thing coming out of speakers yet is silence! So what about finding a nice piece of music (sometimes abbreviated BGM) and playing it natively with Android NDK? OpenSL ES provides the necessary stuff to read music files such as MP3s.

Project DroidBlaster_Part7-1 can be used as a starting point for this part. The resulting project is provided with this book under the name DroidBlaster_Part7-2.

Time for action – playing background music

Let's improve the code written in the previous part to read and play an MP3 file:

1. MP3 files are opened by OpenSL ES using a POSIX file descriptor, pointing to the file. Improve `jni/ResourceManager.cpp` created in the previous chapters by injecting a new structure `ResourceDescriptor` and appending a new method `descript()`:

```
#ifndef _PACKT_RESOURCE_HPP_
#define _PACKT_RESOURCE_HPP_

#include "Types.hpp"

#include <android_native_app_glue.h>

namespace packt {
    struct ResourceDescriptor {
        int32_t mDescriptor;
        off_t mStart;
        off_t mLength;
    };
```

```
class Resource {
public:
    ...

    off_t getLength();
    const void* bufferize();

    ResourceDescriptor descript();

private:
    ...
};
}
#endif
```

2. Implementation in `ResourceManager.cpp`, of course, makes use of the asset manager API to open the descriptor and fill a `ResourceDescriptor` structure:

```
...
namespace packt {
    ...
    ResourceDescriptor Resource::descript() {
        ResourceDescriptor lDescriptor = { -1, 0, 0 };
        AAsset* lAsset = AAssetManager_open(mAssetManager, mPath,
                                            AASSET_MODE_UNKNOWN);
        if (lAsset != NULL) {
            lDescriptor.mDescriptor = AAsset_openFileDescriptor(
                lAsset, &lDescriptor.mStart, &lDescriptor.
mLength);
            AAsset_close(lAsset);
        }
        return lDescriptor;
    }
}
```

3. Go back to `jni/SoundService.hpp` and define two methods, `playBGM()` and `stopBGM()`, to play a background music.

   Also declare an OpenSL ES object for the music player along with the following interfaces:

   ❑ `SLPlayItf`: This plays and stops music files
   ❑ `SLSeekItf`: This controls position and looping

```
. . .
namespace packt
{
    class SoundService {
    public:
        . . .

        status playBGM(const char* pPath);
        void stopBGM();

    . . .

    private:
        . . .

        SLObjectItf mBGMPlayerObj; SLPlayItf mBGMPlayer;
        SLSeekItf mBGMPlayerSeek;
    };
}
#endif
```

4. Start implementing jni/SoundService.cpp. Include Resource.hpp to get access to asset file descriptors. Initialize new members in constructor and update stop() to stop the background music automatically (or some users are not going to be happy!):

```
#include "SoundService.hpp"
#include "Resource.hpp"
#include "Log.hpp"

namespace packt {
    SoundService::SoundService(android_app* pApplication) :
        mApplication(pApplication),
        mEngineObj(NULL), mEngine(NULL),
        mOutputMixObj(NULL),
        mBGMPlayerObj(NULL), mBGMPlayer(NULL), mBGMPlayerSeek(NULL)
    {}

    . . .

    void SoundService::stop() {
        stopBGM();
```

```
            if (mOutputMixObj != NULL) {
                (*mOutputMixObj)->Destroy(mOutputMixObj);
                mOutputMixObj = NULL;
            }
            if (mEngineObj != NULL) {
                (*mEngineObj)->Destroy(mEngineObj);
                mEngineObj = NULL; mEngine = NULL;
            }
        }
    ...
```

5. Enrich `SoundService.cpp` with playback features by implementing `playBGM()`.
First we need to describe our audio setup through two main structures:
`SLDataSource` and `SLDataSink`. The first describes the audio input channel
and the second, the audio output channel.

Here, we configure the data source as a **MIME** source so that file type gets detected
automatically from file descriptor. File descriptor is, of course, opened with a call to
`ResourceManager::descript()`.

Data sink (that is, destination channel) is configured with the `OutputMix` object
created in the first part of this chapter while initializing OpenSL ES engine
(and which refers to default audio output, that is, speakers or headset):

```
    ...
    status SoundService::playBGM(const char* pPath) {
        SLresult lRes;

        Resource lResource(mApplication, pPath);
        ResourceDescriptor lDescriptor = lResource.descript();
        if (lDescriptor.mDescriptor < 0) {
            Log::info("Could not open BGM file");
            return STATUS_KO;
        }

        SLDataLocator_AndroidFD lDataLocatorIn;
        lDataLocatorIn.locatorType = SL_DATALOCATOR_ANDROIDFD;
        lDataLocatorIn.fd          = lDescriptor.mDescriptor;
        lDataLocatorIn.offset      = lDescriptor.mStart;
        lDataLocatorIn.length      = lDescriptor.mLength;

        SLDataFormat_MIME lDataFormat;
        lDataFormat.formatType     = SL_DATAFORMAT_MIME;
```

```
lDataFormat.mimeType        = NULL;
lDataFormat.containerType = SL_CONTAINERTYPE_UNSPECIFIED;

SLDataSource lDataSource;
lDataSource.pLocator = &lDataLocatorIn;
lDataSource.pFormat  = &lDataFormat;

SLDataLocator_OutputMix lDataLocatorOut;
lDataLocatorOut.locatorType = SL_DATALOCATOR_OUTPUTMIX;
lDataLocatorOut.outputMix   = mOutputMixObj;

SLDataSink lDataSink;
lDataSink.pLocator = &lDataLocatorOut;
lDataSink.pFormat  = NULL;
...
```

6. Then create the OpenSL ES audio player. As always with OpenSL ES objects, instantiate it through the engine first and then realize it. Two interfaces SL_IID_PLAY and SL_IID_SEEK are imperatively required:

```
...
const SLuint32 lBGMPlayerIIDCount = 2;
const SLInterfaceID lBGMPlayerIIDs[] =
    { SL_IID_PLAY, SL_IID_SEEK };
const SLboolean lBGMPlayerReqs[] =
    { SL_BOOLEAN_TRUE, SL_BOOLEAN_TRUE };

lRes = (*mEngine)->CreateAudioPlayer(mEngine,
    &mBGMPlayerObj, &lDataSource, &lDataSink,
    lBGMPlayerIIDCount, lBGMPlayerIIDs, lBGMPlayerReqs);
if (lRes != SL_RESULT_SUCCESS) goto ERROR;
lRes = (*mBGMPlayerObj)->Realize(mBGMPlayerObj,
    SL_BOOLEAN_FALSE);
if (lRes != SL_RESULT_SUCCESS) goto ERROR;

lRes = (*mBGMPlayerObj)->GetInterface(mBGMPlayerObj,
    SL_IID_PLAY, &mBGMPlayer);
if (lRes != SL_RESULT_SUCCESS) goto ERROR;
lRes = (*mBGMPlayerObj)->GetInterface(mBGMPlayerObj,
    SL_IID_SEEK, &mBGMPlayerSeek);
if (lRes != SL_RESULT_SUCCESS) goto ERROR;
...
```

7. Finally, using the play and seek interfaces, switch the playback in loop mode (that is, music keeps playing) from the track beginning (that is, 0 ms) until its end (SL_TIME_UNKNOWN) and then start playing (SetPlayState() with SL_PLAYSTATE_PLAYING).

```
...
        lRes = (*mBGMPlayerSeek)->SetLoop(mBGMPlayerSeek,
            SL_BOOLEAN_TRUE, 0, SL_TIME_UNKNOWN);
        if (lRes != SL_RESULT_SUCCESS) goto ERROR;
        lRes = (*mBGMPlayer)->SetPlayState(mBGMPlayer,
            SL_PLAYSTATE_PLAYING);
        if (lRes != SL_RESULT_SUCCESS) goto ERROR;

        return STATUS_OK;

    ERROR:
        return STATUS_KO;
    }
...
```

8. The last method stopBGM() is shorter. It stops and then destroys the player:

```
...
    void SoundService::stopBGM() {
        if (mBGMPlayer != NULL) {
            SLuint32 lBGMPlayerState;
            (*mBGMPlayerObj)->GetState(mBGMPlayerObj,
                &lBGMPlayerState);
            if (lBGMPlayerState == SL_OBJECT_STATE_REALIZED) {
                (*mBGMPlayer)->SetPlayState(mBGMPlayer,
                    SL_PLAYSTATE_PAUSED);

                (*mBGMPlayerObj)->Destroy(mBGMPlayerObj);
                mBGMPlayerObj = NULL;
                mBGMPlayer = NULL;
                mBGMPlayerSeek = NULL;
            }
        }
    }
```

9. Copy an MP3 file into the `assets` directory and name it `bgm.mp3`.

 File `bgm.mp3` is provided with this book in `Chapter7/Resource`.

10. Finally, in `jni/DroidBlaster.cpp`, start music playback right after `SoundService` is started:

```cpp
#include "DroidBlaster.hpp"
#include "Log.hpp"

namespace dbs {
    ...
    packt::status DroidBlaster::onActivate() {
        packt::Log::info("Activating DroidBlaster");

        if (mGraphicsService->start() != packt::STATUS_OK) {
            return packt::STATUS_KO;
        }
        if (mSoundService->start() != packt::STATUS_OK) {
            return packt::STATUS_KO;
        }

        mSoundService->playBGM

        mBackground.spawn();
        mShip.spawn();

        mTimeService->reset();
        return packt::STATUS_OK;
    }

    void DroidBlaster::onDeactivate() {
        mGraphicsService->stop();
        mSoundService->stop();
    }
    ...
}
```

What just happened?

We have discovered how to play a music clip from an MP3 file. Playback loops until the game is terminated. When using a MIME data source, the file type is auto-detected. Several formats are currently supported format in Gingerbread including Wave PCM, Wave alaw, Wave ulaw, MP3, Ogg Vorbis and so on. MIDI playback is currently not supported.

You may be surprised to see that, in the example, `startBGM()` and `stopBGM()` recreates and destroys the audio player, respectively. The reason is that there is currently no way to change a MIME data source without completely recreating the OpenSL ES `AudioPlayer` object. So although this technique is fine to play a long clip, it is not adapted for playing short sound dynamically.

The way the sample code is presented here is typical of how OpenSL ES works. The OpenSL ES engine object, that kind of object factory, creates an `AudioPlayer` object which cannot do much in that state. First, it needs to be realized to allocate necessary resources. But that is not enough. It needs to retrieve the right interfaces, like the `SL_IID_PLAY` interface to change audio player state to playing/stopped. Then OpenSL API can be effectively used.

That is quite some work, taking into account result verification (as any call is susceptible to fail), which kind of clutters the code. Getting inside this API can take a little bit more time than usual, but once understood, these concepts become rather easy to deal with.

Playing sounds

The technique presented to play BGM from a MIME source is very practical but sadly, not flexible enough. Recreating an `AudioPlayer` object is not necessary and accessing asset files each time is not good in term of efficiency.

So when it comes to playing sounds quickly in response to an event and generating them dynamically, we need to use a sound buffer queue. Each sound is preloaded or even generated into a memory buffer, and placed into a queue when playback is requested. No need to access a file at runtime!

A sound buffer, in current OpenSL ES Android implementation, can contain **PCM** data. PCM, which stands for **Pulse Code Modulation**, is a data format dedicated to the representation of digital sounds. It is the format used in CD and in some Wave files. A PCM can be Mono (same sound on all speakers) or Stereo (different sound for left and right speakers if available).

PCM is not compressed and is not efficient in terms of storage (just compare a musical CD with a data CD full of MP3). But this format is lossless and offers the best quality. Quality depends on the sampling rate: analog sounds are represented digitally as a series of *measure* (that is, sample) of the sound signal.

A sound sample at 44100 Hz (that is 44100 *measures* per second) has a better quality but also takes more place than a sound sampled at 16000 Hz. Also, each measure can be represented with a more or less fine degree of precision (the encoding). On current Android implementation:

- A sound can use 8000 Hz, 11025 Hz, 12000 Hz, 16000 Hz, 22050 Hz, 24000 Hz, 32000 Hz, 44100 Hz, or 48000 Hz sampling,
- A sample can be encoded on 8-bit unsigned or 16-bit signed (finer precision) in **little-endian** or **big-endian**.

In the following step-by-step tutorial, we are going to use a raw PCM file encoded over 16-bit in little-endian.

Project DroidBlaster_Part7-2 can be used as a starting point for this part. The resulting project is provided with this book under the name DroidBlaster_Part7-3.

Time for action – creating and playing a sound buffer queue

First, let's create a new object to hold sound buffers:

1. In `jni/Sound.hpp`, create a new class `Sound` to manage a sound buffer. It features a method `load()` to load a PCM file and `unload()` to release it:

```
#ifndef _PACKT_SOUND_HPP_
#define _PACKT_SOUND_HPP_

class SoundService;

#include "Context.hpp"
#include "Resource.hpp"
#include "Types.hpp"

namespace packt {
    class Sound {
    public:
        Sound(android_app* pApplication, const char* pPath);

        const char* getPath();

        status load();
        status unload();
```

```
        private:
            friend class SoundService;

        private:
            Resource mResource;
            uint8_t* mBuffer; off_t mLength;
    };
}
#endif
```

2.   Sound loading implementation is quite simple: it creates a buffer with the same size as the PCM file and loads all file content in it:

```
#include "Sound.hpp"
#include "Log.hpp"

#include <png.h>
#include <SLES/OpenSLES.h>
#include <SLES/OpenSLES_Android.h>
#include <SLES/OpenSLES_AndroidConfiguration.h>

namespace packt {
    Sound::Sound(android_app* pApplication, const char* pPath) :
        mResource(pApplication, pPath),
        mBuffer(NULL), mLength(0)
    {}

    const char* Sound::getPath() {
        return mResource.getPath();
    }

    status Sound::load() {
        status lRes;

        if (mResource.open() != STATUS_OK) {
            return STATUS_KO;
        }

        mLength = mResource.getLength();
        mBuffer = new uint8_t[mLength];
        lRes = mResource.read(mBuffer, mLength);
        mResource.close();

        if (lRes != STATUS_OK) {
            Log::error("Error while reading PCM sound.");
```

```
            return STATUS_KO;
        } else {
            return STATUS_OK;
        }
    }

    status Sound::unload() {
        delete[] mBuffer;
        mBuffer = NULL; mLength = 0;

        return STATUS_OK;
    }
}
```

We can manage sound buffers in the dedicated sound service.

3. Open `SoudService.hpp` and create a few new methods:

- ❑ `registerSound()` to load and manage a new sound buffer
- ❑ `playSound()` to send a sound buffer to the sound play queue
- ❑ `startSoundPlayer()` to initialize the sound queue when `SoundService` starts

A sound queue can be manipulated through `SLPlayItf` and `SLBufferQueueItf` interfaces. Sound buffers are stored in fixed-size C++ array:

```
#ifndef _PACKT_SOUNDSERVICE_HPP_
#define _PACKT_SOUNDSERVICE_HPP_

#include "Sound.hpp"
#include "Types.hpp"

...

namespace packt {
    class SoundService {
    public:
        ...
        Sound* registerSound(const char* pPath);
        void playSound(Sound* pSound);

    private:
        status startSoundPlayer();

    private:
```

```
    . . .
        SLObjectItf mPlayerObj; SLPlayItf mPlayer;
        SLBufferQueueItf mPlayerQueue;
        Sound* mSounds[32]; int32_t mSoundCount;
    };
}
#endif
```

4. Now, open `jni/SoundService.cpp` implementation file. Update `start()` to call `startSoundPlayer()` and load sound resources registered with `registerSound()`. Also create a destructor to release these resources when application exits:

```
. . .
namespace packt {
    SoundService::SoundService(android_app* pApplication) :
        . . .,
        mPlayerObj(NULL), mPlayer(NULL), mPlayerQueue(NULL),
        mSounds(), mSoundCount(0)
    {}

    SoundService::~SoundService() {
        for (int32_t i = 0; i < mSoundCount; ++i) {
            delete mSounds[i];
            mSoundCount = 0;
        }
    }

    status SoundService::start() {
        . . .

        if (startSoundPlayer() != STATUS_OK) goto ERROR;

        for (int32_t i = 0; i < mSoundCount; ++i) {
            if (mSounds[i]->load() != STATUS_OK) goto ERROR;
        }
        return STATUS_OK;

    ERROR:
        packt::Log::error("Error while starting SoundService");
        stop();
        return STATUS_KO;
    }

    . . .
```

```
Sound* SoundService::registerSound(const char* pPath) {
    for (int32_t i = 0; i < mSoundCount; ++i) {
        if (strcmp(pPath, mSounds[i]->getPath()) == 0) {
            return mSounds[i];
        }
    }

    Sound* lSound = new Sound(mApplication, pPath);
    mSounds[mSoundCount++] = lSound;
    return lSound;
}
...
```

5. Write `startSoundPlayer()`, beginning with the `SLDataSource` and `SLDataSink` to describe the input and output channel. On the opposite to the BGM player, the data format structure is not `SLDataFormat_MIME` (to open an MP3 file) but a `SLDataFormat_PCM` with sampling, encoding, and endianness information. Sounds need to be Mono (that is, only one sound channel for both left and right speakers when available). The queue is created with the Android-specific extension `SLDataLocator_AndroidSimpleBufferQueue()`:

...

```
status SoundService::startSoundPlayer() {
    SLresult lRes;

    // Set-up sound audio source.
    SLDataLocator_AndroidSimpleBufferQueue lDataLocatorIn;
    lDataLocatorIn.locatorType =
        SL_DATALOCATOR_ANDROIDSIMPLEBUFFERQUEUE;
    // At most one buffer in the queue.
    lDataLocatorIn.numBuffers = 1;

    SLDataFormat_PCM lDataFormat;
    lDataFormat.formatType = SL_DATAFORMAT_PCM;
    lDataFormat.numChannels = 1; // Mono sound.
    lDataFormat.samplesPerSec = SL_SAMPLINGRATE_44_1;
    lDataFormat.bitsPerSample = SL_PCMSAMPLEFORMAT_FIXED_16;
    lDataFormat.containerSize = SL_PCMSAMPLEFORMAT_FIXED_16;
    lDataFormat.channelMask = SL_SPEAKER_FRONT_CENTER;
    lDataFormat.endianness = SL_BYTEORDER_LITTLEENDIAN;

    SLDataSource lDataSource;
    lDataSource.pLocator = &lDataLocatorIn;
    lDataSource.pFormat = &lDataFormat;
```

```
SLDataLocator_OutputMix lDataLocatorOut;
lDataLocatorOut.locatorType = SL_DATALOCATOR_OUTPUTMIX;
lDataLocatorOut.outputMix = mOutputMixObj;

SLDataSink lDataSink;
lDataSink.pLocator = &lDataLocatorOut;
lDataSink.pFormat = NULL;
```

...

6. Then, in `startSoundPlayer()`, create and realize the sound player. We are going to need its `SL_IID_PLAY` and also `SL_IID_BUFFERQUEUE` interface now available thanks to the data locator configured in previous step:

...

```
const SLuint32 lSoundPlayerIIDCount = 2;
const SLInterfaceID lSoundPlayerIIDs[] =
    { SL_IID_PLAY, SL_IID_BUFFERQUEUE };
const SLboolean lSoundPlayerReqs[] =
    { SL_BOOLEAN_TRUE, SL_BOOLEAN_TRUE };

lRes = (*mEngine)->CreateAudioPlayer(mEngine, &mPlayerObj,
    &lDataSource, &lDataSink, lSoundPlayerIIDCount,
    lSoundPlayerIIDs, lSoundPlayerReqs);
if (lRes != SL_RESULT_SUCCESS) goto ERROR;
lRes = (*mPlayerObj)->Realize(mPlayerObj, SL_BOOLEAN_FALSE);
if (lRes != SL_RESULT_SUCCESS) goto ERROR;

lRes = (*mPlayerObj)->GetInterface(mPlayerObj, SL_IID_PLAY,
    &mPlayer);
if (lRes != SL_RESULT_SUCCESS) goto ERROR;
lRes = (*mPlayerObj)->GetInterface(mPlayerObj,
    SL_IID_BUFFERQUEUE, &mPlayerQueue);
if (lRes != SL_RESULT_SUCCESS) goto ERROR;
```

...

7. To finish with `startSoundPlayer()`, start the queue by setting it in the playing state. This does not actually mean that a sound is played. The queue is empty so that would not be possible. But if a sound gets enqueued, then it is automatically played:

...

```
lRes = (*mPlayer)->SetPlayState(mPlayer,
    SL_PLAYSTATE_PLAYING);
if (lRes != SL_RESULT_SUCCESS) goto ERROR;
```

```
        return STATUS_OK;

    ERROR:
        packt::Log::error("Error while starting SoundPlayer");
        return STATUS_KO;
    }
...
```

8. Update method `stop()` to destroy the sound player and free sound buffers:

```
...
    void SoundService::stop() {
        stopBGM();

        if (mOutputMixObj != NULL) {
            (*mOutputMixObj)->Destroy(mOutputMixObj);
            mOutputMixObj = NULL;
        }
        if (mEngineObj != NULL) {
            (*mEngineObj)->Destroy(mEngineObj);
            mEngineObj = NULL; mEngine = NULL;
        }

        if (mPlayerObj != NULL) {
            (*mPlayerObj)->Destroy(mPlayerObj);
           mPlayerObj = NULL; mPlayer = NULL; mPlayerQueue = NULL;
        }

        for (int32_t i = 0; i < mSoundCount; ++i) {
            mSounds[i]->unload();
        }
    }
...
```

9. Terminate `SoundService` by writing `playSound()`, which first stops any sound being played and then enqueue the new sound buffer to play:

```
...
    void SoundService::playSound(Sound* pSound) {
        SLresult lRes;
        SLuint32 lPlayerState;
        (*mPlayerObj)->GetState(mPlayerObj, &lPlayerState);
        if (lPlayerState == SL_OBJECT_STATE_REALIZED) {
            int16_t* lBuffer = (int16_t*) pSound->mBuffer;
            off_t    lLength = pSound->mLength;
```

```
        // Removes any sound from the queue.
        lRes = (*mPlayerQueue)->Clear(mPlayerQueue);
        if (lRes != SL_RESULT_SUCCESS) goto ERROR;

        // Plays the new sound.
        lRes = (*mPlayerQueue)->Enqueue(mPlayerQueue, lBuffer,
            lLength);
        if (lRes != SL_RESULT_SUCCESS) goto ERROR;
    }
    return;

ERROR:
    packt::Log::error("Error trying to play sound");
    }
}
```

Let's play a sound file when the game starts:

10. Store a reference to sound buffer in file `jni/DroidBlaster.hpp`:

```
#ifndef _PACKT_DROIDBLASTER_HPP_
#define _PACKT_DROIDBLASTER_HPP_

#include "ActivityHandler.hpp"
#include "Background.hpp"
#include "Context.hpp"
#include "GraphicsService.hpp"
#include "Ship.hpp"
#include "Sound.hpp"
#include "SoundService.hpp"
#include "TimeService.hpp"
#include "Types.hpp"

namespace dbs {
    class DroidBlaster : public packt::ActivityHandler {
        ...

    private:
        ...
        Background mBackground;
        Ship mShip;
        packt::Sound* mStartSound;
    };
}
#endif
```

11. Finally, play the sound in `jni/DroidBlaster.cpp` when the application is activated:

```
#include "DroidBlaster.hpp"
#include "Log.hpp"

namespace dbs {
    DroidBlaster::DroidBlaster(packt::Context* pContext) :
        mGraphicsService(pContext->mGraphicsService),
        mSoundService(pContext->mSoundService),
        mTimeService(pContext->mTimeService),
        mBackground(pContext), mShip(pContext),
        mStartSound(mSoundService->registerSound("start.pcm"))
    {}

    packt::status DroidBlaster::onActivate() {
        ...
        mSoundService->playBGM("bgm.mp3");
        mSoundService->playSound(mStartSound);

        mBackground.spawn();
        mShip.spawn();
        ...
    }
}
```

What just happened?

We have discovered how to preload sounds in a buffer and play them as needed. What differentiates the sound playing technique from the BGM one showed earlier is the use of a buffer queue. A buffer queue is exactly what its name reveals: a FIFO (First In, First Out) collection of sound buffers played one after the other. Buffers are *enqueued* for playback when all previous buffers are played.

Buffers can be recycled. This technique is essential in combination with streaming files: two or more buffers are filled and sent to the queue. When first buffer has finished playing, the second one starts while the first buffer is filled with new data. As soon as possible, the first buffer is enqueued before the queue gets empty. This process repeats forever until playback is over. In addition, buffers are raw data and can thus be processed or filtered on the fly.

In the present tutorial, because `DroidBlaster` does not need to play more than one sound at once and no form of streaming is necessary, the buffer queue size is simply set to one buffer (step 5, `lDataLocatorIn.numBuffers = 1;`). In addition, we want new sounds to pre-empt older ones, which explains why queue is systematically cleared. Your OpenSL ES architecture should be of course adapted to your needs. If it becomes necessary to play several sounds simultaneously, then several audio players (and therefore buffer queues) should be created.

Sound buffers are stored in the PCM format, which does not self-describe its internal format. Sampling, encoding, and other format information needs to be selected in the application code. Although this is fine for most of them, a solution, if that is not flexible enough, can be to load a Wave file which contains all the necessary header information.

If you have read carefully the second part of this chapter about playing BGM, you will remember that we have used a MIME data source to load different kind of sound files, Waves included. So why not use a MIME source instead of a PCM source? Well, this is because a buffer queue works only with PCM data. Although improvements can be expected in the future, audio file decoding still need to be performed by hand. Trying to connect a MIME source to a buffer queue (like we are going to do with the recorder) will cause an `SL_RESULT_FEATURE_UNSUPPORTED` error.

OpenSL ES has been updated in NDK R7 and now allows decoding compressed files such as MP3 files to PCM buffers.

Exporting PCM sounds with Audacity

A great open source tool to filter and sequence sounds is **Audacity**. It allows altering sampling rate and modifying channels (Mono/Stereo). Audacity is able to export as well as import sound as raw PCM data.

Event callback

It is possible to detect when a sound has finished playing using callbacks. A callback can be set up by calling the `RegisterCallback()` method on a queue (but other type of objects can also register callbacks) like in the following example:

```
...

namespace packt {
    class SoundService {
        ...
```

```
      private:
          static void callback_sound(SLBufferQueueItf pObject,
              void* pContext);
          ...
      };
}
#endif
```

For example, the callback can receive this, that is, a SoundService self reference, to allow processing with any *contextual* information, if needed. Although this is facultative, an event mask is set up to ensure callback is called only when event SL_PLAYEVENT_HEADATEND (player has finished playing the buffer) is triggered. A few others play events are available in OpenSLES.h:

```
      ...

namespace packt {
      ...
      status SoundService::startSoundPlayer() {
          ...


          // Registers a callback called when sound is finished.
          lResult = (*mPlayerQueue)->RegisterCallback(mPlayerQueue,
              callback_sound, this);
          slCheckErrorWithStatus(lResult, "Problem registering player
callback (Error %d).", lResult);
          lResult = (*mPlayer)->SetCallbackEventsMask(mPlayer, SL_
PLAYEVENT_HEADATEND);
          slCheckErrorWithStatus(lResult, "Problem registering player
callback mask (Error %d).", lResult);


          // Starts the sound player
          ...
      }


      void callback_sound(SLBufferQueueItf pBufferQueue, void *context)
      {
          // Context can be casted back to the original type.
          SoundService& lService = *(SoundService*) context;
          ...
          Log::info("Ended playing sound.");
      }
      ...
}
```

Now, when a buffer ends playing, a message is logged. Operations like, for example, enqueuing a new buffer (to handle streaming for example) can be performed.

> **Callback and threading**
>
> Callbacks are like system interruptions or application events: their processing must be short and fast. If advanced processing is necessary, it should not be performed inside the callback but on another thread, native threads being perfect candidates.

Indeed, callbacks are emitted on a system thread, different than the one requesting OpenSL ES services (that is, the native thread in our case). Of course, with threads rise the problem of thread-safety when accessing your own variables from the callback. Although protecting code with mutexes is tempting, they are not always compatible with real-time audio as their effect on scheduling (inversion of priority issues) can disturb playback. Prefer using thread safe technique like a lock-free queue to communicate with callbacks.

Recording sounds

Android devices are all about interactions. And interactions can come not only from touches and sensors, but also from audio input. Most Android devices provide a micro to record sound and allow an application such as the Android desktop search to offer vocal features to record queries.

If sound input is available, OpenSL ES gives access to the sound recorder natively. It collaborates with a buffer queue to take data from the input device and fill an output sound buffer from it. Setup is pretty similar to what has been done with the `AudioPlayer` except that data source and data sink are permuted.

To discover how this works, next the challenge consists in recording a sound when an application starts and playing it when it has finished recording.

>
>
> Project DroidBlaster_Part7-3 can be used as a starting point for this part. The resulting project is provided with this book under the name DroidBlaster_Part7-Recorder.

Have a go hero – recording and playing a sound

Turning `SoundService` into a recorder can be done in four steps:

1. Using `status startSoundRecorder()` initialize the sound recorder. Invoke it right after `startSoundPlayer()`.

2. With `void recordSound()` start recording a sound buffer with device micro. Invoke this method at instances such as when the application is activated in `onActivate()` after background music playback starts.

3. A new callback `static void callback_recorder(SLAndroidSimpleBuffe rQueueItf, void*)` to be notified of record queue events. You have to register this callback so that it is triggered when a recorder event happens. Here, we are interested in *buffer full* events, that is, when the sound recording is finished.

4. `void playRecordedSound()` to play a sound once recorded. Play it at instances such as when sound has finished being recorded in `callback_recorder()`. This is not technically correct because of potential race conditions but is fine for an illustration.

Before going any further, recording requires a specific authorization and, of course, an appropriate Android device (you would not like an application to record your secret conversations behind your back!). This authorization has to be requested in Android manifest:

```
<?xml version="1.0" encoding="utf-8"?>
<manifest xmlns:android="http://schemas.android.com/apk/res/android"
    package="com.packtpub.droidblaster" android:versionCode="1"
    android:versionName="1.0">
    . . .
    <uses-permission android:name="android.permission.RECORD_AUDIO"/>
</manifest>
```

Sounds are recorded with a recorder object created from the OpenSL ES engine, as usual. The recorder offers two interesting interfaces:

◆ `SLRecordItf`: This interface is to start and stop recording. The identifier is `SL_IID_RECORD`.

◆ `SLAndroidSImpleBufferQueueItf`: This manages a sound queue for the recorder. This is an Android extension provided by NDK because current OpenSL ES 1.0.1 specification does not support recording to a queue. The identifier is `SL_IID_ANDROIDSIMPLEBUFFERQUEUE`.

```
const SLuint32 lSoundRecorderIIDCount = 2;
const SLInterfaceID lSoundRecorderIIDs[] =
    { SL_IID_RECORD, SL_IID_ANDROIDSIMPLEBUFFERQUEUE };
```

```
const SLboolean lSoundRecorderReqs[] =
    { SL_BOOLEAN_TRUE, SL_BOOLEAN_TRUE };
SLObjectItf mRecorderObj;
(*mEngine)->CreateAudioRecorder(mEngine, &mRecorderObj,
    &lDataSource, &lDataSink,
    lSoundRecorderIIDCount, lSoundRecorderIIDs,
lSoundRecorderReqs);
```

To create the recorder, you will need to declare your audio source and sink similar to the following one. The data source is not a sound but a default recorder device (like a microphone). On the other hand, the data sink (that is, the output channel) is not a speaker but a sound buffer in PCM format (with the requested sampling, encoding, and endianness). The Android extension SLDataLocator_AndroidSimpleBufferQueue must be used to work with a recorder since standard OpenSL buffer queues cannot be used as with a recorder:

```
SLDataLocator_AndroidSimpleBufferQueue lDataLocatorOut;
lDataLocatorOut.locatorType =
    SL_DATALOCATOR_ANDROIDSIMPLEBUFFERQUEUE;
lDataLocatorOut.numBuffers = 1;

SLDataFormat_PCM lDataFormat;
lDataFormat.formatType = SL_DATAFORMAT_PCM;
lDataFormat.numChannels = 1;
lDataFormat.samplesPerSec = SL_SAMPLINGRATE_44_1;
lDataFormat.bitsPerSample = SL_PCMSAMPLEFORMAT_FIXED_16;
lDataFormat.containerSize = SL_PCMSAMPLEFORMAT_FIXED_16;
lDataFormat.channelMask = SL_SPEAKER_FRONT_CENTER;
lDataFormat.endianness = SL_BYTEORDER_LITTLEENDIAN;

SLDataSink lDataSink;
lDataSink.pLocator = &lDataLocatorOut;
lDataSink.pFormat = &lDataFormat;

SLDataLocator_IODevice lDataLocatorIn;
lDataLocatorIn.locatorType = SL_DATALOCATOR_IODEVICE;
lDataLocatorIn.deviceType = SL_IODEVICE_AUDIOINPUT;
lDataLocatorIn.deviceID = SL_DEFAULTDEVICEID_AUDIOINPUT;
lDataLocatorIn.device = NULL;

SLDataSource lDataSource;
lDataSource.pLocator = &lDataLocatorIn;
lDataSource.pFormat = NULL;
```

To record a sound, you also need to create a sound buffer with an appropriate size according to the duration of your recording. Size depends on the sampling rate. For example, for a record of 2 s with a sampling rate of 44100 Hz and 16-bit quality, sound buffer size would look like the following:

```
mRecordSize   = 44100 * 2
mRecordBuffer = new int16_t[mRecordSize];
```

In `recordSound()`, you can stop the recorder thanks to `SLRecordItf` to ensure it is not already recording and clear the queue. The same process applies to destroy the recorder when application exits.

```
(*mRecorder)->SetRecordState(mRecorder, SL_RECORDSTATE_STOPPED);
(*mRecorderQueue)->Clear(mRecorderQueue);
```

Then you can enqueue a new buffer and start recording:

```
(*mRecorderQueue)->Enqueue(mRecorderQueue, mRecordBuffer,
    mRecordSize * sizeof(int16_t));
(*mRecorder)->SetRecordState(mRecorder,SL_RECORDSTATE_RECORDING);
```

Of course, it would be perfectly possible to just enqueue a new sound so that any current recording is processed to its end (for example, to create a continuous chain of recording). The sound being enqueued would be processed potentially later in that case. All depends on your needs.

You eventually need to know when your sound buffer has finished recording. To do so, register a callback triggered when a recorder event happens (for example, a buffer has been filled). An event mask should be set to ensure callback is called only when a buffer has been filled (`SL_RECORDEVENT_BUFFER_FULL`). A few others are available in `OpenSLES.h` but not all are supported (`SL_RECORDEVENT_HEADATLIMIT`, and so on):

```
(*mRecorderQueue)->RegisterCallback(mRecorderQueue,
                                    callback_recorder, this);
(*mRecorder)->SetCallbackEventMask(mRecorder,
                                   SL_RECORDEVENT_BUFFER_FULL);
```

Finally, when `callback_recorder()` is triggered, just stop recording and play the recorded buffer with `playRecordedSound()`. The recorded buffer needs to be enqueued in the audio player's queue for playback:

```
(*mPlayerQueue)->Enqueue(mPlayerQueue, mRecordBuffer,
    mRecordSize * sizeof(int16_t));
```

Playing recorded sound directly from a callback is nice to perform quick and simple tests. But to implement such a mechanism properly, more advanced thread-safe technique (preferably lock-free) is required.

Indeed, in this example, there is a risk of race condition with `SoundService` destructor (which destroys the queue used in the callback).

Summary

In this chapter, we saw how to create and realize an OpenSL ES engine connected to an output channel. We played music from an encoded file and saw that an encoded file cannot be loaded in a buffer.

We also played sound buffers in a sound queue. Buffers can either be appended to a queue, in which case they are played with delay, or inserted in replacement of previous sounds, in which case they are played immediately. Finally, we have recorded sound in buffers and played them back.

Should you prefer OpenSL ES over Java APIs? There is no definite answer. Devices evolve at much quieter pace than Android itself. So if your application aims at a large compatibility, that is, Android 2.2 or less, Java APIs are the only solution. On the other hand, if it is planned for later releases, then OpenSL ES is an option to consider, praying that most devices will be migrated to Gingerbread! But you have to be ready to support the cost of possible future evolutions.

If all you need is a nice high-level API, then Java APIs may suit your requirements better. If you need finer playback or recording control, then there is no significant difference between low-level Java APIs and OpenSL ES. In that case, choice should be architectural: if your code is mainly Java, then you should probably go with Java and reciprocally. If you need to reuse an existing sound-related library, optimize performance or perform intense computations, like sound filtering on the fly, then OpenSL ES is probably the right choice. There is no garbage collector overhead and aggressive optimization is favored in the native code.

Whatever choice you make, know that Android NDK has a lot more to offer. After rendering graphics with Open GL ES and playing sound with OpenSL ES, the next chapter will take care of handling input natively: keyboard, touches, and sensors.

8
Handling Input Devices and Sensors

Android is all about interaction. Admittedly, that means feedback, through graphics, audio, vibrations, and so on. But there is no interaction without input! The success of today's smart-phones takes its root in their multiple and modern input possibilities: touch screens, keyboard, mouse, GPS, accelerometer, light detector, sound recorder, and so on. Handling and combining them properly is a key to enrich your application and and to make it successful.

Although Android handles many input peripherals, the Android NDK has long been very limited in their support, not to say good for nothing, until the release of R5! We can now access them directly through a native API. Examples of available devices are:

- Keyboard, either physical (with a slide-out keyboard) or virtual (which appears on screen)
- Directional pad (up, down, left, right, and action buttons), often abbreviated D-Pad
- Trackball (optical ones included)
- Touch screen, which has made the success of modern smart-phones
- Mouse or Track Pad (since NDK R5, but available on Honeycomb devices only)

We can also access hardware sensors, for example:

- Accelerometer, which measures linear acceleration applied to a device.
- Gyroscope, which measures angular velocity. It is often combined with the magnetometer to compute orientation accurately and quickly. Gyroscope has been introduced recently and is not available on most devices yet.

- Magnetometer, which gives the ambient magnetic field and thus (if not perturbed) cardinal direction.

- Light sensor, for example, to automatically adapt screen luminosity.

- Proximity sensor, for example, to detect ear distance during a call.

In addition to hardware sensors, "software sensors" have been introduced with Gingerbread. These sensors are derived from hardware sensor's data:

- Gravity sensor, to measure the gravity direction and magnitude

- Linear acceleration sensor, which measures device "movement" excluding gravity

- Rotation vector, which indicates device orientation in space

Gravity sensor and linear acceleration sensor are derived from the accelerometer. On the other hand, rotation vector is derived from the magnetometer and the accelerometer. Because these sensors are generally computed over time, they usually incur a slight delay to get up-to-date values.

To familiarize more deeply with input devices and sensors, this chapter teaches how to:

- Handle screen touches

- Detect keyboard, D-Pad, and trackball events

- Turn the accelerometer sensor into a joypad

Interacting with Android

The most emblematic innovation of today's smart phones is the touch screen, which has replaced the now antique mice. A touch screen detects, as its name suggests, touches made with fingers or styluses. Depending on the quality of the screen, several touches (also referred as **cursors** in Android) can be handled, de-multiplying interaction possibilities.

So let's start this chapter by handling touch events in DroidBlaster. To keep the example simple, we will only handle one touch. The goal is to move the ship in the direction of a touch. The farther the touch is, the faster goes the ship. Beyond a pre-defined range, ship speed reaches a top limit.

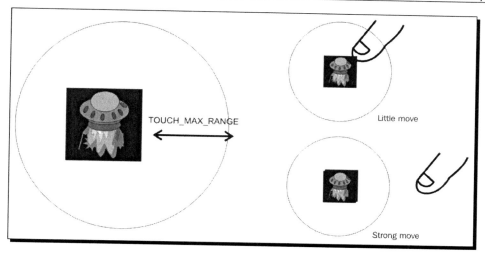

The final project structure will look as shown in the following diagram:

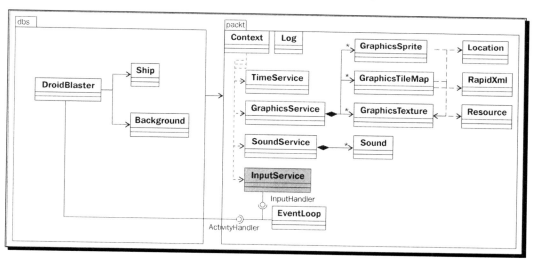

 Project DroidBlaster_Part7-3 can be used as a starting point for this part. The resulting project is provided with this book under the name DroidBlaster_Part8-1.

Time for action – handling touch events

Let's begin with the plumber to connect Android input event queue to our application.

1. In the same way we created an `ActivityHandler` to process application events in *Chapter 5, Writing a Native Application*, create a class `InputHandler`, in a new file `jni/InputHandler.hpp` to process the input events. Input API is declared in `android/input.h`.

2. Create a `onTouchEvent()` to handle touch events. These events are packaged in an `AInputEvent` structure defined in Android include files. Other input peripherals will be added later in this chapter:

```
#ifndef _PACKT_INPUTHANDLER_HPP_
#define _PACKT_INPUTHANDLER_HPP_

#include <android/input.h>

namespace packt {
    class InputHandler {
    public:
        virtual ~InputHandler() {};

        virtual bool onTouchEvent(AInputEvent* pEvent) = 0;
    };
}
#endif
```

3. Modify `jni/EventLoop.hpp` header file to include and handle an `InputHandler` instance. Like with activity event, define an internal method `processInputEvent()` triggering a static callback `callback_input()`:

```
#ifndef _PACKT_EVENTLOOP_HPP_
#define _PACKT_EVENTLOOP_HPP_

#include "ActivityHandler.hpp"
#include "InputHandler.hpp"
#include "Types.hpp"

#include <android_native_app_glue.h>

namespace packt {
    class EventLoop {
    public:
        EventLoop(android_app* pApplication);
```

```
        void run(ActivityHandler* pActivityHandler,
            InputHandler* pInputHandler);

    protected:
        ...
        void processAppEvent(int32_t pCommand);
        int32_t processInputEvent(AInputEvent* pEvent);
        void processSensorEvent();

    private:
        ...
        static void callback_event(android_app* pApplication,
            int32_t pCommand);
        static int32_t callback_input(android_app* pApplication,
            AInputEvent* pEvent);

    private:
        ...
        android_app* mApplication;
        ActivityHandler* mActivityHandler;
        InputHandler* mInputHandler;
    };
}
#endif
```

4. We need to process input events in `jni/EventLoop.cpp` source file and notify the associated `InputHandler`.

First, connect the Android input queue to our `callback_input()`. The `EventLoop` itself (that is, `this`) is passed anonymously through the `userData` member of the `android_app` structure. That way, callback is able to delegate input processing back to our own object, that is, to `processInputEvent()`.

Touch screen events are of the type `MotionEvent` (as opposed to key events). They can be discriminated according to their source (`AINPUT_SOURCE_TOUCHSCREEN`) thanks to Android native input API (here, `AInputEvent_getSource()`):

> Note how `callback_input()` and by extension `processInputEvent()` return an integer value (which is in fact a Boolean). This value indicates that an input event (for example, a pressed button) has been processed by the application and does not need to be processed further by the system. For example, return 1 when the back button is pressed to stop event processing and prevent activity from getting terminated.

```cpp
#include "EventLoop.hpp"
#include "Log.hpp"

namespace packt {
    EventLoop::EventLoop(android_app* pApplication) :
        mEnabled(false), mQuit(false),
        mApplication(pApplication),
        mActivityHandler(NULL), mInputHandler(NULL) {
        mApplication->userData = this;
        mApplication->onAppCmd = callback_event;
        mApplication->onInputEvent = callback_input;
    }

    void EventLoop::run(ActivityHandler* pActivityHandler,
                        InputHandler* pInputHandler) {
        int32_t lResult;
        int32_t lEvents;
        android_poll_source* lSource;

        // Makes sure native glue is not stripped by the linker.
        app_dummy();
        mActivityHandler = pActivityHandler;
        mInputHandler    = pInputHandler;

        packt::Log::info("Starting event loop");
        while (true) {
            // Event processing loop.
            ...
    }

    ...

    int32_t EventLoop::processInputEvent(AInputEvent* pEvent) {
        int32_t lEventType = AInputEvent_getType(pEvent);
        switch (lEventType) {
        case AINPUT_EVENT_TYPE_MOTION:
            switch (AInputEvent_getSource(pEvent)) {
            case AINPUT_SOURCE_TOUCHSCREEN:
                return mInputHandler->onTouchEvent(pEvent);
                break;
            }
            break;
        }
```

```
            return 0;
        }

        int32_t EventLoop::callback_input(android_app* pApplication,
          AInputEvent* pEvent) {
          EventLoop& lEventLoop = *(EventLoop*) pApplication->userData;
          return lEventLoop.processInputEvent(pEvent);
        }
    }
```

Plumber is ready. Let's handle these events concretely.

5. To analyze touch events, create a `InputService` class in `jni/InputService.hpp` implementing our `InputHandler`. It contains a `start()` method to realize necessary initializations and implements `onTouchEvent()`.

More interestingly, `InputService` provides `getHorizontal()` and `getVertical()` methods, which indicate the virtual joypad direction. Direction is defined between the touch point and a reference point (which will be the ship).

We also need to know window height and width (reference values, which come from `GraphicsService`) to handle coordinate conversions:

```
#ifndef _PACKT_INPUTSERVICE_HPP_
#define _PACKT_INPUTSERVICE_HPP_

#include "Context.hpp"
#include "InputHandler.hpp"
#include "Types.hpp"

#include <android_native_app_glue.h>

namespace packt {
    class InputService : public InputHandler {
    public:
        InputService(android_app* pApplication,
          const int32_t& pWidth, const int32_t& pHeight);

        float getHorizontal();
        float getVertical();
        void setRefPoint(Location* pTouchReference);

        status start();

    public:
```

```cpp
        bool onTouchEvent(AInputEvent* pEvent);

    private:
        android_app* mApplication;

        float mHorizontal, mVertical;

        Location* mRefPoint;
        const int32_t& mWidth, &mHeight;
    };
}
#endif
```

6. Now, the interesting part: `jni/InputService.cpp`. First, define the constructor, destructor, getters, and setters.

Input service needs a `start()` method to clear state members:

```cpp
#include "InputService.hpp"
#include "Log.hpp"

#include <android_native_app_glue.h>
#include <cmath>

namespace packt {
    InputService::InputService(android_app* pApplication,
            const int32_t& pWidth, const int32_t& pHeight) :
        mApplication(pApplication),
        mHorizontal(0.0f), mVertical(0.0f),
        mRefPoint(NULL), mWidth(pWidth), mHeight(pHeight)
    {}

    float InputService::getHorizontal() {
        return mHorizontal;
    }

    float InputService::getVertical() {
        return mVertical;
    }

    void InputService::setRefPoint(Location* pTouchReference) {
        mRefPoint = pTouchReference;
    }

    status InputService::start() {
```

```
      mHorizontal = 0.0f, mVertical = 0.0f;
      if ((mWidth == 0) || (mHeight == 0)) {
          return STATUS_KO;
      }
      return STATUS_OK;
}
```

The effective event processing comes in `onTouchEvent()`. Horizontal and vertical directions are computed according to the distance between the reference point and the touch point. This distance is restricted by `TOUCH_MAX_RANGE` to an arbitrary range of 65 pixels. Thus, ship max speed is reached when reference-to-touch point distance is beyond `TOUCH_MAX_RANGE` pixels. Touch coordinates are retrieved thanks to `AMotionEvent_getX()` and `AMotionEvent_getY()` when finger moves. Direction vector is reset to `0` when no more touch is detected:

Beware that the way touch events are fired is not homogeneous among devices. For example, some devices emit events continuously while finger is down whereas others only emit them when finger moves. In our case, we could re-compute movement each frame instead of when an event is triggered to get a more predictable behavior.

. . .

```
    bool InputService::onTouchEvent(AInputEvent* pEvent) {
        const float TOUCH_MAX_RANGE = 65.0f; // In pixels.

        if (mRefPoint != NULL) {
          if (AMotionEvent_getAction(pEvent)
                        == AMOTION_EVENT_ACTION_MOVE) {
            // Needs a conversion to proper coordinates
            // (origin at bottom/left). Only lMoveY needs it.
            float lMoveX = AMotionEvent_getX(pEvent, 0)
                        - mRefPoint->mPosX;
            float lMoveY = mHeight - AMotionEvent_getY(pEvent, 0)
                        - mRefPoint->mPosY;
            float lMoveRange = sqrt((lMoveX * lMoveX)
                                + (lMoveY * lMoveY));

            if (lMoveRange > TOUCH_MAX_RANGE) {
              float lCropFactor = TOUCH_MAX_RANGE / lMoveRange;
              lMoveX *= lCropFactor; lMoveY *= lCropFactor;
            }

            mHorizontal = lMoveX / TOUCH_MAX_RANGE;
```

```
            mVertical    = lMoveY / TOUCH_MAX_RANGE;
        } else {
            mHorizontal = 0.0f; mVertical = 0.0f;
        }
    }
    return true;
}
}
```

7. Insert `InputService` into the `Context` structure in `jni/Context.hpp`.

```
#ifndef _PACKT_CONTEXT_HPP_
#define _PACKT_CONTEXT_HPP_

#include "Types.hpp"

namespace packt {
    class GraphicsService;
    class InputService;
    class SoundService;
    class TimeService;

    struct Context {
        GraphicsService* mGraphicsService;
        InputService*    mInputService;
        SoundService*    mSoundService;
        TimeService*     mTimeService;
    };
}
#endif
```

Finally, let's react to touch events in the game itself.

8. Get the `InputService` back in `jni/DroidBlaster.hpp`:

```
#ifndef _PACKT_DROIDBLASTER_HPP_
#define _PACKT_DROIDBLASTER_HPP_

#include "ActivityHandler.hpp"
#include "Background.hpp"
#include "Context.hpp"
#include "InputService.hpp"
#include "GraphicsService.hpp"
#include "Ship.hpp"

...
```

```
namespace dbs {
    class DroidBlaster : public packt::ActivityHandler {
    public:
        ...

    private:
        packt::InputService*    mInputService;
        packt::GraphicsService* mGraphicsService;
        packt::SoundService*    mSoundService;
        packt::TimeService*     mTimeService;
        ...
    };
}
#endif
```

9. InputService is started in `jni/DroidBlaster.cpp` when the activity is activated. Because it calls `ANativeWindow_lock()` to retrieve window height and width, `InputService` needs to be started before `GraphicsService` to avoid a deadlock:

```
#include "DroidBlaster.hpp"
#include "Log.hpp"

namespace dbs {
    DroidBlaster::DroidBlaster(packt::Context* pContext) :
        mInputService(pContext->mInputService),
        mGraphicsService(pContext->mGraphicsService),
        mSoundService(pContext->mSoundService),
        ...
    {}

    packt::status DroidBlaster::onActivate() {
        if (mGraphicsService->start() != packt::STATUS_OK) {
            return packt::STATUS_KO;
        }
        if (mInputService->start() != packt::STATUS_OK) {
            return packt::STATUS_KO;
        }
        ...
    }

    ...

    packt::status DroidBlaster::onStep() {
```

```
        mTimeService->update();

        mBackground.update();
        mShip.update();

        // Updates services.
        if (mGraphicsService->update() != packt::STATUS_OK) {
            ...
        }
    }
}
```

10. The `InputService` is used by the `Ship` class to reposition. Open `jni/Ship.hpp` and associate it with the `InputService` and `TimeService`. The ship position is moved according to user input and time step in a new method `update()`:

```cpp
#ifndef _DBS_SHIP_HPP_
#define _DBS_SHIP_HPP_

#include "Context.hpp"
#include "InputService.hpp"
#include "GraphicsService.hpp"
#include "GraphicsSprite.hpp"
#include "Types.hpp"

namespace dbs {
    class Ship {
    public:
        Ship(packt::Context* pContext);

        void spawn();
        void update();

    private:
        packt::InputService* mInputService;
        packt::GraphicsService* mGraphicsService;
        packt::TimeService* mTimeService;

        packt::GraphicsSprite* mSprite;
        packt::Location mLocation;
        float mAnimSpeed;
    };
}
#endif
```

11. The reference point from which distance to the touch is computed is initialized with the ship position. During update, ship is moved toward the touch point according to the time step and the direction calculated in `InputService` class:

```
#include "Ship.hpp"
#include "Log.hpp"


namespace dbs {
    Ship::Ship(packt::Context* pContext) :
        mInputService(pContext->mInputService),
        mGraphicsService(pContext->mGraphicsService),
        mTimeService(pContext->mTimeService),
        mLocation(), mAnimSpeed(8.0f) {
        mSprite = pContext->mGraphicsService->registerSprite(
            mGraphicsService->registerTexture("ship.png"), 64, 64,
            &mLocation);
        mInputService->setRefPoint(&mLocation);
    }


    ...


    void Ship::update() {
      const float SPEED_PERSEC = 400.0f;
      float lSpeed = SPEED_PERSEC * mTimeService->elapsed();

      mLocation.translate(mInputService->getHorizontal() * lSpeed,
                          mInputService->getVertical() * lSpeed);
    }
}
```

12. Finally, update the `android_main()` method in `jni/Main.cpp` to build an instance of `InputService` and pass it to the event processing loop:

```
#include "Context.hpp"
#include "DroidBlaster.hpp"
#include "EventLoop.hpp"
#include "InputService.hpp"
#include "GraphicsService.hpp"
#include "SoundService.hpp"
#include "TimeService.hpp"


void android_main(android_app* pApplication) {
    packt::TimeService lTimeService;
    packt::GraphicsService lGraphicsService(pApplication,
        &lTimeService);
```

```
packt::InputService lInputService(pApplication,
    lGraphicsService.getWidth(),lGraphicsService.getHeight());
packt::SoundService lSoundService(pApplication);

packt::Context lContext = { &lInputService, &lGraphicsService,
    &lSoundService, &lTimeService };

packt::EventLoop lEventLoop(pApplication);
dbs::DroidBlaster lDroidBlaster(&lContext);
lEventLoop.run(&lDroidBlaster, &lInputService);
}
```

What just happened?

We have created a simple example of an input system based on touch events. The ship flies toward the touch point at a speed dependent on the touch distance. Yet, many improvements are possible such as taking into account screen density and size, following one specific pointer...

Touch screen event coordinates are absolute. Their origin is in the upper-left corner of the screen (on the opposite of OpenGL which is on the lower-left corner). If screen rotation is authorized by an application, the origin will stay on the upper, left whether the screen is in portrait or landscape mode.

To implement it, we have connected our event loop to the input event queue provided by the `native_app_glue` module. This queue is internally represented as an Unix pipe, like the activity event queue. Touch screen events are embedded in an `AInputEvent` structure, which stores also other kind of input events. Input events can be handled with the functions declared in `android/input.h`. Input event types can be discriminated using `AInputEvent_getType()` and `AInputEvent_getSource()` methods (note the `AInputEvent_` prefix). Methods related to touch events are prefixed by `AMotionEvent_`.

The touch API is rather rich. Many details can be requested such as (non-exhaustively):

`AMotionEvent_getAction()`	To detect whether a finger is entering in contact with the screen, leaving it, or moving over the surface. The result is an integer value composed of the event type (on byte 1, for example, `AMOTION_EVENT_ACTION_DOWN`) and a pointer index (on byte 2, to know which finger the event refers to).

`AMotionEvent_getX()`
 	
`AMotionEvent_getY()`
	To retrieve touch coordinates on screen, expressed in pixels as a float (sub-pixel values are possible).

`AMotionEvent_getDownTime()`
 	
`AMotionEvent_getEventTime()`
	To retrieve how much time finger has been sliding over the screen and when the event has been generated in nanoseconds.

`AMotionEvent_getPressure()`
 	
`AMotionEvent_getSize()`
	To detect how careful users are with their device. Values usually range between 0.0 and 1.0 (but may exceed it). Size and pressure are generally closely related. Behavior can vary greatly and be noisy depending on hardware.

`AMotionEvent_getHistorySize()`
 	
`AMotionEvent_getHistoricalX()`
 	
`AMotionEvent_getHistoricalY()`
 	
. . .
	Touch events of type `AMOTION_EVENT_ACTION_MOVE` can be grouped together for efficiency purpose. These methods give access to these "historical points" that occurred between previous and current events.

Have a look at `android/input.h` for an exhaustive list of methods.

If you look more deeply at `AMotionEvent` API, you will notice that some events have a second parameter `pointer_index`, which ranges between 0 and the number of active pointers. Indeed, most touch screens today are multi-touch! Two or more fingers on a screen (if hardware supports it) are translated in Android by two or more pointers. To manipulate them, look at:

`AMotionEvent_getPointerCount()`	To know how many fingers touch the screen.
`AMotionEvent_getPointerId()`	To get a pointer unique identifier from a pointer index. This is the only way to track a particular pointer (that is, finger) over time, as its index may change when fingers touch or leave the screen.

Do not rely on hardware

If you followed the story of the (now prehistoric!) Nexus One, then you know that it came out with an hardware defect. Pointers were often getting mixed up, two of them exchanging one of their coordinates. So be always prepared to handle hardware specificities or hardware that behaves incorrectly!

Detecting keyboard, D-Pad, and Trackball events

The most common input device among all is the keyboard. This is true for Android too. An Android keyboard can be physical: in the device front face (like traditional blackberries) or on a slide-out screen. But a keyboard can also be virtual, that is, emulated on the screen at the cost of a large portion of space taken. In addition to the keyboard itself, every Android device should include a few physical buttons (sometimes emulated on screen) such as **Menu**, **Home**, **Search**, and so on.

A much less common type of input device is the Directional-Pad. A D-Pad is a set of physical buttons to move up, down, left, or right and a specific action/confirmation button. Although they often disappear from recent phones and tablets, D-Pads remain one of the most convenient ways to move across text or UI widgets. D-Pads are often replaced by trackballs. Trackballs behave similarly to a mouse (the one with a ball inside) that would be upside-down. Some trackballs are analogical, but others (for example, optical ones) behave as a D-Pad (that is, all or nothing).

To see how they work, let's use these peripherals to move our space ship in DroidBlaster. The Android NDK now allows handling all these input peripherals on the native side. So let's try them!

Project `DroidBlaster_Part8-1` can be used as a starting point for this part. The resulting project is provided with this book under the name `DroidBlaster_Part8-2`.

Time for action – handling keyboard, D-Pad, and trackball, natively

First, let's handle keyboard and trackball events.

1. Open jni/`InputHandler.hpp` and add keyboard and trackball event handlers:

```
#ifndef _PACKT_INPUTHANDLER_HPP_
#define _PACKT_INPUTHANDLER_HPP_

#include <android/input.h>

namespace packt {
    class InputHandler {
    public:
        virtual ~InputHandler() {};

        virtual bool onTouchEvent(AInputEvent* pEvent) = 0;
        virtual bool onKeyboardEvent(AInputEvent* pEvent) = 0;
        virtual bool onTrackballEvent(AInputEvent* pEvent) = 0;
    };
}
#endif
```

2. Update method `processInputEvent()` inside the existing file jni/`EventLoop.cpp` to redirect keyboard and trackball events to `InputHandler`.

   Trackballs and touch events are assimilated to motion events and can be discriminated according to their source. On the opposite side, key events are discriminated according to their type. Indeed, there exist two dedicated APIs for `MotionEvents` (the same for trackballs and touch events) and for `KeyEvents` (identical for keyboard, D-Pad, and so on):

```
#include "EventLoop.hpp"
#include "Log.hpp"

namespace packt {
    ...
    int32_t EventLoop::processInputEvent(AInputEvent* pEvent) {
```

```
        int32_t lEventType = AInputEvent_getType(pEvent);
        switch (lEventType) {
        case AINPUT_EVENT_TYPE_MOTION:
            switch (AInputEvent_getSource(pEvent)) {
            case AINPUT_SOURCE_TOUCHSCREEN:
                return mInputHandler->onTouchEvent(pEvent);
                break;

            case AINPUT_SOURCE_TRACKBALL:
                return mInputHandler->onTrackballEvent(pEvent);
                break;
            }
            break;

        case AINPUT_EVENT_TYPE_KEY:
            return mInputHandler->onKeyboardEvent(pEvent);
            break;
        }
        return 0;
    }
    ...
}
```

3. Now, modify the `jni/InputService.hpp` file to override these new methods... also define an `update()` method to react to pressed keys. We are interested in the menu button that is going to cause the application to exit:

```
#ifndef _PACKT_INPUTSERVICE_HPP_
#define _PACKT_INPUTSERVICE_HPP_

...

namespace packt {
    class InputService : public InputHandler {
    public:
        ...
        status start();
        status update();

    public:
        bool onTouchEvent(AInputEvent* pEvent);
        bool onKeyboardEvent(AInputEvent* pEvent);
        bool onTrackballEvent(AInputEvent* pEvent);
```

```
        private:
            ...
            Location* mRefPoint;
            int32_t mWidth, mHeight;

            bool mMenuKey;
        };
    }
    #endif
```

4. Now, update the class constructor `jni/InputService.cpp` and implement method `update()` to exit when the menu button is pressed:

```
#include "InputService.hpp"
#include "Log.hpp"

#include <android_native_app_glue.h>
#include <cmath>

namespace packt {
    InputService::InputService(android_app* pApplication,
            const int32_t& pWidth, const int32_t& pHeight) :
        mApplication(pApplication),
        mHorizontal(0.0f), mVertical(0.0f),
        mRefPoint(NULL), mWidth(pWidth), mHeight(pHeight),
        mMenuKey(false)
    {}

    ...

    status InputService::update() {
        if (mMenuKey) {
            return STATUS_EXIT;
        }
        return STATUS_OK;
    }
    ...
```

5. Still in `InputService.cpp`, process keyboard events in `onKeyboardEvent()`. Use:
  - ❏ `AKeyEvent_getAction()` to get event type (that is, pressed or not).
  - ❏ `AKeyEvent_getKeyCode()` to get the button identity.

In the following code, when left, right, up, or down buttons are pressed, `InputService` compute corresponding direction into fields `mHorizontal` and `mVertical` defined in previous part. Movement starts when button is down and stops when it is up.

We also process the Menu button here, when it gets unpressed:

 This code works only on devices with a D-Pad, which is the case of the emulator. Note however that due to Android fragmentation, reaction may differ according to hardware.

```cpp
...
bool InputService::onKeyboardEvent(AInputEvent* pEvent) {
    const float ORTHOGONAL_MOVE = 1.0f;

    if (AKeyEvent_getAction(pEvent) == AKEY_EVENT_ACTION_DOWN) {
        switch (AKeyEvent_getKeyCode(pEvent)) {
        case AKEYCODE_DPAD_LEFT:
            mHorizontal = -ORTHOGONAL_MOVE;
            break;
        case AKEYCODE_DPAD_RIGHT:
            mHorizontal = ORTHOGONAL_MOVE;
            break;
        case AKEYCODE_DPAD_DOWN:
            mVertical = -ORTHOGONAL_MOVE;
            break;
        case AKEYCODE_DPAD_UP:
            mVertical = ORTHOGONAL_MOVE;
            break;
        case AKEYCODE_BACK:
            return false;
        }
    } else {
        switch (AKeyEvent_getKeyCode(pEvent)) {
        case AKEYCODE_DPAD_LEFT:
        case AKEYCODE_DPAD_RIGHT:
            mHorizontal = 0.0f;
            break;
        case AKEYCODE_DPAD_DOWN:
        case AKEYCODE_DPAD_UP:
            mVertical = 0.0f;
            break;
        case AKEYCODE_MENU:
```

```
                mMenuKey = true;
                break;
            case AKEYCODE_BACK:
                return false;
            }
        }
        return true;
    }
    . . .
```

6. Similarly, process trackball events in a new method `onTrackballEvent()`. Retrieve trackball magnitude with `AMotionEvent_getX()` and `AMotionEvent_getY()`. Because some trackballs do not offer a gradated magnitude, the movement is quantified with plain constants. Possible noise is ignored with an arbitrary trigger threshold:

When using trackball that way, the ship moves until a "counter-movement" (for example, requesting to go to the right when going left) or action button is pressed (last `else` section):

 For a wide audience application, code should be adapted to handle hardware capabilities and specificities such as gradated values of analogical trackballs.

```
. . .
    bool InputService::onTrackballEvent(AInputEvent* pEvent) {
        const float ORTHOGONAL_MOVE = 1.0f;
        const float DIAGONAL_MOVE   = 0.707f;
        const float THRESHOLD       = (1/100.0f);

        if (AMotionEvent_getAction(pEvent)
                    == AMOTION_EVENT_ACTION_MOVE) {
            float lDirectionX = AMotionEvent_getX(pEvent, 0);
            float lDirectionY = AMotionEvent_getY(pEvent, 0);
            float lHorizontal, lVertical;

            if (lDirectionX < -THRESHOLD) {
                if (lDirectionY < -THRESHOLD) {
                    lHorizontal = -DIAGONAL_MOVE;
                    lVertical   = DIAGONAL_MOVE;
                } else if (lDirectionY > THRESHOLD) {
                    lHorizontal = -DIAGONAL_MOVE;
                    lVertical   = -DIAGONAL_MOVE;
```

```
                } else {
                    lHorizontal = -ORTHOGONAL_MOVE;
                    lVertical   = 0.0f;
                }
            } else if (lDirectionX > THRESHOLD) {
                if (lDirectionY < -THRESHOLD) {
                    lHorizontal = DIAGONAL_MOVE;
                    lVertical   = DIAGONAL_MOVE;
                } else if (lDirectionY > THRESHOLD) {
                    lHorizontal = DIAGONAL_MOVE;
                    lVertical   = -DIAGONAL_MOVE;
                } else {
                    lHorizontal = ORTHOGONAL_MOVE;
                    lVertical   = 0.0f;
                }
            } else if (lDirectionY < -THRESHOLD) {
                lHorizontal = 0.0f;
                lVertical   = ORTHOGONAL_MOVE;
            } else if (lDirectionY > THRESHOLD) {
                lHorizontal = 0.0f;
                lVertical   = -ORTHOGONAL_MOVE;
            }

            // Ends movement if there is a counter movement.
            if ((lHorizontal < 0.0f) && (mHorizontal > 0.0f)) {
                mHorizontal = 0.0f;
            } else if((lHorizontal > 0.0f)&&(mHorizontal < 0.0f)){
                mHorizontal = 0.0f;
            } else {
                mHorizontal = lHorizontal;
            }

            if ((lVertical < 0.0f) && (mVertical > 0.0f)) {
                mVertical = 0.0f;
            } else if ((lVertical > 0.0f) && (mVertical < 0.0f)) {
                mVertical = 0.0f;
            } else {
                mVertical = lVertical;
            }
        } else {
            mHorizontal = 0.0f; mVertical = 0.0f;
        }
        return true;
    }
}
```

Let's finish by making a slight modification to the game itself.

7. Finally, edit `DroidBlaster.cpp` and update `InputService` at each iteration:

```cpp
#include "DroidBlaster.hpp"
#include "Log.hpp"

namespace dbs {
    ...
    packt::status DroidBlaster::onStep() {
        mTimeService->update();

        mBackground.update();
        mShip.update();

        if (mInputService->update()     != packt::STATUS_OK) {
            return packt::STATUS_KO;
        }
        if (mGraphicsService->update() != packt::STATUS_OK) {
            return packt::STATUS_KO;
        }
        return packt::STATUS_OK;
    }
    ...
}
```

What just happened?

We have extended our input system to handle the keyboard, D-Pad, and trackball events. D-Pad can be considered as a keyboard extension and is processed the same way. Indeed, D-Pad and keyboard events are transported in the same structure (`AInputEvent`) and handled by the same API (prefixed with `AKeyEvent`). The following table lists the main key event methods:

`AKeyEvent_getAction()`	Indicate if button is down (`AKEY_EVENT_ACTION_DOWN`) or released (`AKEY_EVENT_ACTION_UP`). Note that multiple key actions can be emitted in batch (`AKEY_EVENT_ACTION_MULTIPLE`).
`AKeyEvent_getKeyCode()`	To retrieve the actual button being pressed (defined in `android/keycodes.h`), for example, `AKEYCODE_DPAD_LEFT` for the left button.
`AKeyEvent_getFlags()`	Key events can be associated with one or more flags that give various information on the event like `AKEY_EVENT_LONG_PRESS`, `AKEY_EVENT_FLAG_SOFT_KEYBOARD` for event originated from an emulated keyboard.
`AKeyEvent_getScanCode()`	Is similar to a key code except that this is the raw key ID, dependent and different from device to device.
`AKeyEvent_getMetaState()`	Meta states are flags that indicate if some modifier keys like *Alt* or *Shift* are pressed simultaneously (for example, `AMETA_SHIFT_ON`, `AMETA_NONE`, and so on).
`AKeyEvent_getRepeatCount()`	Indicates how many times the button event occurred, usually when you leave button down.
`AKeyEvent_getDownTime()`	To know when a button was pressed.

Although some of them (especially optical ones) behave like a D-Pad, trackballs are not using the same API. Actually, trackballs are handled through the `AMotionEvent` API (like touch events). Of course, some information provided for touch events is not always available on trackballs. The most important functions to look at are:

`AMotionEvent_getAction()`	To know if an event represents a move action (as opposed to a press action).
`AMotionEvent_getX()` `AMotionEvent_getY()`	To get trackball movement.
`AKeyEvent_getDownTime()`	To know if trackball is pressed (like D-Pad action button). Currently, most trackballs use an all-or-nothing pressure to indicate the press event.

Something tricky with trackballs, that may not be obvious at first, is that no event up is generated to indicate that trackball has finished moving. Moreover, trackball events are generated as a series (as a burst) which makes it harder to detect when movement is finished. There is no easy way to handle this except using a manual timer and checking regularly that no event has happened for a sufficient amount of time.

> **Again, do not rely on an expected behaviour**
> Never expect peripherals to behave exactly the same on all phones. Trackballs are a very good example: they can either indicate a direction like an analogical pad or a straight direction like a D-Pad (for example, optical trackballs). There is currently no way to differentiate device characteristics from the available APIs. The only solutions are to either calibrate device and configure it at runtime or save a kind of device database.

Have a go hero – displaying software keyboard

An annoying problem with the Android NDK and `NativeActivity` is that there is no easy way to display a virtual keyboard. And of course, without a virtual keyboard, nothing can be keyed in. This is where the JNI skills you have gained by reading *Chapter 3* and *Chapter 4* come to the rescue.

The piece of Java code to show or hide the keyboard is rather concise:

```
InputMethodManager mgr = (InputMethodManager)
        myActivity.getSystemService(Context.INPUT_METHOD_SERVICE);
mgr.showSoftInput(pActivity.getWindow().getDecorView(), 0);
...

mgr.hideSoftInput(pActivity.getWindow().getDecorView(), 0);
```

Write the equivalent JNI code in four steps:

1. First, create a `JNI` helper class which:

    ❏ Takes an `android_app` instance and attaches the `JavaVM` during construction. The `JavaVM` is provided in member `activity->vm` of `android_app`.

    ❏ Detaches the `JavaVM` when class gets destroyed.

    ❏ Offers helper methods to create and delete global references like implemented in *Chapter 4, Calling Back Java from Native Code* (`makeGlobalRef()` and `deleteGlobalRef()`).

    ❏ Provides getters to a `JNIEnv` cached on VM attachment and the `NativeActivity` instance provided in member `activity->clazz` of `android_app`.

2. Then, write a `Keyboard` class which receives a `JNI` instance in parameter and cache all the necessary `jclass`, `jmethodID`, and `jfieldID` to execute the piece of Java code presented above. This is similar to the `StoreWatcher` in *Chapter 4, Calling Back Java from Native Code*, but in C++ this time.

   Define methods to:

   ❑ Cache JNI elements. Call it when `InputService` is initialized to handle error cases properly and report a status.

   ❑ Release global references when application is deactivated.

   ❑ Show and hide the keyboard by executing the JNI methods cached earlier.

3. Instantiate both the `JNI` and the `Keyboard` classes in your `android_main()` method and pass the latter to your `InputService`.

4. Open the virtual keyboard when the menu key is pressed instead of leaving the game. Finally, detect keys that are pressed on the virtual keyboard. For example, try to detect the key `AKEYCODE_E` to exit the game.

 The final project is provided with this book in DroidBlaster_Part8-2-Keyboard.

Probing device sensors

Handling input devices is essential to any application, but probing sensors is important for the smartest one! The most spread sensor among Android game applications is the accelerometer.

An **accelerometer**, as its name suggests, measures the linear acceleration applied to a device. When moving a device up, down, left, or right, the accelerometer gets excited and indicates an acceleration vector in 3D space. Vector is expressed relative to screen default orientation. Coordinates system is relative to device natural orientation:

◆ X axis points left

◆ Y points up

◆ Z points from back to front

Axes become inverted if device is rotated (for example, Y points left if the device is rotated 90 degrees clockwise).

A very interesting feature of accelerometers is that they undergo a constant acceleration: gravity, around 9.8m/s2 on earth. For example, when lying flat on a table, acceleration vector indicates -9.8 on the Z-axis. When straight, it indicates the same value on Y axis. So assuming device position is fixed, device orientation on two axes in space can be deduced from the gravity acceleration vector. Magnetometer is still required to get full device orientation in 3D space.

 Remember that accelerometers work with linear acceleration. They allow detecting translation when device is not rotating and partial orientation when device is fixed. But both movements cannot be combined without a magnetometer and/or gyroscope.

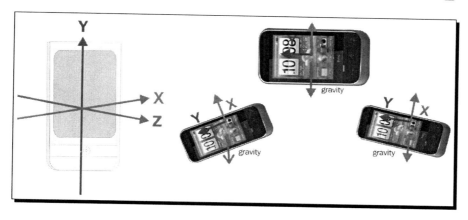

The final project structure will look as shown in the following diagram:

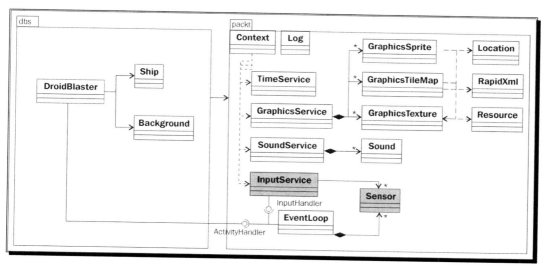

> Project DroidBlaster_Part8-2 can be used as a starting point for this part. The resulting project is provided with this book under the name DroidBlaster_Part8-3.

Time for action – turning your device into a joypad

First, we need to handle sensor events in the event loop.

1. Open `InputHandler.hpp` and add a new method `onAccelerometerEvent()`. Include `android/sensor.h` official header for sensors.

    ```
    #ifndef _PACKT_INPUTHANDLER_HPP_
    #define _PACKT_INPUTHANDLER_HPP_

    #include <android/input.h>
    #include <android/sensor.h>

    namespace packt {
        class InputHandler {
        public:
          virtual ~InputHandler() {};

          virtual bool onTouchEvent(AInputEvent* pEvent) = 0;
          virtual bool onKeyboardEvent(AInputEvent* pEvent) = 0;
          virtual bool onTrackballEvent(AInputEvent* pEvent) = 0;
          virtual bool onAccelerometerEvent(ASensorEvent* pEvent) = 0;
        };
    }
    #endif
    ```

2. Update `jni/EventLoop.hpp` class by adding a static callback dedicated to sensors named `callback_sensor()`. This method delegates processing to member method `processSensorEvent()`, which redistributes events to `InputHandler` instance.

    A sensor event queue is represented by an `ASensorManager` opaque structure. On the opposite of the activity and input event queues, the sensor queue is not managed by the `native_app_glue` module (as seen in *Chapter 5, Writing a Fully Native Application*). We need to set it up ourselves with an `ASensorEventQueue` and an `android_poll_source`:

    ```
    #ifndef _PACKT_EVENTLOOP_HPP_
    #define _PACKT_EVENTLOOP_HPP_
    ```

```
    ...

    namespace packt {
        class EventLoop {
            ...
        protected:
            ...

            void processAppEvent(int32_t pCommand);
            int32_t processInputEvent(AInputEvent* pEvent);
            void processSensorEvent();

        private:
            friend class Sensor;

            static void callback_event(android_app* pApplication,
                int32_t pCommand);
            static int32_t callback_input(android_app* pApplication,
                AInputEvent* pEvent);
            static void callback_sensor(android_app* pApplication,
                android_poll_source* pSource);

        private:
            ...
            ActivityHandler* mActivityHandler;
            InputHandler* mInputHandler;

            ASensorManager* mSensorManager;
            ASensorEventQueue* mSensorEventQueue;
            android_poll_source mSensorPollSource;
        };
    }
    #endif
```

3. Modify file `jni/EventLoop.cpp`, starting with its constructor:

```
#include "EventLoop.hpp"
#include "Log.hpp"

namespace packt {
    EventLoop::EventLoop(android_app* pApplication) :
        mEnabled(false), mQuit(false),
        mApplication(pApplication),
        mActivityHandler(NULL), mInputHandler(NULL),
```

```
        mSensorPollSource(), mSensorManager(NULL),
        mSensorEventQueue(NULL) {
      mApplication->userData = this;
      mApplication->onAppCmd = callback_event;
      mApplication->onInputEvent = callback_input;
  }
...
```

4. When starting an EventLoop in activate(), create a new sensor queue and attach it with ASensorManager_createEventQueue() so that it gets polled with the activity and input event queues. LOOPER_ID_USER is a slot defined inside native_app_glue to attach a custom queue to the internal glue Looper (see *Chapter 5, Writing a Fully Native Application*. The glue Looper already has two internal slots (LOOPER_ID_MAIN and LOOPER_ID_INPUT handled transparently). Sensors are managed through a central manager ASensorManager which can be retrieved using ASensorManager_getInstance().

In the deactivate() method, destroy the sensor event queue without mercy with method ASensorManager_destroyEventQueue():

```
...
    void EventLoop::activate() {
        if ((!mEnabled) && (mApplication->window != NULL)) {
            mSensorPollSource.id = LOOPER_ID_USER;
            mSensorPollSource.app = mApplication;
            mSensorPollSource.process = callback_sensor;
            mSensorManager = ASensorManager_getInstance();
            if (mSensorManager != NULL) {
              mSensorEventQueue = ASensorManager_createEventQueue(
                    mSensorManager, mApplication->looper,
                    LOOPER_ID_USER, NULL, &mSensorPollSource);
                if (mSensorEventQueue == NULL) goto ERROR;
            }

            mQuit = false; mEnabled = true;
            if (mActivityHandler->onActivate() != STATUS_OK) {
                goto ERROR;
            }
        }
        return;

ERROR:
    mQuit = true;
```

```
        deactivate();
        ANativeActivity_finish(mApplication->activity);
    }

    void EventLoop::deactivate() {
        if (mEnabled) {
            mActivityHandler->onDeactivate();
            mEnabled = false;

            if (mSensorEventQueue != NULL) {
                ASensorManager_destroyEventQueue(mSensorManager,
                    mSensorEventQueue);
                mSensorEventQueue = NULL;
            }
            mSensorManager = NULL;
        }
    }
    ...
```

5. Finally, redirect sensor events to the handler in `processSensorEvent()`.
Sensor events are wrapped in an `ASensorEvent` structure. This structure
contains a `type` field to identify the sensor the event originates from
(here, to keep accelerometer events):

```
    ...
    void EventLoop::processSensorEvent() {
        ASensorEvent lEvent;
        while (ASensorEventQueue_getEvents(mSensorEventQueue,
                                    &lEvent, 1) > 0) {
            switch (lEvent.type) {
            case ASENSOR_TYPE_ACCELEROMETER:
                mInputHandler->onAccelerometerEvent(&lEvent);
                break;
            }
        }
    }

    void EventLoop::callback_sensor(android_app* pApplication,
        android_poll_source* pSource) {
        EventLoop& lEventLoop = *(EventLoop*) pApplication->userData;
        lEventLoop.processSensorEvent();
    }
}
```

6. Create a new file `jni/Sensor.hpp` as follows. The `Sensor` class is responsible for the activation (with `enable()`) and deactivation (with `disable()`) of the sensor. Method `toggle()` is a wrapper to switch the sensor state.

This class works closely with `EventLoop` to process sensor messages (actually, this code could have been integrated in `EventLoop` itself). Sensors themselves are wrapped in an `ASensor` opaque structure and have a type (a constant defined in `android/sensor.h` identical to the ones in `android.hardware.Sensor`):

```cpp
#ifndef _PACKT_SENSOR_HPP_
#define _PACKT_SENSOR_HPP_

#include "Types.hpp"

#include <android/sensor.h>

namespace packt {
    class EventLoop;

    class Sensor {
    public:
        Sensor(EventLoop& pEventLoop, int32_t pSensorType);

        status toggle();
        status enable();
        status disable();

    private:
        EventLoop& mEventLoop;
        const ASensor* mSensor;
        int32_t mSensorType;
    };
}
#endif
```

7. Implement `Sensor` in `jni/Sensor.cpp` file and write `enable()` in three steps:

- ❑ Get a sensor of a specific type with `ASensorManager_getDefaultSensor()`.

- ❑ Then, enable it with `ASensorEventQueue_enableSensor()` so that the event queue receives related events.

❑ Set the desired event rate with `ASensorEventQueue_setEventRate()`. For a game, we typically want measures close to real time. The minimum delay is queried with `ASensor_getMinDelay()` and setting it to a lower value results in failure.

Obviously, we should perform this setup only when the sensor event queue is ready. Sensor is deactivated in `disable()` with `ASensorEventQueue_disableSensor()` thanks to the sensor instance retrieved previously.

```cpp
#include "Sensor.hpp"
#include "EventLoop.hpp"
#include "Log.hpp"

namespace packt {
    Sensor::Sensor(EventLoop& pEventLoop, int32_t pSensorType):
        mEventLoop(pEventLoop),
        mSensor(NULL),
        mSensorType(pSensorType)
    {}

    status Sensor::toggle() {
        return (mSensor != NULL) ? disable() : enable();
    }

    status Sensor::enable() {
        if (mEventLoop.mEnabled) {
            mSensor = ASensorManager_getDefaultSensor(
                mEventLoop.mSensorManager, mSensorType);
            if (mSensor != NULL) {
                if (ASensorEventQueue_enableSensor(
                        mEventLoop.mSensorEventQueue, mSensor) < 0) {
                    goto ERROR;
                }

                int32_t lMinDelay = ASensor_getMinDelay(mSensor);
                if (ASensorEventQueue_setEventRate(mEventLoop
                        .mSensorEventQueue, mSensor, lMinDelay) < 0) {
                    goto ERROR;
                }
            } else {
                packt::Log::error("No sensor type %d", mSensorType);
            }
        }
    }
```

```
        return STATUS_OK;

    ERROR:
        Log::error("Error while activating sensor.");
        disable();
        return STATUS_KO;
    }

    status Sensor::disable() {
        if ((mEventLoop.mEnabled) && (mSensor != NULL)) {
            if (ASensorEventQueue_disableSensor(
                mEventLoop.mSensorEventQueue, mSensor) < 0) {
                goto ERROR;
            }
            mSensor = NULL;
        }
        return STATUS_OK;

    ERROR:
        Log::error("Error while deactivating sensor.");
        return STATUS_KO;
    }
}
```

Sensors are connected to our event loop. Let's handle sensor events in our input service.

8. Manage the accelerometer sensor in `jni/InputService.hpp`. Add a method `stop()` to disable sensors when service stops:

```
#ifndef _PACKT_INPUTSERVICE_HPP_
#define _PACKT_INPUTSERVICE_HPP_

#include "Context.hpp"
#include "InputHandler.hpp"
#include "Sensor.hpp"
#include "Types.hpp"

#include <android_native_app_glue.h>

namespace packt {
    class InputService : public InputHandler {
    public:
        InputService(android_app* pApplication,
```

```
        Sensor* pAccelerometer,
     const int32_t& pWidth, const int32_t& pHeight);

   status start();
   status update();
   void stop();
   ...


  public:
     bool onTouchEvent(AInputEvent* pEvent);
     bool onKeyboardEvent(AInputEvent* pEvent);
     bool onTrackballEvent(AInputEvent* pEvent);
     bool onAccelerometerEvent(ASensorEvent* pEvent);

  private:
     ...
     bool mMenuKey;

     Sensor* mAccelerometer;
   };
}
#endif
```

9. Rewrite `update()` to toggle the accelerometer when the menu button is pressed (instead of leaving the application). Implement `stop()` to disable sensors when application is stopped (and save battery):

```
...
namespace packt {
   InputService::InputService(android_app* pApplication,
       Sensor* pAccelerometer,
        const int32_t& pWidth, const int32_t& pHeight) :
       mApplication(pApplication),
       mHorizontal(0.0f), mVertical(0.0f),
       mRefPoint(NULL), mWidth(pWidth), mHeight(pHeight),
       mMenuKey(false),
       mAccelerometer(pAccelerometer)
   {}

   ...

   status InputService::update() {
       if (mMenuKey) {
           if (mAccelerometer->toggle() != STATUS_OK) {
```

```
                return STATUS_KO;
            }
        }

        mMenuKey = false;
        return STATUS_OK;
    }

    void InputService::stop() {
        mAccelerometer->disable();
    }
...
```

10. Here is the core code which computes direction from the accelerometer captured values. In the following code, X and Z axis express the roll and the pitch respectively. We check for both, the roll and the pitch, whether the device is in a neutral orientation (that is, CENTER_*) or sloping to the extreme (MIN_* and (MAX_*). Z values need to be inverted:

 Android devices can be naturally portrait-oriented (most smart-phones if not all) or landscape-oriented (mostly tablets). This has an impact on applications which require portrait or landscape mode: axes are not aligned the same way. Use y-axis (that is, vector.y) instead of x axis in the following piece for landscape oriented devices.

```
...
    bool InputService::onAccelerometerEvent(ASensorEvent* pEvent) {
        const float GRAVITY  =  ASENSOR_STANDARD_GRAVITY / 2.0f;
        const float MIN_X    = -1.0f; const float MAX_X = 1.0f;
        const float MIN_Y    =  0.0f; const float MAX_Y = 2.0f;
        const float CENTER_X = (MAX_X + MIN_X) / 2.0f;
        const float CENTER_Y = (MAX_Y + MIN_Y) / 2.0f;

        float lRawHorizontal = pEvent->vector.x / GRAVITY;
        if (lRawHorizontal > MAX_X) {
            lRawHorizontal = MAX_X;
        } else if (lRawHorizontal < MIN_X) {
            lRawHorizontal = MIN_X;
        }
        mHorizontal = CENTER_X - lRawHorizontal;

        float lRawVertical = pEvent->vector.z / GRAVITY;
```

```
            if (lRawVertical > MAX_Y) {
                lRawVertical = MAX_Y;
            } else if (lRawVertical < MIN_Y) {
                lRawVertical = MIN_Y;
            }
            mVertical = lRawVertical - CENTER_Y;

            return true;
        }
    }
```

11. In `jni/DroidBlaster.cpp`, call `stop()` to ensure sensors get disabled:

```
#include "DroidBlaster.hpp"
#include "Log.hpp"

namespace dbs {
    ...
    void DroidBlaster::onDeactivate() {
        packt::Log::info("Deactivating DroidBlaster");
        mGraphicsService->stop();
        mInputService->stop();
        mSoundService->stop();
    }
    ...
}
```

Let's terminate by initializing the input service properly after all the modifications are done.

12. Finally, initialize the accelerometer in `jni/Main.hpp`. Because they are closely related, move the `EventLoop` initialization line on top:

```
...
#include "GraphicsService.hpp"
#include "InputService.hpp"
#include "Sensor.hpp"
#include "SoundService.hpp"
#include "TimeService.hpp"
#include "Log.hpp"

void android_main(android_app* pApplication) {
    packt::EventLoop lEventLoop(pApplication);
    packt::Sensor lAccelerometer(lEventLoop,
        ASENSOR_TYPE_ACCELEROMETER);
```

```
        packt::TimeService lTimeService;
        packt::GraphicsService lGraphicsService(pApplication,
            &lTimeService);
        packt::InputService lInputService(pApplication,
    &lAccelerometer,
            lGraphicsService.getWidth(),lGraphicsService.getHeight());
        packt::SoundService lSoundService(pApplication);

        packt::Context lContext = { &lGraphicsService, &lInputService,
            &lSoundService, &lTimeService };

        dbs::DroidBlaster lDroidBlaster(&lContext);
        lEventLoop.run(&lDroidBlaster, &lInputService);
    }
```

What just happened?

We have created an event queue to listen to sensor events. Events are wrapped in an
`ASensorEvent` structure, defined in `android/sensor.h`. This structure provides the:

◆ Sensor event origin, that is, which sensor produced this event.

◆ Sensor event occurrence time.

◆ Sensor output value. This value is stored in a union structure, that is, you
  can use either one of the inside structures (here, we are interested in the
  `acceleration` vector).

The same `ASensorEvent` structure is used for any Android sensor:

```
typedef struct ASensorEvent {
    int32_t version;
    int32_t sensor;
    int32_t type;
    int32_t reserved0;
    int64_t timestamp;
    union {
        float           data[16];
        ASensorVector   vector;
        ASensorVector   acceleration;
        ASensorVector   magnetic;
        float           temperature;
        float           distance;
        float           light;
        float           pressure;
    };
```

```
        int32_t reserved1[4];
} ASensorEvent;

typedef struct ASensorVector {
    union {
        float v[3];
        struct {
            float x;
            float y;
            float z;
        };
        struct {
            float azimuth;
            float pitch;
            float roll;
        };
    };
    int8_t status;
    uint8_t reserved[3];
} ASensorVector;
```

In our example, the accelerometer is set up with the lowest event rate possible, which may vary between devices. It is important to note that sensor event rate has a direct impact on battery saving! So use a rate that is sufficient for your application. `ASensor_` API offers some method to query available sensors and their capabilities: `ASensor_getName()`, `ASensor_getVendor()`, `ASensor_getMinDelay()`, and so on.

Sensors have a unique identifier, defined in `android/sensor.h`, which is the same on all Android devices: `ASENSOR_TYPE_ACCELEROMETER`, `ASENSOR_TYPE_MAGNETIC_FIELD`, `ASENSOR_TYPE_GYRISCOPE` `ASENSOR_TYPE_LIGHT`, `ASENSOR_TYPE_PROXIMITY`. Additional sensors may exist and be available even if they are not named in `android/sensor.h` header. On Gingerbread, this is the case of the gravity sensor (identifier 9), the linear acceleration sensor (identifier 10) and the rotation vector (identifier 11).

The sense of orientation

The rotation vector sensor, successor of the now deprecated orientation vector, is essential in Augmented Reality application. It gives you device orientation in 3D space. Combined with the GPS, it allows locating any object through the eye of your device. The rotation sensor provides a data vector, which can be translated to an OpenGL view matrix thanks to the `android.hardware.SensorManager` class (see its source code). An example is provided with this book in `DroidBlaster_Part8-3-Orientation`.

Have a go hero – Handling screen rotation

There is sadly no way to get device rotation relative to screen natural orientation with native APIs. Thus, we need to rely on JNI to get current rotation properly. The piece of Java code to detect screen rotation is the following:

```
WindowManager mgr = (InputMethodManager)
        myActivity.getSystemService(Context.WINDOW_SERVICE);
int rotation = mgr.getDefaultDisplay().getRotation();
```

Rotation values are can be ROTATION_0, ROTATION_90, ROTATION_180, or ROTATION_270 (provided in the Java class Surface). Write the equivalent JNI code in four steps:

1. Create a Configuration class which takes an android_app as constructor parameter and whose only purpose is to provide the rotation value.

2. In Configuration constructor, attach the JavaVM, retrieve the rotation, and finally detach the VM.

3. Instantiate both the Configuration class in your android_main() method and pass it to your InputService to get rotation value.

4. Write a utility method toScreenCoord() to convert canonical sensor coordinates (that is, in the natural orientation referential) to screen coordinates:

```
void InputService::toScreenCoord(screen_rot pRotation,
    ASensorVector* pCanonical, ASensorVector* pScreen) {
    struct AxisSwap {
        int8_t mNegX; int8_t mNegY;
        int8_t mXSrc;     int8_t mYSrc;
    };
    static const AxisSwap lAxisSwaps[] = {
        {  1, -1, 0, 1},   // ROTATION_0
        { -1, -1, 1, 0},   // ROTATION_90
        { -1,  1, 0, 1},   // ROTATION_180
        {  1,  1, 1, 0}};  // ROTATION_270
    const AxisSwap& lSwap = lAxisSwaps[pRotation];

    pScreen->v[0] = lSwap.mNegX * pCanonical->v[lSwap.mXSrc];
    pScreen->v[1] = lSwap.mNegY * pCanonical->v[lSwap.mYSrc];
    pScreen->v[2] = pCanonical->v[2];
}
```

This piece of code comes from an interesting document about sensors on the NVidia developer site at http://developer.download.nvidia.com/tegra/docs/ tegra_android_accelerometer_v5f.pdf.

5. Finally, fix `onAccelerometerEvent()` to reverse accelerometer axis according to the current screen rotation. Just call the utility method and use resulting X and Z axes.

 The final project is provided with this book in DroidBlaster_Part8-3-Keyboard.

Summary

In this chapter, we learnt different ways to interact with Android natively using input and sensors. We discovered how to handle touch events. We also read key events from keyboard and D-Pad and processed trackballs motion events. Finally, we have turned the accelerometer into a Joypad. Because of Android fragmentation, expect specificities in input device's behavior and be prepared to adapt your code.

We have already been far in the capabilities of Android NDK in terms of application structure, graphics, sound, input, and sensors. But reinventing the wheel is not a solution! In the next chapter, we are going to unleash the real power of Android by porting existing libraries.

Porting Existing Libraries to Android

There are two main reasons why one would be interested in the Android NDK: first, for performance, and second, for portability. In the previous chapters, we have seen how to access main native Android APIs from native code for efficiency purposes. In this chapter, we are going to bring the whole C/C++ ecosystem to Android. Well, at least discovering the path, as decades of C/C++ development would be difficult to fit the limited memory of mobile devices anyway! Indeed, C and C++ are still some of the most widely used programming languages nowadays.

*In previous NDK releases, portability was limited due to the partial support of C++, especially **Exceptions** and **Run-Time Type information** (or **RTTI**, a basic C++ reflection mechanism to get data types at runtime such as* `instanceof` *in Java). Any library requiring them could not be ported without modifying their code or installing a custom NDK (the **Crystax NDK**, rebuilt by the community from official sources and available at* `http://www.crystax.net/`*). Hopefully, many of these restrictions have been lifted in NDK R5 (except wide character support).*

In this chapter, in order to port existing code to Android, we are going to learn how to:

- Activate the **Standard Template Library** and **Boost** framework
- Enable **exceptions** and **Run Time Type Information** (or **RTTI**)
- Compile two open source libraries: **Box2D** and **Irrlicht**
- Write **Makefiles** to compile modules

By the end of this chapter, you should understand the native building process and know how to use Makefiles appropriately.

Developing with the Standard Template Library

The **Standard Template Library** (or **STL**) is a normalized library of containers, iterators, algorithms, and helper classes, to ease most common programming operations: dynamic arrays, associative arrays, strings, sorting, and so on. This library gained reconnaissance among developers over years and is widely spread. Developing in C++ without the STL is like coding with one hand behind to the back!

Until NDK R5, no STL was included. The whole C++ ecosystem was only one step ahead, but not yet reachable. With some efforts, compiling an STL implementation (for example, STLport), for which exceptions and RTTI were optional, was possible, but only if the code built upon did not require these features (unless building with the Crystax NDK). Anyway, this nightmare is over, as STL and exceptions are now officially included. Two implementations can be chosen:

- ◆ **STLport**, a multiplatform STL, which is probably one of the most portable implementations, well accepted among open source projects
- ◆ **GNU STL** (more commonly **libstdc++**), the official GCC STL

The STLport version included in the NDK R5 does not support exceptions (RTTI being supported from NDK R7) but can be used either as a shared or a static library. On the other hand, GNU STL supports exceptions but is currently available as a static library only.

In this first part, let's embed STLport in DroidBlaster to ease collection management.

> Project `DroidBlaster_Part8-3` can be used as a starting point for this part. The resulting project is provided with this book under the name `DroidBlaster_Part9-1`.

Time for action – embedding GNU STL in DroidBlaster

1. Create a `jni/Application.mk` file beside `jni/Android.mk` and write the following content. That's it! Your application is now STL-enabled, thanks to this single line:

   ```
   APP_STL = stlport_static
   ```

   Of course, enabling the STL is useless, if we do not actively use it in our code. Let's take advantage of this opportunity to switch from asset files to external files (on a `sdcard` or internal memory).

2. Open the existing file, `jni/Resource.hpp`, and:

- ❑ Include the `fstream` stl header to read files.
- ❑ Replace the Asset management members with an `ifstream` object (that is, an input file stream). We are also going to need a buffer for the `bufferize()` method.
- ❑ Remove the `descript()` method and the `ResourceDescriptor` class. Descriptors work with the Asset API only.

```
#ifndef _PACKT_RESOURCE_HPP_
#define _PACKT_RESOURCE_HPP_

#include "Types.hpp"

#include <fstream>

namespace packt {
    ...

    class Resource {
        ...

    private:
        const char* mPath;
        std::ifstream mInputStream;
        char* mBuffer;
    };
}

#endif
```

3. Open the corresponding implementation file `jni/Resource.cpp`. Replace the previous implementation, based on the asset management API with STL streams. Files will be opened in binary mode (even the tile map XML file that is going to be directly buffered in memory). To read the file length, we can use the `stat()` POSIX primitive. Method `bufferize()` is emulated with a temporary buffer:

```
#include "Resource.hpp"
#include "Log.hpp"

#include <sys/stat.h>

namespace packt {
    Resource::Resource(android_app* pApplication, const char*
pPath):
```

```
                    mPath(pPath), mInputStream(), mBuffer(NULL)
    {}

    status Resource::open() {
        mInputStream.open(mPath, std::ios::in | std::ios::binary);
        return mInputStream ? STATUS_OK : STATUS_KO;
    }

    void Resource::close() {
        mInputStream.close();
        delete[] mBuffer; mBuffer = NULL;
    }

    status Resource::read(void* pBuffer, size_t pCount) {
        mInputStream.read((char*)pBuffer, pCount);
        return (!mInputStream.fail()) ? STATUS_OK : STATUS_KO;
    }

    const char* Resource::getPath() {
        return mPath;
    }

    off_t Resource::getLength() {
        struct stat filestatus;
        if (stat(mPath, &filestatus) >= 0) {
            return filestatus.st_size;
        } else {
            return -1;
        }
    }

    const void* Resource::bufferize() {
        off_t lSize = getLength();
        if (lSize <= 0) return NULL;

        mBuffer = new char[lSize];
        mInputStream.read(mBuffer, lSize);
        if (!mInputStream.fail()) {
            return mBuffer;
        } else {
            return NULL;
        }
    }
}
```

These changes to the reading system should all be transparent. Except one.

4. Background music was previously played through an asset descriptor. Now, we provide a real file. So, in `jni/SoundService.cpp`, change the data source by replacing the `SLDataLocator_AndroidFD` structure with `SLDataLocation_URI`.

The file location has to be prefixed with `file://`, when it comes from the `sdcard` (it could also be, for example, `http://`, if the file was coming from a server). To help building the final URI, concatenate the prefix and the path using STL strings. The file is still an MP3, so the data format does not change:

```cpp
#include "SoundService.hpp"
#include "Resource.hpp"
#include "Log.hpp"

#include <string>

namespace packt {
    ...

    status SoundService::playBGM(const char* pPath) {
        SLresult lRes;
        Log::info("Opening BGM %s", pPath);

        SLDataLocator_URI lDataLocatorIn;
        std::string lPath = std::string("file://") + pPath;
        lDataLocatorIn.locatorType = SL_DATALOCATOR_URI;
        lDataLocatorIn.URI = (SLchar*) lPath.c_str();

        SLDataFormat_MIME lDataFormat;
        lDataFormat.formatType    = SL_DATAFORMAT_MIME;
        ...

        return STATUS_OK;

    ERROR:
        return STATUS_KO;
    }
    ...
}
```

5. Copy resources in your `asset` directory to your sdcard (or internal memory, depending on your device) in the directory `droidblaster` (for example, `/sdcard/droidblaster`).

Almost all Android devices can store files in an additional storage location mounted in directory `/sdcard`. "Almost" is the important word here... Since the first Android G1, the meaning of "sdcard" has changed. Some recent devices have an external storage that is in fact internal (e.g. flash memory on some tablets), and some others have a second storage location at their disposal (although in most cases, the second storage is mounted inside `/sdcard`). Moreover, path `/sdcard` is not engraved into the marble...

To detect safely the additional storage location, the only solution is to rely on JNI, by calling `android.os.Environment.getExternalStorageDirectory()`. You can also check that storage is available with `getExternalStorageState()`. Note that the word "External" in API method names is here for historical reasons only.

Replace paths to resources in each file that needs one (change the path if necessary):

- ❏ `/sdcard/droidblaster/tilemap.png` in `jni/Background.cpp`.
- ❏ `/sdcard/droidblaster/tilemap.tmx` in `jni/Background.cpp`.
- ❏ `/sdcard/droidblaster/start.pcm` in `jni/DroidBlaster.cpp`.
- ❏ `/sdcard/droidblaster/bgm.mp3` in `jni/DroidBlaster.cpp`.
- ❏ `/sdcard/droidblaster/ship.png` in `jni/Ship.cpp`.

6. Run the application. Noticed it? Everything runs like before!

Now, let's take advantage of the STL to give some company to our lonely ship.

7. First, let's create a little randomization helper macro in existing file `jni/Type.hpp`:

```
#ifndef _PACKT_TYPES_HPP_
#define _PACKT_TYPES_HPP_

#include <stdint.h>
#include <cstdlib>

namespace packt {
    ...
}

#define RAND(pMax) (float(pMax) * float(rand()) / float(RAND_MAX))

#endif
```

8. The random value generator has to be initialized first, with a seed. A possible solution is to set the seed value to the current time in `jni/TimeService.cpp`:

```cpp
#include "TimeService.hpp"
#include "Log.hpp"

#include <cstdlib>

namespace packt {
    TimeService::TimeService() :
        mElapsed(0.0f),
        mLastTime(0.0f) {
        srand(time(NULL));
    }
    ...
}
```

9. Create a new header file `jni/Asteroid.hpp`, similar to the one used for the Ship game object, to represent a dangerous and frightening asteroid:

```cpp
#ifndef _DBS_ASTEROID_HPP_
#define _DBS_ASTEROID_HPP_

#include "Context.hpp"
#include "GraphicsService.hpp"
#include "GraphicsSprite.hpp"
#include "Types.hpp"

namespace dbs {
    class Asteroid {
    public:
        Asteroid(packt::Context* pContext);

        void spawn();
        void update();

    private:
        packt::GraphicsService* mGraphicsService;
        packt::TimeService* mTimeService;

        packt::GraphicsSprite* mSprite;
        packt::Location mLocation;
        float mSpeed;
    };
}

#endif
```

10. Implement the `Asteroid` class in `jni/Asteroid.cpp`. An asteroid is represented with a sprite loaded at construction time.

The `Asteroid` game object itself is initialized in `spawn()`, above the top of the screen (that is, they are initially hidden). Asteroids are distributed randomly over screen width and have a random animation and movement speed.

During frame processing in `update()`, asteroids fall from top to bottom, according to their speed. When they reach the bottom, they are recreated.

```cpp
#include "Asteroid.hpp"
#include "Log.hpp"

namespace dbs {
    Asteroid::Asteroid(packt::Context* pContext) :
        mTimeService(pContext->mTimeService),
        mGraphicsService(pContext->mGraphicsService),
        mLocation(), mSpeed(0.0f) {
        mSprite = pContext->mGraphicsService->registerSprite(
            mGraphicsService->registerTexture(
                "/sdcard/droidblaster/asteroid.png"),
            64, 64, &mLocation);
    }

    void Asteroid::spawn() {
        const float MIN_SPEED = 4.0f;
        const float MIN_ANIM_SPEED = 8.0f, ANIM_SPEED_RANGE = 16.0f;

        mSpeed = -RAND(mGraphicsService->getHeight()) - MIN_SPEED;
        float lPosX = RAND(mGraphicsService->getWidth());
        float lPosY = RAND(mGraphicsService->getHeight())
                      + mGraphicsService->getHeight();
        mLocation.setPosition(lPosX, lPosY);

        float lAnimSpeed = MIN_ANIM_SPEED + RAND(ANIM_SPEED_RANGE);
        mSprite->setAnimation(8, -1, lAnimSpeed, true);
    }

    void Asteroid::update() {
        mLocation.translate(0.0f, mTimeService->elapsed() * mSpeed);
        if (mLocation.mPosY <= 0) {
            spawn();
        }
    }
}
```

11. Open the `jni/DroidBlaster.hpp` header and include the `vector` header, the most common STL container that encapsulates C arrays. Then, declare a vector of asteroid pointers (prefixed with the `std` namespace):

```
#ifndef _PACKT_DROIDBLASTER_HPP_
#define _PACKT_DROIDBLASTER_HPP_

#include "ActivityHandler.hpp"
#include "Asteroid.hpp"
#include "Background.hpp"
#include "Context.hpp"
. . .
#include "Types.hpp"

#include <vector>

namespace dbs {
    class DroidBlaster : public packt::ActivityHandler
    {
        . . .
    private:
        . . .

        Background mBackground;
        Ship mShip;
        std::vector<Asteroid*> mAsteroids;
        packt::Sound* mStartSound;
    };
}

#endif
```

12. Finally, open `jni/DroidBlaster.cpp`. Include this new container in the constructor initialization list and insert `Asteroid` instances with method `push_back()`.

Then, in the destructor, we can iterate through the vector using an `iterator` to release every vector entry. Syntax is a bit more tedious, but gives more flexibility:

```
#include "DroidBlaster.hpp"
#include "Log.hpp"

namespace dbs {
    DroidBlaster::DroidBlaster(packt::Context* pContext) :
```

```
        mGraphicsService(pContext->mGraphicsService),
        mInputService(pContext->mInputService),
        mSoundService(pContext->mSoundService),
        mTimeService(pContext->mTimeService),
        mBackground(pContext), mShip(pContext), mAsteroids(),
        mStartSound(mSoundService->registerSound(
                        "/sdcard/droidblaster/start.pcm")) {
    for (int i = 0; i < 16; ++i) {
        mAsteroids.push_back(new Asteroid(pContext));
    }
}

DroidBlaster::~DroidBlaster() {
    std::vector<Asteroid*>::iterator iAsteroid =
                    mAsteroids.begin();
    for (; iAsteroid < mAsteroids.end() ; ++iAsteroid) {
        delete *iAsteroid;
    }
    mAsteroids.clear();
}
...
```

13. Still in `jni/DroidBlaster.cpp`, apply the same iteration technique to initialize asteroid game objects (in `onActivate()`) and iterate each frame (in `onStep()`):

```
    ...
    packt::status DroidBlaster::onActivate() {
        ...

        mBackground.spawn();
        mShip.spawn();
        std::vector<Asteroid*>::iterator iAsteroid =
                        mAsteroids.begin();
        for (; iAsteroid < mAsteroids.end() ; ++iAsteroid) {
            (*iAsteroid)->spawn();
        }

        mTimeService->reset();
        return packt::STATUS_OK;
    }

    ...
```

```
packt::status DroidBlaster::onStep() {
    mTimeService->update();

    mBackground.update();
    mShip.update();
    std::vector<Asteroid*>::iterator iAsteroid =
                    mAsteroids.begin();
    for (; iAsteroid < mAsteroids.end(); ++iAsteroid) {
        (*iAsteroid)->update();
    }

    // Updates services.
    ...
    return packt::STATUS_OK;
}
...
}
```

14. Copy the `asteroid.png` sprite sheet to your `droidblaster` storage directory.

 File `asteroid.png` is provided with this book in `Chapter9/Resource`.

What just happened?

We have seen how to access a binary file located on the SD-Card through STL streams. All asset files became simple files on the additional storage. This change can be made almost transparent at the exception of OpenSL ES MIME player, which needs a different locator. We have also seen how to manipulate STL strings and avoid using the complex C string manipulation primitives.

Finally, we have implemented a set of `Asteroid` game objects managed inside an STL container `vector`, instead of a raw C array. STL containers automatically handle memory management (array resizing operations and so on). File access happens like on any Unix file systems, SD-Card being available from a mount point (located generally, but not always, in `/sdcard`).

 SD-card storage should always be considered for applications with heavy resource files. Indeed, installing heavy APK causes trouble on memory-limited devices.

Android and endianness

Beware of platform and file endianness with external files. Although all official Android devices are little-endian, there is no guarantee this will remain true (for example, there exist some unofficial ports for Android on other CPU architectures). ARM supports both little-and big-endian encoding, whereas x86 (available since NDK R6) are little-endian only. Endian encoding is convertible, thanks to POSIX primitives declared in `endian.h`.

We have linked STLport as a static library. But, we could have linked it dynamically, or linked to the GNU STL. Which choice to make depends on your needs:

- No exceptions or RTTI needed, but STL required by several libraries: In that case, if a consequent subset of STL features is necessary, `stlport_shared` should be used.

- No exceptions or RTTI needed and STL used by a single library or only a small subset required: Consider using `stlport_static` instead, as memory usage may be lower.

- Exception handling or RTTI are needed: Link against `gnustl_static`.

Since NDK R7, RTTI are supported by STLport, but not exceptions.

STL is definitely a huge improvement that avoids repetitive and error-prone code. Many open source libraries require it and can now be ported without much trouble. More documentation about it can be found at `http://www.cplusplus.com/reference/stl` and on SGI's website (publisher of the first STL), at `http://www.sgi.com/tech/stl`.

Static versus shared

Remember that shared libraries need to be loaded manually at runtime. If you forget to load one of them, an error is raised, as soon as dependent libraries (or the application) are loaded. As it is not possible to predict in advance which functions are going to be called, they are loaded entirely in memory, even if most of their contents remain unused.

On the other hand, static libraries are de facto loaded with dependent libraries. Indeed, static libraries do not really exist as such. They are copied into dependent libraries during linking. The drawback is that binary code may get duplicated in each library, and memory is thus wasted. However, since the linker knows precisely which part of the library gets called from the embedding code, it can copy only what is needed, resulting in a limited size after compilation.

Also remember that a Java application can load shared libraries only (which can be themselves linked against either shared or static libraries). With a native activity, the main shared library is specified through the `android.app.lib_name` property, in the application manifest. Libraries referenced from another library must be loaded manually before. The NDK does not do this itself.

Shared libraries can be loaded easily, using `System.loadLibrary()` in a JNI application. But, a `NativeActivity` is transparent. So, if you decide to use shared libraries, then the only solution is to write your own Java activity, inheriting from `NativeActivity` and invoking the appropriate `loadLibrary()` directives. For instance, below is what DroidBlaster activity would look like, if we were using `stlport_shared` instead:

```
package com.packtpub.droidblaster

import android.app.NativeActivity

public class MyNativeActivity extends NativeActivity {
    static {
        System.loadLibrary("stlport_shared");
        System.loadLibrary("droidblaster");
    }
}
```

STL performances

When developing for performance, a standard STL container is not always the best choice, especially in terms of memory management and allocation. Indeed, STL is an all-purpose library, written for common cases. Alternative libraries should be considered for performance-critical code. A few examples are:

- **EASTL**: An STL replacement library, developed by Electronic Arts, and developed with gaming in mind. Only 50 percent of the projects have been released (as part of the EA open source program), which are nevertheless highly interesting. An extract is available in the repository `https://github.com/paulhodge/EASTL`. A must-read paper detailing EASTL technical details can be found on the Open Standards website at `http://www.open-std.org/jtc1/sc22/wg21/docs/papers/2007/n2271.html`.

- **RDESTL**: It is an open source subset of the STL, based on the EASTL technical paper, which was published several years before EASTL code release. The code repository can be found at `http://code.google.com/p/rdestl/`.

- **Google SparseHash**: For a high performance associative array library (note that **RDESTL** is also quite good at that).

This is far from exhaustive. Just define your exact needs to make the most appropriate choice.

Compiling Boost on Android

If STL is the most common framework among C++ programs, Boost probably comes right after. A real Swiss army knife, this toolkit contains a profusion of utilities to handle most common needs, and even more! The most popular features of Boost are smart pointers, an encapsulation of raw pointers in a reference-counting class to handle memory allocation, and deallocation automatically. They avoid most memory leaks or pointer misuse for almost free.

Boost, like STL, is mainly a template library, which means that no compilation is needed for most of its modules. For instance, including the smart pointer header file is enough to use them. However, a few of its modules need to be compiled as a library first (for example, the threading module).

We are now going to see how to build Boost on the Android NDK and replace raw, unmanaged pointers with smarter ones.

 Project `DroidBlaster_Part9-1` can be used as a starting point for this part. The resulting project is provided with this book, under the name `DroidBlaster_Part9-2`.

Time for action – embedding Boost in DroidBlaster

1. Download Boost from `http://www.boost.org/` (version 1.47.0, in this book).

    The Boost 1.47.0 archive is provided with this book in directory `Chapter09/Library`.

2. Uncompress the archive into `${ANDROID_NDK}/sources`. Name the directory `boost`.

3. Open a command line window and go to the `boost` directory. Launch `bootstrap.bat` on Windows or the `./bootstrap.sh` script on Linux and Mac OS X, to build **b2**. This program, previously named **BJam**, is a custom building tool similar to **Make**.

4. Open the file `boost/tools/build/v2/user-config.jam`. This file is, like its name suggests, a configuration file that can be set up to customize Boost compilation.

   ```
   Update user-config.jam. Initial content contains only comments
   and can be erased:
   import os ;
   ```

```
if [ os.name ] = CYGWIN || [ os.name ] = NT {
    androidPlatform = windows ;
}
else if [ os.name ] = LINUX {
    androidPlatform = linux-x86 ;
}
else if [ os.name ] = MACOSX {
    androidPlatform = darwin-x86 ;
}
...
```

5. Compilation is performed statically. BZip is deactivated, because it is unavailable, by default, on Android (we could however compile it separately):

```
...
modules.poke : NO_BZIP2 : 1 ;
...
```

6. Compiler is reconfigured to use the NDK GCC toolchain (`g++`, `ar`, and `ranlib`) in static mode (the `ar` archiver being in charge of creating the static library). Directive `sysroot` indicates which Android API release to compile and link against. The specified directory is located in the NDK and contains include files and libraries specific to this release:

```
...
ANDROID_NDK = ../.. ;

using gcc : android4.4.3 :
    $(ANDROID_NDK)/toolchains/arm-linux-androideabi-4.4.3/
prebuilt/$(androidPlatform)/bin/arm-linux-androideabi-g++ :
    <archiver>$(ANDROID_NDK)/toolchains/arm-linux-
androideabi-4.4.3/prebuilt/$(androidPlatform)/bin/arm-linux-
androideabi-ar
    <ranlib>$(ANDROID_NDK)/toolchains/arm-linux-androideabi-4.4.3/
prebuilt/$(androidPlatform)/bin/arm-linux-androideabi-ranlib

    <compileflags>--sysroot=$(ANDROID_NDK)/platforms/android-9/
arch-arm
    <compileflags>-I$(ANDROID_NDK)/sources/cxx-stl/gnu-libstdc++/
include
    <compileflags>-I$(ANDROID_NDK)/sources/cxx-stl/gnu-libstdc++/
libs/armeabi/include
...
```

7. A few options have to be defined to tweak Boost compilation:

- ❑ NDEBUG to deactivate debug mode
- ❑ BOOST_NO_INTRINSIC_WCHAR_T to indicate the lack of support for wide chars
- ❑ BOOST_FILESYSTEM_VERSION is set to 2, because the latest version of Boost FileSystem module (version 3) brings incompatible changes related to wide chars
- ❑ no-strict-aliasing to disable optimizations related to type aliasing
- ❑ -02 to specify optimization level

. . .

```
<compileflags>-DNDEBUG
<compileflags>-D__GLIBC__
<compileflags>-DBOOST_NO_INTRINSIC_WCHAR_T
<compileflags>-DBOOST_FILESYSTEM_VERSION=2
<compileflags>-lstdc++
<compileflags>-mthumb
<compileflags>-fno-strict-aliasing
<compileflags>-O2
    ;
```

8. With the previously opened terminal, still in the boost directory, launch compilation using the command line below. We need to exclude two modules not working with the NDK:

- ❑ The **Serialization** module, which requires wide characters (not supported by the official NDK yet)
- ❑ **Python**, which requires additional libraries not available on the NDK by default

```
b2 --without-python --without-serialization toolset=gcc-
android4.4.3 link=static runtime-link=static target-os=linux
--stagedir=android
```

9. Compilation should take quite some time, but eventually it will fail! Launch compilation a second time to find the error message hidden inside thousands of lines the first time. You should get a **::statvfs has not been declared**... This problem is related to boost/libs/filesystem/v2/src/v2_operations.cpp. This file, normally at line 62, includes the sys/statvfs.h system header. However, the Android NDK provides sys/vfs.h instead. We have to include it in v2_operations.cpp:

Android is (more or less) a Linux with its own specificities. If a library does not take them into account (yet!), expect to encounter these kinds of annoyances frequently.

```
. . .
# else // BOOST_POSIX_API
#    include <sys/types.h>
#    if !defined(__APPLE__) && !defined(__OpenBSD__) \
                            && !defined(__ANDROID__)
#       include <sys/statvfs.h>
#       define BOOST_STATVFS statvfs
#       define BOOST_STATVFS_F_FRSIZE vfs.f_frsize
#    else
#ifdef __OpenBSD__
#       include <sys/param.h>
#elif defined(__ANDROID__)
#       include <sys/vfs.h>
#endif
#       include <sys/mount.h>
#       define BOOST_STATVFS statfs
. . .
```

10. Compile again. No message **...failed updating X targets...** should appear this time. Libraries are compiled in ${ANDROID_NDK}/boost/android/lib/.

11. Several other incompatibilities may appear when using the various modules of Boost. For example, if you prefer to generate a random number with Boost and decide to include boost/random.hpp, you will encounter a compilation error related to endianness. To fix it, add a definition for Android in boost/boost/detail/endian.hpp, **at line 34:**

```
. . .
#if defined (__GLIBC__) || defined(__ANDROID__)
# include <endian.h>
# if (__BYTE_ORDER == __LITTLE_ENDIAN)
#   define BOOST_LITTLE_ENDIAN
. . .
```

 The patches applied in previous steps are provided with this book in directory Chapter09/Library/boost_1_47_0_android, along with compiled binaries.

12. Still in the `boost` directory, create a new `Android.mk` file to declare the newly compiled libraries as Android modules. It needs to contain one module declaration per module. For example, define one library `boost_thread`, referencing the static library `android/lib/libboost_thread.a`. Variable `LOCAL_EXPORT_C_INCLUDES` is important to automatically append boost includes when referenced from a program:

```
LOCAL_PATH:= $(call my-dir)

include $(CLEAR_VARS)

LOCAL_MODULE:= boost_thread
LOCAL_SRC_FILES:= android/lib/libboost_thread.a
LOCAL_EXPORT_C_INCLUDES := $(LOCAL_PATH)

include $(PREBUILT_STATIC_LIBRARY)
```

More modules can be declared in the same file with the same set of lines (for example, `boost_iostreams`, etc.).

Android.mk is provided in `Chapter09/Library/boost_1_47_0_android`.

Now, let's use Boost in our own project.

13. Go back to the DroidBlaster project. To include Boost in an application, we need to link with an STL implementation supporting exceptions. Thus, we need to replace STLport with GNU STL (available as a static library only) and activate exceptions:

```
APP_STL        := gnustl_static
APP_CPPFLAGS := -fexceptions
```

14. Finally, open your `Android.mk` file and include a Boost module to check that everything works. For example, try the Boost thread module:

```
LOCAL_PATH := $(call my-dir)

include $(CLEAR_VARS)

LS_CPP=$(subst $(1)/,,$(wildcard $(1)/*.cpp))
LOCAL_MODULE     := droidblaster
LOCAL_SRC_FILES := $(call LS_CPP,$(LOCAL_PATH))
LOCAL_LDLIBS    := -landroid -llog -lEGL -lGLESv1_CM -lOpenSLES
```

```
LOCAL_STATIC_LIBRARIES := android_native_app_glue png boost_thread

include $(BUILD_SHARED_LIBRARY)

$(call import-module,android/native_app_glue)
$(call import-module,libpng)
$(call import-module,boost)
```

DroidBlaster is now Boost-enabled! First, let's see if exceptions work.

15. Edit `jni/GraphicsTilemap.cpp`. Remove the RapidXML error handling block and replace the call to `setjmp()` with a C++ `try/catch`. Catch a `parse_error` exception:

```
...
namespace packt {
    ...
    int32_t* GraphicsTileMap::loadFile() {
        ...
            mResource.close();
        }
        try {
            lXmlDocument.parse<parse_default>(lFileBuffer);
        } catch (rapidxml::parse_error& parseException) {
            packt::Log::error("Error while parsing TMX file.");
            packt::Log::error(parseException.what());
            goto ERROR;
        }

        ...
    }
}
```

Now, we could use smart pointers to manage memory allocation and deallocation automatically.

16. Boost and STL tends to cause a proliferation of unreadable definitions. Let's simplify their use by defining custom smart pointer and vector types with the `typedef` keyword in `jni/Asteroid.hpp`. The vector type contains smart pointers instead of raw pointers:

```
#ifndef _DBS_ASTEROID_HPP_
#define _DBS_ASTEROID_HPP_

#include "Context.hpp"
#include "GraphicsService.hpp"
```

```
#include "GraphicsSprite.hpp"
#include "Types.hpp"

#include <boost/shared_ptr.hpp>
#include <vector>

namespace dbs {
    class Asteroid {
    ...
    public:
        typedef boost::ptr <Asteroid> ptr;
        typedef std::vector<shared> vec;
        typedef vec::iterator vec_it;
    }
}

#endif
```

17. Open `jni/DroidBlaster.hpp` and remove the `vector` header inclusion (now included in `jni/Asteroid.hpp`). Use the newly defined type `Android::vec`:

```
...
namespace dbs {
    class DroidBlaster : public packt::ActivityHandler {
        ...
    private:
        ...
        Background mBackground;
        Ship mShip;
        Asteroid::vec mAsteroids;
        packt::Sound* mStartSound;
    };
}

#endif
```

18. Every iterator declaration involving asteroids now needs to be switched with the new 'typedefed' types. Code is not much different except one thing... Look carefully: the destructor is now empty! All pointers are deallocated automatically by Boost:

```
#include "DroidBlaster.hpp"
#include "Log.hpp"

namespace dbs {
    DroidBlaster::DroidBlaster(packt::Context* pContext) :
```

```
        ... {
        for (int i = 0; i < 16; ++i) {
            Asteroid::ptr lAsteroid(new Asteroid(pContext));
            mAsteroids.push_back(lAsteroid);
        }
    }

    DroidBlaster::~DroidBlaster()
    {}

    packt::status DroidBlaster::onActivate() {
        ...
        mBackground.spawn();
        mShip.spawn();

        Asteroid::vec_it iAsteroid = mAsteroids.begin();
        for (; iAsteroid < mAsteroids.end() ; ++iAsteroid) {
            (*iAsteroid)->spawn();
        }

        mTimeService->reset();
        return packt::STATUS_OK;
    }

    ...

    packt::status DroidBlaster::onStep() {
        mTimeService->update();

        mShip.update();
        Asteroid::vec_it iAsteroid = mAsteroids.begin();
        for (; iAsteroid < mAsteroids.end(); ++iAsteroid) {
            (*iAsteroid)->update();
        }

        if (mGraphicsService->update() != packt::STATUS_OK) {
        ...
        return packt::STATUS_OK;
    }
}
```

What just happened?

We have fixed a minor issue with Boost code and written the proper configuration to compile it. Finally, we have discovered one of Boost's most famous (and helpful!) features: smart pointers. But Boost provides much more. See its documentation, located at `http://www.boost.org/doc/libs`, to discover its full richness. You can find information about Android issues on the bug tracker.

We have compiled Boost manually, using its dedicated building tool b2, customized to use the NDK tool chain. Then, prebuilt static libraries have been published using an `Android.mk` and imported into a final application with NDK `import-module` directive. Every time Boost is updated or a modification is made, code has to be manually compiled again with b2. Only the final prebuilt library is imported into client application with `PREBUILT_STATIC_LIBRARY` directive (and the shared library equivalent `PREBUILT_SHARED_LIBRARY`). On the other hand, `BUILD_STATIC_LIBRARY` and `BUILD_SHARED_LIBRARY` would recompile the whole module each time a new client application imports it or changes its own compilation settings (for example, when switching `APP_OPTIM` from debug to release in `Application.mk`).

To make Boost work, we have switched from STLport to GNU STL, which is currently the only one to support exceptions. This replacement occurs in the `Application.mk` file, by replacing `stlport_static` with `gnustl_static`. Exceptions and RTTI are activated very easily by appending `-fexceptions` and `-frtti`, respectively, to the `APP_CPPFLAGS` directive in the same file, or the `LOCAL_CPPFLAGS` of the concerned library. By default, Android compiles with `-fno-exceptions` and `-fno-rtti` flags.

A problem? Clean!

It happens often, especially when switching from one STL to another, that libraries do not get recompiled well. Sadly, this results in rather weird and obscure undefined link errors. If you have a doubt, just clean your project from the **Eclipse** menu | **Project/Clean...** or the command `ndk-build clean`, in your application root directory.

Exceptions have the reputation of making the compiled code bigger and less efficient. They prevent the compiler from performing some clever optimizations. However, whether exceptions are worse than error checking or even no check at all is a highly debatable question. In fact, Google's engineers dropped them in first releases because GCC 3.x generated poor exception handling code for ARM processors. However, the build chain now uses GCC 4.x, which does not suffer from this flaw. Compared to manual error checking and handling of exceptional cases, penalty should not be significant most of the time, assuming exceptions are used for exceptional cases only. Thus, the choice of exceptions or not is up to you (and your embedded libraries)!

Exception handling in C++ is not easy and imposes a strict discipline! They must be used strictly for exceptional cases and require carefully designed code. Have a look at the **Resource Acquisition Is Initialization** (abbreviated **RAII**) idiom to properly handle them.

Have a go hero – threading with Boost

DroidBlaster is now a bit safer, thanks to smart pointers. However, smart pointers are based on template files. There is no need to link against Boost modules to use them. So, to check if this works, modify the `DroidBlaster` class to launch a Boost thread updates asteroids in the background. The thread must be run in a separate method (for example, `updateBackground()`). You can launch the thread itself from `onStep()` and join it (that is, wait for the thread to terminate its task) before the `GraphicsService` draws its content:

```
...
    #include <boost/thread.hpp>
...


    void DroidBlaster::updateThread() {
        Asteroid::vec_it iAsteroid = mAsteroids.begin();
        for (; iAsteroid < mAsteroids.end(); ++iAsteroid) {
            (*iAsteroid)->update();
        }
    }

packt::status DroidBlaster::onStep() {
    mTimeService->update();

        boost::thread lThread(&DroidBlaster::updateThread, this);
    mBackground.update();
    mShip.update();
        lThread.join();

    if (mGraphicsService->update() != packt::STATUS_OK) {
        ...
    }
...
```

The final result is available in project DroidBlaster_Part9-2-Thread, provided with this book.

If you have experience with threads, this piece of code will probably make you jump out of your chair. Indeed, this is the best example of what should not be done with threads because:

- Functional division (for example, one service in its own thread) is generally not the best way to achieve threading efficiently.

- Only a few mobile processors are multi-cores (but this fact is changing really fast). Thus, creating a thread on a single processor will not improve performance, except for blocking operations such as I/O.

- Multi-cores can have more than just 2 cores! Depending on the problem to solve, it can be a good idea to have as many threads as cores.

- Creating threads on demand is not efficient. Thread pools are a better approach.

 Threading is a really complex matter and should be taken it into account early in your design. The Intel developer website (`http://software.intel.com/`) provides lots of interesting resources about threading and a library named **Threading Building Block**, which is a good reference in design terms (but not ported on Android, yet, despite some progress).

Porting third-party libraries to Android

With the Standard Template Library and Boost in our basket, we are ready to port almost any library to Android. Actually, many third-party libraries have been already ported and many more are coming. But when nothing is available, we have to rely on our own skills to port them. In this final part, we are going to compile two of them:

- **Box2D**: It is a highly popular open source physics simulation engine, embedded in many 2D games such as Angry Birds (quite a good reference!). It is available in several languages, Java included. But, its primary language is C++.

- **Irrlicht**: It is a real-time open source 3D engine. It is cross-platform and offers DirectX, OpenGL, and GLES bindings.

We are going to use them in the next chapter to implement the DroidBlaster physics layer and brings graphics to the third dimension.

 Project DroidBlaster_Part9-2 can be used as a starting point for this part. The resulting project is provided with this book, under the name DroidBlaster_Part9-3.

Time for action – compiling Box2D and Irrlicht with the NDK

First, let's try to port Box2D on the Android NDK.

 The Box2D 2.2.1 archive is provided with this book, in directory `Chapter09/Library`.

1. Go to `http://www.box2d.org/` and download the Box2D source archive (2.2.1 in this book). Uncompress it into `${ANDROID_NDK}/sources/` and name the directory `box2d`.

2. Create and open an `Android.mk` file in the root of the `box2d` directory. Save the current directory inside the `LOCAL_PATH` variable. This step is always necessary, because an NDK build system may switch to another directory at any time during compilation.

    ```
    LOCAL_PATH:= $(call my-dir)
    ...
    ```

3. Then, list all Box2D source files to compile. We are interested in source file name only, which can be found in `${ANDROID_NDK}/sources/box2d/Box2D/Box2D`. Use the `LS_CPP` helper function to avoid copying each filename.

    ```
    ...
    LS_CPP=$(subst $(1)/,,$(wildcard $(1)/$(2)/*.cpp))
    BOX2D_CPP:= $(call LS_CPP,$(LOCAL_PATH),Box2D/Collision) \
                $(call LS_CPP,$(LOCAL_PATH),Box2D/Collision/Shapes) \
                $(call LS_CPP,$(LOCAL_PATH),Box2D/Common) \
                $(call LS_CPP,$(LOCAL_PATH),Box2D/Dynamics) \
                $(call LS_CPP,$(LOCAL_PATH),Box2D/Dynamics/Contacts) \
                $(call LS_CPP,$(LOCAL_PATH),Box2D/Dynamics/Joints) \
                $(call LS_CPP,$(LOCAL_PATH),Box2D/Rope)
    ...
    ```

4. Then, write the Box2D module definition for a static library. First, call the `$ (CLEAR_VARS)` script. This script has to be included before any module definition, to remove any potential change made by other modules and avoid any unwanted side effects. Then, define the following settings:

    ❑   Module name in `LOCAL_MODULE`: Module name is suffixed with `_static` to avoid a name clash with the shared version we are going to define right after.

    ❑   Module source files in `LOCAL_SRC_FILES` (using `BOX2D_CPP` defined previously).

❏ Include file directory provided to clients in `LOCAL_EXPORT_C_INCLUDES`.

❏ Include file used internally for module compilation in `LOCAL_C_INCLUDES`. Here, client include files and compilation include files are the same (and are often the same in other libraries), so reuse `LOCAL_EXPORT_C_INCLUDES`, defined previously:

```
...
include $(CLEAR_VARS)

LOCAL_MODULE:= box2d_static
LOCAL_SRC_FILES:= $(BOX2D_CPP)
LOCAL_EXPORT_C_INCLUDES := $(LOCAL_PATH)
LOCAL_C_INCLUDES := $(LOCAL_EXPORT_C_INCLUDES)
...
```

5. Finally, request Box2D module compilation as a static library, as follows:

```
...
include $(BUILD_STATIC_LIBRARY)
...
```

6. The same process can be repeated to build a shared library by selecting a different module name and invoking `$(BUILD_SHARED_LIBRARY)`, instead:

```
...
include $(CLEAR_VARS)

LOCAL_MODULE:= box2d_shared
LOCAL_SRC_FILES:= $(BOX2D_CPP)
LOCAL_EXPORT_C_INCLUDES := $(LOCAL_PATH)
LOCAL_C_INCLUDES := $(LOCAL_EXPORT_C_INCLUDES)

include $(BUILD_SHARED_LIBRARY)
```

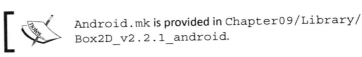

Android.mk is provided in `Chapter09/Library/Box2D_v2.2.1_android`.

7. Open DroidBlaster `Android.mk` and link against `box2d_static`, by appending it to `LOCAL_STATIC_LIBRARIES`. Provide its directory with directive `import-module`. Remember that modules are found, thanks to the NDK_MODULE_PATH variable, which points by default to `${ANDROID_NDK}/sources`:

```
LOCAL_PATH := $(call my-dir)

include $(CLEAR_VARS)
```

```
LS_CPP=$(subst $(1)/,,$(wildcard $(1)/*.cpp))
LOCAL_MODULE     := droidblaster
LOCAL_SRC_FILES := $(call LS_CPP,$(LOCAL_PATH))
LOCAL_LDLIBS     := -landroid -llog -lEGL -lGLESv1_CM -lOpenSLES
LOCAL_STATIC_LIBRARIES:=android_native_app_glue png boost_thread \
                        box2d_static

include $(BUILD_SHARED_LIBRARY)

$(call import-module,android/native_app_glue)
$(call import-module,libpng)
$(call import-module,boost)
$(call import-module,box2d)
```

8. Optionally, activate include file resolution for Box2D (as seen in *Chapter 2, Creating, Compiling, and Deploying Native Projects*). To do so, in Eclipse **Project properties**, go to section **C/C++ General/Paths and Symbols** and then the **Includes** tab, and add Box2d directory `${env_var:ANDROID_NDK}/sources/box2d`.

9. Launch DroidBlaster compilation. Box2D gets compiled without errors.

Now, let's compile Irrlicht. Irrlicht is currently not supporting Android in its official branch. The iPhone version, which implements an OpenGL ES driver, is still on a separate branch (and does not include Android support). However, it is possible to adapt this branch to make it work with Android (let's say, in a few hours, for experienced programmers).

But there is another solution: an Android fork initiated by developers from IOPixels (see `http://www.iopixels.com/`). It is ready to compile with the NDK and takes advantage of a few optimizations. It works quite well, but is not as up-to-date as the iPhone branch.

10. Check out the Irrlicht for Android repository, from Gitorious. This repository can be found at `http://girotious.org/irrlichtandroid/irrlichtandroid`. To do so, install GIT (`git` package, on Linux) and execute the following command:

```
> git clone git://gitorious.org/irrlichtandroid/irrlichtandroid.git
```

> 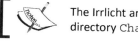 The Irrlicht archive is provided with this book, in directory `Chapter09/Library`.

11. The repository is on the disk. Move it to `${ANDROID_NDK}/sources` and name it `irrlicht`.

12. The main directory contains a ready-to-use Android project that makes use of JNI to communicate with Irrlicht on the native side. Instead, we are going to adapt this package to make use of NDK R5 native activities.

13. Go to `${ANDROID_NDK}/sources/irrlicht/project/jni` and open `Android.mk`.

14. Again, makefile starts with a `$(call my-dir)` directive, to save the current path, and `$(CLEAR_VARS)`, to erase any pre-existing values:

```
LOCAL_PATH := $(call my-dir)

include $(CLEAR_VARS)
. . .
```

15. After that, we define all the source files to compile. And there are lots of them! Nothing needs to be changed, apart from the `Android` variable. Indeed, this port of Irrlicht communicates with a Java application through JNI and gives you some places to append your own simulation code.

But, what we want is to compile Irrlicht as a module. So, let's get rid of the useless JNI binding and rely on the client application for EGL initialization. Update the `ANDROID` directive to keep only:

- ❑ `importgl.cpp`, which gives the option to bind dynamically to GLES runtime.

- ❑ `CIrrDeviceAndroid.cpp`, which is an empty stub. It delegates EGL initialization to the client. In our case, it is going to be performed by our `GraphicsService`:

```
. . .
IRRMESHLOADER = CBSPMeshFileLoader.cpp CMD2MeshFileLoader.cpp . . .

. . .
ANDROID = importgl.cpp CIrrDeviceAndroid.cpp
. . .
```

16. Then comes the module definition. Variable `LOCAL_ARM_MODE` can be removed, as these settings will be set globally, in our own application, with the `Application.mk` file. Of course, it is not forbidden to use a custom setting when needed:

```
. . .
LOCAL_MODULE := irrlicht

#LOCAL_ARM_MODE    := arm
. . .
```

17. Remove the -03 flag from `LOCAL_CFLAGS`, in the original file. This option specifies the level of optimization (here, aggressive). However, it can be set up at application level too.

`ANDROID_NDK` flag is specific to this Irrlicht port and is necessary to set up OpenGL. It works in conjunction with `DISABLE_IMPORTGL`, which disables the dynamic loading of the OpenGL ES system library, at runtime. This would be useful if we wanted to let users choose the renderer at runtime (for example, to allow selecting GLES 2.0 renderer). In that case, the GLES 1 system library would not be loaded uselessly:

```
. . .
LOCAL_CFLAGS := -DANDROID_NDK -DDISABLE_IMPORTGL
LOCAL_SRC_FILES := $(IRRLICHT_CPP)
. . .
```

18. Insert `LOCAL_EXPORT_C_INCLUDES` and `LOCAL_C_INCLUDES`, to indicate which include directory to use for library compilation and which one client applications need. The same goes for linked libraries (`LOCAL_EXPORT_LDLIBS` and `LOCAL_LDLIBS`). Keep only GLESv1_CM. The Irrlicht source folder, which contains include files needed during Irrlicht compilation only, is not appended to the export flags:

```
. . .
LOCAL_EXPORT_C_INCLUDES := $(LOCAL_PATH)/../include \
                           $(LOCAL_PATH)/libpng
LOCAL_C_INCLUDES := $(LOCAL_EXPORT_C_INCLUDES) $(LOCAL_PATH)
LOCAL_EXPORT_LDLIBS := -lGLESv1_CM -lz -ldl -llog
LOCAL_LDLIBS := $(LOCAL_EXPORT_LDLIBS)
. . .
```

19. Finally, modify Irrlicht to compile as a static library. We could also compile it as a shared library. But, because of Irrlicht's size after compilation, static mode is advised. In addition, it is going to be linked with `DroidBlaster.so` only:

```
. . .
include $(BUILD_STATIC_LIBRARY)
```

Android.mk is provided in `Chapter09/Library/irrlicht_android`.

20. Now, we need to configure what parts of Irrlicht we want to keep and which part we are not interested in. Indeed, size is an important matter with mobile development, and the raw Irrlicht library is actually more than 30mb.

As we are basically going to read OBJ meshes and PNG files and display them with GLES 1.1, everything else can be deactivated. To do so, use `#undef` directives in `${ANDROID_NDK}/irrlicht/project/include/IrrCompileConfig.h`, and keep only a few `#define` where needed:

- Target Android with GLES1 only (no GLES 2 or software renderer). DroidBlaster requires only non-compressed files read from the file system:

```
#define _IRR_COMPILE_WITH_ANDROID_DEVICE_
#define _IRR_COMPILE_WITH_OGLES1_
#define _IRR_OGLES1_USE_EXTPOINTER_
#define _IRR_MATERIAL_MAX_TEXTURES_ 4
#define __IRR_COMPILE_WITH_MOUNT_ARCHIVE_LOADER_
```

- Irrlicht embeds a few libraries of its own, such as, `libpng`, `lijpeg`, and so on:

```
#define _IRR_COMPILE_WITH_OBJ_WRITER_
#define _IRR_COMPILE_WITH_OBJ_LOADER_
#define _IRR_COMPILE_WITH_PNG_LOADER_
#define _IRR_COMPILE_WITH_PNG_WRITER_
#define _IRR_COMPILE_WITH_LIBPNG_
#define _IRR_USE_NON_SYSTEM_LIB_PNG_

#define _IRR_COMPILE_WITH_ZLIB_
#define _IRR_USE_NON_SYSTEM_ZLIB_
#define _IRR_COMPILE_WITH_ZIP_ENCRYPTION_
#define _IRR_COMPILE_WITH_BZIP2_
#define _IRR_USE_NON_SYSTEM_BZLIB_
#define _IRR_COMPILE_WITH_LZMA_
```

- Debug mode can be undef when a application gets released:

```
#define _DEBUG
```

 The modified `IrrCompileConfig.h` is provided with this book, in directory `Chapter09/Library/irrlicht_android`.

21. Finally, append Irrlicht library to DroidBlaster. We need to remove `libpng` from `LOCAL_LDLIBS` because, from now, DroidBlaster is going to use Irrlicht's `libpng`, instead of the one we compiled (which is too recent for Irrlicht):

```
...
LOCAL_STATIC_LIBRARIES:=android_native_app_glue png boost_thread \
                        box2d_static irrlicht
```

```
include $(BUILD_SHARED_LIBRARY)

$(call import-module,android/native_app_glue)
$(call import-module,libpng)
$(call import-module,boost)
$(call import-module,box2d)
$(call import-module,irrlicht/project/jni)
```

22. Optionally, activate include file resolution for Irrlicht (as done with Box2D previously). The directory is `${env_var:ANDROID_NDK}/sources/irrlicht`.

23. Launch compilation and watch Irrlicht getting compiled. It may take quite some time!

What just happened?

We have compiled two open source libraries with the Android NDK, thus reusing the many wheels already created by the community! We will see, in next chapter, how to develop code with them. There are two main steps involved when porting a library to Android:

1. Adapting library code to Android if necessary.
2. Writing build scripts (that is, makefiles) to compile code with the NDK toolchain.

The first task is generally necessary for libraries accessing system libraries, such as Irrlicht with OpenGL ES. It is obviously the hardest and most non-trivial task. In that case, always consider:

◆ Making sure required libraries exist. If not, port them before. For instance, the main Irrlicht branch cannot be used on Android because renderers are only DirectX and OpenGL (not ES). Only the iPhone branch provides a GLES renderer.

◆ Looking for the main configuration include file. One is often provided (such as `IrrCompileConfig.h` for Irrlicht) and is a good place to tweak enabled/disabled features or remove unwanted dependencies.

◆ Giving attention to system-related macros (that is, `#ifdef _LINUX ...`), which are one of the first places to change in code. Generally, one will need to define macros such as `_ANDROID_` and insert them where appropriate.

◆ Commenting non-essential code, at least to check if the library can compile and its core features work.

The second task, building scripts, is easier, although tedious. You should choose building the import module dynamically, when compiling your application, as opposed to a prebuilt library, like we did with Boost. Indeed, on-demand compilation allows tweaking compilation flags on all included libraries (like optimization flags or ARM mode) from your main `Application.mk` project file.

Prebuilt libraries are only interesting to redistribute binaries, without delivering code, or to use a custom build system. In the latter case, the NDK toolchain is used in the so-called standalone mode (that is, Do It Yourself mode!) detailed in the Android NDK documentation. But, the default `ndk-build` command is, of course, considered a better practice, to make future evolutions simpler.

Libraries are produced in `<PROJECT_DIR>/libs`. Intermediate binary files are available in `<PROJECT_DIR>/obj`. Module size in the latter place is quite impressive. That would not be viable if NDK toolchain was not **stripping** them when producing final APK. Stripping is the process of discarding unnecessary symbols from binaries. Combined with static linking, this reduces the size of DroidBlaster binaries from 60 MB to just 3 MB.

GCC optimization levels

There are 5 main optimization levels in GCC:

1. **-O0**: It disables any optimization. This is automatically set by the NDK when `APP_OPTIM` is set to `debug`.

2. **-O1**: It allows basic optimizations without increasing compilation time too much. These optimizations do not require any speed-space tradeoffs, which mean that they produce faster code without increasing executable size.

3. **-O2**: It allows advanced optimization (including `-O1`), but at the expense of compilation time. Like `-O1`, these optimizations do not require speed-space tradeoffs. This is the default level when `APP_OPTIM` is set to the `release` option, when releasing an application.

4. **-O3**: To perform aggressive optimizations (including `-O2`), which can increase executable size, such as **function inlining**. This is generally profitable, but sometimes, counterproductive (for example, increasing memory usage can also increase cache misses).

5. **-Os**: To optimize compiled code size (a subset of `-O2`) before speed.

Although `-O2` is generally the way to go for release mode, `-O3` should also be considered for performance critical code. `-O` flags being just shortcuts for the various GCC optimization flags, enabling `-O2` and with additional fine-grain flags (for example, `-finline-functions`) is an option. Anyway, the best way to find the best choice is still performing benchmarking! To get more information about the numerous GCC optimization options, have a look at `http://gcc.gnu.org/`.

Mastering Makefiles

Android makefiles are an essential piece of the NDK building process. Thus, it is important to understand the way they work, to build and manage a project properly.

Makefile variables

Compilation settings are defined though a set of predefined NDK variables. We have already seen the three most important ones: LOCAL_PATH, LOCAL_MODULE, and LOCAL_SRC_FILES. But many others exist. We can differentiate four types of variables, each with a different prefix: LOCAL_, APP_, NDK_, and PRIVATE_.

* APP_ variables refer to application-wide options and are set in Application.mk

* LOCAL_ variables are dedicated to individual module compilation and are defined in Android.mk files

* NDK_ are internal variables that usually refer to environment variables (for example, NDK_ROOT, NDK_APP_CFLAGS or NDK_APP_CPPFLAGS)

* PRIVATE_ prefixed variables are for NDK internal use only

Here is an almost exhaustive list:

LOCAL_PATH	To specify the source files, root location. Must be defined before include $(CLEAR_VARS).
LOCAL_MODULE	To define module name.
LOCAL_MODULE_FILENAME	To override default name of the compiled module, that is, lib<module name>.so for shared libraries lib<module name>.a for static libraries. No custom file extensions can be specified, so that .so or .a remains appended.
LOCAL_SRC_FILES	To define source files to compile, each separated by a space and relative to LOCAL_PATH.
LOCAL_C_INCLUDES	To specify header file directories for both C and C++ languages. The directory can be relative to the ${ANDROID_NDK} directory, but unless you need to include a specific NDK file, you are advised to use absolute path (which can be built from Makefile variables such as $(LOCAL_PATH)).
LOCAL_CPP_EXTENSION	To change default C++ file extension that is .cpp (for example, cc or cxx). Extension is necessary for GCC to discriminate between files, according to their language.
LOCAL_CFLAGS, LOCAL_CPPFLAGS, LOCAL_LDLIBS	To specify any options, flags, or macro definitions, for compilation and linking. The first one works for both C and C++, the second one is for C++ only, and the last one is for the linker.

`LOCAL_SHARED_LIBRARIES,`
 	
 `LOCAL_STATIC_LIBRARIES`
	To declare a dependency with other modules (not system libraries), shared and static modules, respectively.

`LOCAL_ARM_MODE,`
 	
 `LOCAL_ARM_NEON,`
 	
 `LOCAL_DISABLE_NO_` `EXECUTE,`
 	
 `LOCAL_FILTER_ASM`
	Advanced variables dealings with processors and assembler/binary code generation. They are not necessary for most programs.

`LOCAL_EXPORT_CFLAGS,`
 	
 `LOCAL_EXPORT_CPPFLAGS,`
 	
 `LOCAL_EXPORT_LDLIBS`
	To define additional options or flags in import modules that should be appended to clients options. For example, if a module A defines
	
	 LOCAL_EXPORT_LDLIBS := -llog
	
	 because it needs an Android logging module, then a module B that depends on A will be automatically linked to `-llog`.
	
	 `LOCAL_EXPORT_` variables are not used when compiling the module that exports them. If required, they also need to be specified in their LOCAL counterpart.

Makefile Instructions

Although these advanced features are marginally needed, Makefile is a real language with programming instructions and functions. First, know that makefiles can be broken down into several sub-makefiles, included with the instruction `include`.

Variable initialization comes in two flavours:

◆ Simple affectation : This expands variables at the time that they are initialised.

◆ Recursive affectation : This re-evaluates the affected expression, each time it is called.

The following conditional and loop instructions are available: `ifdef/endif`, `ifeq/endif`, `ifndef/endif`, `for…in/do/done`. For example, to display a message only when a variable is defined, do:

```
ifdef my_var
    # Do something...
endif
```

More advanced stuff, such as functional `if`, `and`, `or`, are at your disposal, but are rarely used. Make also provides some useful built-in functions:

`$(info <message>)`	Allows printing messages to the standard output. This is the most essential tool when writing makefiles! Variables inside information messages are allowed.
`$(warning <message>)`, `$(error <message>)`	Allows printing a warning or a fatal error that stops compilation. These messages can be parsed by Eclipse.
`$(foreach <variable>, <list>, <operation>)`	To perform an operation on a list of variables. Each element of the list is expanded in the first argument variable, before the operation is applied on it.
`$(shell <command>)`	To execute a command outside of Make. This brings all the power of Unix Shell into Makefiles but is heavily system-dependent. Avoid it if possible.
`$(wildcard <pattern>)`	Select files and directory names according to a pattern.
`$(call <function>)`	Allows evaluating a function or macro. One macro we have seen is `my-dir`, which returns the directory path of the last executed Makefile. This is why LOCAL_PATH := `$(call my-dir)` is systematically written at the beginning of each `Android.mk` file, to save in the current Makefile directory.

With the `call` directive, custom functions can easily be written. These functions look somewhat similar to recursively affected variables, except that arguments can be defined: `$(1)` for first argument, `$(2)` for second argument, and so on. A call to a function can be performed in a single line:

```
my_function=$(<do_something> ${1},${2})
$(call my_function,myparam)
```

Strings and files manipulation functions are available too:

`$(join <str1>, <str2>)`	Concatenates two strings.
`$(subst <from>, <replacement>,<string>)`, `$(patsubst <pattern>, <replacement>,<string>)`	Replaces each occurrence of a substring by another. The second one is more powerful, because it allows using patterns (which must start with "%").

`$(filter <patterns>, <text>)`
 	
`$(filter-out <patterns>, <text>)`
	Filter strings from a text matching patterns. This is useful for filtering files. For example, the following line filters any C file:
	
	$(filter %.c, $(my_source_list))

`$(strip <string>)`	Removes any unnecessary whitespace.
`$(addprefix <prefix>,<list>)`, `$(addsuffix <suffix>, <list>)`	Append a prefix and suffix, respectively, to each element of the list, each element being separated by a space.
`$(basename <path1>, <path2>, ...)`	Returns a string from which file extensions are removed.
`$(dir <path1>, <path2>)`, `$(notdir <path1>, <path2>)`	Extracts respectively the directory and the filename in a path, respectively
`$(realpath <path1>, <path2>, ...)`, `$(abspath <path1>, <path2>, ...)`	Return both canonical paths of each path argument, except that the second one does not evaluate symbolic links.

This is just really an overview of what Makefiles are capable of. For more information, refer to the full Makefile documentation, available at `http://www.gnu.org/software/make/manual/make.html`. If you are allergic to Makefiles, have a look at CMake. CMake is a simplified Make system, already building many open source libraries on the market. A port of CMake on Android is available at `http://code.google.com/p/android-cmake`.

Have a go hero – mastering Makefiles

We can play in a variety of ways with Makefiles:

- Try the affectation operator. For example, write down the following piece of code which uses the = operator in your `Android.mk` file:

```
my_value    := Android
my_message := I am an $(my_value)
$(info $(my_message))
my_value    := Android eating an apple
$(info $(my_message))
```

- Watch the result when launching compilation. Then do the same using =.Print current optimization mode. Use `APP_OPTIM` and internal variable, `NDK_APP_CFLAGS`, and observe the difference between `release` and `debug` modes:

```
$(info Optimization level: $(APP_OPTIM) $(NDK_APP_CFLAGS))
```

- Check that variables are properly defined, for example:

```
ifndef LOCAL_PATH
    $(error What a terrible failure! LOCAL_PATH not defined...)
endif
```

- Try to use the `foreach` instruction to print the list of files and directories inside the project's root directory and its `jni` folder (and make sure to use recursive affectation):

```
ls = $(wildcard $(var_dir))
dir_list := . ./jni
files := $(foreach var_dir, $(dir_list), $(ls))
```

- Try to create a macro to log a message to the standard output and its time:

```
log=$(info $(shell date +'%D %R'): $(1))
$(call log,My message)
```

- Finally, test the `my-dir` macro behaviour, to understand why `LOCAL_PATH :=  $(call my-dir)` is systematically written at the beginning of each `Android.mk`:

```
$(info MY_DIR     =$(call my-dir))
include $(CLEAR_VARS)
$(info MY_DIR     =$(call my-dir))
```

Summary

The present chapter introduced a fundamental aspect of the NDK: portability. Thanks to the recent improvements in the building toolchain, the Android NDK can now take advantage of the vast C/C++ ecosystem. It unlocks the door of a productive environment where code is shared with other platforms with the aim of creating new cutting-edge applications efficiently. More specifically, we learnt how to enable, include, and compile STL and Boost and use them in our own code. We also enabled exceptions and RTTI, and selected the appropriate STL implementation. Then, we ported Open Source libraries to Android. Finally, we discovered how to write makefiles with advanced instructions and features.

In the next chapter, these foundations will allow us to integrate a collision system and to develop a new 3D graphics system.

10
Towards Professional Gaming

We have seen in the previous chapter how to port third-party libraries to Android. More specifically, we have compiled two of them: Box2D and Irrlicht. In this chapter, we are going one step further by implementing them concretely in our sample application DroidBlaster. This is the outcome of all the effort made and all the stuff learned until now. This chapter highlights the path toward the concrete realization of your own application. Of course, there is still a very long way to go... but if the slope is steep, the road is straight!

By the end of this chapter, you should be able to do the following:

- Simulate physics and handle collisions with Box2D
- Display 3D graphics with Irrlicht

Simulating physics with Box2D

We have handled collisions or physics and with good cause! This is a rather complex subject, involving maths, numerical integration, software optimization, and so on. To answer these difficulties, physics engine have been invented on the model of 3D engine, and Box2D is one of them. This open source engine, initiated by Erin Catto in 2006, can simulate rigid body movements and collisions in a 2D environment. Bodies are the essential element of Box2D and are characterized by:

- A geometrical **shape** (polygons, circles, and so on)
- Physics properties (such as **density**, **friction**, **restitution**, and so on)
- Movement **constraints** and **joints** (to link bodies together and restrict their movement)

All these bodies are orchestrated inside a **World**, which steps simulation according to time.

In previous chapters, we have created `GraphicsService`, a `SoundService`, and `InputService`. This time, let's implement `PhysicsService` with Box2D.

 Project DroidBlaster_Part9-3 can be used as a starting point for this part. The resulting project is provided with this book under the name DroidBlaster_Part10-Box2D.

Time for action – simulating physics with Box2D

Let's encapsulate Box2D simulation in a dedicated service first:

1. First, create `jni/PhysicsObject.hpp` and insert Box2D main include file. Class `PhysicsObject` exposes a location and a collision flag publicly. It holds various Box2D properties defining a physical entity:

   - A reusable **body definition** to define how to simulate a body (static, with rotations).
   - A **body** to represent a body instance in the simulated world.
   - A **shape** to detect collisions. Here use a circle shape.
   - A **fixture** to bind a shape to a body and define a few physics properties.

   The class `PhysicsObject` is set up with `initialize()` and refreshed with `update()` after each simulation step. Method `createTarget()` will help us create a joint for the ship.

```
#ifndef PACKT_PHYSICSOBJECT_HPP
#define PACKT_PHYSICSOBJECT_HPP

#include "PhysicsTarget.hpp"
#include "Types.hpp"

#include <boost/smart_ptr.hpp>
#include <Box2D/Box2D.h>
#include <vector>

namespace packt {
    class PhysicsObject {
    public:
        typedef boost::shared_ptr<PhysicsObject> ptr;
        typedef std::vector<ptr> vec; typedef vec::iterator vec_it;
    public:
        PhysicsObject(uint16 pCategory, uint16 pMask,
```

```
         int32_t pDiameter, float pRestitution, b2World* pWorld);
      PhysicsTarget::ptr createTarget(float pFactor);

      void initialize(float pX, float pY,
         float pVelocityX, float pVelocityY);
      void update();

      bool mCollide;
      Location mLocation;

   private:
      b2World* mWorld;
      b2BodyDef mBodyDef; b2Body* mBodyObj;
      b2CircleShape mShapeDef; b2FixtureDef mFixtureDef;
   };
}
#endif
```

2. Implement `jni/PhysicsObject.cpp` constructor to initialize all Box2D properties.

   The body definition describes a dynamic body (as opposed to static), awake (that is, actively simulated by Box2D), and which cannot rotate (a property especially important for polygon shapes, meaning that it is always pointing upward).

   Also note how we save a `PhysicsObject` self reference in `userData` field, in order to access it later inside Box2D callbacks

3. Define body shape, which we approximate to a box. Box2D requires half dimension, from object's center to its borders.

```
#include "PhysicsObject.hpp"
#include "Log.hpp"

namespace packt {
    PhysicsObject::PhysicsObject(uint16 pCategory, uint16 pMask,
       int32_t pDiameter, float pRestitution, b2World* pWorld) :
      mLocation(), mCollide(false), mWorld(pWorld),
      mBodyDef(), mBodyObj(NULL), mShapeDef(), mFixtureDef() {
        mBodyDef.type = b2_dynamicBody;
        mBodyDef.userData = this;
        mBodyDef.awake = true;
        mBodyDef.fixedRotation = true;

        mShapeDef.m_p = b2Vec2_zero;
        mShapeDef.m_radius = pDiameter / (2.0f * SCALE_FACTOR);
   ...
```

4. Body fixture is the *glue* which brings together body definition, shape, and also physical properties. We also use it to set body category and mask. This allows us to filter collisions between objects according to their category (for instance, asteroids must collide with the ship but not between themselves). There is one category per bit.

Finally, effectively instantiate your body inside the Box2D physical world:

```
. . .
        mFixtureDef.shape = &mShapeDef;
        mFixtureDef.density = 1.0f;
        mFixtureDef.friction = 0.0f;
        mFixtureDef.restitution = pRestitution;
        mFixtureDef.filter.categoryBits = pCategory;
        mFixtureDef.filter.maskBits = pMask;
        mFixtureDef.userData = this;

        mBodyObj = mWorld->CreateBody(&mBodyDef);
        mBodyObj->CreateFixture(&mFixtureDef);
        mBodyObj->SetUserData(this);
    }
. . .
```

5. Then take care of mouse joint creation in `createTarget()`.

When `PhysicsObject` is initialized, coordinates are converted from DroidBlaster referential to Box2D one. Indeed, Box2D performs better with smaller coordinates.

When Box2D has finished simulating, each `PhysicsObject` instance converts coordinates computed by Box2D back into DroidBlaster coordinates referential:

```
. . .
    PhysicsTarget::ptr PhysicsObject::createTarget(float pFactor)
{
        return PhysicsTarget::ptr(
            new PhysicsTarget(mWorld, mBodyObj, mLocation,
pFactor));
    }

    void PhysicsObject::initialize(float pX, float pY,
        float pVelocityX, float pVelocityY) {
        mLocation.setPosition(pX, pY);
        b2Vec2 lPosition(pX / SCALE_FACTOR, pY / SCALE_FACTOR);
        mBodyObj->SetTransform(lPosition, 0.0f);
        mBodyObj->SetLinearVelocity(b2Vec2(pVelocityX,
pVelocityY));
    }
```

```
void PhysicsObject::update() {
    mLocation.setPosition(
        mBodyObj->GetPosition().x * SCALE_FACTOR,
        mBodyObj->GetPosition().y * SCALE_FACTOR);
    }
}
```

6. Now, create `jni/PhysicsService.hpp` header and again insert the Box2D include file. Make `PhysicsService` inherit from `b2ContactListener`. A contact listener gets notified about new collisions each time the simulation is updated. Our `PhysicsService` inherits one of its method named `BeginContact()`.

Define constants and member variables. Iteration constants determine the simulation accuracy. Variable `mWorld` represents the whole Box2D simulation which contains all the physical bodies we are going to create:

```
#ifndef PACKT_PHYSICSSERVICE_HPP
#define PACKT_PHYSICSSERVICE_HPP

#include "PhysicsObject.hpp"
#include "TimeService.hpp"
#include "Types.hpp"

#include <Box2D/Box2D.h>

namespace packt {
    class PhysicsService : private b2ContactListener {
    public:
        PhysicsService(TimeService* pTimeService);

        status update();
        PhysicsObject::ptr registerEntity(uint16 pCategory,
            uint16 pMask, int32_t pDiameter, float pRestitution);

    private:
        void BeginContact(b2Contact* pContact);

    private:
        TimeService* mTimeService;
        PhysicsObject::vec mColliders;
        b2World mWorld;

        static const int32_t VELOCITY_ITER = 6;
        static const int32_t POSITION_ITER = 2;
    };
}
#endif
```

7. In the `jni/PhysicsService.cpp` source file, write `PhysicsService` constructor. Initialize the world, setting the first parameter to a zero vector (type `b2vec`). This vector represents the gravity force, which is not necessary in DroidBlaster. Finally, register the service as a listener of contact/collision event. This way, each time simulation is stepped, `PhysicsService` gets notified through callbacks.

Destroy Box2D resources in the destructor. Box2D uses its own internal (de)allocator.

Also implement `registerEntity()` to encapsulate physics object creation:

```
#include "PhysicsService.hpp"
#include "Log.hpp"

namespace packt {
    PhysicsService::PhysicsService(TimeService* pTimeService) :
      mTimeService(pTimeService),
      mColliders(), mWorld(b2Vec2_zero) {
        mWorld.SetContactListener(this);
    }

    PhysicsObject::ptr PhysicsService::registerEntity(
        uint16 pCategory, uint16 pMask, int32_t pDiameter,
        float pRestitution) {
        PhysicsObject::ptr lCollider(new PhysicsObject(pCategory,
            pMask, pDiameter, pRestitution, &mWorld));
        mColliders.push_back(lCollider);
        return mColliders.back();
    }
    . . .
```

8. Write the `update()` method. First, it clears collision flags buffered in `BeginContact()` during previous iteration. Then simulation is performed by calling `Step()` with a time period and iterations constants define simulation accuracy. Finally, `PhysicsObject` is updated (that is, location extracted from Box2D into our own `Location` object) according to simulation results. Box2D is going to handle mainly collisions and simple movements. So fixing velocity and position iterations to 6 and 2, respectively, is sufficient.

```
    . . .
    status PhysicsService::update() {
        PhysicsObject::vec_it iCollider = mColliders.begin();
        for (; iCollider < mColliders.end() ; ++iCollider) {
            (*iCollider)->mCollide = false;
        }
```

```
        // Updates simulation.
        float lTimeStep = mTimeService->elapsed();
        mWorld.Step(lTimeStep, VELOCITY_ITER, POSITION_ITER);

        // Caches the new state.
        iCollider = mColliders.begin();
        for (; iCollider < mColliders.end() ; ++iCollider) {
            (*iCollider)->update();
        }
        return STATUS_OK;
    }
...
```

9. The method `BeginContact()` is a callback inherited by `b2ContactListener` to notify about new collisions between bodies, two at a time (named A and B). Event information is stored in a `b2contact` structure, which contains various properties, such as friction and restitution, and the two bodies involved through their fixture, which themselves contain a reference to our own `PhysicsObject` (the `UserData` property set in `GraphicsObject`). We can use this link to switch the `PhysicsObject` collision flag when Box2D detects one:

```
...
    void PhysicsService::BeginContact(b2Contact* pContact) {
        void* lUserDataA = pContact->GetFixtureA()->GetUserData();
        if (lUserDataA != NULL) {
            ((PhysicsObject*)(lUserDataA))->mCollide = true;
        }
        void* lUserDataB = pContact->GetFixtureB()->GetUserData();
        if (lUserDataB != NULL) {
            ((PhysicsObject*)(lUserDataB))->mCollide = true;
        }
    }
}
```

10. Finally, create `jni/PhysicsTarget.hpp` to encapsulate Box2D mouse joints. The ship will follow the direction specified in `setTarget()`. To do so, we need a multiplier (`mFactor`) to simulate a target point from the input service output vector.

 Mouse joints are usually good to simulate dragging effects or for test purposes. They are easy to use but implementing a precise behavior with them is difficult.

```
#ifndef PACKT_PHYSICSTARGET_HPP
#define PACKT_PHYSICSTARGET_HPP
```

```
#include "Types.hpp"
#include <boost/smart_ptr.hpp>
#include <Box2D/Box2D.h>

namespace packt {
    class PhysicsTarget {
    public:
        typedef boost::shared_ptr<PhysicsTarget> ptr;

    public:
        PhysicsTarget(b2World* pWorld, b2Body* pBodyObj,
            Location& pTarget, float pFactor);
        void setTarget(float pX, float pY);

    private:
        b2MouseJoint* mMouseJoint;
        float mFactor; Location& mTarget;
    };
}
#endif
```

11. The source counterpart is `jni/PhysicsTarget.cpp` to encapsulate a Box2D mouse joint. The ship will follow the direction specified in `setTarget()` each frame.

```
#include "PhysicsTarget.hpp"
#include "Log.hpp"

namespace packt {
    PhysicsTarget::PhysicsTarget(b2World* pWorld, b2Body* pBodyObj,
        Location& pTarget, float pFactor):
      mFactor(pFactor), mTarget(pTarget) {
        b2BodyDef lEmptyBodyDef;
        b2Body* lEmptyBody = pWorld->CreateBody(&lEmptyBodyDef);

        b2MouseJointDef lMouseJointDef;
        lMouseJointDef.bodyA = lEmptyBody;
        lMouseJointDef.bodyB = pBodyObj;
        lMouseJointDef.target = b2Vec2(0.0f, 0.0f);
        lMouseJointDef.maxForce = 50.0f * pBodyObj->GetMass();
        lMouseJointDef.dampingRatio = 1.0f;
        lMouseJointDef.frequencyHz = 3.5f;
        mMouseJoint = (b2MouseJoint*)
            pWorld->CreateJoint(&lMouseJointDef);
    }
```

```
void PhysicsTarget::setTarget(float pX, float pY) {
  b2Vec2 lTarget((mTarget.mPosX + pX * mFactor) / SCALE_FACTOR,
        (mTarget.mPosY + pY * mFactor) / SCALE_FACTOR);
      mMouseJoint->SetTarget(lTarget);
    }
  }
```

12. Finally, add the `PhysicsService` to `jni/Context.hpp` like all the other services created in previous chapters.

We can now go back to our asteroids and simulate them with our new physics service.

13. In `jni/Asteroid.hpp`, replace location and speed by `PhysicsObject` instance:

```
...
#include "PhysicsService.hpp"
#include "PhysicsObject.hpp"
...
namespace dbs {
    class Asteroid {
        ...
    private:
        ...
        packt::GraphicsSprite* mSprite;
        packt::PhysicsObject::ptr mPhysics;
    };
}
```

14. Makes use of this new physics object in `jni/Asteroid.cpp` source file. Physics properties are registered with a category and mask. Here, Asteroids are declared as belonging to category 1 (`0X1` in hexadecimal notation) and only bodies in group 2 (`0X2` in hexadecimal) are considered when evaluating collisions.

To spawn an asteroid, replace speed with the notion of velocity (expressed in m/s).

Because asteroid direction will change when a collision occurs, asteroids are spawn when they go outside the main area in `update()`:

```
#include "Asteroid.hpp"
#include "Log.hpp"

namespace dbs {
    Asteroid::Asteroid(packt::Context* pContext) :
      mTimeService(pContext->mTimeService),
      mGraphicsService(pContext->mGraphicsService) {
        mPhysics = pContext->mPhysicsService->registerEntity(
```

```
                    0X1, 0x2, 64, 1.0f);
            mSprite = pContext->mGraphicsService->registerSprite(
                mGraphicsService->registerTexture(
                        "/sdcard/droidblaster/asteroid.png"),
                64, 64, &mPhysics->mLocation);
        }

    void Asteroid::spawn() {
      const float MIN_VELOCITY = 1.0f, VELOCITY_RANGE=19.0f;
      const float MIN_ANIM_SPEED = 8.0f, ANIM_SPEED_RANGE=16.0f;

      float lVelocity = -(RAND(VELOCITY_RANGE) + MIN_VELOCITY);
      float lPosX = RAND(mGraphicsService->getWidth());
      float lPosY = RAND(mGraphicsService->getHeight())
                    + mGraphicsService->getHeight();
      mPhysics->initialize(lPosX, lPosY, 0.0f, lVelocity);

      float lAnimSpeed = MIN_ANIM_SPEED + RAND(ANIM_SPEED_RANGE);
      mSprite->setAnimation(8, -1, lAnimSpeed, true);
        }

    void Asteroid::update() {
      if ((mPhysics->mLocation.mPosX < 0.0f) ||
        (mPhysics->mLocation.mPosX > mGraphicsService->getWidth()) ||
        (mPhysics->mLocation.mPosY < 0.0f) ||
        (mPhysics->mLocation.mPosY > mGraphicsService->getHeight()*2)){
                spawn();
          }
        }
    }
```

15. Modify the `jni/Ship.hpp` header file in the same way as asteroids:

```
...
#include "PhysicsService.hpp"
#include "PhysicsObject.hpp"
#include "PhysicsTarget.hpp"
...
namespace dbs {
    class Ship {
        ...
```

```
    private:
        ...
        packt::GraphicsSprite* mSprite;
        packt::PhysicsObject::ptr mPhysics;
        packt::PhysicsTarget::ptr mTarget;
    };
}
```

16. Rewrite `jni/Ship.cpp` with the new `PhysicsObject`. Ship is added to category 2 and is marked as colliding with category 1 only (that is, asteroids). Velocity and movement is entirely managed by Box2D. We can now check in `update()` if an asteroid collided:

```cpp
#include "Ship.hpp"
#include "Log.hpp"

namespace dbs {
    Ship::Ship(packt::Context* pContext) :
        mInputService(pContext->mInputService),
        mGraphicsService(pContext->mGraphicsService),
        mTimeService(pContext->mTimeService) {
            mPhysics = pContext->mPhysicsService->registerEntity(
                0x2, 0x1, 64, 0.0f);
            mTarget = mPhysics->createTarget(50.0f);
            mSprite = pContext->mGraphicsService->registerSprite(
                mGraphicsService->registerTexture(
                        "/sdcard/droidblaster/ship.png"),
                64, 64, &mPhysics->mLocation);
            mInputService->setRefPoint(&mPhysics->mLocation);
    }

    void Ship::spawn() {
        mSprite->setAnimation(0, 8, 8.0f, true);
        mPhysics->initialize(mGraphicsService->getWidth()  * 1 / 2,
            mGraphicsService->getHeight() * 1 / 4, 0.0f, 0.0f);
    }

    void Ship::update() {
        mTarget->setTarget(mInputService->getHorizontal(),
          mInputService->getVertical());
        if (mPhysics->mCollide) {
            packt::Log::info("Ship has been touched");
        }
    }
}
```

Finally, let's instantiate and run our physics service.

17. Modify `jni/DroidBlaster.hpp` to hold `PhysicsService` instance:

```
...
#include "PhysicsService.hpp"
...
namespace dbs {
    class DroidBlaster : public packt::ActivityHandler {
        ...
    private:
        packt::GraphicsService* mGraphicsService;
        packt::InputService*    mInputService;
        packt::PhysicsService*  mPhysicsService;
        packt::SoundService*    mSoundService;
        ...
    };
}
```

18. Update `PhysicsService` each time the game is stepped:

```
namespace dbs {
    ...
    packt::status DroidBlaster::onStep()
    {
        ...
        if (mInputService->update() != packt::STATUS_OK) {
            return packt::STATUS_KO;
        }
        if (mPhysicsService->update() != packt::STATUS_OK) {
            return packt::STATUS_KO;
        }
        return packt::STATUS_OK;
    }
    ...
}
```

19. Finally, instantiate `PhysicsService` in the application's main method:

```
...
#include "PhysicsService.hpp"
...

void android_main(android_app* pApplication) {
    ...
```

```
packt::PhysicsService lPhysicsService(&lTimeService);
packt::SoundService lSoundService(pApplication);

packt::Context lContext = { &lGraphicsService, &lInputService,
    &lPhysicsService, &lSoundService, &lTimeService };
...
}
```

What just happened?

We have created a physical simulation using Box2D physics engine. We have seen how to do the following:

- Define a physical representation of entities (ships and asteroids)
- Step a simulation and detect/filter collisions between entities
- Extracted simulation state (that is, coordinates) to feed graphics representation

The central point of access in Box2D is b2World, which stores a collection of bodies to simulate. A Box2D body is composed of the following:

- b2BodyDef: This defines the body type (b2_staticBody, b2_dynamicBody, and so on) and initial properties like its position, angle (in radians), and so on.
- b2Shape: This is used for collision detection and to derive body mass from its density and can be a b2PolygonShape, b2CircleShape, and so on
- b2FixtureDef: This links together a body shape, a body definition, and its physical properties, such as density
- b2Body: This is a body instance in the world (that is, on per game object), created from a body definition, a shape, and a fixture

Bodies are characterized by a few physical properties:

- Shape: This represents a circle in DroidBlaster, although a polygon or box could also be used.
- Density: This is in kg/m², to compute body mass depending on its shape and size. Value should be greater or equal to 0.0. A bowling ball has a bigger density than a soccer ball.
- Friction: This property shows how much a body slides on another (for example, a car on a road or on an icy path). Values are typically in the range 0.0 to 1.0, where 0.0 implies no friction and 1.0 means strong friction.
- Restitution: This property shows how much a body reacts to a collision, for example, a bouncing ball. Value 0.0 means no restitution and 1.0 full restitution.

When running, bodies are subject to the following:

- Forces: This make bodies move linearly.
- Torques: This represents *rotational force* applied on a body.
- Damping: This is similar to friction but it does not occur only when a body is in contact with another. It can be considered as the effect of air friction slowing down a body.

Box2D is tuned for worlds containing objects at a scale from 0.1 to 10 (unit in meters). When used outside this range, again numerical approximation can make simulation inaccurate. Thus, it is very necessary to scale coordinates from the Box2D referential, where object should to be kept in the (rough) range [0.1, 10] and, to the game or directly to the graphics referential. This is where SCALE_FACTOR is used for coordinate transformation.

Box2D memory management

Box2D uses its own allocators to optimize memory management. So to create and destroy Box2D objects, one needs to systematically use the provided factory methods (CreateX(), DestroyX()). Most of the time, Box2D will manage memory automatically for you. When an object is destroyed, all related *child objects* get destroyed (for instance, the bodies are destroyed when the world is destroyed). But if you need to get rid of your objects earlier, and thus manually, then always destroy them.

More on collision detection

Several ways of detecting and handling collisions exist in Box2D. The most basic one consists in checking all contacts stored in the world or in a body after they are updated. But this can result in missed contacts that happen surreptitiously during Box2D internal iterations.

A better way we have seen to detect contacts is the b2ContactListener, which can be registered on the world object. Four callbacks can be overridden:

- BeginContact(b2Contact): This is to detect when two bodies enter in collision.
- EndContact(b2Contact): This is the counterpart of BeginContact(), which indicates when bodies are not in collision any more. A call to BeginContact() is always followed by a matching EndContact().
- PreSolve(b2Contact, b2Manifold): This is called after a collision is detected but before collision resolution, that is, before impulse resulting from the collision is computed. The b2Manifold structure holds information about contact points, normals, and so on in a single place.
- PostSolve(b2Contact, b2ContactImpulse): This is called after actual impulse (that is, physical reaction) has been computed by Box2D.

The first two callbacks are interesting to trigger game logic (for example, entity destruction). The last two are interesting to alter physics simulation (more specifically to ignore some collisions by *disabling* a contact) while it is being computed or to get more accurate details about it. For instance, use `PreSolve()` to create a one-sided platform to which an entity collides only when it falls from above (not when it jumps from below). Use `PostSolve()` to detect collision strength and calculate damages accordingly.

Methods `PreSolve()` and `PostSolve()` can be called several times between `BeginContact()` and `EndContact()`, which can be called themselves from zero to several times during one world update. A contact can begin during one simulation step and terminate several steps after. In that case, event solving callbacks will be occurring continuously during in-between steps. As many collisions can occur while stepping simulation, callbacks can be called lot of times and should be as efficient as possible.

When analyzing collisions inside `BeginContact()` callback, we have buffered a collision flag. This is necessary because Box2D reuses the `b2Contact` parameter passed when a callback is triggered. In addition, as these callbacks are called while simulation is computed, physics bodies cannot be destroyed at that instance but only after simulation stepping is over. Thus, it is highly advised to copy any information gathered there for post-processing (for example, to destroy entities).

Collision modes

I would like to point out that Box2D offers a so-called **bullet** mode that can be activated on a body definition using corresponding Boolean member:

```
mBodyDef.bullet = true;
```

This mode is necessary for fast moving objects like bullets! By default, Box2D uses **Discrete Collision Detection,** which considers bodies at their final position for collision detection, missing any body located between initial and final positions. But for a fast moving body, the whole path followed should be considered. This is more formally called **Continuous Collision Detection**. Obviously, **CCD** is expensive and should be used with parsimony:

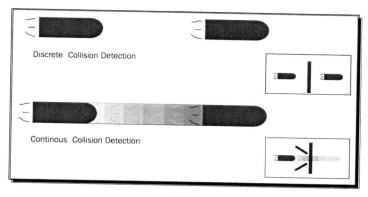

We sometimes want to detect when bodies overlap without generating collisions (like a car reaching the finish line): this is called a **sensor**. A sensor can be easily set by setting `isSensor` Boolean member to `true` in the fixture:

```
mFixtureDef.isSensor = true;
```

A sensor can be queried with a listener through `BeginContact()` and `EndContact()` or by using `IsTouching()` shortcut on a `b2Contact` class.

Collision filtering

Another important aspect of collision is about... not colliding! Or more precisely about filtering collisions... A kind of filtering can be performed in `PreSolve()` by disabling contacts. This is the most flexible and powerful solution but also the most complex.

But as we have seen it, filtering can be performed in a more simple way by using categories and masks technique. Each body is assigned one or more category (each being represented by one bit in a short integer, the `categoryBits` member) and a mask describing categories of body they can collide with (each filtered category being represented by a bit set to 0, the `maskBits` member):

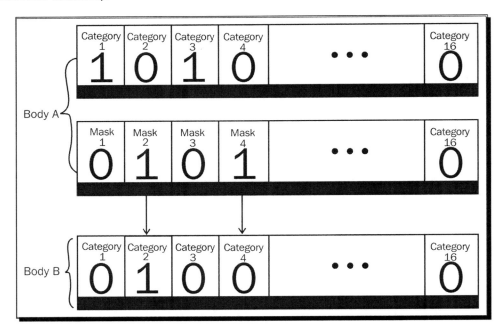

In the preceding figure, Body A is in category 1 and 3 and collide with bodies in categories 2 and 4, which is the case for this poor body B unless its mask filters collision with body A categories (that is, 1 and 3). In other words, both the bodies A and B must agree to collide!

Box2D also has a notion of collision groups. A body has a collision group set to any of the following:

◆ Positive integer: This means others bodies with the same collision group value can collide

◆ Negative integer: This means others bodies with the same collision group value are filtered

This could have been a solution, although less flexible than categories and masks, to avoid collision between asteroids in DroidBlaster. Note that groups are filtered before categories.

A more flexible solution than category/group filters is the class `b2ContactFilter`. This class has a method `ShouldCollide(b2Fixture, b2Fixture)` that you can customize to perform your own filtering. Actually, category/group filtering are themselves implemented that way.

More resources about Box2D

This was a short introduction to Box2D, which is capable of much more! We have left the following in the shadow:

◆ Joints: two bodies linked together

◆ Raycasting: to query a physics world (for example, which location is a gun pointing toward).

◆ Contact properties: normals, impulses, manifolds, and so on

Box2D has a really nice documentation with much useful information that can be found at `http://www.box2d.org/manual.html`. Moreover, Box2D is packaged with a test bed directory (in `Box2D/Testbed/Tests`) featuring many use cases. Have a look to get a better understanding of its capabilities. Because physics simulations can sometime be rather tricky, I also encourage you to visit Box2D forum, which is quite active, at `http://www.box2d.org/forum/`.

Running a 3D engine on Android

DroidBlaster now includes a nice and shiny physics engine. Now, let's run the Irrlicht engine, created by a game developer Nikolaus Gebhardt in 2002. This engine supports many features:

◆ OpenGL ES 1 and (partially) Open GL ES 2 support

◆ **2D graphics** capabilities

◆ Support many images and mesh files formats (**PNG**, **JPEG**, **OBJ**, **3DS**, and so on)

- ◆ Import **Quake** levels in **BSP** format
- ◆ **Skinning** to deform and animate meshes with bones
- ◆ **Terrain** rendering
- ◆ Collision handling
- ◆ **GUI** system

And even much more. Now, let's add a new dimension to `DroidBlaster` by running Irrlicht GLES 1.1 renderer with the fixed rendering pipeline.

 Project DroidBlaster_Part10-Box2D can be used as a starting point for this part. The resulting project is provided with this book under the name DroidBlaster_Part10-Irrlicht.

Time for action – rendring 3D graphics with Irrlicht

1. First, let's get rid of all unnecessary stuff. Remove `GraphicsSprite`, `GraphicsTexture`, and `GraphicsTileMap` and `Background` header and source files in the `jni` folder.

First, we need to clean up the code and rewrite the graphics service.

2. Create a new file `jni/GraphicsObject.hpp`, which includes `Irrlicht.h` header.

`GraphicsObject` encapsulates an Irrlicht scene node, that is, an object in the 3D world. Nodes can form a hierarchy, child nodes moving accordingly to their parent (for example, a turret on a tank) and inheriting some of their properties (for example, visibility).

We also need a reference to a location in our own coordinate format (coming from our Box2D `PhysicsService`) and the name of the mesh, and texture resources we need:

```
#ifndef PACKT_GRAPHICSOBJECT_HPP
#define PACKT_GRAPHICSOBJECT_HPP

#include "Types.hpp"

#include <boost/shared_ptr.hpp>
#include <irrlicht.h>
#include <vector>

namespace packt {
    class GraphicsObject {
    public:
```

```
        typedef boost::shared_ptr<GraphicsObject> ptr;
        typedef std::vector<ptr> vec;
        typedef vec::iterator vec_it;

    public:
        GraphicsObject(const char* pTexture, const char* pMesh,
            Location* pLocation);

        void spin(float pX, float pY, float pZ);

        void initialize(irr::scene::ISceneManager* pSceneManager);
        void update();

    private:
        Location* mLocation;
        irr::scene::ISceneNode* mNode;
        irr::io::path mTexture; irr::io::path mMesh;
    };
}
#endif
```

3. In `jni/GraphicsObject.cpp`, write the class constructor.

Create a `spin()` method that will be used to animate asteroids with a continuous rotation. First, remove any previous animation potentially set. Then, create a rotation animator applied to the Irrlicht node. Finally, free animator resources (with `Drop()`):

```
#include "GraphicsObject.hpp"
#include "Log.hpp"

namespace packt {
    GraphicsObject::GraphicsObject(const char* pTexture,
      const char* pMesh, Location* pLocation) :
      mLocation(pLocation), mNode(NULL),
      mTexture(pTexture), mMesh(pMesh)
    {}

    void GraphicsObject::spin(float pX, float pY, float pZ) {
        mNode->removeAnimators();
        irr::scene::ISceneNodeAnimator* lAnimator =
            mNode->getSceneManager()->createRotationAnimator(
                irr::core::vector3df(pX, pY, pZ));
        mNode->addAnimator(lAnimator);
        lAnimator->drop();
    }

    . . .
```

4. Initialize Irrlicht resources in the corresponding method `initialize()`. First, load the requested 3D mesh and its texture according to their path on disk. If resources are already loaded, Irrlicht takes care of reusing them. Then, create a scene node attached to the 3D world. It must contain the newly loaded 3D mesh with the newly loaded texture applied on its surface. Although this is not compulsory, meshes are going to be lighted dynamically (`EMF_LIGHTING` flag). Lights will be set up later.

    Finally, we need an `update()` method whose only purpose is to convert coordinates from DroidBlaster referential to Irrlicht referential, which are almost identical (both indicate the object center with the same scale), almost because Irrlicht needs a third dimension. Obviously, it will be possible to use Irrlicht coordinates everywhere:

    ```
    ...
    void GraphicsObject::initialize(
        irr::scene::ISceneManager* pSceneManager) {
        irr::scene::IAnimatedMesh* lMesh =
            pSceneManager->getMesh(mMesh);
        irr::video::ITexture* lTexture = pSceneManager->
            getVideoDriver()->getTexture(mTexture);

        mNode = pSceneManager->addMeshSceneNode(lMesh);
        mNode->setMaterialTexture(0, lTexture);
        mNode->setMaterialFlag(irr::video::EMF_LIGHTING, true);
    }

    void GraphicsObject::update() {
        mNode->setPosition(irr::core::vector3df(
            mLocation->mPosX, 0.0f, mLocation->mPosY));
    }
    }
    ```

5. Open existing file `jni/GraphicsService.hpp` to replace the older code with Irrlicht. `GraphicsService` requires quite some change! Clean up all the stuff about `GraphicsSprite`, `GraphicsTexture`, `GraphicsTileMap`, and `TimeService`.

    Then, insert Irrlicht main include file in place of previous graphics headers.

    Replace previous registration methods with a `registerObject()` similar to the one we created in `PhysicsService`. It takes a mesh and texture file path in parameters and returns a `GraphicsObject` defined as follows:

    ```
    #ifndef _PACKT_GRAPHICSSERVICE_HPP_
    #define _PACKT_GRAPHICSSERVICE_HPP_

    #include "GraphicsObject.hpp"
    #include "TimeService.hpp"
    #include "Types.hpp"

    #include <android_native_app_glue.h>
    ```

```
#include <irrlicht.h>
#include <EGL/egl.h>

namespace packt {
    class GraphicsService {
    public:
        ...
        GraphicsObject::ptr registerObject(const char* pTexture,
            const char* pMesh, Location* pLocation);

    protected:
        ...
...
```

6. Declare Irrlicht-related member variables and a vector to store all `GraphicsObject` that will be displayed on screen. Irrlicht central class is `IrrlichtDevice`, which gives access to any Irrlicht features. `IVideoDriver` is also an important class which abstracts 2D/3D graphical operations and resource management. `ISceneManager` handles the simulated 3D world:

```
...
    private:
        ...
        EGLContext mContext;

        irr::IrrlichtDevice* mDevice;
        irr::video::IVideoDriver* mDriver;
        irr::scene::ISceneManager* mSceneManager;

        GraphicsObject::vec mObjects;
    };
}
#endif
```

7. In `jni/GraphicsService.cpp` source file and update class constructor, EGL setup remains as before. Indeed, the Irrlicht-to-Android glue code (CirrDeviceAndroid) is an empty stub. Initialization is left to the client (originally on the Java side) which is performed by our own code natively in `start()`.

   So this part does not change much: just request a depth buffer to blend 3D objects properly and remove `loadResources()` as Irrlicht now takes care of that.

   When application stops, releases Irrlicht resources with a call to `Drop()`:

```
...
namespace packt {
    GraphicsService::GraphicsService(android_app* pApplication,
                                     TimeService* pTimeService) :
        ...
```

```
        mContext(EGL_NO_SURFACE),
        mDevice(NULL), mObjects()
{}
...
status GraphicsService::start() {
    ...
    const EGLint lAttributes[] = {
        EGL_RENDERABLE_TYPE, EGL_OPENGL_ES_BIT,
        EGL_BLUE_SIZE, 5, EGL_GREEN_SIZE, 6, EGL_RED_SIZE, 5,
        EGL_DEPTH_SIZE, 16, EGL_SURFACE_TYPE, EGL_WINDOW_BIT,
        EGL_NONE
    };
    ...
}

void GraphicsService::stop() {
    mDevice->drop();

    if (mDisplay != EGL_NO_DISPLAY) {
        ...
    }
}
...
```

8. Now comes the interesting part: `setup()`. First, initialize Irrlicht by invoking `createDevice()` factory method. The important parameter is `EDT_OGLES1` which indicates which renderer to use for rendering. The additional parameters describe window properties (dimensions, bit depth, and so on).

Then, set up Irrlicht so that it accesses resources through files (resources could also be compressed in an archive) relative to `/sdcard/droidblaster` directory. Finally, retrieve the video driver and the scene manager that we are often going to use:

```
void GraphicsService::setup() {
    mDevice = irr::createDevice(irr::video::EDT_OGLES1,
        irr::core::dimension2d<irr::u32>(mWidth, mHeight), 32,
        false, false, false, 0);

    mDevice->getFileSystem()->addFolderFileArchive(
        "/sdcard/droidblaster/");
    mDriver = mDevice->getVideoDriver();
    mSceneManager = mDevice->getSceneManager();
    ...
```

9. In `setup()`, prepare the scene with a light for dynamic mesh lighting (the last parameter being the light range) and a camera positioned to simulate a top view (values are empirical). As you can see, every object of a 3D world is considered as a node in the scene manager, a light as well as a camera, or anything else:

. . .

```
mSceneManager->setAmbientLight(
  irr::video::SColorf(0.85f,0.85f,0.85f));

mSceneManager->addLightSceneNode(NULL,
  irr::core::vector3df(-150, 200, -50),
  irr::video::SColorf(1.0f, 1.0f, 1.0f), 4000.0f);

irr::scene::ICameraSceneNode* lCamera =
  mSceneManager->addCameraSceneNode();
lCamera->setTarget(
  irr::core::vector3df(mWidth/2, 0.0f, mHeight/2));
lCamera->setUpVector(irr::core::vector3df(0.0f, 0.0f, 1.0f));
lCamera->setPosition(
  irr::core::vector3df(mWidth/2, mHeight*3/4, mHeight/2));
```
. . .

10. Instead of a tile map, we are going to create particles to simulate a background star field. To do so, create a new particle system node, emitting particles randomly from a *virtual* box located on top of the screen. Depending on the rate chosen, more or less particles are emitted. The lifetime leaves enough time for particles to cross the screen from their emission point from the top to the bottom. Particles can have different sizes (from 1.0 to 8.0). When we are done setting up the particle emitter, we can release it with `drop()`:

. . .

```
irr::scene::IParticleSystemSceneNode* lParticleSystem =
    mSceneManager->addParticleSystemSceneNode(false);
irr::scene::IParticleEmitter* lEmitter =
  lParticleSystem->createBoxEmitter(
  // X, Y, Z of first and second corner.
  irr::core::aabbox3d<irr::f32>(
    -mWidth * 0.1f, -300, mHeight * 1.2f,
    mWidth * 1.1f, -100, mHeight * 1.1f),
  // Direction and emit rate.
  irr::core::vector3df(0.0f,0.0f,-0.25f), 10.0f, 40.0f,
  // darkest and brightest color
```

```
                irr::video::SColor(0,255,255,255),
                irr::video::SColor(0,255,255,255),
                // min and max age, angle
                8000.0f, 8000.0f, 0.0f,
                // min and max size.
                irr::core::dimension2df(1.f,1.f),
                irr::core::dimension2df(8.f,8.f));
        lParticleSystem->setEmitter(lEmitter);
        lEmitter->drop();
...
```

11. To finish with the star field, set up particle texture (here `star.png`) and graphical properties (transparency is needed but not the Z-buffer nor lighting). When everything is ready, you can initialize all `GraphicsObjects` referenced by game objects:

```
...
        lParticleSystem->setMaterialTexture(0,
            mDriver->getTexture("star.png"));
        lParticleSystem->setMaterialType(
            irr::video::EMT_TRANSPARENT_VERTEX_ALPHA);
        lParticleSystem->setMaterialFlag(
            irr::video::EMF_LIGHTING, false);
        lParticleSystem->setMaterialFlag(
            irr::video::EMF_ZWRITE_ENABLE, false);

        GraphicsObject::vec_it iObject = mObjects.begin();
        for (; iObject < mObjects.end() ; ++iObject) {
            (*iObject)->initialize(mSceneManager);
        }
    }
...
```

12. The important method of `GraphicsService` is `update()`. First, update each `GraphicsObject` to refresh its position in the Irrlicht referential.

Then, run the device to process nodes (for example, to emit particles). Then draw the scene between a call to `beingScene()` (with a background color set to black here) and `endScene()`. Scene drawing is delegated to the scene manager and its internal nodes.

Finally, rendered scene can be displayed on screen as usual:

```
...
    status GraphicsService::update() {
        GraphicsObject::vec_it iObject = mObjects.begin();
        for (; iObject < mObjects.end() ; ++iObject) {
            (*iObject)->update();
        }
```

```
        if (!mDevice->run()) return STATUS_KO;
        mDriver->beginScene(true, true,
irr::video::SColor(0,0,0,0));
        mSceneManager->drawAll();
        mDriver->endScene();

        if (eglSwapBuffers(mDisplay, mSurface) != EGL_TRUE) {
            ...
    }
...
```

To finish with `GraphicsService`, implement `registerObject()` method:

```
...
    GraphicsObject::ptr GraphicsService::registerObject(
      const char* pTexture, const char* pMesh, Location* pLocation) {
        GraphicsObject::ptr lObject(new GraphicsObject(mSceneManager,
            pTexture, pMesh, pLocation));
        mObjects.push_back(lObject);
        return mObjects.back();
    }
}
```

The graphics module now renders scene with Irrlicht. So let's update game entities accordingly.

13. Modify `jni/Asteroid.hpp` to reference a `GraphicsObject` instead of a sprite:

```
...
#include "GraphicsService.hpp"
#include "GraphicsObject.hpp"
#include "PhysicsService.hpp"
...

namespace dbs {
    class Asteroid {
        ...
    private:
        packt::GraphicsService* mGraphicsService;
        packt::TimeService* mTimeService;

        packt::GraphicsObject::ptr mMesh;
        packt::PhysicsObject::ptr mPhysics;
    };
}
#endif
```

14. Edit `jni/Asteroid.cpp` counterpart to register a `GraphicsObject`.

When an asteroid is recreated, its spin is updated with the corresponding method. We do not need an animation speed anymore:

```cpp
. . .
namespace dbs {
    Asteroid::Asteroid(packt::Context* pContext) :
        mTimeService(pContext->mTimeService),
        mGraphicsService(pContext->mGraphicsService) {
            mPhysics = pContext->mPhysicsService->registerEntity(
                0X1, 0x2, 64, 1.0f);
            mMesh = pContext->mGraphicsService->registerObject(
                "rock.png", "asteroid.obj", &mPhysics->mLocation);
    }

    void Asteroid::spawn() {
        . . .
        mPhysics->initialize(1PosX, 1PosY, 0.0f, 1Velocity);

        float 1SpinSpeed = MIN_SPIN_SPEED + RAND(SPIN_SPEED_RANGE);
        mMesh->spin(0.0f, 1SpinSpeed, 0.0f);
    }
    . . .
}
```

15. Also update `jni/Ship.hpp` header file, as done for asteroids:

```cpp
. . .
#include "GraphicsService.hpp"
#include "GraphicsObject.hpp"
#include "PhysicsService.hpp"
. . .

namespace dbs {
    class Ship {
        . . .
    private:
        . . .
        packt::TimeService* mTimeService;
```

```
        packt::GraphicsObject::ptr mMesh;
        packt::PhysicsObject::ptr mPhysics;
        packt::PhysicsTarget::ptr mTarget;
    };
}


#endif
```

16. Change `Ship.cpp` to register a static mesh. Remove animation stuff in `spawn()`:

```
...
namespace dbs {
    Ship::Ship(packt::Context* pContext) :
        ... {
        mPhysics = pContext->mPhysicsService->registerEntity(
            0x2, 0x1, 64, 0.0f);
        mTarget = mPhysics->createTarget(50.0f);
        mMesh = pContext->mGraphicsService->registerObject(
            "metal.png", "ship.obj", &mPhysics->mLocation);
        mInputService->setRefPoint(&mPhysics->mLocation);
    }


    void Ship::spawn() {
        mPhysics->initialize(mGraphicsService->getWidth() * 1 / 2,
            mGraphicsService->getHeight() * 1 / 4, 0.0f, 0.0f);
    }
    ...
}
```

We are almost done. Do not forget to remove references to Background in the `DroidBlaster` class.

17. Before running the application, 3D meshes and textures need to be copied on the SD Card, in `/sdcard/droidblaster` directory given to Irrlicht at step 8. This path may have to be adapted depending on your device SD Card mount point (like explained in Chapter 9, *Porting Existing Libraries to Android*).

 Resource files are provided with this book in `Chapter10/Resource`.

What just happened?

We have seen how to embed and reuse a 3D engine in an Android application to display 3D graphics. If you run DroidBlaster on your Android device, you should obtain the following result. Asteroids look nicer in 3D and the star field gives a simple and nice depth impression:

Irrlicht main entry point is the `IrrlichtDevice` class, from which we have been able to access anything in the engine, few of them are as follows:

- `IVideoDriver`, which is a shell around the graphics renderer, managing graphics resources, such as textures
- `ISceneManager`, which manages the scene through a hierarchical tree of nodes

In other words, you draw a scene using the video driver and indicate the entities to display, their position, and properties through the scene manager (which manages a 3D world through nodes).

> **Memory management in Irrlicht**
>
> Internally, Irrlicht uses reference counting to manage object lifetime properly. The rule of thumb is simple: when a factory method contains `create` (for example, `createDevice()`) in its name, then there must be a matching call to `drop()` to release resources.

More specifically, we have used mesh nodes to display ship and asteroids, the later being animated through an animator. We have used a simple rotation animator but more are provided (to animate objects over a path, for collisions, and so on).

> **3D modeling with Blender**
>
> The best open source 3D authoring tool nowadays is Blender. Blender can model meshes, texture them, export them, generate lightmaps, and many other things. More information and the program itself can be found at `http://www.blender.org/`.

More on Irrlicht scene management

Let's linger a bit on the scene manager which is an important aspect of Irrlicht. As exposed during the step-by-step tutorial, a node basically represents an object in the 3D world, but not always a visible one. Irrlicht features many kinds of custom nodes:

- `IAnimatedMeshSceneNode`: This is the most basic node. It renders a 3D mesh to which one or more textures (for multi-texturing) can be attached. As it is stated by its name, such a node can be animated with key frames and bones (for example, when using Quake `.md2` format).

- `IBillboardSceneNode`: This displays a sprite inside a 3D world (that is, a textured plane which always faces the camera).

- `ICameraSceneNode`: This is the node through which you can see the 3D world. Thus, this is a non-visible node.

- `ILightSceneNode`: This illuminates world objects. We are talking here about dynamic lighting, calculated on meshes per frames. This can be expensive and should be activated only if necessary. Light-mapping, which can be described as, an interesting technique to avoid expensive light calculation.

- `IParticleSceneNode`: This emits particles like we have done to simulate a star field.

- `ITerrainSceneNode`: This renders an outdoor terrain (with hills, moutains, ...) from an heightmap. It provides automatic Level of Detail (or LOD) handling for depending on the distance of the terrain chunk.

Nodes have a hierarchical structure and can be attached to a parent. Irrlicht also provides some spatial indexing (to cull meshes quickly) such as **Octree** or **BSP** to cull meshes in complex scenes. Irrlicht is a rich engine and I encourage you to have a look at its documentation available at `http://irrlicht.sourceforge.net/`. Its forum is also quite active and helpful.

Summary

This chapter demonstrated the re-usability possibilities offered by the Android NDK. It is a step forward to the creation of the professional applications with an emphasize on something essential in this fast-moving mobile world: productivity.

More specifically, we saw how to simulate a physical world by porting Box2D and how to display 3D graphics with the existing engine, Irrlicht. We highlighted the path towards the creation of professional applications using the NDK as a leverage. But do not expect all C/C++ libraries to be ported so easily.

Talking about paths, we are almost at the end. The next, and last, chapter introduces advanced techniques to debug and troubleshoot NDK applications and make you fully prepared for Android development.

11

Debugging and Troubleshooting

This introduction to the Android NDK would not be complete without approaching some more advanced topics: debugging and troubleshooting code. Indeed, C/C++ are complex languages that can fail in many ways.

I will not lie to you: NDK debugging features are rather rubbish yet. It is often more practical and fast to rely on simple log messages. This is why debugging is presented in this last chapter. But still, a debugger can save quite some time in complex programs or even worse... crashing programs! But even in that case, there exist alternative solutions.

More specifically, we are going to discover how to do the following:

◆ Debug native code with **GDB**

◆ Interpret a **stack trace** dump

◆ Analyze program performances with **GProf**

Debugging with GDB

Because Android NDK is based on the GCC toolchain, Android NDK includes GDB, the GNU Debugger, to allow starting, pausing, examining, and altering a program. On Android and more generally on embedded devices, GDB is configured in client/server mode. The program runs on a device as a server and a remote client, the developer's workstation connects to it and sends debugging commands as for a local application.

GDB itself is a command-line utility and can be cumbersome to use manually. Hopefully, GDB is handled by most IDE and especially CDT. Thus, Eclipse can be used directly to add breakpoints and inspect a program, only if it has been properly configured before!

Indeed, Eclipse can insert breakpoints easily in Java as well as C/C++ source files by clicking in the gutter, to the text editor's left. Java breakpoints work out of the box thanks to the ADT plugin, which manages debugging through the Android Debug Bridge. This is not true for CDT which is naturally not *Android-aware*. Thus, inserting a breakpoint will just do nothing unless we manage to configure CDT to use the NDK's GDB, which itself needs to be bound to the native Android application to debug.

Debugger support has improved among NDK releases (for example, debugging purely native threads was not working before). Although it is getting more usable, in NDK R5 (and even R7), situation is far from perfect . But, it can still help! Let's see now concretely how to debug a native application.

Time for action – debugging DroidBlaster

Let's enable debugging mode in our application first:

1. The first important thing to do but really easy to forget is to activate the debugging flag in your Android project. This is done in the application manifest `AndroidManifest.xml`. Do not forget to use the appropriate SDK version for native code:

```xml
<?xml version="1.0" encoding="utf-8"?>
<manifest ...>
    <uses-sdk android:minSdkVersion="10"/>
    <application ...
                android:debuggable="true">
    ...
```

2. Enabling debug flag in manifest automatically activates debug mode in native code. However, APP_OPTIM flag also controls debug mode. If it has been manually set in `Android.mk`, then check that its value is set to `debug` (and not `release`) or simply remove it:

```
APP_OPTIM    := debug
```

First, let's configure the GDB client that will connect to the device:

3. Recompile the project. Plug your device in or launch the emulator. Run and leave your application. Ensure the application is loaded and its PID available. You can check it by listing processes using the following command. One line should be returned:

```
$ adb shell ps |grep packtpub
```

```
 File  Edit  View  Search  Terminal  Help
app_46    611   117   98884  23568 ffffffff afd0c75c t com.packtpub.droidblaster
```

4. Open a terminal window and go to your project directory. Run the `ndk-gdb` command (located in `$ANDROID_NDK` folder, which should already be in your `$PATH`):

```
$ ndk-gdb
```

This command should return no message and create three files in `obj/local/armeabi`:

- `gdb.setup`: This is a configuration file generated for GDB client.

- `app_process`: This file is retrieved directly from your device. It is a system executable file (that is, **Zygote**, see Chapter 2, *Creating, Compiling, and Deploying Native Projects*), launched when system starts up and forked to start a new application. GBD needs this reference file to find its marks. It is in some way the binary entry point of your app.

- `libc.so`: This is also retrieved from your device. It is the Android standard C library (commonly referred as **bionic**) used by GDB to keep track of all the native threads created during runtime.

 Append `-verbose` flag to have a detailed feedback on what `ndk-gdb` does. If `ndk-gdb` complains about an already running debug session, then re-execute ndk-gdb with the `-force` flag. Beware, some devices (especially HTC ones) do not work in debug mode unless they are rooted with a custom ROM (for example, they return a **corrupt installation** error).

5. In your project directory, copy `obj/local/armeabi/gdb.setup` and name it `gdb2.setup`. Open it and remove the following line which requests GDB client to connect to the GDB server running on the device (to be performed by Eclipse itself):

```
target remote :5039
```

6. In the Eclipse main menu, go to **Run | Debug Configurations...** and create a new Debug configuration in the **C/C++ Application** item called `DroidBlaster_JNI`. This configuration will start GDB client on your computer and connect to the GDB Server running on the device.

7. In the **Main** tab, set:

- **Project** to your own project directory (for example, `DroidBlaster_Part8-3`).

❑ **C/C++ Application** to point to `obj/local/armeabi/app_process` using the **Browse** button (you can use either an absolute or a relative path).

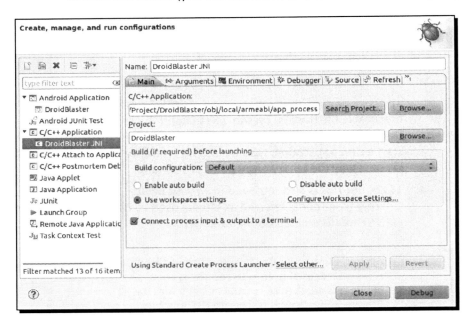

8. Switch launcher type to **Standard Create Process Launcher** using the link **Select other...** at the bottom of the window:

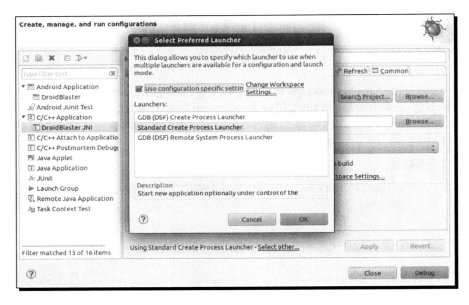

9. Go to the debugger file and set:

- ❑ **Debugger** type to **gdbserver**.

- ❑ **GDB debugger** to ${ANDROID_NDK}/toolchains/arm-linux-androideabi-4.4.3/prebuilt/linux-x86/bin/arm-linux-androideabi-gdb.

- ❑ **GDB command file** to point to the gdb2.setup file located in obj/local/armeabi/ (you can use either an absolute or a relative path).

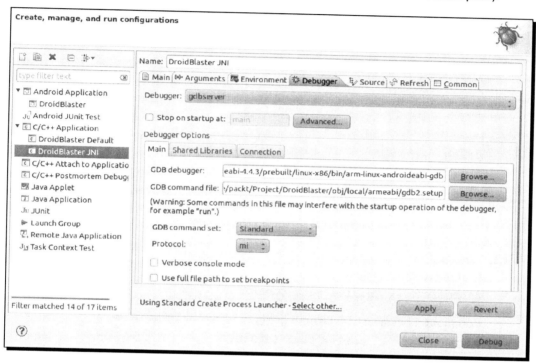

10. Go to the **Connection** tab and set **Type** to **TCP**. Default value for **Host name or IP address** and **Port number** can be kept (**localhost** d **5039**).

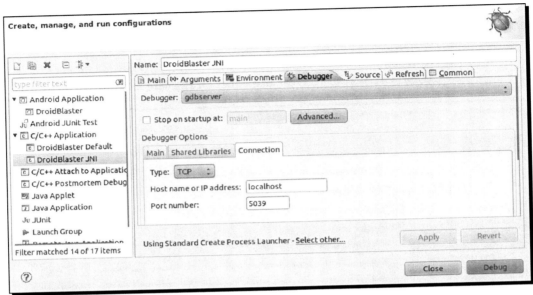

Now, let's configure Eclipse to run GDB server on the device:

11. Make a copy of `$ANDROID_NDK/ndk-gdb` and open it with a text editor. Find the following line:

```
$GDBCLIENT -x `native_path $GDBSETUP`
```

Comment it because GDB client is going to be run by Eclipse itself:

```
#$GDBCLIENT -x `native_path $GDBSETUP`
```

12. In the Eclipse main menu, go to **Run | External Tools | External Tools Configurations...** and create a new configuration `DroidBlaster_GDB`. This configuration will launch GDB server on the device.

13. In the **Main** tab, set:

- **Location** pointing to our modified `ndk-gdb` in `$ANDROID_NDK`. You can use **Variables...** button to define Android NDK location in a more generic way (that is, `${env_var:ANDROID_NDK}/ndk-gdb`).
- **Working directory** to your application directory location (for example, `${workspace_loc:/DroidBlaster_Part8-3}`)

❑ Optionally, set the **Arguments** textbox:

❑ `--verbose`: To see in details what happens in the Eclipse console.

❑ `-force`: To kill automatically any previous session.

❑ `-start`: To let GDB Server start the application instead of getting attached to the application after it has been started. This option is interesting if you debug native code only and not Java but it can cause troubles with the emulator (such as to leave the back button).

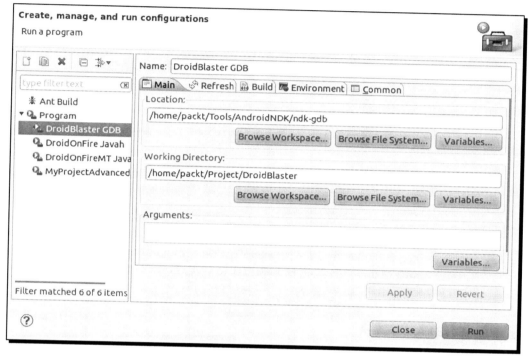

We are done with configuration.

14. Now, launch your application as usual (as shown in Chapter 2, *Creating, Compiling, and Deploying Native Projects*).

15. Once application is started, launch the external tool configuration **DroidBlaster GDB** which is going to start GDB server on the device. GDB server receives debug commands sent by the remote GDB client and debugs your application *locally*.

16. Open `jni/DroidBlaster.cpp` and set a breakpoint on the first line of `onStep()` (`mTimeService->update()`) by double-clicking on the gutter on the text editor's left (or right-clicking and selecting **Toggle breakpoint**).

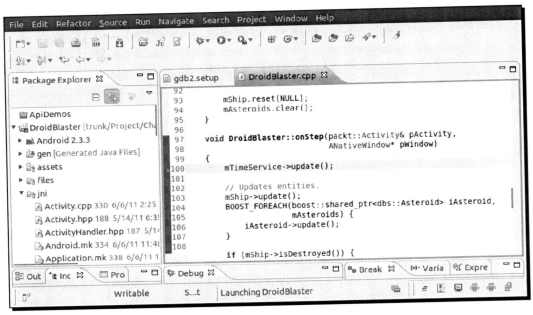

17. Finally, launch DroidBlaster JNI C/C++ application configuration to start GDB client. It relays debug commands from Eclipse CDT to GDB server over a socket connection. From the developer's point of view, this is almost like debugging a local application.

What just happened?

If set up properly, application freezes after a few seconds and Eclipse focuses into the *break-pointed* line. It is now possible to step into, step out, step over a line of code or resume application. For assembly-addict, an instruction stepping mode can also be activated.

Now, enjoy the benefit of this modern productivity tool, that is, a debugger. However, as you are going or maybe are already experiencing, beware that debugging on Android is rather slow (because it needs to communicate with the remote Android device) and somewhat unstable though it works well most of the time.

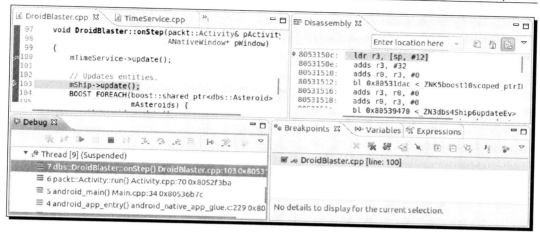

If the configuration process is a bit complicated and tricky, the same goes for the launch of a debug session. Remember the three necessary steps:

1. Start the Android application (whether from Eclipse or your device).

2. Then, launch GDB server on the device (that is, the DroidBlaster_GDB configuration here) to attach it to the application locally.

3. Finally, start GDB client on your computer (that is, the DroidBlaster_JNI configuration here) to allow CDT to communicate with the GDB server.

4. Optionally, start the GDB server with the `-start` flag to make it launch the application itself and omit the first step.

 Beware `gdb2.setup` may be removed while cleaning your project directory. When debugging stops working, this should be the second thing to check, after making sure that `ndk-gdb` is up and running.

However, there is an annoying limitation about this procedure: we are interrupting the program while it is already running. So how to stop on a breakpoint in initialization code and debug it (for example in `jni/DroidBlaster.cpp` on `onActivate()`)? There are two solutions:

♦ Leave your application and launch the GDB client. Android does not manage memory as it is in Windows, Linux, or Mac OS X: it kills applications only when memory is needed. Processes are kept in memory even after user leaves. As your application is still running, GDB server remains started and you can quietly start your client debugger. Then, just start your application from your device (not from Eclipse, which would kill it).

◆ Take a pause when the application starts... in the Java code! However, from a fully native application, you will need to create a `src` folder for Java sources and add a new `Activity` class extending `NativeActivity`. Then you can put a breakpoint on a static initializer block.

Stack trace analysis

No need to lie. I know it happened. Do not be ashamed, it happened to all of us... your program crashed, without a reason! You think probably the device is getting old or Android is broken. We all made that reflection but ninety-nine percent of the time, we are the ones to blame!

Debuggers are the tremendous tool to look for problems in your code. But they work in *real time* when programs run. They assume you know where to look for. With problems that cannot be reproduced easily or that already happened, debuggers become sterile.

Hopefully, there is a solution: a few utilities embedded in the NDK help to analyse ARM stack traces. Let's see how they work.

Time for action – analysing a crash dump

1. Let's introduce a fatal bug in the code. Open `jni/DroidBlaster.cpp` and modify method `onActivate()` as follows:

    ```
    . . .
        void DroidBlaster::onActivate() {
            . . .
            mTimeService = NULL;
            return packt::STATUS_KO;
        }
    . . .
    ```

2. Open the **LogCat** view (from **Window | Show View | Other...**) in Eclipse and then run the application. Not pretty for a candid Android developer! A crash dump appeared in the logs:

    ```
    . . .
    *** *** *** *** *** *** *** *** *** *** *** *** *** *** *** ***
    Build fingerprint: 'htc_wwe/htc_bravo/bravo:2.3.3/...
    pid: 1723, tid: 1743  >>> com.packtpub.droidblaster <<<
    signal 11 (SIGSEGV), code 1 (SEGV_MAPERR), fault addr 0000000c
     r0 a9df2e71  r1 40815c8d  r2 7cb9c28d  r3 00000000
    . . .
    ```

```
  ip a3400000   sp 45102830   lr 00000016   pc 80410a2c   cpsr 00000030
  d0   6f466e6961476e6f   d1   000000040000390
  . . .
  scr 20000012
          #00   pc 00010a2c   /data/data/com.packtpub.droidblaster/
  lib/libdroidblaster.so
          #01   pc 00009fcc   /data/data/com.packtpub.droidblaster/
  lib/libdroidblaster.so
  . . .
          #06   pc 00011618   /system/lib/libc.so
  code around pc:
  80410a0c 00017ad4 00000000 b084b510 9b019001
  . . .
  code around lr:
  stack:
      451027f0   00000000
      451027f4   45102870
      451027f8   804110f5   /data/data/com.packtpub.droidblaster/lib/
  libdroidblaster.so
  . . .
```

This dump contains useful information about the current program state. First it describes the error that happened: a SIGSEGV, also known as a **segmentation fault**. If you look at the faulty address, that is, `0000000c`, you will see that it is close to NULL. This is an important hint!

Then we have information about ARM register states (`rX`, `dX`, `ip`, `sp`, `lr`, `pc`, and so on). But what we are interested in comes right after this: information about where the program was when it got interrupted. These lines are highlighted in the extract above and can be identified by the words `pc` written on the line and an hexadecimal number after it. The latter expresses the **Program Counter** location, that is, which instruction was executed when problem occurred. Note that this memory address is relative to the containing library. With this piece of information, we know exactly on which instruction problem occurred... in the binary code!

3. We need somehow to translate this binary address into something understandable to a normal human being. The first solution is to disassemble completely the `.so` library.

    Open a terminal window and go to your project directory. Then execute the **objdump** command located in the executable directory of the NDK toolchain:

    ```
    $ $ANDROID_NDK/toolchains/arm-linux-androideabi-4.4.3/prebuilt/
    linux-x86/bin/arm-linux-androideabi-objdump -S
        ./obj/local/armeabi/libdroidblaster.so > ~/disassembler.dump
    ```

4. This command disassembles the library and outputs each assembler instruction and location accompanied with the source C/C++ code. Open the output file with a text editor and if you look carefully, you will find the same address than the one in the crash dump, next to `pc`:

```
. . .
    void TimeService::update()
    {
    10a14:    b510              push    {r4, lr}
    10a16:    b084              sub     sp, #16
    10a18:    9001              str     r0, [sp, #4]
        double lCurrentTime = now();
    10a1a:    9b01              ldr     r3, [sp, #4]
    10a1c:    1c18              adds    r0, r3, #0
    10a1e:    f000 f81f         bl      10a60 <_
ZN5packt11TimeService3nowEv>
    10a22:    1c03              adds    r3, r0, #0
    10a24:    1c0c              adds    r4, r1, #0
    10a26:    9302              str     r3, [sp, #8]
    10a28:    9403              str     r4, [sp, #12]
        mElapsed = (lCurrentTime - mLastTime);
    10a2a:    9b01              ldr     r3, [sp, #4]
    10a2c:    68dc              ldr     r4, [r3, #12]
    10a2e:    689b              ldr     r3, [r3, #8]
    10a30:    9802              ldr     r0, [sp, #8]
    10a32:    9903              ldr     r1, [sp, #12]
. . .
```

5. As you can see, problem seems to occur when executing `mService->update()` in `jni/TimeService.cpp` instruction because of the wrong object address inserted in step 1.

6. Disassembled dump file can become quite big. For this version of `droidblaster.so`, it should be around 3 MB. But it could become tenth MB, especially when libraries such as Irrlicht are involved! In addition, it needs to be regenerated each time library is updated.

Hoperfully, another utility named **addr2line**, located in the same directory as `objdump`, is available. Execute the following command with the `pc` address at the end, where `-f` shows function names, `-C` demangles them and `-e` indicates the input library:

```
$ $ANDROID_NDK/toolchains/arm-linux-androideabi-4.4.3/prebuilt/
linux-x86/bin/arm-linux-androideabi-addr2line -f -C
            -e ./obj/local/armeabi/libdroidblaster.so 00010a2c
```

This gives immediately the corresponding C/C++ instruction and its location in its source file:

```
File  Edit  View  Search  Terminal  Help
packt::TimeService::update()
/home/packt/Project/DroidBlaster_Part8-3/jni/TimeService.cpp:25
```

7. Since version R6, Android NDK provides **ndk-stack** in its root directory. This utility does what we have done manually using an Android log dump. Coupled with the ADB, which is able to display Android logs while in real time, crashes can be analyzed without a move (except your eyes!).

Simply run the following command from a terminal window to decipher crash dumps automatically:

```
$ adb logcat | ndk-stack -sym ./obj/local/armeabi
********* Crash dump: **********
Build fingerprint: 'htc_wwe/htc_bravo/bravo:2.3.3/
GRI40/96875.1:user/release-keys'
pid: 1723, tid: 1743  >>> com.packtpub.droidblaster <<<
signal 11 (SIGSEGV), code 1 (SEGV_MAPERR), fault addr 0000000c
Stack frame #00  pc 00010a2c  /data/data/com.packtpub.
droidblaster/lib/libdroidblaster.so: Routine update in /home/
packt/Project/Chapter11/DroidBlaster_Part11/jni/TimeService.cpp:25
Stack frame #01  pc 00009fcc  /data/data/com.packtpub.
droidblaster/lib/libdroidblaster.so: Routine onStep in /home/
packt/Project/Chapter11/DroidBlaster_Part11/jni/DroidBlaster.
cpp:53
Stack frame #02  pc 0000a348  /data/data/com.packtpub.
droidblaster/lib/libdroidblaster.so: Routine run in /home/packt/
Project/Chapter11/DroidBlaster_Part11/jni/EventLoop.cpp:49
Stack frame #03  pc 0000f994  /data/data/com.packtpub.
droidblaster/lib/libdroidblaster.so: Routine android_main in /
home/packt/Project/Chapter11/DroidBlaster_Part11/jni/Main.cpp:31
. . .
```

What just happened?

We have used ARM utilities embedded in the Android NDK to locate the origin of an application crash. These utilities constitute an inestimable help and should be considered as your first-aid kit when a bad crash happens.

However, if they can help you finding the "where", it is another kettle of fish to find the "why". As you can see in the piece of code at step 4, understanding why LDR instruction (whose goal is to load in a register, some data from memory, constants, or other registers) fails is not trivial. This is where your programmer intuition (and possibly knowledge of assembly code) comes into play.

More on crash dumps

For general culture, let's linger briefly on what is provided in the LogCat crash dump. A crash dump is not dedicated only to overly talented developers or people seeing red-dressed girl in binary code, but also to those who have a minimum knowledge of assemblers and the way ARM processors work. The goal of this trace is to give as much information as possible on the current state of the program at the time it crashed:

- The first line gives the build fingerprint, which is a kind of an identifier indicating the device/Android release currently running. This information is interesting when analyzing dumps from various origins.

- The second line indicates the **PID**, process identifier, which uniquely identify an application on Unix system, and the **TID**, which is the thread identifier. It can be the same as the process identifier when crash occurs on the main thread.

- The third line shows the crash origin represented as a signal, here a classic segmentation fault (**SIGSEGV**).

- Then, processor's register values are dumped, where:

  - rX: This is an integer register.

  - dX: This is a floating point register.

  - fp (or r11): The Frame Pointer holds a fixed location on the stack during a routine call (in conjunction with the Stack Pointer).

  - ip (or r12): The **intra procedure call scratch register** may be used with some subroutine calls, for example, when the linker needs a veneer (a small piece of code) to aim at a different memory area when branching (a branch instruction to jump somewhere else in the memory requires an offset argument relative to current location, allowing a branching range of a few MB only, not the full memory).

  - sp (or r13): This is the **stack pointer,** which saves location of the top of the stack.

  - lr (or r14): The **link register** generally saves program counter's value temporarily to restore it later. A typical example of its use is a function call which jumps somewhere in the code and then go back to its previous location. Of course, several chained subroutine calls requires the link register to be stacked.

❑ pc (or r15): This represents the **program counter** which holds the address of next instruction to execute. Program counter is just incremented when executing a sequential code to fetch next instruction but is altered by branching instructions (if/else, a C/C++ function calls, and so on).

❑ cpsr: The **Current Program Status Register** contains a few flags about the current processor working mode and some additional bit flags for condition codes (such as N for an operation which resulted in a negative value, Z for a 0 or equality result, and so on), interrupts, and instruction set (Thumb or ARM).

◆ Crash dump also contains a few memory words around PC (that is, the block of instructions around) and LR (for previous location).

◆ Finally, a dump of the raw call stack is logged.

Just a convention

Remember that the use of registers is mainly a convention. For example, Apple iOS uses r7 as a frame pointer instead of r12... So always be very careful when reusing existing code!

Performance analysis

If debugging tools are still imperfect, I have to advise you that profiling tools are rather immature... when they even work! Actually, there is no real official support from Google for memory or performance profiler, except in the emulator. This may change soon or later. But right now, those who like to tweak code and analyse each instruction may starve. This is particularly true when developing with a non-developer or non-rooted phone.

Hopefully, a few solutions exist and some are coming. Let's cite the following one:

◆ **Valgrind**: This is probably the most famous open source profiler which can monitor not only performance but also memory and cache usage. This utility is currently being ported to Android. With some tweaking, it is possible to make it work on a developer or rooted phone in ArmV7 mode. It is one of the best hopes for Android.

◆ **Android-NDK-Profiler:** This is a port of **Gprof** on Android. It is a simple and basic profiler which works by instrumenting and sampling code at runtime. It is the simplest solution to profile performance and does not require any specific hardware.

◆ **OProfile** is a system-wide profiler which inserts its code in the system kernel (which thus needs to be updated) to collect profiling data with a low overhead. It is more complicated to install and requires a developer or rooted phone to work but works quite well and does instrument code. It is a much better solution to profile code for free if you have proper hardware at your disposal.

◆ The commercial development suite **ARM DS-5** and its **StreamLine** performance analyzer may become an interesting option.

◆ Open GL ES Profilers from manufacturers: **Adreno Profiler** for Qualcomm, **PerfHUD ES** for NVidia and **PVRTune** for PowerVR. These profilers are hardware-specific. The choice depends on your phone. These tools are however essential to see what is happening under the GLES hood.

We are not going to evoke the emulator profiler here because of its inability to emulate programs properly at an effective speed (especially when using GLES). But know that it exists. Instead, we are now going to discover the interesting Android-NDK-Profiler, an alternative Gprof-based profiler ported on Android by Richard Quirk (see `http://quirkygba.blogspot.com/` for more information). Android-NDK-Profiler requires a device running at least Android Gingerbread.

Project DroidBlaster_Part8-3 can be used as a starting point for this part. The resulting project is provided with this book under the name DroidBlaster_Part11.

Time for action – running GProf

Let's try to profile our own application code:

1. Open a browser window and navigate to the Android-NDK-Profiler homepage at `http://code.google.com/p/android-ndk-profiler/`. Go to the **Downloads** section and save the latest release (3.1 at the time of writing) on your computer.

2. Unzip archive in `$ANDROID_NDK/sources/android-ndk-profiler`. This archive contains an Android Makefile and two libraries: one for Arm V5 and one for Arm V7.

3. Turn Android-NDK-Profiler into a full android module (see highlighted lines). The main missing point is the export of `prof.h` file that we are going to include in our code.

This Makefile uses the `$TARGET_ARCH_ABI` variable to select the right library version (Arm V5/V7) automatically according to what is defined in `Application.mk` (`APP_ABI= armeabi, armeabi-v7a`). It also filters some optimization options which could interfere with it (for Thumb as well as ARM code):

```
LOCAL_PATH:= $(call my-dir)

TARGET_thumb_release_CFLAGS := $(filter-out -ffunction-
sections,$(TARGET_thumb_release_CFLAGS))
```

```
TARGET_thumb_release_CFLAGS := $(filter-out -fomit-frame-
pointer,$(TARGET_thumb_release_CFLAGS))
TARGET_CFLAGS := $(filter-out -ffunction-sections,$(TARGET_
CFLAGS))


# include libandprof.a in the build
include $(CLEAR_VARS)
LOCAL_MODULE := andprof
LOCAL_SRC_FILES := $(TARGET_ARCH_ABI)/libandprof.a
LOCAL_EXPORT_C_INCLUDES := $(LOCAL_PATH)/
include $(PREBUILT_STATIC_LIBRARY)
```

4. Android-NDK-Profiler can now be included in a normal native library. Let's append it to DroidBlaster_Part8-3 (you can use any other version you want).

Add the optimization filter like done in profiler's own Makefile. Since compilation is done in thumb mode by default, keep only related lines. Then include -pg parameter which inserts additional instruction necessary to the profiler. Finally, include profiler module as usual:

```
LOCAL_PATH := $(call my-dir)

TARGET_thumb_release_CFLAGS := $(filter-out -ffunction-
sections,$(TARGET_thumb_release_CFLAGS))
TARGET_thumb_release_CFLAGS := $(filter-out -fomit-frame-
pointer,$(TARGET_thumb_release_CFLAGS))
TARGET_CFLAGS := $(filter-out -ffunction-sections,$(TARGET_
CFLAGS))

include $(CLEAR_VARS)

LS_CPP=$(subst $(1)/,,$(wildcard $(1)/*.cpp))
LOCAL_CFLAGS      := -DRAPIDXML_NO_EXCEPTIONS -pg
LOCAL_MODULE      := droidblaster
LOCAL_SRC_FILES   := $(call LS_CPP,$(LOCAL_PATH))
LOCAL_LDLIBS      := -landroid -llog -lEGL -lGLESv1_CM -lOpenSLES

LOCAL_STATIC_LIBRARIES := android_native_app_glue png andprof

include $(BUILD_SHARED_LIBRARY)

$(call import-module,android/native_app_glue)
$(call import-module,libpng)
$(call import-module,android-ndk-profiler)
```

5. To run the profiler, we need to include a profiler start up and shut down function in the code. Open `jni/Main.cpp` and insert them at the beginning and end of `android_main()`. Set sample frequency to 6000 thanks to a predefined environment variable `CPUPROFILE_FREQUENCY`:

```
...
#include <cstdlib>
#include <prof.h>

void android_main(struct android_app* pApplication)
{
    setenv("CPUPROFILE_FREQUENCY", "60000", 1);
    monstartup("droidblaster.so");

    // Run game services and event loop.
    ...
    lEventLoop.run(&lDroidBlaster, &lInputService);

    moncleanup();
}
```

6. Finally, allow application to write on a storage in `AndroidManifest.xml`:

```
<?xml xmlns:android="http://schemas.android.com/apk/res/android"
    package="com.packtpub.droidblaster" android:versionCode="1"
    android:versionName="1.0">
    ...
    <uses-permission
            android:name="android.permission.WRITE_EXTERNAL_
STORAGE"/>
</manifest>
```

7. Recompile `DroidBlaster` project. It now includes all the necessary instructions to start profiler and generate profiling information.

8. Run project on a device. Log messages are generated between profiler startup and shutdown. Make sure application completely dies by pressing the back button, a pause being not sufficient:

```
INFO/threaded_app(3553): Start: 0x97270
INFO/PROFILING(3553): Profile droidblaster.so 80400000-8043d000: 0
INFO/PROFILING(3553): 0: parent: carrying on
INFO/PACKT(3553): Creating GraphicsService
...
```

```
INFO/PACKT(3553): Exiting event loop
INFO/PROFILING(3553): parent: moncleanup called
INFO/PROFILING(3553): 1: parent: done profiling
INFO/PROFILING(3553): writing gmon.out
INFO/PROFILING(3598): child: finished monitoring
INFO/PACKT(3553): Destructing DroidBlaster
```

9. After application is terminated, retrieve file gmon.out generated in the /sdcard folder of your device (depending on your device, storage may be mounted in another directory) and save it in your project directory. Do not forget to activate USB Mass Storage mode to see files from your computer.

10. From a terminal window located in your project directory where gmon.out is saved, open a terminal and run gprof analyser located beside NDK ARM toolchain binaries:

```
$ ANDROID_NDK/toolchains/arm-linux-androideabi-4.4.3/prebuilt/
linux-x86/bin/arm-linux-androideabi-gprof obj/local/armeabi/
libdroidblaster.so
```

This command generates a textual output that you can redirect to a file. It contains all profiling results. The first part (flat profile) is the consolidated result with top functions which seem to take time. The second part is the *raw* index from which the first part is calculated:

```
Flat profile:


Each sample counts as 1.66667e-05 seconds.
  %   cumulative   self              self     total
 time   seconds   seconds    calls  us/call  us/call  name
 18.64     0.00      0.00                              png_read_
filter_row
 13.56     0.00      0.00    15847     0.01     0.02  packt::Graph
icsService::update()
 10.17     0.00      0.00    15847     0.01     0.01  packt::Graph
icsSprite::draw(float)
 10.17     0.00      0.00        1   100.00   566.67
packt::EventLoop::run(...)
  8.47     0.00      0.00    15847     0.01     0.03
dbs::DroidBlaster::onStep()
  5.08     0.00      0.00    15847     0.00     0.00
packt::GraphicsTileMap::draw()
...
```

```
   index % time    self  children   called    name
                                              <spontaneous>
   [1]     57.6    0.00    0.00               android_main [1]
                   0.00    0.00      1/1
packt::EventLoop::run(...) [2]
                   0.00    0.00      1/1          packt::EventLoop:
:EventLoop(android_app*) [469]
                   0.00    0.00      1/1          packt::Sensor::Se
nsor(packt::EventLoop&, int) [466]
                   0.00    0.00      1/1          packt::TimeServic
e::TimeService() [433]
                   0.00    0.00      1/1          packt::GraphicsSe
rvice::GraphicsService(...) [456]
   ...
```

What just happened?

We have compiled Android-NDK-Profiler project as an NDK module and appended it to our own project. We turned profiling on with the help of two exported methods `monstartup()` and `moncleanup()`. The profiling result is written to `gmon.out` file on the SD Card (thus requiring write access) that can be parsed by the NDK `gprof` utility.

The output file contains a summary for each function hit by the sampler: the flat profile. More specifically, it indicates the following:

- `index`: This identifies an entry in the index computed from and written after the flat profile.

- `% time`: This represents the fragment of time spent in the function compared to the total program execution times.

- `cumulative seconds`: This is the accumulated total time spent in the function and all the function above in the table (using self seconds).

- `self seconds`: This is the accumulated total time spent in the function itself over its multiple execution.

- `calls`: This represents the total number of calls to a function. This is the only information which is really accurate.

- `self s/call`: This is the average time spent in one execution of the function. This column depends on sample hits and is not reliable.

- `total s/call`: This is the same as `self s/call` but cumulated with the time spent in sub-functions too. This column is also depends on sample hits.

Note that functions in which no *apparent* time is spent (which does not mean they are never called) are not mentioned unless `-z` is appended to command-line options.

How it works

To profile a piece code, GCC compiler instruments your code when option -pg is appended to compilation options. Instrumentation relies on a routine named mcount () (more formerly __gnu_mcount_nc()) which is inserted at the beginning of each function to gather information about its caller and compute call count indicator. The role of Android-NDK-Profiler here is to implement this routine which is not provided by the Android NDK.

More advanced profiling information is extracted by sampling the PC counter at constant intervals (100hz by default), in order to detect which function the program is currently running (and derive the call stack). From a theoretical point of view, the more a function takes time to run, the bigger is the probability that a sample hits it.

To do so, Android-NDK-Profiler creates a separate thread to collect timing information and a new fork process to interrupt native code and record samples. To do so, it requires the ability to attach to a parent process which only works from Android 2.3 Gingerbread. Thus, if you see the following message in Android logs, profiling information will not get collected accurately:

```
INFO/PROFILING(3588): child: could not attach 3584
```

GProf is a mature (not to say antic) tool which has limitations. First, GProf instrumentation is intrusive. It affects performance and potentially cache usage which result in perturbations. Moreover, it does not measure time spent in I/O which is often a good place to look for bottlenecks and does not handle recursion. Finally, because it uses sampling and makes some assumption about code (for example, a function is assumed to use more or less the same time to run for each call), GProf does not give very accurate results and needs many samples to increase accuracy. This makes it difficult to analyze results properly, when they are not misleading.

Although it is far from perfect, GProf is still easy to set up and can be a good start in profiling.

ARM, thumb, and NEON

Compiled native C/C++ code on current Android ARM devices follows an **Application Binary Interface (ABI)**. An ABI specifies the binary code format (instruction set, calling conventions, and so on). GCC translates code into this binary format. ABIs are thus strongly related to processors. The target ABI can be selected in the Application.mk file with the property APP_ABI. There exist four main ABIs supported on Android:

- **thumb:** This is the default option which should be compatible with all ARM devices. Thumb is a special instruction set which encodes instructions on 16-bit instead of 32 to improve code size (useful for devices with constrained memory). The instruction set is severely restricted compared to ArmEABI.

- **armeabi** (Or Arm v5): This should run on all ARM devices. Instructions are encoded on 32-bit but may be more concise than Thumb code. Arm v5 does not support advanced extensions like floating point acceleration and is thus slower than Arm v7.

- **armeabi-v7a**: This supports extensions such as Thumb-2 (similar to Thumb but with additional 32-bit instructions) and VFP plus some optional extensions such as NEON. Code compiled for Arm V7 will not run on Arm V5 processors.

- **x86**: This is for *PC-like* architectures (that is, Intel/AMD). There is no official device that existed at the time this book was written but an unofficial open source initiative exists.

It is possible to compile code, for example, for Arm V5 and V7 at the same time, the most appropriate binaries are selected at installation time.

Android provides a `cpu-features.h` API (with `android_getCpuFamily()` and `android_getCpuFeatures()` methods) to detect available features on the host device at runtime. It helps in detecting the CPU (ARM, X86) and its capabilities (ArmV7 support, NEON, VFP).

Performance is one of the main criteria to develop with the Android NDK. To achieve this, ARM created a SIMD instruction set (acronym Single Instruction Multiple Data, that is, process several data in parallel with one instruction) called NEON which has been introduced along with the VFP (the floating point accelerated unit).

NEON is not available on all chips (for example, Nvidia Tegra 2 does not support it) but is quite popular in intensive multimedia application. They are also a good way to compensate the weak VFP unit of some processors (for example, Cortex-A8).

NEON code can be written in a separate assembler file, in a dedicated `asm volatile` block with assembler instructions or in a C/C++ file or as intrinsics (NEON instructions encapsulated in a GCC C routine). Intrinsics should be used with much care as GCC is often unable to generate efficient machine code (or requires lots of *tricky* hints). Writing real assembler code is generally advised.

NEON and modern processors are not easy to master. The Internet is full of examples to get inspiration from. For example, have a look at `code.google.com/p/math-neon/` for an example of math library implemented with NEON. Reference technical documentation can be found on the ARM website at `http://infocenter.arm.com/`.

Summary

In this last chapter, we have seen advanced techniques to troubleshoot bugs and performance issues. More specifically, we have debugged our code with the native code debugger, which is slow and complex to set up but is a real life saver.

We have also executed NDK Arm utilities to decipher crash dumps. They are the ultimate solution when a crash already occurred.

Finally, we have profiled our code to analyze performances with GProf. This solution is limited but can give an interesting overview.

With these tools in hand, you are now ready to venture out into the NDK jungle. And if you are adventurous, you can dive head first in ARM assembler to improve performances drastically . However, beware this is useful only when targeting the right pieces of code (the famous 20%!). Do not forget that optimizing a bad algorithm will never make it good, and a good algorithm even without optimization can make a huge difference.

Afterword

Throughout this book, you have learnt the essentials to get started and overlooked the paths to follow to go further. You now know the key elements to tame these little powerful monsters and start exploiting their full power. However, there is still a lot to learn, but the time and space lacks. Anyway, the only way to master a technology is to practice and practice again. I hope you enjoy the journey and that you feel armed up for the mobile challenge. So my best advice now is to gather your fresh knowledge and all your amazing ideas, beat them up in your mind and bake them with your keyboard!

Where we have been

We have seen concretely how to create native projects with Eclipse and the NDK. We have learnt how to embed a C/C++ library in Java applications through JNI and how to run native code without writing a line of Java.

We have tested multimedia capabilities of the Android NDK with OpenGL ES and OpenSL ES, which are becoming a standard in mobility (of course, after omitting Windows Mobile). We have even interacted with our phone input peripherals and apprehended the world through its sensors.

Moreover, the Android NDK is not only related to performance but also to portability. Thus, we have reused the STL framework, its best companion Boost, and ported third-party libraries almost seamlessly. We now have powerful 3D and physics engines in our hands!

Finally, we have seen how to debug native code (and that was not so simple) and analyze program crashes and performance.

Where you can go

Eclipse with ADT and CDT plugins is great. But their integration is not absolutely natural. Debugging operations are a bit complex and not everybody will be satisfied with the lack of advanced profiling tools. But some alternatives are emerging, such as the Nvidia Tegra Development Pack (http://developer.nvidia.com/tegra-android-development-pack) for glad Tegra device owners. ARM DS-5 (http://www.arm.com/products/tools/software-tools/ds-5/) can also become an interesting option for professional development. An open source initiative exists to bring Android features to Visual Studio (http://code.google.com/p/vs-android/). The Android ecosystem is full of life and quickly evolving.

A subject that is partially outside the scope of this book is the emulation of application on a PC. Here I am not talking about the Android emulator, which runs an Android OS image on a system virtualizer, I am talking about *native emulation*, that is, running an application directly on your Linux, Mac, or Windows computer. This is the best solution to make all your usual programming tools available, Valgrind (to analyze memory leaks) being probably the most useful example. Have a look at the PowerVR SDK (http://www.imgtec.com/powervr/insider/) to emulate OpenGL ES on your PC. Obviously, there is no real alternative to emulate the native Android framework. This approach works quite well but requires a real design effort to keep apart common code from OS-specific code. But this is worth the effort as you can definitely gain some productivity and, even better, ease the porting of your C/C++ to other OS (you know what I am talking about!).

We have ported a few libraries, but a lot more are out there and waiting to get ported. Actually, many of them work without the need of a code revamp. They just need to be recompiled. For those interested in 3D physics, Bullet (http://bulletphysics.org/) is an example of the engine that can be ported right away in a few minutes. The C/C++ ecosystem has existed for several decades now and is full of richness. Some libraries have been specifically designed for mobile devices. A great framework that you should definitely have a look at if you want to write mobile games, is Unity (http://unity3d.com/).

And if you really want to get your hand dirty in the guts of Android, I encourage you to have a look at the Android platform code itself, available at http://source.android.com/. It is not a piece of cake to download, compile, or even deploy it, but this is the only way to get an in-depth understanding of Android internals and sometimes the only way to find out where these annoying bugs are coming from!

Where to find help

The Android community is really active and following are the places to find useful information:

◆ The Android Google group (`http://groups.google.com/group/android-developers`) and the Android NDK group (`http://groups.google.com/group/android-ndk`) where you can get some help, sometimes from the Android team member.

◆ The Android Developer BlogSpot (`http://android-developers.blogspot.com/`) where you can find fresh and official information about Android development.

◆ Google IO (`http://www.google.com/events/io/2011`, 2009 and 2010 sessions are also available) for great Android video talks performed by Google's engineers.

◆ Google Code (`http://code.google.com/hosting/`) for lots of NDK example applications. Just type **NDK** in the search engine and let Google be your friend.

◆ The NVidia Developer Centre (`http://developer.nvidia.com/category/zone/mobile-development`) for Tegra but also general resources about Android and the NDK.

◆ The Qualcomm Developer Network (`https://developer.qualcomm.com/`) to find information about the NVidia main competitor. The Qualcomm's Augmented Reality SDK is especially promising.

◆ Anddev (`http://www.anddev.org/`) is an active Android forum with an NDK section.

◆ Stack Overflow (`http://stackoverflow.com/`) is not dedicated to Android but here you can ask questions and get accurate answers.

◆ Marakana Website (`http://marakana.com/tutorials.html`) provides many interesting resources about Android and especially video talks.

◆ Packt Website (`http://www.packtpub.com/`), a bit of self-promotion for the many resources available there about Android, Irrlicht, and open source software.

This is just the beginning

Creating an application is only part of the path. Publishing and selling is another. This is, of course, outside the scope of this book but handling fragmentation and testing compatibility with various target devices can be a real difficulty that needs to be taken seriously. Beware, problems start occurring when you start dealing with hardware specificities (and there are lots of them) like we have seen with input devices. These issues are, however, not specific to the NDK. If incompatibilities exist in a Java application, then native code will not do better. Handling various screen sizes, loading appropriately sized resources, and adapting to device capabilities are things that you will eventually need to deal with. But that should be manageable.

In few words, there are a lot of marvellous but also painful surprises to discover. But Android and mobility is still a fallow land that needs to be modelled. Look at the evolution of Android from its earliest version to the latest one to be convinced. Revolution does not take place every day so do not miss it!

Good luck.

Index

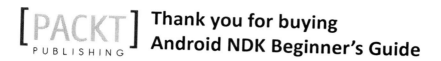

Thank you for buying
Android NDK Beginner's Guide

About Packt Publishing

Packt, pronounced 'packed', published its first book "Mastering phpMyAdmin for Effective MySQL Management" in April 2004 and subsequently continued to specialize in publishing highly focused books on specific technologies and solutions.

Our books and publications share the experiences of your fellow IT professionals in adapting and customizing today's systems, applications, and frameworks. Our solution-based books give you the knowledge and power to customize the software and technologies you're using to get the job done. Packt books are more specific and less general than the IT books you have seen in the past. Our unique business model allows us to bring you more focused information, giving you more of what you need to know, and less of what you don't.

Packt is a modern, yet unique publishing company, which focuses on producing quality, cutting-edge books for communities of developers, administrators, and newbies alike. For more information, please visit our website: www.PacktPub.com.

Writing for Packt

We welcome all inquiries from people who are interested in authoring. Book proposals should be sent to author@packtpub.com. If your book idea is still at an early stage and you would like to discuss it first before writing a formal book proposal, contact us; one of our commissioning editors will get in touch with you.

We're not just looking for published authors; if you have strong technical skills but no writing experience, our experienced editors can help you develop a writing career, or simply get some additional reward for your expertise.

Android User Interface Development

ISBN: 978-1-84951-448-4   Paperback:304 pages

Quickly design and develop compelling user interfaces for your Android applications

1. Leverage the Android platform's flexibility and power to design impactful user-interfaces

2. Build compelling, user-friendly applications that will look great on any Android device

3. Make your application stand out from the rest with styles and themes

4. A practical Beginner's Guide to take you step-by-step through the process of developing user interfaces to get your applications noticed!

Android Application Testing Guide

ISBN: 978-1-84951-350-0   Paperback: 332 pages

Build intensively tested and bug free Android applications

1. The first and only book that focuses on testing Android applications

2. Step-by-step approach clearly explaining the most efficient testing methodologies

3. Real world examples with practical test cases that you can reuse

Please check **www.PacktPub.com** for information on our titles

Android 3.0 Animations

ISBN: 978-1-84951-528-3   Paperback:304 pages

Bring your Android applications to life with stunning animations

1. The first and only book dedicated to creating animations for Android apps.

2. Covers all of the commonly used animation techniques for Android 3.0 and lower versions.

3. Create stunning animations to give your Android apps a fun and intuitive user experience.

4. A step-by-step guide for learning animation by building fun example applications and games.

Android 3.0 Application Development Cookbook

ISBN: 978-1-84951-294-7   Paperback: 272 pages

Over 70 working recipes covering every aspect of Android development

1. Written for Android 3.0 but also applicable to lower versions

2. Quickly develop applications that take advantage of the very latest mobile technologies, including web apps, sensors, and touch screens

3. Part of Packt's Cookbook series: Discover tips and tricks for varied and imaginative uses of the latest Android features

Please check **www.PacktPub.com** for information on our titles

Lightning Source UK Ltd.
Milton Keynes UK
UKOW021200270412

191595UK00003B/41/P

9 781849 6915